The Hero's Children

By the same author

The Long Birth (novel)
Secker & Warburg, 1967

Paul Neuburg

The Hero's Children

The Post-War Generation in Eastern Europe

William Morrow & Company, Inc.
NEW YORK 1973

For friends over there

Neuburg, Paul
    The hero's children.

    Bibliography: p.
        1. Youth—Europe, Eastern. 2. Young adults—Europe, Eastern.
3. Europe, Eastern—Social conditions. 4. Communism and society. I.
Title.
HQ799.E9N47 1973   301.43′1′0947   72-121
ISBN 0-688-00138-6
ISBN 0-688-05138-3 (pbk.)

Contents

Preface

Though born in Hungary in 1939, I have lived for fifteen years in Britain and have become to a large extent a westerner. This was brought home to me most clearly during my first trip through Eastern Europe, in 1968. In the spring and summer of that year I spent three months there collecting material for a series of articles, later published in the *Daily Telegraph Magazine*, on the generation that had grown up since the war in the five countries that border on Russia.

I had set out with a number of questions to which I wanted to find answers through interviews with people aged thirty or less in all walks of life. The questions were those that westerners usually ask themselves if they think at all about the new East Europeans, brought up in circumstances and an atmosphere very different from what the rest of the world has known. What has this unique experience done to youth there? What do they believe in? Have they become Communists, atheists, conformists, revolutionary romantics, stubborn resisters, sheer materialists? What have the twists and turns of official hagiography done to any beliefs they ever had? Are they nationalists, internationalists, simple patriots, carefree cosmopolitans, total cynics about the problem? And so on.

One of the things I found out early on during my trip was that many of these questions had been naïve, and some only half-relevant to the daily life and thinking of most young people there. Politics, and their unique experience in the last twenty-five years, mattered, but in quite other ways. My questions had been western questions which, for want of better information, at least in part accepted the description East European countries had been giving of themselves. Now I find that when people confront me with the same questions about the youth of Eastern Europe, if I want to be truthful in my reply, it is either very long, or it makes them feel foolish. As foolish as I felt, in the first weeks of that trip.

This was embarrassing, but from the point of view of the present book it has been a good thing. It forced me to think much more about this East European generation, and about what was new, what traditional and what generally human in them and in the situations with which they and their governments were having to cope.

I could not do this without first working out for myself the main peculiarities of their tradition and present situation. This took some time, but as I proceeded I became more and more convinced that it was my best way back into the mind of the generation to which by birth I belonged. I also returned for a second trip a year later, and a third one in 1970, to find that my meetings with people whom I had got to know during my initial visit, and others too, proved much deeper and more fruitful – both because I knew more about the realities of their situation and because meanwhile, by sheer coincidence, my East European generation had been made to reflect on those realities by the invasion of Czechoslovakia in August 1968. In fact, just as the invasion had once again aroused western interest in Eastern Europe, it had also made young people there realize that they were heirs to a situation that had prevailed between the Black Sea and the Baltic for centuries.

The book which has now emerged is very different from the one I originally set out to write. Instead of being an extended report of a single journey through Eastern Europe it is based on three such journeys and further encounters with young East Europeans visiting the West, and thus contains a good deal more live material. In addition, it draws on a number of surveys and studies of young people's attitudes undertaken by sociologists and other researchers in Eastern Europe itself. And the whole thing is set in a more detailed historical background than I originally intended to provide, because I am now convinced that without enough information of this kind very little of interest can be said about today's young East Europeans. If it was necessary for me to study this background in order to understand the generation to which by birth I belonged and with which I was able to re-establish live contact, it will be indispensable for born westerners who are trying to understand the same generation in its own terms by reading a book.

In brief, I have written something far more ambitious than I had set out to write. It will be for the reader, and for those who have studied Eastern Europe far longer than I have, to judge how far I have succeeded. But I can at least set out here the main ideas that I will attempt to put across.

The central idea is that of the Party as Hero, and the young as the Hero's Children. This is far from being pure fancy. Ever since its foundation by Lenin in 1903 the Party has seen itself, consistently with Marx's own vision, as the anointed Hero of a World Revolution from which mankind's rebirth to a higher state of economic, social, political and spiritual harmony was to result. And as this Hero of a Perfect Future, it has all along claimed the young for its own natural vanguard against the older generations, embodying mankind's sadly imperfect past. In addition, the Party's self-centred ideology – and the centralist methods which Lenin worked out for it in the underground days and which it has essentially retained ever since – designate it as a Hero in absolute command first of its membership, and then of every country it may rule on behalf of the World Proletariat and History, once again claiming the young as its vanguard. This centralism (called 'democratic centralism' by Lenin) is what defines the Party as the Party. It is either Hero in central charge, or it is nothing – which is why every time the Party's heroic position has been threatened in any East European country during the last twenty-five years it has reacted as though to mortal danger.

As Hero in charge of Eastern Europe, however, the Party has found itself having to cope with a task that is relatively mundane compared to that of World Revolution. That is to say, the task of turning the region, with the exception of Czechoslovakia a largely agrarian one, into the kind of industrialized corner of the globe where according to Marx's prophecy the Revolution should have taken place.

In this more prosaic aim, the Party has to a considerable extent succeeded. It has also achieved a great deal in bringing about economic, social and educational homogeneity. But its genuine successes in these fields have produced new circumstances and attitudes that are in no way conducive to revolutionary behaviour. They have thus made the realization of the Party's prime heroic aim not more but less likely. In fact the Party is now in the paradoxical position of a Hero pressing on with mundane aims foisted on it by the situation it meant to overturn, and achieving successes that are bound only to diminish the bases of its claim to heroic power, and the loyalty of the young.

To explain this idea in more detail, I have set myself five tasks that are almost as ambitious.

1 To show how far the idea of the élite as Hero in command of a country is germane to Eastern Europe. It is important to realize that though imposed on the region in 1945–8 by Soviet armed power, the Party did not appear there as some alien Don Quixote, but as heir to an established tradition, of which it has become the ultimate embodiment. Ultimate both because no previous ruling élite has set itself such heroic tasks or ruled in such an absolute manner, and because, thanks as much to the Party's own achievements as to its failures, no more such heroes are likely to follow.

2 To show the ways in which the Party, again true to local tradition, has been presenting itself as the people's vanguard on the road to rebirth, naturally entitled to the loyalty of each new generation. Though full of seeming absurdities, the Party's vast propaganda effort has been not only generally consistent with this idea, but also in many ways fascinating and in some ways irresistible. Most important, however, it is far from dead. Despite its failures, the Party and especially its hardliners do not consider it quixotic at all.

Part of the reason for this is the social distance between many of those in charge and those who are to be convinced. But a more important reason lies, as I shall try to explain, in that superb device of self-justification and deception – dialectics. In the case of the Party faithful, it allows magnification of the Party's successes as inherent in historical progress, and minimization of its failures as due only to mistakes and hostile manoeuvres, so isolating believers from those elements of reality which might destroy their faith.

3 To describe as fully as possible the daily life and concerns of the young in Eastern Europe today. This still remains the main purpose of the book, for two reasons. One is that while many good studies have been written about political and cultural developments in Eastern Europe few have attempted to show the western reader how life is going on underneath. The other is that nobody fully aware of the circumstances and complexities of life as lived by the young there could imagine propaganda from above achieving the kind of successes the Party has claimed for itself, or even provoking the kind of stark resistance described in some counter-claims.

It is because they have remained relatively unfamiliar with life in Eastern Europe, I think, that so many westerners in the 1950s, and to some extent ever since, have seen young East Europeans as either suffused with enthusiasm or burning with resentment of Party rule. What social distance and dialectics have done for the Party faithful in Eastern Europe, geographical distance and their awe of Communism (at times mixed with or replaced by admiration) seem to have done for many people in the West.

4 To go a level further down, as it were. That is, to show that even while the Party has achieved only partial successes in shaping the outlook of young East Europeans from above, it has effected basic changes in their lives, and thus their thinking, from below. These changes have affected material circumstances and opportunities as much as the atmosphere of families and schools, and the conventions and quality of everyday existence. But if young East Europeans themselves have been mostly unable to control the changes wrought in their lives and thinking from below, these have been even further beyond the control of the Party. In fact, though many of the results now visible are to the Party's genuine credit, just as many appear to be not to its liking.

5 To point out the ways that young East Europeans, having grown up in an environment changed in this manner, seem likely to adopt for coping with their new circumstances and with the Party as Hero in charge.

The attempt to present all this in one book has naturally forced on me a mixture of styles. As is already the case in this preface, throughout what follows personal impressions will be found to alternate with political and other kinds of reflection and theory, and to be complemented with the opinion of other researchers. But I think this mixture of styles will be true both to my own experience of the subject, and to the life of the young in Eastern Europe itself, shot through as it is with the results of changes deliberately engineered by theoreticians.

Starting with impressions and live interviews, then setting these within a general framework, and testing my conclusions against those drawn by others, I will in fact be taking the reader through the experience of most visitors to Eastern Europe who have become interested enough to want to find out more about the background of what they have seen. It is also how the majority of today's western experts on the region have proceeded. That is, by examining first what they knew as their own or their parents' native environment, and thus of personal importance to them, or becoming impassioned on a visit and remaining engrossed for years if not for ever, despite all the rude political events and nearly insoluble complexities that may drive them to despair.

Still more important, young East Europeans themselves experience life in a mixed way. Though they may not be aware of the full ideological background of what is happening to them, they know that a good deal of it has to do, directly or indirectly, with ideology. Not only is this impressed on them at all times by propaganda, but they see it to be true as much in the policies of positive discrimination governing their entry to secondary and higher education as in the wage structures awaiting them at work, or the kind of music they can hear on the radio, to mention only three examples.

Quite simply, nothing is so characteristic of the centralism which defines the Party as the awareness of itself which it generates in those it rules – for the better as much as for the worse, and often in ways that have to do largely with organization. For instance, even the most genuinely popular magazines read by today's young East Europeans contain, side by side, articles on pop music and film stars, on the good life in the people's army, on the breeding of pigeons, on preparations for the coming Youth League Congress or the implementation of the policies proclaimed at the last one, plus a correspondence column in which – in the more liberal countries – a controversy about the rights and wrongs of positive discrimination may be raging, alongside a huge list of potential pen-friends abroad and advertisements for chocolate, soft drinks and young people's fashions. And to have all this in a single publication rather than five different ones, each devoted to pop music, army life and so on, will be accepted by most readers as corresponding on the one hand to their normal range of interests and on the other to the realities of the centralist universe around them. Discussing their existence from a similarly wide range of angles and in an inevitably mixed range of styles, I do not therefore feel I am doing violence to the way they experience life.

As I have mentioned, my initial journey through Eastern Europe was sponsored by the *Daily Telegraph Magazine*, to whose editor I remain most grateful. I was given direct financial assistance, in the shape of a generous grant, by the Arts Council of Great Britain in the year 1970–1.

During my first visit to Eastern Europe I was helped with introductions by the press sections of the foreign ministries of the People's Republic of Bulgaria, the Polish People's Republic and the Socialist Republic of Romania, whom I wish to thank here for their co-operation. I am also grateful to the director and staff of the research departments of Radio Free Europe for allowing me to browse through their invaluable library of reference material on Eastern Europe, and to make use of their research papers and surveys, references to which are acknowledged in the notes. For help with translations I should like to thank Mrs Olga Kovaly, Miss M. M. and Miss K. Slepokoura.

I should like to thank Penguin Books for permission to quote from *The Monument* by Antonin Brousek published in a translation by G. Theiner in *New Writing in Czechoslovakia* (1969); and from *Leave Us Alone* by Tadeusz Rozewicz, translated by Czeszlaw Miłosz in *Post-War Polish Poetry* (1970).

I should also like to thank the proprietors of *East Europe* (the magazine formerly entitled *News From Behind the Iron Curtain*)

Preface

for permission to quote from the articles mentioned in the notes
on pp. 365–8.

I have had most valuable advice on a substantial part of the
manuscript from Mr Zoltán Szabó. Of great help were the com-
ments made on various parts of the book by Mr Peter Brent,
Dr David Caute, Mr Richard Davy, Miss Jenny Hargreaves, Mr
Don Honeyman, Miss Ruth Isakaroff, Mr J. K. and Mr Andrew
Stypulkowski. I am grateful to my editors, Mr James Landis and
Mr John Jolliffe, for their patience and good advice, and greatly
obliged to Mrs Joslyn Pyne and Miss Vivienne Menkes for the
conscientious and, in my view, very fruitful work they have done
on the text. And I would like to thank most sincerely Marika,
Joe and Craig, who saw me through some difficult times in
completing this book, as three true friends.

Part I

The Hero

Introduction
I think my best way of beginning to describe the situation into
which today's young East Europeans were born will be to
approach it, as any westerner would, from the outside. In particular, by defining the way I intend to use the comparative term
'western' (and 'West' and 'westerners') throughout the rest of
this book. This will not only avoid some confusion, but will also
help to put what seems to me peculiar to Eastern Europe, and to
young people there today, into a sharper light.

Writing in London, by West I shall mean the handful of mostly
Anglo-Saxon countries of north-western Europe and North
America, forming an important but otherwise small part of the
world; countries which their geographical good luck has placed
around the northern Atlantic, thus both saving them from the
nomad invasions and a good many of the continental pressures
that have plagued even their culturally closest neighbours in
Europe, and enabling them to become the trader nations of the
modern era. As a result, they now constitute the most homogeneously developed part of the world. Economic progress and
consequent mobility have, largely without intervention by the
State, reduced the difference between the countryside and the
towns, and between social strata, to an extent unknown anywhere
else. This has on the whole coincided with the spread of education
and the extension of political rights, diminishing in both spheres
the monopoly of former ruling strata and at the same time pre-
venting the entrenchment of the military and the bureaucracy
who, in underdeveloped societies, are often turned into effective
élites by being at least half-educated and organized bodies.

All this is, of course, relative. In economic development the
countries of the West may be overtaken by others, but nowhere
else has development been more steady and less fraught with
sudden upheavals. As regards geographical and social homogeneity, in the West too differences between the countryside and

the towns and between social strata prevail, but these are generally nowhere near as sharp as, say, in the Mediterranean countries or in Mexico, to go no further. There is in the West, too, a cultural and a political élite, in semi-permanent positions, but the distance between them and the rest of each nation is not as great and the divisions not as rigid as are those between intellectuals and oligarchs on the one hand, and at best half-literate and nominally enfranchised masses on the other in, say, much of South America. And even though in the West, too, the civil service and the military wield considerable influence and may strive for more, neither their power nor their hopes of increasing it are equal to those of the bureaucracy even in Italy, or of the generals in the Greece or Nigeria of today.

Now, Greece is an East European country. Only external alignments make it seem close to the West. Geographically as well as in its development and in its social and political traditions it belongs in the region which to most people today means the five Communist countries whose young generation I shall be describing (and, to a somewhat lesser extent, Yugoslavia and Albania). In fact, had the Communists won the armed struggle in Greece which followed the Second World War, the country would now count as part of Eastern Europe. But they lost, as the Hungarian and Polish Communists lost in the struggles following the First World War, to the nationalist forces, from whose victory there has resulted a political system at best half-democratic and at worst wholly dominated by the military.

This was also what had happened during the inter-war period not just in Hungary and Poland but in all my five countries, with the exception of Czechoslovakia. Indeed, the present situation in Greece is politically and in certain other ways too very similar to that prevailing in the four non-democratic countries of Eastern Europe before the Second World War, and in another (though to my mind more hopeful) form throughout the region since.

Essential to this situation is the phenomenon of an élite corps in undisputed charge of each country, trying to rally the masses in what are proposed as various states of emergency. Any form of the proposition may be rhetorical or genuine, or both, and the masses may or may not accept it, or may do so only halfheartedly. But in every case its purpose is to centre loyalties on the élite as Hero, embodying the vital essence and consciousness of the collective, itself proposed as a beleaguered Individual. In terms dating back to Plato (and already criticized by Aristotle as open to abuse) the élite is posited as the manifest Universal of the collective, to whose Will all the latter's component individuals must in their own interests subordinate themselves.

Basic Patterns

The main difference between the heroic propositions of prewar East European élites and those of the Party has been that by the collective the first meant the nation and the second meant the people. The difference is not just nominal. The first is an essentially separatist, the second an internationalist notion. Beyond that, in Eastern Europe much more than the West, the first originally meant the ruling strata, and the second, the masses underneath.

One reason for this was the underdeveloped economic and social situation of the area, which maintained a virtual caste system. But another equally important reason had to do with the way in which the ideas of nationhood and democracy together reached Eastern Europe in the nineteenth century.

At that time, whereas in the generally independent countries of the West economic and social development had made the realization of liberal political ideas possible, Eastern Europe was both a retarded region and one whose countries were all either dominated or directly ruled by foreign powers. As a result, the idea of *Liberté*, sweeping through the educated classes of the continent after the French Revolution, had to be interpreted there not only as freedom from internal oppression for the individuals composing the people, but also as freedom from foreign rule for the nation-collective as an Individual.

The two, however, meant different things, and to some people they were opposites. The internal oppressors constituted the politically enfranchised 'nation', and while in several countries this nation readily enough proposed itself as the collective's Hero commanding the struggle against foreign rule, only an insignificant minority of its members chose to become the people's heroes against the native ruling strata. The ones who did very

The Hero's Children

often found themselves rejected by those strata in turn (on occasions as 'anti-national').

And it was the nationalist rather than the democratic version of the heroic idea that the regimes of the 1920s and 1930s embraced in the four eastern countries of the region. By contrast, when the Party got into power in 1945–8, though in several East European countries it was a good deal less popular than the pre-war regimes had been, and though it retained many of the bureaucratic features and merely exaggerated the militant postures of its predecessors, in its basic policies it proved to have the interests of the actual people, rather than those of any historic 'nation', at heart.

This is, of course, putting it very broadly. But before I go on to explain myself in more detail I draw the reader's attention to the maps on pages 16 and 17, and the chronological table on pages 18–21, which serve as the framework of what I am about to say.

The maps will provide a guide to the histories of foreign conquest that form the most memorable part of each East European country's experience. It will also show the shifting of frontiers at the end of the First World War, separating large minority populations from their mother nations and so preparing the ground for Eastern Europe's involvement in the Second World War, which brought a further shifting of frontiers and populations. In the chronological table I have concentrated on the 1918–45 period, and within that on events and figures that are either essential to an understanding of the historical background of this book or are actually mentioned by my interviewees.

As can be seen from the map and the table, the vision of the collective in a state of emergency and in need of a Hero to lead and save it is rooted in Eastern Europe in starkest historical reality. External pressure and lasting foreign rule form the major experience of each nation. Worse, by the beginning of the nineteenth century several were, or saw themselves as being, on the verge of losing their cultural identities, that is, becoming extinct nations; (the more so as the enfranchised 'nation' usually spoke the language of the foreign oppressor, or French or Latin, while only the people, who at that time counted for little, kept alive the native tongue and customs). This is why most of the nationalist move-

14

ments first took the form of cultural revivals, and even as political phenomena for ever retained a vision of the nation-collective engaged in producing its own rebirth through liberation, and regaining its former stature and territorial greatness.

This was also one of the main reasons why poets, writers, grammarians and other users of the language, and later intellectuals in general, became so prominent first in the nationalist movements and then in the revolutions and wars of independence. To some extent this was a secularization of the work which the clergy had been doing for centuries and indeed carried on during the romantic era, both as champions of the people's spirituality against alien religions which imperial oppressors tried to impose to cement their rule, and also at times as actual warrior leaders.* But whereas most political nationalists of the region remained true members of the internal ruling strata in striving for independence rather than democracy, the intellectuals, having begun as champions of the people's language and culture against both the internal and external oppressor, emerged instead as democrats, founding a tradition that has lasted to this day.

Not all the nations of Eastern Europe, however, reacted to the mortal threat in a heroic way. In fact controversies raged between adherents of the 'heroic' (romantic) and 'realistic' (positivistic) concepts of nationalism inside several of the national élites themselves, with circumstances swaying the majority of each one way or the other from time to time. Though both the heroic and the realistic nationalists were concerned with seeing the nation be reborn to its former greatness, they differed radically on how this should be brought about. The first saw the main threat in outside menace, and advocated attempting to liberate the nation at all costs, and perhaps developing the country afterwards; the second envisaged going to work on internal underdevelopment, and then taking a suitable opportunity to assert the nation's independence.

* The Bulgarian and Romanian national revival movements both began with priests doing pioneering work on the nation's language and history, and throughout the region the clergy remained important in nationalist conspiracies, and even in the wars of independence. In Poland, of whose three rulers Russia was Orthodox and Prussia Protestant, Catholic services often developed into nationalist demonstrations.

EASTERN EUROPE
IN 1914

0   50   100   200 miles

Poland: Partitioned between Russia, Prussia and Austria 1795; reborn as country 1917–18, gaining territories until 1922, when of her 27 million people, 4 million were Ukrainians, 1 million Byelorussians and 1 million Germans; divided between Germany and Soviet Union 1939; reborn, 'moved' 130 miles westward 1945.

Czechoslovakia: Born 1918 out of Czech lands of Bohemia and Moravia (under Habsburg rule since end of sixteenth century) and Slovakia (under Hungarian rule since tenth century); between wars contained 3·2 million Germans and 700,000 Hungarians in a population of about 14 million; 1938–39 Sudetenland awarded to Germany, Slovakia secedes, Czech lands occupied by Germans; reborn as country 1945.

Hungary: Overrun in 1526 by Turks, who took central parts, the west coming under Habsburgs, who gained total control at end of seventeenth century; be-

came semi-equal partner in Austria-Hungary 1867, with minority populations about half of the total; gained independence 1918, losing three-fifths of former territory and two-thirds of former population to neighbours.

Romania: Born 1859 out of Principalities of Wallachia and Moldavia, under Turks since fifteenth century, with Russian overlordship since 1820s; achieved full independence 1878, incorporated Transylvania (under Hungarian rule since eleventh century) in 1918-20; between wars contained 1·5 million Hungarians, 750,000 Germans, 1 million Ukrainians and Russians; lost Bessarabia to Soviet Union 1944.

Bulgaria: Oldest kingdom of area; overrun by Turks late fourteenth century; gains virtual independence 1878, full sovereignty 1908; in Second Balkan War 1913, lost Macedonia to Serbia and Dobruja to Romania which, despite efforts in both world wars, were only partly recovered.

17

TABLE I

	EXTERNAL POWERS AND EVENTS	POLAND	CZECHOSLOVAKIA	HUNGARY	ROMANIA	BULGARIA
PRE-1914	Imperial rule over parts of Eastern Europe by Turkey, from 1370s to 1908; Austria, from early 16th century to 1918; Russia, from 1772 to 1917; Prussia, from 1772 to 1918.	Conspiratorial movements against Russian rule culminated in 1830–31 rebellion and war of independence, defeat resulting in loss of some remaining aspects of sovereignty; rest of these lost in second war of independence, 1863–64, followed by intense Russification in eastern parts and intense Germanisation in west, but also rapid economic development.	National revival movement in Czech lands from 1790s, in Slovakia somewhat later; after defeat in Prague rebellion (1848), economic development and social homogenisation proceed in Czech lands; while in politics moderate nationalism holds sway; turn of century saw rise of Realist Party, headed by T. G. Masaryk, subsequent founder of republic.	Linguistic revival movement of 1790s took reformist political character in 1820s but remained blind to rights of non-Magyar population; same blindness a major cause of defeat in 1848–49 war of independence; ensuing period of repression ended in Compromise with Austria (1867), which ushered in period of economic development.	National revival movement from 1800s onwards; small revolution in 1848, put down by Turkey at Russian insistence; semi-independent constitution of 1864 liberal, but remains unimplemented; from 1870s onwards some economic development occurs, chiefly authoritarian governments in power, with nationalism the only bond between them and masses.	National revival movement from 1760s onwards; in 19th century, moderate nationalists envisage economic and political modernisation under Turkish rule, radicals put independence first; major revolt in 1876, savagely suppressed ('Bulgarian atrocities'); following 1878, semi-independent country remains in hands of autocrats, but three decades of economic development ensued; the results largely wiped out by near-continuous war between 1912 and 1918.

WORLD WAR I	Germany and Austria-Hungary (Central Powers) war with Russia (allied to France and Britain in West) over domination of Eastern Europe.	Poles taken into war as soldiers in three imperial armies, while Pilsudski's Polish Legions fight Russia as Poland's main enemy; collapse of empires brings rebirth of country.	Czechs and Slovaks taken into war by Austria-Hungary, deserted in large numbers to enemy side, while Masaryk's Prague group plots with émigrés in West to bring about independence.	As one of Central Powers, suffered defeat, with disastrous peace treaties imposed on it by western Allies.	Originally neutral, drawn to Allied side in 1916 through promise of Transylvania and half of Hungarian Plain; emerged as victor.	Joined Central Powers with aim of recouping losses suffered in 1912–13 Balkan Wars, but suffers defeat.
INTER-WAR PERIOD	1917 Russian Revolution ends reign of tsars. 1918 Defeat throws Germany into chaos, reduces Austria to a small central European country. 1922 Mussolini becomes fascist Prime Minister of Italy. 1926–27 Stalin's rise in Russia, with internal and external policies of Socialism in One Country becoming dominant; First Five Year Plan 1928, with first series of 'sabotage' trials,	1919–21 Polish–Soviet War ends in Pilsudski's victory with large territorial gains in east, and Pilsudski a national hero. 1920–26 While minimal land reforms leave rural poverty acute, country's financial situation grows critical, and its parliament anarchical. 1926 Pilsudski's coup d'état; new constitution grants him semi-dictatorial powers, but democratic parties retain	October 1918 Independent republic declared. April 1919 Land reforms dispose of all estates over 375 acres. 1920 Democratic constitution, the only one in area to remain in practice until World War II; but its centralised rather than federal structure is opposed by Slovaks, who come to support the autonomist Slovak People's Party of Fathers Hlinka and Tiso, while German population is set	March–August 1919 Bela Kun's Commune flounders in red terror. November 1919 Admiral Horthy's counter-revolutionary regime, having unleashed white terror throughout the country, takes power in Budapest. 1920–24 Under Count Bethlen, electoral laws effectively deprive peasantry of suffrage, while land-reforms remain minimal, but inflation is replaced with economic	1920 General Averescu's government puts through sizeable land reforms but deals firmly with Communists and imposes martial law and censorship. 1926 Bratianu, leader of liberals, promulgates electoral law with built-in advantages for government. 1928 Following Bratianu's death Maniu's National Peasant Party gains chance to win 90 per cent of seats in free elections, and then to relax censorship and	1920 Agrarian leader Stamboliiski becomes Prime Minister with great majority, divides among peasants all estates over 75 acres and pursues conciliatory policies towards country's neighbours. June 1923 Irredentist organisation allied to officer's group stages coup d'état; Stamboliiski killed. September 1923 Communist-led rising, suppressed in bloodshed, and followed by reign of terror and

EXTERNAL POWERS AND EVENTS	POLAND	CZECHOSLOVAKIA	HUNGARY	ROMANIA	BULGARIA
start of forcible collectivisation 1929. **1929** Crash on Wall Street, effect overtaking Europe from 1930 onwards, and lasting in Eastern Europe till late thirties. **1933** Hitler's rise in Germany; subsequent German economic penetration of south-eastern Europe, coupled with encouragement and financing of German minority rights movements and local fascist groups. **September 1938** Munich agreement by Germany, Italy, France, Britain dismembers Czechoslovakia. **March 1939** Britain guarantees Poland's territorial integrity.	influence and an era of stability ensues. **1929-30** Pilsudski's rule hardens, effected through loyal officer corps, with huge bureaucracy underneath, while impact of world financial crisis helps radicalise opposition both Left and Right. **1935** Pilsudski's death leaves his colonels in charge of country; new electoral laws make government defeat impossible. **1938** Poland participates in dismemberment of Czechoslovakia. **1st September 1939** German invasion of Poland, followed by Russian invasion 17th September. By 21st September, whole country	against its inclusion in state. **1929** Following period of prosperity and relative calm, Hitlerite influence becomes manifest in election of eight Nazi candidates by Sudeten Germans to Czechoslovak parliament; effects of world financial crisis and of Hitler's rise to power in Germany further aggravate situation. **May 1935** German *Heimatfront*, autonomist, anti-semitic, strongly pro-Nazi, emerges as largest single party in elections; belated attempts to satisfy demands of German population have no effect, and Slovak autonomists also grow restive. **28 September 1938**	reconstruction and right-wing extremism is curbed. **1931** Effects of world financial crisis end Bethlen's era. **1932-35** Gömbös, new Prime Minister, seeks Hitler's and Mussolini's support for Hungary's territorial claims, but in internal policies his fascist demagoguery is tamed by situation he inherited. **November 1938** Hungary is awarded (mostly Magyar-inhabited) Slovakian areas by Hitler and Mussolini. **May 1939** Fascists gain 25 per cent of popular vote. **August 1940** Hungary is awarded northern Transylvania by	police rule; 1930, Maniu resigns. **1932** Fascist Iron Guard, active since mid-twenties, gains first two seats in parliament. **1937** Maniu makes pact with Guard, which gets 16 per cent of votes, with 9 per cent going to semi-fascistic National Christian Party led by poet Octavian Goga, who is asked by King Carol to form government; affair ends in King taking power in his own hands. **August 1940** Popular reaction to Vienna Award undermines Carol's rule, he abdicates in favour of son, actual power going to General Antonescu and Iron	assassinations. **1926-31** Under semi-liberal government, era of consolidation prevails, but is brought to end by impact of world financial crisis. **May 1934** Second coup d'état by military group; all parties disbanded, full censorship imposed, secondary education curtailed. **1935** King Boris takes power. **1938** While nationalist agitation grows, Bulgaria signs non-aggression pact with neighbours, as price of being allowed to re-arm. **1940** Germany forces Romania to return Southern Dobruja to Bulgaria.

August 1939 German–Soviet Pact with secret clause on partitioning of Poland. September 1939 German attack on Poland starts Second World War.	occupied.	Munich agreement dismembers Czechoslovakia.	Hitler.	Guard. November 1940–January 1941 Iron Guard violence, suppressed by Antonescu with aid of army, gives him chance to take power alone.	German troops having established bases for operations against Greece and Yugoslavia, 1941, country declares war on western Allies only; September 1944 becomes neutral, then, under Soviet pressure, declares war on Germany.
Germany (with Bulgaria, Romania, Hungary and Slovakia on its side) overruns Czech lands and Poland, before invading Soviet Union, by which (allied to France, Britain and U.S. in West) it is eventually defeated.	After being shared out between Germany and Soviet Union, comes entirely under German rule following invasion of Soviet Union June 1941; powerful resistance movement; country loses 1/5 of population between 1939 and 1945.	March 1939, Czech lands occupied by Germany, whose protectorate they remain until late 1944, showing little resistance; Slovakia, autonomous but vassal of Germany, develops resistance movement.	Having annexed territory from neighbours, country declares war on Soviet Union after German invasion of latter; its attempts to make contacts with Allies, and then to get out of war, provoke German invasion, March 1944.	Invades Soviet Union with Germany and carves new province for itself out of conquered territory, but, with Soviet troops invading it, changes sides in August 1944.	

WORLD WAR II

These controversies have, as I shall explain, continued under various forms in Eastern Europe to the present day.

During the nineteenth century the Poles and the Hungarians opted on the whole for heroism. They mounted long wars of independence, which they lost, but from which the vision of re-birth through combat against impossible odds still accrued to the national tradition. Between these two 'heroic' nations the Czechs, who rose only briefly in 1848, developed a philosophy of 'realism' which their more flamboyant neighbours have never been able to forgive them. In Bulgaria, where military risings throughout the nineteenth century culminated in a savagely suppressed rebellion in 1876, the issue continued to be debated until the acquisition of independence, while in the Romanian Principalities it had little time to be defined before the attainment of sovereignty in 1859.

In more recent years, whereas the prewar élites in the four non-democratic countries of the region took the heroic view, with militant postures and rhetoric in foreign affairs and, internally, efforts to preserve the *status quo* rather than promote change, the Party since 1945-8 has proved a realist. This must be immediately qualified, however, by saying that at least some of the measures instituted by prewar élites had the realistic purpose of economic development in mind, while many of the Party's own economic targets, and the centralist methods used in the attempt to achieve them, have been nothing short of heroically insane.

Let me give an example of the first. For a period in prewar Romania nationalism manifested itself not only in a lot of noise, but also in autarchic policies of development. However hard these were on the peasantry, who thus had to buy home-produced industrial goods at much higher prices than imported ones would have cost, their aim was to finance the growth of native industry. Examples from the postwar period I shall discuss shortly, but in general every East European Party in the Stalinist era not only engaged in violent rhetoric about external and internal 'enemies', and terror against the latter, but also set itself and the people titanic tasks in the economy. After Stalin, and especially from the late fifties onwards, differences appeared that separated the various Parties of the region, and various factions within them, into groups that may be called heroic-centralist on the one hand and realistic-decentralizing on the other, if the reader will forgive these unwieldy names. On the whole, though centralism is inherent in the Party's vision of itself as an élite indisputably and for ever in charge, individual Parties and factions now take their positions in the spectrum not so much for ideological reasons as according to how acute they consider the emergency situations of their countries to be, due to underdevelopment and the lack of managerial brains. Where the heroic-centralist vision is close enough to the truth, as in the two least developed countries in the south, the damage done by centralism is less than it has been in, for instance, Czechoslovakia – by far the most developed and homogeneously educated country of the region.

A version of the same 'developmental map' of Eastern Europe actually provides the basic clues to why the various nations adopted 'heroic', 'realistic' or half-way attitudes in the first place, though these may have been ascribed afterwards simply to their 'national characters'. The same developmental map has also underlain the 'behavioural map' of the region ever since the nineteenth century, and not least during the lifetime of the present generation. In other words, the postures adopted in the era of national revival have, due to versions of the original reasons, characterized these nations ever since.

To begin with, the postures were taken up by the enfranchised élites ('nations') and only in imitation of them, if at all, by their peoples. As such, they reflected the way in which any particular élite saw its own situation, historically and in the nineteenth century, and within the internal and external context. In the four eastern countries, economic and social retardation had kept the élite, consisting mainly of landowners, almost totally separate from the people. It was also culturally, and in the large minority areas of Hungary and Poland and throughout Bulgaria nationally, alien from the masses which politically it ruled. Such an alienated élite was bound to prefer that whatever liberty emerged should be its own freedom to rule the people alone, rather than the people's freedom to shake off its rule. In fact one of the reasons why the Romanian élite developed no distinct concept of nationalism was that it habitually sided with the foreign oppressor with a view to securing firmer control for itself over the people. This was also why in both Romania and Bulgaria the heroic concept of nationalism triumphed only after foreign rule, with the crumbling of the Ottoman Empire, had been withdrawn, leaving the local élites in charge and in need of rallying the people.

Hungary and Poland, however, had native landowning classes, possessing far more political rights than their southern equivalents and looking back to military traditions famous throughout Europe.* In other words, there were established and relatively secure élites, with a good deal to lose to both the foreign oppressor on the one hand and the people on the other, and all too inclined to react heroically to pressure or violence from both. In fact the inability of these élites to bring themselves either to compromise with the foreign oppressor and so secure the maximum possible gains, or to give the peasants land and so have a large enough popular army at their disposal, were two major causes of their defeat in their wars of independence.

The situation in the Czech lands (joined by Slovakia only on the foundation of T. G. Masaryk's republic at the end of the First World War) was wholly different from that in the four eastern countries. The native landowning classes had been dispossessed in the seventeenth century by victorious Austria. More important, a mainly German-speaking burgher stratum had developed the area – especially Bohemia – into a centre of manufacture and industry, which had one of the most homogeneous societies in the whole of Europe by the time the nationalist movement began to gather momentum. As a result the movement found its leaders not in aristocrats but in middle-class intellectuals, and its troops not in any gentry but in the middle and lower-middle classes and the beginnings of an urban proletariat. The social distance between the élite, its prime troops and the people underneath being thus much smaller than anywhere else in the region, the nationalist movement both acquired and managed to retain a more demo-

* Poland was wiped off the map only in 1795, and then retained a separate parliament until 1831 and various aspects of sovereignty until 1864. Hungary, which had a parliament throughout, came under direct Austrian administration following defeat in 1849, but then gained semi-sovereignty, and full power over its minorities, in 1867.

cratic political character, a preference for the idea of economic and social development over heroic gestures, and a good deal of the commoner's readiness to compromise, as opposed to the flamboyance, and often arrogance, of the aristocracy and the gentry. All this found final embodiment at the turn of the century in Masaryk's philosophy of Realism, which then became basic to the republic he founded and led as president until shortly before his death in 1937.

Between the wars, when all of the five countries of Eastern Europe were independent, their behaviour can be said to have corresponded closely to their 'characters'. Czechoslovakia remained a democracy, based in all spheres on the idea of compromise. In the other countries the heroic attitudes, by then hallowed with the memory of revolutions and battles lost and won, and beautiful romantic poetry as well as some hideous songs of hatred for the nation's enemies, were taken over by the groups assuming authoritarian power.

The most important reason for this behavioural contrast between the countries of Eastern Europe lay, however, not in their 'characters', but in the economic, social and political situations holding them captive. Basically, these were versions of the situations which had generated the postures of their élites in the first place. It may even be said that the good and bad luck of the countries of the region, which had already separated the Czech lands from the rest while they were all under foreign rule, lasted them through the First World War and their two decades of independence.

Economically, while Czechoslovakia prospered or at worst wanted, the four eastern countries remained indigent or grew delirious with hunger. The First World War never touched the Czech lands and only provided work and further stimulus for their developed industries. By contrast, it physically devastated Poland and Romania, economically ruined Bulgaria (already weakened by the 1912–13 Balkan wars) and brought defeat and the loss of nearly all its previous markets and sources of raw materials to Hungary, then the industrial centre of the Carpathian Basin. Within a decade came the Depression. This affected Czechoslovakia badly enough, but it caught the four eastern countries of the region, where the peasantry constituted half to four-fifths of the population in the 'price scissors' (with world agricultural prices sinking further and taking longer to recover than industrial ones) from whose deadly grip the three southern ones were freed only by Germany beginning to buy their produce in exchange for industrial goods in the later thirties, as part of a policy of economic penetration. To have Hitler as their saviour then landed them in the Second World War.

Socially, in Czechoslovakia homogenization was furthered by the departure of the Hungarian landowning class from Slovakia and by some of the most sweeping land reforms in the region, which broke up all the large estates. In the four eastern countries, however, the distance between the strata mostly survived. Of the three countries where land reforms would have been needed, Poland, Hungary and Romania, only in the last were any significant ones introduced, and even these hardly made an impression on the numbers of landless and more often than not unemployed labourers in the countryside. In Bulgaria there was a large and relatively prosperous small-holder stratum, and the two northern countries by then had a noticeable industrial proletariat; but in all countries upward social mobility, especially through education, remained a dream for the masses. What there was of a middle class either derived from the gentry or was a reproduction of itself. In the three northern countries, and especially Poland, it also consisted, in a very significant measure, of Jews, whom most of the rest feared and at the very least disliked as aliens.

Politically, whereas Czechoslovakia remained a full democracy up to its dismemberment at Munich in 1938, in the four eastern countries authoritarianism of one kind or another reigned, and grew progressively more authoritarian. They had parliaments in which the largest class of the nation, the peasantry, was badly underrepresented either from the start, as in Hungary and Romania, or within a few years, as in Bulgaria and Poland. And even though other classes could make themselves heard to a considerable extent, as the years wore on each country found itself ever more firmly in the hands of the bureaucracy and above that a secret or open military junta or, as in Romania, the king and later a general.

It was natural for such regimes to display heroic attitudes, both as a matter of conviction and in order to rally the people they oppressed by diverting popular resentment on to 'enemies'.* The people in any case were so distressed by their circumstances, and often so mad with hunger, that they were already looking for scapegoats in alien forces and phenomena. It was enough for the inter-war regimes to encourage such tendencies to turn them into defensive passions and hysterias.

The three most important of these passions were irredentism (and its complement, full integrationism in the countries which had gained rather than lost territories, and with them minorities, in the war) anti-Bolshevism and anti-Semitism. All three, seeing the nation-collective as an Individual threatened by external enemies and by corruptive elements in its own body, were sub-variants of nineteenth-century heroic nationalism, whose powerful heritage they took over and exploited to the hilt.

There was, once again, least trace of them in Czechoslovakia, where the situation in no way compelled their encouragement from above and did much less to help their popular growth than in the four eastern countries. Tacit attempts to integrate the minorities were made, but these minorities enjoyed far more rights than in any other country of the region. Whatever Masaryk or anyone else thought of Bolshevism, the Communists were not just un-persecuted but possessed one of the four largest parties in parliament. And anti-Semitism, though appreciable, especially in Slovakia, had found an outspoken enemy in Masaryk himself.

In the four eastern countries, however, at least one and on occasions all three sub-variants of nationalism were both encouraged from above and rampant at the popular level. Irredentism was strongest in Hungary and Bulgaria, which had lost territories

---

* Part of the reason for this was, paradoxically, that these regimes were more democratic in their social composition than the previous élites had been. Their members had in most cases attained positions in the bureaucracy or the military through combinations of merit and nepotism rather than sheer inheritance. But being thus inferior versions of nineteenth-century aristocrats and intellectuals, they were all the more eager to imitate the manners of the established ruling strata in both politics and social life, and all the less generous towards the people into whose ranks they were afraid they might sink, or from which they had just emerged.

and populations, and full integrationism in Poland and Romania. Anti-Bolshevism was vivid in Poland, following the 1919 Polish-Soviet war and the attempt to spread Communism to the country on the point of bayonets; it enjoyed equal vigour in Hungary following the disastrous 1919 Commune, and in Romania following territorial conflicts with Communard Hungary and later territorial disputes with the Soviet Union; it was also fairly strong among the middle and upper classes in Bulgaria, who had approved of the bloody 1923 *coup d'état* as putting an end to the peasant-Bolshevik dictatorship of Alexandar Stamboliiski.

Anti-Semitism was the ugliest of the sub-variants in that it was aimed at people closely surrounded by their persecutors, rather than at 'enemies' living in wholly separate groups or beyond the borders. As far as encouragement from above was concerned, the Hungarian regime indulged in this immediately after the 1919 Commune (a striking percentage of whose commissars had been Jewish) and intermittently afterwards, as did the Romanian regime; it was used least in Poland, where Marshal Piłsudski's main opposition came from the Right, and was a lot more anti-Semitic than he seemed to be. In Bulgaria, which had few Jews and a tradition of tolerance towards them since Turkish days, anti-Semitism was never fostered at all.

Almost independent of official attitudes, however, anti-Semitism was a popular passion in the three northern countries where, as I have mentioned, Jews made up a significant proportion of the upper-middle and middle classes and were especially strong in business and the professions. As such they were hated by many of their native competitors. At the same time the lower-middle classes and parts of the urban proletariat and of the peasantry regarded the Jews as the cause of all the misery resulting from the First World War and the Depression, which were thought to have benefited alien capital only. Besides being capitalists and professionals, Jews were also prominent in the Communist movement at all levels, and this seemed to give substance to the idea of a vast Jewish pincer operation aimed at the Christian nations of the earth, each standing as a mortally beleaguered Individual.

And whatever the actual regimes did about any of these sub-variants of nationalism, all were furiously propagated, in combination with social demagogy, by Fascist movements, and to great effect. In Poland, Fascism ruled a section of the largest opposition party and groups to the right of it, and in both Hungary and Romania elections in the late thirties brought Fascist parties a full 25 per cent of the popular vote.

The regimes themselves, though called fascistic by the Communists who replaced them, were conservative-authoritarian in outlook. They made occasional use of the nationalist hysterias, but mostly for the purpose of establishing or maintaining what they regarded as God-given order. They never entertained the mad territorial dreams of the Fascist movements, let alone spoke of exterminating or even expropriating the Jews, even if they thought it every decent man's duty to dislike them. In fact they used middle-class fears of Fascism rather as they used general fears of Bolshevism, to confirm themselves in power.

Altogether, though they posited the nation as a beleaguered Individual and themselves as its commanding Hero, their interpretation of the role became increasingly paternal. With the blessing of the Church, they upheld the social *status quo* as the best defensive order of each nation, in the manner of fathers meaning to preserve the structure of indigent families in a most insecure world. They were also accepted as such by substantial segments of each population, in whose own social units, from the family and the school community to the labouring gang and the micro-societies of factory and office, the same kind of economic strains, traditions of management and sense of close danger maintained the same sort of authoritarian structure and attitudes. In this sense, the national-authoritarian State as a whole expressed the conservatism of its parts.

However, neither the internal nor the external situation of the four eastern countries of the region favoured the survival of authoritarian conservatism. Internally, they needed rapid economic development and radical social changes. As the national-authoritarian regimes envisaged little of either, in due course the worst-off and so most desperate sections of the people were bound to look for alternatives. This was why the Fascist movements (which were free to propagate their extremism, whereas the Communists were banned in the three southern countries and allowed only under another name in Poland) made such gains in the course of the thirties.

Externally, the region formed the buffer between the two extremist powers of the period, Stalin's Russia and Hitler's Germany. Both tried their hardest to exploit the internal tensions of each country, which the regimes tried only to contain, and the inter-country tensions of the region as a whole. Russia's appeal was minimal, due to grave mistakes by the Communists in Poland and Hungary in 1918–19, alienating national sentiments and antagonizing the peasantry, and further mistakes by native Communists and by the Russians in the 1920s and 1930s, alienating trade union movements and further enraging nationalists and peasants.

Germany, however, having long been a source of ideas and technical know-how, emerged to make superb use of both its own advantages and the problems plaguing Eastern Europe. It came as an economic saviour to the three southern countries, and offered all necessary aid to their regimes, while encouraging, advising and financing both the Fascist movements and the German minority movements of the region, though the two agreed only in their anti-Semitism and of course disagreed as regards irredentism and integration. Germany thus acquired genuine popularity and the actual allegiance of Hungary and Bulgaria and – at first less definitely but in the end more positively – Romania, while she still showed herself friendly to Poland, and staked claims only on the German-inhabited parts of the Czech lands, so pleasing both the minority there and the national separatists of Slovakia. As a result, by the time Czechoslovakia was deprived of its German-speaking areas at Munich in the autumn of 1938, and then broken in two, Hitler had the southern three and a half of the region's five countries on his side, and enjoyed the co-operative neutrality of Poland, leaving him free to invade the Czech lands in the following spring. Next, he joined hands with Stalin (in accordance with the German-Soviet Treaty of August 1939) to wipe Poland off the map in September, so starting the Second World War.

It was Hitler's defeat in this which left room for his chief rival, Stalin, to go to work on the region. The Red Army's arrival in Eastern Europe in pursuit of the Germans in 1944–5 and its domination of the area since in accordance with the Teheran and

Yalta agreements between Churchill, Roosevelt and Stalin have
been chiefly responsible for the present version of the Hero, the
Communist Party, being in charge there. Though in Czechoslovakia there had long been a strong Party, not even there could
it have attained power democratically, let alone suppressed all its
rivals, without reliance on Russian armed pressure. Elsewhere,
Russia directly imposed the Party, as will be explained in more
detail shortly.

Stalinism

Of course the situation in the four eastern countries had long
needed transforming in ways which could be envisaged only by
a revolutionary élite. Nor could there be much doubt about the
identity of this élite: of the alternatives available, rational considerations clearly favoured the Communists over the Fascists.
In fact it is a safe enough conjecture that if the Communists had
not alienated national sentiments and antagonized the peasantry
in 1918–19, they could have had the field to themselves much
earlier – as indeed they did in Russia, for precisely those reasons.*
And even after its disastrous attempts to gain power had ended in
the Party being driven underground and into exile, its ideology
retained the allegiance of significant minorities among the professional intelligentsia and – especially in Poland – the proletariat
(in addition to remaining a broadly based movement in Czechoslovakia).

The reasons for the appeal of revolutionary Marxism, particularly to segments of the intelligentsia in Eastern Europe, were
not far to seek. As an ideology, it combined some of the most
appealing elements of the native tradition with many of the most
worthwhile, and locked these into a system claiming 'scientific'
validity, which the tradition lacked.

* Contrary to Lenin's express advice, the Polish Communists in 1918–19
quite simply denounced their country's new-born independence, and both they
and the Hungarian Communists in 1919 set about nationalizing estates *en bloc*
rather than distributing them to the peasants. Lenin himself, however, gave the
peasants land in order to rally them against the landlords, and in the Civil War
posited the Bolsheviks as Russia's defensive command against foreign intervention and its allies, the Whites, so enlisting patriotism, on which the Party
there has been drawing ever since.

On the one hand it was clearly revivalistic, and infinitely heroic. Its dialectical vision of history as mankind's inexorable progress towards its own rebirth in perfection magnified the vision of national history instilled in every East European child since his schooldays. At the same time, it prophesied, as the penultimate episode of the process of rebirth, a vast revolution, to be executed by the proletariat under the leadership of its conscious élite and inevitably changing the world for ever.

On the other hand it was democratic, and realistic to the point of materialism. It championed the people as part of mankind instead of what it denounced as the upper-class concept of the nation, and though this alienated from it the nationalists among the intelligentsia, it also gained for Marxism the unswerving allegiance of the anti-nationalist democrats. (This was the chief reason, beyond its appeal to their sympathies for the oppressed and their Messianic heritage, why Marxism was embraced by so many Jews, themselves unattached to the nationalist establishments.) And it put the emphasis on economic development as basic to all other forms of development in society, and on rational and socially conscious planning as a precondition of the rebirth it prophesied. It thus proposed that an élite in charge on behalf of an ideal future should both aim at bringing about a heroic rebirth, and get down to solving the material and social problems that have plagued the people in the past.

And all this it presented within the framework of Dialectical Materialism, unquestionably the most fascinating and at first sight most convincing intellectual apparatus any revivalist or social-revolutionary movement had ever possessed. Indeed its materialism, its intellectuality, its revivalist visions and its revolutionary prophecies all contributed to its fascination and its powers of conviction. In essence it proposed that nothing less than laws inherent in Matter compelled the world and within it mankind to move inexorably through imperfect stages of (economic, social, political and spiritual) development, until they achieved perfection in socialism and then Communism, whose vanguard in the present was the Party. It thus anointed the conscious élite as in every sense, and for the most rational-seeming reasons, the Hero of the Universe.

Of course this presented the most presumptuous idealism as deterministic materialism, but that only enhanced the appeal of the combination. In fact, the essential paradox of Communist ideology was turned into a dynamic and apparently consistent whole through the dialectical method central to Marxism, whereby everything is declared to include its own opposite, and the observer becomes free to choose which of the opposites in anything he prefers at any point of an argument even with himself. Against this, especially while the argument remained theoretical, no reasoning could avail. The practical consequences of proposing the Party on the one hand as the Vanguard of Perfection and Rationality Incarnate and on the other as History's Hero and the Champion of Progress (that is, as simultaneously the Platonic Ideal Being and the Motor of Aristotelian Becoming) were duly inflicted on its members when it assumed total power, and with it total responsibility for all the ways in which its words and actions contradicted each other. But while the Party was underground or at most a parliamentary group in Eastern Europe, and ruled a single foreign country in the midst of 'hostile capitalist encirclement', the paradox remained part of its illogical appeal, which devotees employed the fiercest dialectics to uphold rather than to question.

This was the more so as they themselves were encircled badly enough, and without a hope of attaining power. In Czechoslovakia the Party could remain legal only as long as it played the parliamentary game. In the other four countries, where it had alienated popular support, it was also facing national-authoritarian regimes and their military, against which no leftist intellectual élite stood a chance. Thus it is literally true to say that the Red Army, sweeping the region clear not only of the Germans but also of every other military force, and establishing itself as dominant, was the main instrument of heaving the Party into power.

Nor could there be much doubt about this in Eastern Europe during the transitional period of 1945–8. In Bulgaria, Romania and Poland, Communist or closely sympathetic governments had been established through direct, and indeed unconcealable, Russian intervention by 1946. In Hungary democracy survived until the spring of 1947 and in Czechoslovakia until February

1948, but there too the key Ministry of the Interior, of Information, of Land Distribution, and so on had all had to be given to Communists, at Russian insistence. In fact, several East European leaders in the early fifties directly acknowledged the major role Russian help had played in the Party's ever attaining power. The Polish constitution, adopted in 1952, still carries in its preamble the acknowledgement: 'The historic victory of the Union of Soviet Socialist Republics over fascism liberated Polish soil, *enabled the Polish working people to take power into their own hands*, and established conditions for the national rebirth of Poland within new and just frontiers.'*[1]

It must be added, however, that whereas in 1919 the Communists had through their heroic disregard of local complexities alienated every population they had tried to rally, in 1945–8 they proved more realistic and emerged as a far more serious force. Instead of nationalizing estates, they made themselves the champions of land reform, in some countries following directly in the wake of the Red Army's advance westwards. Instead of rushing ahead to impose dictatorship, they engaged in various, often subtle manoeuvres to ally some democratic parties to themselves, even while their police forces and storm-trooping youth groups broke up the meetings of others. They also gained supporters with a speed that was remarkable in view of the memory they had left behind in 1919. In the 1945 free elections in Hungary they polled 17 per cent of the popular vote, and in the still mainly free 1946 elections in Czechoslovakia they achieved a victorious 38 per cent. Meanwhile, the size of Party membership throughout the region was growing apace. In Poland, for example, the numbers increased from 30,000 in 1944 to 550,000 by late 1946, and 820,000 by 1947, that is, before the Party had assumed total power.

* Italics mine. This last point refers to Poland ceding to Russia the territories in the east which Piłsudski's victory in the 1919 Polish-Soviet War had secured for her, and being compensated with formerly German territories in the west, whose population of some eight million she could expel (see map, p. 17). But as the result was to combine hatred of the Germans for their behaviour during the war with fears of German revanchism, this 'rebirth within new frontiers' also tied Poland to Russian protection, and hence to the Party Russia favoured.

A part of this support came from opportunists, who wisely foresaw that a Russian presence meant a Communist future. But Communism also held a genuine appeal for sections of the peasantry, who were grateful for land and trusted in the Party's promises that no collectivization would follow; for the industrial proletariat, whom the Party proposed to make the leading element in society; and above all for the radical intelligentsia, among whom Communism had always found its most ardent and faithful supporters.

Nor were Communist policies, as proposed partially ever since 1945 and revealed in full on the Party's assumption of power, wholly unsuited to the four eastern countries of the region. The nationalization of the economy, the proposed transformation of society, the democratization of the general and higher educational system, the extension of welfare measures and of unprecedented privileges to the manual-working strata, all gained Communism a good deal more support than hostility. The Party's programmes of rapid development, with industrial investment far in excess of that envisaged for agriculture, and heavy industrial investment well in excess of that directed towards the consumer industries, also seemed to be at least an attempt to deal with the area's backwardness and to avoid the disasters of the thirties. Though a number of economic realists were opposed to these plans from the outset, more heroically minded experts approved of their targets, and the promise of national achievements certainly appealed to popular feelings. Even collectivization, begun in 1949, was recognized by economists as necessary if agriculture were ever to reach the standards of efficiency long since attained on the consolidated farmlands of the West. And of course idealistic Party members and sympathizers, both in Eastern Europe and abroad, could regard the nationalization of the economy almost down to the last ice-cream stand, and the collectivization campaign, as part of the progress of Eastern Europe towards the new age of mankind, in whose collectivist spirit the people was being powerfully re-educated at the same time.

What, however, ruined the Party's effort in the economy as much as in every other sphere was the mad heroism of its targets and the heroic centralism of its methods. The two were closely connected, indeed formed one of those dialectical wholes dear to the Party's theoreticians. This will be explained in greater detail below. But first it must be made clear why heroic centralism was bound to overtake the Party in a mad form during the fifties, and to remain in one form or another characteristic of its stance throughout Eastern Europe to this day.

Basically, heroic centralism is what defines the Party as the Party. There are three main reasons for this, of which one is ideological, one historical and one practical.

Ideologically, the demand for the maximum amount of centralized planning is essential to Marxist economics. At the same time, Marx's whole vision owes its systematic appearance to the fact that everything is connected to everything else within the universe round a single centre, namely, the idea of inexorable progress through history towards mankind's rebirth. As the conscious élite of the proletarian revolution is the ultimate champion of this progress, and as the idea resides in the élite's own consciousness (which is what defines it as the élite), the vision in fact centres the whole of the universe and its motion round the minds of a group of people, at the centre of which one man – Marx – is dominant. This proposition is as infinitely centralistic and prophetic as it is open to being abused by any one of the prophet's followers at the absolute centre.

Historically, Marxism was brought to triumph by a man whose main achievement lay, precisely, in the most brilliant abuse of prophetic centralism. He did so first to establish himself at the head of a group of revolutionaries, then to appropriate a vast popular upheaval on behalf of that élite group – said to be representing the proletariat and history – and finally to establish the same élite to the exclusion of all other groups emerging from the revolution, in charge of a vast country, which through its heirs the same élite has ruled since.

Essential to all of Lenin's tactics (and to the Party's own since his day) were two things. One was the principle of 'democratic centralism' which, from 1903 onwards, subordinated the Party to the decisions of its Central Committee, led by a caucus, itself ruled by Lenin. The other was the dialectical method of defending the decisions of the leader, the caucus, the Central Committee and then the Party against all comers, at any level, be they the worst reactionaries or the most convinced Marxists, by denouncing them as enemies of the Party, the proletariat, the people, the revolution and history altogether. This joined the dialectical vision of history which Marx and Engels had taken from Hegel and turned into Dialectical Materialism, to the dialectical defence of the Party at the centre of all its opponents, as History's Hero (and if necessary, the Leader at the Party's centre as History's Mind). Once again, no stance could have been more prophetic and none more open to abuse, but Lenin abused the ideas and tactics he had introduced for a worthwhile purpose. This purpose entailed finalizing the overthrow of the then most oppressive regime in Europe, and then imposing on Russia a band of zealots whose transformatory work the country badly needed.

It was the third, practical, reason which then drove heroic centralism to its logical extremes, lying beyond the borders of sanity. This practical reason derived from the difficulties the Bolsheviks of Russia encountered in their transformatory work, and from the way in which after Lenin's death Stalin tried to turn to practical advantage the difficulties of the Party and the country he emerged to rule.

In the late twenties Stalin declared, without much exaggeration, that Russia, as the single country of socialism, and the Party in heroically forlorn charge of it, were facing a quadruple war situation. They were at war with the country's own economic backwardness, on the defensive against 'hostile capitalist encirclement', threatened internally by the 'enemies of the people', and struggling to overcome the educational and cultural retardation of Russia's masses. In all four of these situations the people, and in their command the Party, had to fight or be overwhelmed, and defeat in any one meant death in all.

Once again, there could be little question about the tactical brilliance of the idea. It effectively combined the heroic-nationalist vision which Stalin's colleagues in charge of the four underdeveloped countries of Eastern Europe were also promoting, with the heroic-dialectical vision of history in which Russia suddenly figured as the Lone Vanguard of the Future threatened by the Forces of the World's Past, for the purpose of inducing heroism in the work of the country's development. This heroism it did induce. But next to that it also induced heroic insanity in planning, insane centralism in the effort to realize plans, and literally murder in dealing with anyone who had the misfortune to appear to be an enemy at any level. In other words, it was not just open to abuse, but bound to end in madness and so undermine many of its own benefits, inflict enormous suffering on the people which it drove into heroic work, and inevitably come round to devouring the majority of zealots who had begun by seeing themselves as the heroic command of the quadruple war effort. And it would have done so even without Stalin's personal paranoia and cruelty acting as catalysts to the whole process.

This then, was the form of Party centralism which the Red Army and its generalissimo imposed on the countries of Eastern Europe in 1945–8. And it was made even worse by two things. One had to do with the byzantine proportions which every one of its features, including Stalin's own megalomania, had acquired during the years since 1927. The other, with the conviction that had meanwhile been instilled into Communists throughout the world, that their fidelity to the cause must be measured by the degree of their subservience to the Russian Party, and at its centre, Stalin. The two together led to the copying of all the Central Hero's methods, which by then were at best only half-sane, as an act of faith in Historical Progress.

As heroic centralism meant Party rule over everything, its insanity was bound to become pervasive. In the economy, it led to the making of plans which, though obsessed both with vast targets and with giving every enterprise instructions on the minutest details of production, ignored not only the demands of the market, and costs, as a matter of policy, but often also the sheer availability of manpower and even raw materials. At the same time, as centrally made decisions had the full support of the political apparatus and its machinery of terror, there arose a situation in which mistakes could be made and magnified but rarely corrected. While iron-fast plans and the demand for sheer tonnage killed individual initiative and all sense of responsibility, living standards sank and shops were emptied of even essential goods, making the people feel that it was being forced to commit economic suicide. In agriculture, the collectivization drive ignored in the same heroically centralist way not only the peasantry's predictable unwillingness to part with land for which it had been yearning for centuries, but also the utter lack of the investments and machinery needed to make farming collectives work. As a result, psychological and physical terror of often insane proportions had to be employed to herd peasants into collectives, while agricultural production fell, not to achieve even prewar standards for years.

Politically, it was inherent in the Party being the Party that it should allow at best only the nominal survival of its competitors. But while its being thus identified with the State made it ever more bureaucratic as an organization, the Party also grew isolated as Hero at the centre of a system originally designed to connect it with every section of the people it claimed to represent and sought to command. Having assumed full power, the Party had also taken hold of all social organizations from trade unions to the smallest club of lepidopterists, so as to convey its message through them to the people. This was what Lenin had called turning mass organizations into 'transmission systems' of Party propaganda. Getting hold of these organizations had, however, amounted mostly to changing their constitutions and names and their functionaries, who from then on depended for their survival not on the allegiance of the people they were meant to guide and represent, but on the Party's favour. Predictably enough, the Party soon found itself surrounded with figures orating its message to an ever less credulous population, and mouthing the same propaganda back to the Party as if it were the people's genuine response.

A similar situation arose in culture and propaganda. The Party allowed only those who, sincerely or otherwise, presented its own heroically inspired and to the same extent insane picture of life, to make any contact with their public. In due course, the effort proved largely counterproductive and not only antagonized the already unconvinced majority of intellectuals themselves, but also shook the faith of the very important Communist minority among them.

This was especially tragic from the point of view of a Party which had always found its most fervent adherents among the professional intelligentsia and which, as Rationality Incarnate, had all along regarded as its natural allies every man of intellect and indeed every particle of truth about the world that the people had a chance to absorb (which is why *Pravda*, 'Truth', had ever been called *Pravda*, and why under Lenin all but directly anti-Soviet manifestations in culture could thrive). But ever worse alienation became inevitable when under Stalin intellectuals were pressed into service as mere war artists, obliged on pain not just of isolation but often of hunger and occasionally of death, to let the muses fall silent, and sacrifice truth as the first casualty.

All failures in the economy, as well as the resentment these and the Party's conduct in politics and all other spheres produced, were blamed by it on 'enemy manoeuvres'. The idea, once more presenting the collective as Plato's Individual surrounded by complex and intractable hostility, was accepted by many Party members, and even a substantial part of each population, as explaining at least partly what otherwise seemed largely insane. As such, it was used to justify the heavy sentences imposed for shop-floor laxity and the bloody purging of managements, the almost open war on the private peasantry and the vast campaigns against 'saboteurs', the ever-growing power of the secret police and the ever-widening circle of arrests, the existential blackmail or physical torture employed to make people inform on themselves and each other, and the vast show trials, in which the people's heroic defence of itself was supposed to reach its climax.

Altogether, the Stalinist period became the ultimate in the heroic-authoritarian experience of the peoples of Eastern Europe. Though the Party's economic policies aimed more realistically at development, and though its social intentions were far more democratic than those of the prewar élites, its situation as ruler was much the same. Posing as the supreme command of each economically and politically beleaguered collective, it was, instead of a military-bureaucratic regime blessed by the Church, a quasi-religious and equally bureaucratic regime upheld by the police. And the two main ways in which it differed from its predecessors only made its political rule harder to impose and harder, too, for the people to endure.

No native regimes that any of the peoples of Eastern Europe had known had ever tried to rule their economic, social, political, cultural and even personal and inner lives so thoroughly as the Party did. At the same time, no regimes ruling any East European country had ever been so thoroughly ruled from abroad. Indeed never before had all the countries of Eastern Europe been ruled from a single centre. Now they were: what each Party tried to be to its people, Moscow was to each Party. In fact, put in power with the help of Russian arms and thus already regarded as an alien imposition, the further each Party's attempts at total centralism alienated each people, the more totally each Party became dependent for its survival on the Moscow centre. And the more thoroughly each executed the economic and political directives which it was thus in the power of Moscow to impose, the less credibly could each present itself as the defensive command of its own people.

This was yet another 'dialectical whole' imprisoning the Party as Hero. Not even just in theory, but in bloodiest practice. While it tried its hardest to generate collectivist passions through blaming all failures on the 'enemy' abroad and at home, each Party was obliged by its position to denounce and persecute all those among its own members and even leaders who had tried to interfere on their countries' behalf, with the designs of the Moscow centre. This was why in the most important show trials defendants had to face charges – and admit to them either under torture or out of devotion to the cause – that no sane person could reconcile but which the Party, as a mere link in a no longer sane imperial administration, had to press (with the personal paranoia and cruelty of Stalin's local versions acting once again as catalysts). In the 1952 Slansky trials in Czechoslovakia, for instance, members of the same 'conspiratorial centre' were accused of having ruined the economy by sabotaging plans which (without regard to the absence of raw materials) Stalin himself had forced on the country; of having deliberately employed terror since 1948 so as to alienate the people from the Party; and of having tried to find western currency markets for Czechoslovak goods with the intention of selling the country to the enemy. To these and to an assortment of other crimes, for which eleven of the fourteen defendants were hanged, they were said to have been prompted by

Trotskyism, nationalism, cosmopolitanism, Zionism, and the habit of collaborating with the enemy learnt under the German occupation.

Post-Stalin Patterns

The death of Stalin in 1953 deprived the heroic-centralist universe he had established throughout Eastern Europe of its Central Hero. The essential result of this has since been to make the whole of that universe and every one of its units less heroic in their ideology and less centralistic in their methods. The main factors contributing to de-Stalinization in Eastern Europe have been the New Course, initiated by Stalin's immediate successors in Moscow, and affecting both the internal and external aspects of heroic centralism and isolationism; the denunciation of Stalin at the Twentieth Soviet Party Congress in February 1956, and of Stalinism in much broader terms at the Twenty-Second Congress in October 1961, by Krushchev; the admission of practical difficulties and sheer terror which the policies forced by Stalin and his local versions on the Parties of Eastern Europe had created; and reactions to both Stalinism and the changes that followed, among the people, the Party membership and Party leaders themselves throughout the region.

The main effect of de-Stalinization has been the onset of pragmatism (realism). Though the extent of this has differed from country to country and from sphere to sphere, in every case it has consisted of mixtures of rationalization and decentralization, with the quality of the mixture dependent partly on local factors, partly on the personalities and outlook of those in charge, and partly on the kinds of opposition de-Stalinizers have had to face in any sphere.

The spheres affected divide neatly enough in two main groups. One comprises the relationships of the Moscow centre to the Parties of Eastern Europe, and of the whole of Stalin's former empire to the rest of the world; the other, the relationships of each East European Party to the people it has continued to rule, and to the economic and social environment with which Party and people have had to cope together.

As regards the international sphere, Moscow has been allowing the Parties of Eastern Europe much more latitude in both external and internal affairs than Stalin had, while retaining its prerogative to command them as élites in charge of countries separate from the rest of the world. The kind of external defiance which Romania, for example, has been showing in both economic affairs and politics would have been unimaginable in the early 1950s. Similarly, the kind of internal variety now prevalent in the region, with pragmatism bordering on liberalism in Hungary and increasingly in Poland, paternal centralism in Bulgaria, semi-Stalinism in Romania, and harsh, if quixotic, Party rule in Czechoslovakia, was unknown and would have been found intolerable in Stalin's time. Though the present Moscow leadership appears to favour such externally loyal and internally self-sufficient managements as that now ruling in Hungary under János Kádár, and that apparently emerging as a result of Edward Gierek's policies in Poland since December 1970, Romania's very different behaviour has drawn only verbal fire and strong diplomatic pressure, but no Stalin-type purges, let alone armed invasion.

Moscow's rule over Eastern Europe has become not only less centralized but also more rational, in both its ideology and its practice. As regards ideology, though attestations of loyalty to the Soviet Union remain part of what Moscow likes to hear in any major policy speech by an East European leader, only at times of real crisis, such as occurred following the invasion of Czechoslovakia in August 1968, is such loyalty proposed as the prime attribute of a good Communist nowadays. As regards practice, though Moscow exerts pressure on the countries of Eastern Europe to become economically integrated among themselves and with the Soviet Union, the times when the measure of a good Communist negotiator lay in his willingness to sell cheaply to Russia are long past. In fact, not only has it become usual for Moscow to grant large loans and direct aid to East European Parties in times of trouble, as happened after the Hungarian Revolt of October 1956, the invasion of Czechoslovakia in 1968, and the Polish workers' riots in December 1970; it is also by now a perennial complaint of Soviet economists that as the prices of raw materials sink in the world and those of manufactured goods rise, Russia, being an exporter of the first and an importer of the second, is at a constant disadvantage compared to the more developed countries of Eastern Europe.

All this, however, can go only so far. When Moscow considers an East European Party to be in mortal danger of being overwhelmed by democratization, or its own rule over an East European Party to be threatened in ways that could prove mortal to the empire Stalin left behind, it reacts with the utmost force. In fact the two situations where Moscow has militarily intervened since Stalin's death – in Hungary in 1956 and in Czechoslovakia in 1968 – both appeared to combine the two main dangers that it cannot afford to tolerate along its western borders. In both cases the Party was threatened, violently in Hungary and politely in Czechoslovakia, with being reduced to the rank of one among several parties in a parliamentary system; and both countries appeared set to withdraw, immediately or in due course, from the Warsaw Pact, and choose neutrality on the pattern of their western neighbour, Austria. And where Moscow has refrained from direct intervention, it has allowed the threat to be made, implicitly or openly, on its behalf by the local Party. In Poland, whose history between late 1954 and October 1956 had combined Czechoslovak-type peaceful democratization with Hungarian-type street violence, in January 1957, on the eve of the freest elections Eastern Europe has seen under Party rule, the First Secretary of the Party, Wladysław Gomułka, warned the electorate that striking his Party's candidates off the ballot papers would be as good as 'striking Poland off the map of Europe'. In a country reborn only in 1918, and again banished to a bloody limbo between 1939 and 1945, and with the fate of Hungary fresh in everyone's mind, his warning was as good as a Russian invasion. It enabled his Party to return to power, and to re-establish itself once more as Hero in central charge.

In the two southern countries, of which Bulgaria has only seen measured de-Stalinization, and Romania only the denunciation of 'excesses' and the smoothing away of the worst features of heroic centralism, the Party has never been in danger of being swallowed up by the people. Nor has Moscow ever really been in danger of being deserted by the local Party. But should either of these eventualities threaten, Soviet divisions could be expected to appear, and Moscow to set about restoring the *status quo*, within days.

The internal situation, being a version of the external one, has seen much the same kind of changes, themselves subject to the same kind of limitations. In every country, pragmatism consisting of different mixtures of decentralization and rationalization has set in, without any Party showing signs of preparedness to give up its position as Hero in central charge.

Throughout the region, the process began with the denunciation, in violent or muted terms, of 'one-man leadership' and of the 'personality cult' which had accompanied it. By these were meant the political manners and sickening adoration of Stalin as Central Hero within the universe he had established; but the demolition work also encompassed the manners and cult of his local versions, either immediately, or when these people were brought down by events or, worst of all, after they had been called upstairs by God. Where denunciation of one-man leadership and its personality cult grew violent, as in Hungary in 1953–4 and then from the spring of 1956 onwards, and in Poland from late 1954 without much interruption, it became part of a process that ended in situations of mortal danger for the Party in both countries in October 1956, and shook the nerve of its most ardent Stalinists beyond recovery. Where it was perceptible but muted, as in Czechoslovakia and Bulgaria in 1953–4 and then again after the Twentieth Soviet Party Congress in February 1956, it still brought certain changes in personnel and policies and the tone of propaganda; these changes were to be greatly broadened following the Twenty-Second Congress in October 1961, setting in motion processes that led in Czechoslovakia to the Dubček period of 1968. In Romania, where the personality cult of the country's version of Stalin continued until the man's death in 1965, there persisted with it not only one-man leadership but also heroic centralism of a kind closest to Stalin's own, to be eased but never dismantled by the next leader, Nicolae Ceausescu; at the time of writing, he is in fact the only First Secretary in Eastern Europe to have his name chanted at Party and mass meetings by official encouragement.

Decentralization and rationalization have usually developed in phase with de-Stalinization proper, even where groups in agreement with the abolition of one-man leadership have nevertheless managed to retain or even revive aspects of centralism itself as a means of preserving or enhancing their own power. As a result, every East European Party is now more pragmatic than it was under Stalin, and certain policies pursued by some directly negate those of the 1950s.

In the economy, realistic reforms have been at the very least attempted from 1958 onwards. In every case they have combined increased enterprise independence (and in some countries the re-licensing of private small trade to provide services and quality goods) with a stress on the profitability of each enterprise and the marketability of its products, and with material and consumer incentives offered to management, workers and the population at large. This has involved planning in terms of major goals rather than minute details, the dispersal of responsibilities, and at the same time a greatly increased awareness of the demands of the market, and of the real costs of production, the last leading to a serious increase in prices.* In agriculture, though Poland is the only country not to have recommenced collectivization after 1956, a good deal has meanwhile been provided in money and machinery to make farming collectives work. Even more important, in several countries the peasantry has been allowed to sell the produce of its household plots freely on the market instead of having to let the State have it at give-away prices; this has both increased peasant prosperity and greatly improved the supply of food to the towns.

In politics, while the Party has ceased to be the monolith it was under Stalin, it has also either allowed a number of its prerogatives to lapse, or actually delegated a part of its former powers. In the pragmatic countries it now lets expertise prevail over political criteria in personnel selection, and allows mass organiza-

---

* A very unpopular measure, and the more so as it usually came at the start of reforms as a means of raising capital. It provoked violent demonstrations in Hungary in early 1966, serious resentment and a fall in productivity in Czechoslovakia in 1967–8, and finally the December 1970 strikes and workers' riots in Poland which, suppressed at the cost of over two hundred lives, were chiefly responsible for bringing down the once popular Gomułka.

tions a measure of independence. While even in Bulgaria and
Romania popular pressures influence policies often in directly
detectable ways, in Poland the workers' committees became the
most important centres of the people's power in 1970, and in
Hungary the 1966–8 reforms actually gave trade unions the right
to veto management decisions, a right which a number of union
executives have since been using. In Czechoslovakia, where one
of the main features of the process leading to 1968 had been the
disintegration of central political authority, the hard-liners who
replaced Alexander Dubček in April 1969 in due course abrogated
all power; but not even they are as insensitive to the feelings of
the population as the Stalinists of the fifties were.

In culture and propaganda, as I shall explain more fully in the
next chapter, decentralization and rationalization have meant a
relaxing of controls and an increased readiness to admit both
human diversity and particles of truth about the world. While the
Party goes on trying to convey its message to the people, its tone
of voice has become less shrill and its methods more subtle, often
to the point of irresistible manipulation. At the same time,
writers, artists and publicists have been increasingly allowed to
produce at least neutral work and in the pragmatic countries even
to make some critical noises in the manner of a loyal opposition.

The powers of the bureaucratic and police machinery have
also been seriously reduced. The bureaucracy, though as inert
as ever, is now often required to give reasons for its decisions or
delays, and the police cannot simply abuse their prerogatives.
Quite apart from having been purged of their worst Stalinists
(violently in Poland and Hungary, effectively enough in Bulgaria
and Czechoslovakia, and to a considerable extent even in
Romania), they have been publicly denounced for their 'excesses',
and genuinely taught the lesson that sooner or later every population will get its chance to take revenge for cruelties and sheer
lawlessness. While most of the victims of the Stalinist show trials
have now been at the very least partially or by implication rehabilitated, only a very few sentences have been handed down for
political reasons since the end of the wave of arrests and executions
following the Hungarian Revolt of October 1956.

Altogether, the changes in Eastern Europe since Stalin's death have amounted to the Party as Hero giving up its insane ambitions and pure command methods, in favour of compromises with reality, manifest in the people and in the circumstances surrounding the Party and the people together.

At the same time, however, just as Moscow remains the central ruler of Eastern Europe, so the Party remains indisputably Hero in central charge of each East European country. Whatever it decides continues to prevail as the word of the people. If it chooses to halt decentralization in the economy, as it did in 1958-9 in Poland and Czechoslovakia, and again in the mid-sixties in Poland, or even to recentralize, as it did in 1968 in Bulgaria, nothing can stop its decision being made – even if execution may then run up against resistance by the people and opposition from sheer facts. If it decides to return to insanely heroic targeting, as it did in 1958-9 in both Bulgaria and Romania, it still demotes if not purges oppositionists as enemies of the collective, and thinks again only if reality puts up too hard a fight against its plans. And even apart from such special decisions, the Party keeps general control of the economy as a matter of course, both through the retention of all main levers from price and production indices to the right to appoint managers, and through its 'democratic centralist' command of key personnel, the majority of whom are Party members.

In politics, culture and propaganda, too, the Party remains omnipotent. Mass organizations can be legal only if they swear by its programme, and what opposition is allowed must make itself heard either in private conversations whose contents seep to the top through the informer network, or within closed meetings of enterprise committees and Party cells. At normal times, it can come to public notice only between the lines of newspaper articles and of poetry and fiction, in the tone of theatre productions and films, and in learned publications. Propaganda also remains constant and can, without anybody being able to do a thing about it, become deafening. This may happen not only at such critical times as followed the ousting of Alexander Dubček by Czechoslovak hard-liners in April 1969, but even in such otherwise peaceful moments as the start of a vast new ideological campaign in July 1971 in Romania. And diminished though their powers have been, the police continue to spy on the people and control its life more intensely than anywhere not just in the West, but in the whole of the non-Communist world. They can refuse individuals passports and wreck their careers or entire existence even in the now most liberal country, Hungary, and can also turn into fearsome brutes at the bidding of the Party's hard-liners, as happened in Poland in the second half of the sixties, and in Czechoslovakia following April 1969.

Just what kind of course the Party as Hero takes, with a decisive effect on all the spheres it rules, depends mostly on what faction rules the Party. There are two main ones, with allies in posts of importance throughout each country, roughly reproducing the division between realistic and heroic nationalists within the East European élites of the nineteenth century, and versions of these groups since.

The heirs of the first are today's pragmatic–decentralizers. Within and outside the Party, this faction includes middle-aged and older people who either opposed the insanities of Stalinism from the start or learnt its cruel lessons at their own cost, or were shocked into sobriety when de-Stalinization began; it also embraces a younger generation whose members have either been through the same sort of experiences at the beginning of their careers, or acquired pragmatic views as part of a much fuller secondary and higher education offered them by the Party itself.

The front which has thus developed has its radicals and its moderates. Both wings strive for factual assessments of any situation in the country and within every sphere, and for decisions to be taken for practical rather than mythical reasons.* Beyond that, however, the radicals, who became prominent in Czechoslovakia in 1968 to such an extent as to stampede Moscow into military intervention, envisage economic decentralization and the drive for efficiency as inseparable from cultural liberalization and political democratization, enabling the people to manage all of its affairs as far as it possibly can. By contrast, the moderates not

* Among other things, they reject blaming all the problems of Eastern Europe under Party rule on 'Stalinist excesses' and the 'too-close imitation of Soviet models', as this only reverses the Stalinist argument, blaming every difficulty and disaster on 'enemy manoeuvres'.

only wish to go more slowly, but also make every effort to emphasize that while they would decentralize the economy for the sake of better results and allow the people the maximum sense of comfort in culture and propaganda, they do not intend the Party to cease being Hero in central charge throughout Eastern Europe.

The heirs of the heroic nationalists are today's centralists of one shade or another. Among them are, again, older and middle-aged people who either never learnt the lessons of Stalinism (even in opposition), or were promoted in the heroic days for ideological rather than rational reasons to positions which only strong centralism will let them retain; plus a younger generation who either were promoted in the same way or are genuinely convinced that centralism, in combination with the computers now coming into use in Eastern Europe, is the best method of modernization, about which every wing of every faction is enthusiastic.

The centralist front, too, has its radicals and its moderates. Common to both wings is the fact that they are true heirs of the prewar national-authoritarian regimes in that they consist mostly of bureaucrats within the Party and the State economic and cultural administrations, and of army and police officers, whereas their pragmatic opponents come mostly from the academic world and the technical and cultural intelligentsia, with allies inside the Party's higher echelons. But whereas the radical centralists seem genuinely to believe in the need for themselves as fathers of order to guard the collective against such midwives of anarchy as economic revisionists, political liberalizers, cultural westernizers and so on, the moderates are mostly interested in order for the sake of results. And while the two wings may unite in reviving prewar heroic nationalism, and even some of its sub-variants (as anti-Semitism was revived in Poland in the later sixties), so as to rally the people, and may perhaps combine it with ideological fervour to please the Party faithful, only the radicals seem to believe in the enthusiasm they promote. To the moderates it is an instrument, to be discarded when it has served its purpose, often together with the radical figureheads in whom it has become manifest.

The extent to which either the pragmatic-decentralizing or the heroic-centralist faction has managed to get hold of any East European Party has depended chiefly on two things. Of these, one is almost constant, the other almost unpredictable. The first is the economic and social situation of each country, and the measure of centralism its traditions inspire and its present situation seems to compel. This accounts for the outlines of the 'behavioural map' of Eastern Europe today, in that the two least developed countries, Bulgaria and Romania, are ruled by the two most heroically centralist Parties, with the Romanian one actually pursuing autarchic policies in line with those the country knew in the 1920s. By contrast, in Poland the needs of a much more developed economy have been pressing against the ramparts of centralist resistance since 1958, and appear finally to have broken through following the ascent to power of the former technocrat Party secretary of Silesia, Edward Gierek, in December 1970. And in Hungary recognition of the country's need to survive, without almost any industrial raw materials, as a fast-trading nation, has been one of the main factors prompting economic decentralization and the abandonment of former heroic attitudes.

Only Czechoslovakia now has an anomalous system, and this is due to the second factor (which may, however, at any time in the future restore anomaly elsewhere in the region too). This second factor is the history of each East European country since 1953, that is, since the death of the Central Hero forcing identical policies on all of them. To present their histories in brief and immediately comparable detail, I should like here to make use of a second set of chronological tables. Once again, I have concentrated in these on events and figures that either are essential to an understanding of what has happened in Eastern Europe during the conscious lifetime of today's young generation, or are actually mentioned by interviewees.

As is clear from these tables, the Party as Hero in central charge of each East European country and Moscow in central charge of them all are surrounded by complex dynamics, which they have more than once found very difficult to contain. Yet contain them they must, each for reasons existential to both. Only as Hero in central charge of each country can the Party remain the

TABLE 2 – EVENTS SINCE STALIN

SOVIET UNION	POLAND	CZECHOSLOVAKIA	HUNGARY	ROMANIA	BULGARIA
5th March 1953 Stalin dies. **1953–54** Malenkov's New Course attacks one-man leadership, neglect of consumer goods and of agriculture, internal terror and external isolationism. **February 1956** Twentieth Party Congress; Krushchev delivers speech denouncing Stalin's personality cult, and many of his methods. **November 1956** Following Polish and Hungarian events, period of retrenchment begins, with 'revisionism' as main target. **November 1957** Moscow conference of ruling CPs confirms Soviet Union as leader of Socialist Commonwealth; Yugoslavs and	**1953–56** Polish New Course conservative, but stirrings among intellectuals produce most remarkable thaw in Eastern Europe; while secret police become demoralised, Gomulka, arrested in 1948 for advocating Polish Road to Socialism, emerges as symbol of renewal. **June 1956** Following Pozman workers' riots, liberal faction takes workers' side against hard-liners and Russians. **October 1956** Despite Russian opposition, Gomulka brought back to leadership, riding wave of popularity. **January 1957** Voters, given free choice in elections, are warned by Gomulka that striking the Party's	**1953–54** Impact of Stalin's death combines with popular fury at devaluation to cause, June 1953, area's first workers' riots since Communist take-over; but New Course is conservative, and show-trials continue. **June 1956** Novotny, First Secretary of Party since 1953, rejects all important criticism and demands by intellectuals and students, and following October events in Poland and Hungary, goes on neo-Stalinist offensive. **1962–63** In wake of Twenty-second Congress, writers renew attack, while economists – in midst of a full-scale slump – denounce 'cult of the	**July 1953** Imre Nagy, replacing Rákosi as Prime Minister, launches most radical New Course in Eastern Europe. **Late 1954** Rákosi regains power, Nagy's policies and era are denounced. **Spring 1956** Effects of Twentieth Congress put Rákosi on defensive and revive ferment in culture and politics; July, 1956, Rákosi resigns, but in favour of another Stalinist. **23 October 1956** Budapest demonstration in sympathy with Poles develops into Hungarian Revolt; Nagy becomes Prime Minister, but is overwhelmed by task of reconciling popular demands for internal democracy and	**1953–4** Some economic concessions granted, a few labour camps dissolved, and lip-service paid to collective leadership, but Gheorghiu-Dej, the country's Stalin, remains unshaken. **1956** Least effect of Twentieth Congress noted; Dej deals brutally with students and intellectuals actively sympathetic to Hungarian Revolt. **1958** Romania's 'national-Stalinist' course initiated, with country embarking on development of new heavy and light industries of its own instead of agreeing to division of labour within Comecon; police terror remains in force to hold down popular resentment of sacrifices entailed by dictatorial policies, and	**1953–56** Economic concessions offered to the people, concentration camps dissolved and rehabilitations begun, but Vlko Chervenkov, country's Stalin, only cedes First Secretaryship of Party to Todor Zhivkov in 1954, and remains Prime Minister until April 1956. **Spring–Autumn 1956** Serious unrest among intellectuals and students, suppressed in 1957 by Chervenkov as Minister of Culture. **Late 1958** Bulgarian 'Great Leap Forward' begins; astronomical targets set for both industry and agriculture, with realists objecting to these targets denounced as 'anti-people'. **1959–60** 'Great Leap

Chinese demur. **March 1958** Khrushchev becomes undisputed leader, renews stress on consumer industries and agriculture and peaceful co-existence. **1959–60** Beginnings of Sino-Soviet dispute over military versus co-existence. **October 1961** Twenty-second Party Congress; Krushchev launches broad attack on Stalin and Stalinism and gives much freer rein to depictions of Stalinist epoch, including life in concentration camps. **September 1962** Professor Liberman enunciates basic ideas of economic reforms which aim at giving enterprises autonomy and obliging them to survive on their own profits. **October 1962** Cuban missile crisis ends in

candidates off the ballot papers would mean 'striking Poland off the map of Europe'; geopolitical realism thus keeps Party in power. **1957–59** Implementation of economic reforms grinds to a halt, 'revisionism' becomes main enemy, police and secret police regain their pre-1956 strengths. **1961–63** Partisan faction, comprising hard-liners in army, police, veterans' organisations and Party and state apparatus, emerges, with Moczar, deputy Minister of Interior, as figurehead; in next five years it gains support both of nationalists and technical intelligentsia frustrated by economic stagnation, while Gomulka's increasingly autocratic ways lose

plan' as version of personality cult; rehabilitation of virtually all victims of show-trials implicates Novotny, and Slovakia's Party, in which newly rehabilitated people are prominent, goes into near-permanent opposition to Prague. **1966–67** Economic reforms, confused in conception and sabotaged by conservatives, produce chaos, further undermining central authority. **October 1967** Police brutality against student demonstrators unites all factions opposed to Novotny's rule. **January 1968** Novotny replaced with Dubček, head of Slovak Party; start of era of liberalisation from above and criticism from below.

external neutrality, with Russian ideas of a loyal Hungary. **4 November 1956** Revolt crushed by Soviet troops; Kádár put in charge of country; soon, arrests begin, leading to deportations, imprisonment of large numbers, executions, and culminating in trial and execution of Nagy and colleagues in July 1958. **1958–60** While forcible collectivisation is re-started and completed, Kádár's group begins to weed out Stalinists in leadership, to rationalise economic plans, and to gain confidence of people, launching idea 'whoever is not against us is with us'. **1962** Following Twenty-second Congress, de-stalinisation

Party begins to use nationalism for purpose of rallying the people. **December 1961** Following Twenty-second Congress, Dej blames all Stalinist 'excesses' on leaders he purged in 1952, while his own personality cult continues. **1965** Dej dies and is succeeded by Ceausescu; period of some liberalisation begins, partly so as to ease Dej's men out of their posts; defiance of Russia increases, with revival of national cultural heritage widening as complement. **December 1967** Romania announces economic reforms, least radical in area, and most successfully sabotaged by conservatives afraid for their jobs. **April 1968** Dej and his illegal methods

Forward' proves disaster, but forcibly prepares ground for realistic policies in agriculture and far-reaching reform experiments involving enterprise, independence and profit incentives, in rest of economy. **November 1961** Following Twenty-second Congress Zhivkov begins serious de-stalinisation; Chervenkov is ousted from Politburo and after a year, during which Stalinist epoch receives thorough airing in media and arts, he is expelled from Party and many of his important followers are disgraced. **1962–65** Period of general relaxation in atmosphere, leading to announcement of surprisingly courageous economic reforms in December

SOVIET UNION	POLAND	CZECHOSLOVAKIA	HUNGARY	ROMANIA	BULGARIA
political defeat for Khrushchev. **October 1964** His economic policies having run into trouble, Khrushchev is ousted, leadership going to Brezhnev and Kosygin. **August 1968** Invasion of Czechoslovakia, leading to re-affirmation of principle of 'limited sovereignty' within Socialist Commonwealth, now nick-named 'Brezhnev doctrine'; inside Soviet Union, Stalinists take heart. **1969–71** In wake of armed clashes on Chinese border, fresh policy of detente with West launched; Brezhnev becomes clear leader.	him all his former popularity. **March 1968** Countrywide student riots give Moczarists excuse for purging liberals and Jews from important rôles, in favour of their own men, but Gomulka enlists Russian support and retains power. **December 1970** Price increases intended to usher in economic reforms provoke riots suppressed at cost of over 200 lives; Gomulka is replaced by Gierek who purges police and bureaucracy of worst hard-liners, revamps economy, and permits more popular participation in politics.	**April 1968** Party Action Programme promises democratic elections within Party, freedom for social organisations, abolition of censorship and secret police, etc.; Russia and Warsaw Pact neighbours watch situation with increasing alarm. **August 1968** Invasion of Czechoslovakia; Russians, unable to impose puppet government, allow Dubček back to power, but diminish his freedom of action daily. **April 1969** Dubček replaced by Husak; period of slowly worsening repression begins, with purges working from top down through	spreads downwards, frank discussion of Stalinist period in literature and media begins, while non-Party people become admissible to leading jobs. **1963–64** Nearly all political prisoners freed, living standards, especially of peasantry, allowed to rise, visits to West made easier, economic experimentation begins. **1966–68** New Economic Mechanism, comprehensive scheme for decentralisation, put into effect. Autonomy for managements and strongly profit-oriented incentive schemes are combined with greater bargaining power for	denounced by Ceausescu. **August 1968** Alone among Warsaw Pact countries, Romania denounces invasion of Czechoslovakia. **1970–71** External pressures and internal economic problems force Romania to turn back towards Comecon neighbours in trade, and tone down defiance of Warsaw Pact countries. **July 1971** Vast ideological revival campaign begins, bearing marks both of Chinese cultural revolution, and the Stalinist effort of 1950s.	1965. **1966–68** Scope of reforms becomes increasingly narrow in practice, while in culture and media dogmatists re-assert themselves and, making use of Party's effort to rally the people through nationalism, denounce 'revisionism' and 'western influences' in same breath. **1968–71** Events in Czechoslovakia provide conservatives with new arguments; in economy de-centralisation is reversed, while in culture adherence to the principles of Socialist Realism is urged on all.

Party, state and economic apparatus; process culminates in arrest of large numbers of dissidents in late 1971.	unions, wider consumer choices, and latitude in politics and culture, though Party retains control at all levels. 1968–70 Invasion of Czechoslovakia forces caution on leaders and population alike but brings no reversal of policies.

Party as founded by Lenin, and only by maintaining a Communist Party in undisputed charge of each East European country can Moscow save the Soviet Union from the disintegration of its western glacis, and the rebirth of its 'hostile encirclement'. In brief, both are vitally dependent on their maintenance of the *status quo*.

At the same time, however, it is in the nature of the Party's realistic policies of economic and social development to induce change, and so make ever more complex the dynamics the Party means to rule for ever. This is the central paradox of the Party's position in today's Eastern Europe, and the practical embodiment of the paradox that has characterized its ideology all along. It is a Platonic body, irremovable and claiming universal validity of judgement, engaged in the essentially Aristotelian work of transforming the region, and so creating and nourishing forces which its universalist methods, born of a different past, will be increasingly unable to marshal.

It is, however, only in theory that the Party may pose for ever on the one hand as the Vanguard of Perfection and Rationality Incarnate and on the other as History's Hero and the Champion of Progress. In practice, as both the Ideal Being static at the centre of all affairs and the Motor of Becoming inexorably productive of change, it is bound to become ensnared by just the dialectics it thought itself destined to command on behalf of the future.

The human embodiment of the same paradox lies in the Party's relationship with the young, to whom the future inexorably belongs.

Part II

The Hero's Call

To begin with, the Party saw the young as constituting a version of its own heroic self:

'Is it not natural that youth should predominate in our Party, the revolutionary Party?' Lenin wrote in 1906.[1] 'We are the Party of the future, and the future belongs to youth. We are a Party of innovators, and it is always youth who most eagerly follows the innovators. We are a Party that is waging a self-sacrificing struggle against the old rottenness, and youth is always the first to undertake a self-sacrificing struggle.'

This was a romantic view, first propounded by Engels, but consistent with the Party's dialectical ideology. If History amounted to Mankind's inexorable Progress towards its own rebirth in Perfection, then clearly every new generation was that much closer to the Ideal, whose closest version in the present was the Party.

By the time the Party was installed as Hero in central charge of Eastern Europe, it had got itself into the paradoxical position it has held since. From being a revolutionary élite, it had become the sole ruling body within the State. And while it genuinely championed economic and social change, it was already struggling to preserve the political *status quo*.

The paradox was clear in its approach to the young. The Party both claimed youth as its spontaneous vanguard, and imposed on the same vanguard the direst martial discipline. In fact the Party's difficulties in rallying the masses as their Platonic Universal made it only more wistful about the young as its own children and stormtroopers against the old, and at the same time more afraid lest the children should prove as intractable as their parents.

It was in this spirit of romanticism mixed with paranoia that Mátyás Rákosi, the Hungarian version of Stalin, addressed the founding congress of the country's monolithic Working Youth League in Budapest in 1950.

The young were the Party's natural vanguard in fighting the past:

> The struggle against [hostile] elements is not easy, and there can be no quick results. These backward elements are supported by all the capitalist-bred habits, superstitions, prejudices and feelings of selfishness, with which the proletariat itself is tainted and which the enemy is busy trying to keep alive, indeed strengthen. . . . I repeat: at the present stage of development, our worst problem, the greatest obstacle to our progress, is the morass of habits and prejudices inherited from the capitalist days. These we have to overcome as fast as we can, and in this struggle we assign an enormous role to our enthusiastic, vigorous, self-sacrificing and forward-looking youth.[2]

This role, however, the young were to play not as a free volunteer corps, but under strict and unified command:

> Our working youth has so far been prevented by the looseness of its organizations from living up to the example set by the glorious Komsomol, in carrying out its task: to organize and unite under the leadership of our Party the whole of the growing generation, to facilitate the education of a new socialist breed of men, our young troops, and to be everywhere, at work, in study, in disciplinary matters, our vanguard. This organizational problem has been abolished with the present congress, and the youth of Hungary can now charge forward on a broad front and without obstacles along the road leading towards the realization of the great aims of socialism.

And instead of finding this road by themselves, the young were to be steered on to it, and cheered along it, by the Party: 'Compared to [the remoulding of adults], winning the young over to socialism is quite easy. The young generation carries with it many fewer of the old traditions and habits and the casting off of these is made all the easier as the number of those brought up by us is growing every year.' In other words, just as the Party had changed from seeing all men of intellect as its natural allies to pressing them into service as war-artists rose-tinting reality, so instead of letting the young discover spontaneously their identity with the Vanguard of the Future, the Party meant to marshal them as heroically as it meant to rule the rest of the collective, and reality itself.

It was, of course, nothing new in Eastern Europe for an élite either underground or in power to claim the young as the vanguard of a renascent collective. To make this claim was as much part of local tradition as it was for the élite to pose as the collective's Hero, and it had also long been accepted in this way by the young.

Ever since the Polish students and officer cadets had conspired against Russian rule in the 1820s, youth had been in the forefront of East European nationalist movements throughout the nineteenth century. In fact, long before internationalist revivalism had arrived on the scene its nationalist version had developed a distinct youth policy of its own. The Czech gymnastics association Sokol, for example, was founded in 1862 with the express purpose of raising – physically and mentally – a vanguard for nationalism. T. G. Masaryk himself started his career as one of its instructors, and when a serious chance to achieve national independence arose during the First World War, the Prague Plot organized under his leadership could already count on Sokol units being formed as the core of a National Guard.

Following the acquisition of independence, too, youth movements, especially in the heroic countries, retained their spirit of militant revivalism. In Poland, the previously clandestine Riflemen's League, out of which Marshal Piłsudski's famous First World War legions had been formed, was revived in 1919 as one of the country's most powerful youth organizations. The names of many other organizations reflected the same militant spirit. The Polish scout movement was called *Harcerstwo* (after *harcerz*, an archaic term for a lone combatant), the Romanian children's organization *Strajeri* ('Sentrymen') and the main Hungarian youth movement *Levente* (Knights).

These names symbolized the Platonic idea of youth as the self-sacrificing soldiery of collectives erect as Individuals mortally besieged by their neighbours. The propaganda of the organizations accordingly taught the young not just that to die for their country was the highest honour but very often that they belonged to a race surrounded by virtual barbarians, and surviving by the special decree of God. It also taught them, as young soldiers, respect for the social order as the defensive structure of their nations, and perfect submission to the commanding élite. Much the same national-authoritarian spirit pervaded education, whether it was in the hands of the State or in those of the Church, with each other's blessing. And as it was also confirmed by most families, it is not surprising that in Poland, Hungary and Romania a whole generation grew up between the wars to see itself standing, guns in hand, as the only thing between the nation and death and between Eastern barbarity and Christian mankind. In accepting the Platonic idea and subordinating themselves as individuals to their Universal, they also became parts of the Hero, magnificent in the face of mortal danger.

There were, however, two main ways in which the Party's youth effort differed from that of even the fiercest national-authoritarian regimes. Compared to anything previous generations of East Europeans had known, it was far more centralized in organization, and infinitely more heroic both in its aims, and in its claims on the young. In this it was a true reproduction of Stalinism in every other sphere.

Before the Second World War, though the State and its nationalism had made the strongest claim on youth, other influences could also be exerted in organized forms. In most countries various political parties, including the Socialists and, where allowed, the Communists or their front, had their own youth and often even children's organizations, as had the churches, and membership in any of these was voluntary. Where the Church was strong in education, various denominations each had a number of schools. Secondary education varied a great deal according to the traditions of each establishment, and progressive experimentation found scope particularly in Czechoslovakia and Poland.* Universities were generally autonomous, even though pressure might be brought to bear on them in the non-democratic

---

* In fact the spreading of popular education was one of the rare aspects of State policy in which nineteenth-century democratic ideas had largely survived. By the time the present regimes took over, even the highest illiteracy rate, in Romania, had been reduced from 38·2 per cent to 23·7 per cent in seventeen years, while in Poland the rate was about 8 per cent, in Hungary only 4·7 per cent and in Czechoslovakia 2·5 per cent. The last two of these figures were close to those of France and Germany at the time.

countries to remove 'undesirable' members of staff. In addition the whole system was open to the rest of the world, as regards both ideas and, at least for those who could afford it, the possibilities of travel. Following 1945, most of even the previous restrictions disappeared and fertile confusion reigned as regards political and non-political youth movements, philosophies of education and other influences.

With the approach of the year 1948, however, just as in public affairs police rule took over from democracy, so in youth and educational matters monoliths and propaganda took over from spontaneity and enlightenment. What Rákosi meant by removing the obstacles of 'looseness' was in fact the imposition of total centralism.

Youth organizations were all either abolished or merged into the Party's own Youth League. Their former leaders were denounced and in some cases imprisoned, and their more important members remained for years in fear of their past being held against them. This applied not only to, say, a Catholic youth club, but also to many of the former leftist and even some Communist groups, whose adherents could find themselves branded as social democrat traitors, left sectarians, anarchists and so on, and could be imprisoned in the early fifties. The Polish *Harcerstwo* was allowed to keep its name but had to denounce the western Scout movement and its 'false neutralism' (stress on charity rather than class war), while the leaders of the Czechoslovak Scout movement were imprisoned on charges of treason, some to be released and rehabilitated only in the late sixties.

The youth organizations thus turned, like all other social organizations, into 'transmission systems' of the Party's message. Both their paid and their unpaid functionaries were henceforth appointed from above, and legitimized with a show of hands at meetings. The Pioneers became part of school life, with an organization to each form, run by the teacher and his appointee. In secondary schools membership of the Youth League was understood to be obligatory, as no one could get into further education, or better jobs, without League references. And though some functionaries made genuine efforts to cater for the needs of those they had been appointed to rule, most cultural and recreational activities organized by either the Pioneers or the Youth League centred round politics. Beyond that, attendance at a number of directly political meetings and rallies was compulsory for everyone.

Sports clubs were taken over in a similar way, and usually renamed so as to eradicate memory of their 'bourgeois' past. Each club came under the sponsorship of a particular branch of industry or the State administration, and apart from countless speeches on the 'superiority of socialist sport', a strong attempt was made to connect sport with militarism. The mass sports movement – in which old and young did so many press-ups, and ran so many metres, and jumped so high and so long to obtain a badge that it was most advisable to own – was named in each country Ready For Work and Battle, after the Soviet effort of the same name. More important, the clubs with the best facilities usually belonged to the army and the police. In Hungary, the hated Political Police, the AVH, also had a specially well-equipped club of its own. And paramilitary organizations, administered mostly by serving army officers, took over such technical sports and hobbies as gliding, shooting, amateur radio, motorcycling and so on, providing facilities absolutely free.

Education, which had always been more centralized in Eastern Europe than in the Anglo-Saxon countries, became totally so after 1948. Private education was eliminated and church schools, with only marginal exceptions, were nationalized. The teaching body was heavily purged. Some of the people ousted might actually have belonged to Fascist movements, but many more were simply considered dangerous as 'bourgeois elements', or were labelled so by their colleagues to get them out of the way.

Universities lost their autonomy, and their teaching staffs were also purged, together with the student body admitted just prior to 1948, in several countries. The structure of their courses, the subjects to be taught in each course, and often the actual content of lectures were all determined by the ministries of education (or by other ministries, to which a department of a university might have been made directly accountable). Attendance at lectures became compulsory, with unjustified absence resulting in disciplinary action and, later, expulsion. And while the youth organizations were brought under the control of their respective educational establishments, they were also used by the Party to keep staff members of the same establishments in check.

The Party's claim on youth was, if possible, even more comprehensive than the machinery set up to effect it. If each military-bureaucratic regime before the war had posed as each nation's Hero claiming the young for its vanguard, the Party made the same claim as the Hero of Mankind and, indeed, the Universe.

As such, it presented itself as surrounded by infinite hostility, which the young were to fight: 'You must,' said Edward Ochab, Secretary of the Polish Central Committee, speaking to teachers in Warsaw in 1952,

> ... boldly and skilfully unmask the subterfuges of hostile, imperialist, anti-people and anti-national propaganda, stigmatize the agencies of reaction, educate youth in the most profound love of the People's Poland and of the international cause of peace, progress, and socialism, and at the same time instil [in it] a spirit of hatred of the imperialist exploiters, oppressors and genocides.[3]

The propagation of hatred was central to the whole of the Party's heroic claim on the young. Teachers were being endlessly exhorted by their superiors, by ministers of education, by secretaries general of the Party itself, mothers by their women's organizations, fathers by their trade unions, to teach children how to hate. Newspapers for children and young people, and often even school textbooks, carried the most vicious depictions of 'the enemy', and now and again contests were organized for children's own stories and cartoons, illustrating their hatred of the same. Pacifism, tolerance, giving others the benefit of the doubt, and all other forms of 'a generalized love of mankind' (as charity was contemptuously called) were rejected as versions of compromise with the enemy. This was mortal treason, while to reject it was humanity itself: 'It is right that vanguard* pedagogues should teach their pupils to love and hate equally,' wrote the large-circulation daily of the Hungarian People's Front in

* 'Vanguard' is the closest equivalent of an untranslatable adjective (*élenjáró*) which the Party as Hero of Progress appended to everything it thought worthy of promoting (see below).

1952. 'These children should learn the meaning of love and hatred. ... They must be taught to hate those who want to destroy the socialist State. Their hatred should burn as brightly as their love.'[4]

The purpose of this was heroic isolationism, that is, paranoia and heroism producing each other. Nothing could so isolate youth from the enemy as hatred. Nothing could so arouse its heroism in revenge. And hatred of the enemy being love of the self, nothing could so rally it *en masse* round its heroic commanding self, the Party.

Among forms of the enemy, the most obvious one was the West. Internally capitalistic, externally imperialistic, it also presented a military barrier to the progress of socialism in the world. In return, the Party made every effort to isolate East Europeans from its baneful influence. Borders were closed, western papers, books, films, plays, music and art almost entirely banned, and departments of western languages at universities whittled down or expunged. Mail to the West was thoroughly censored and on occasions destroyed, and pressure was put on people to denounce their western friends and relatives, or to denounce the West to them. Listening to western radio stations could involve citizens in unpleasant interrogations and lead to the loss of jobs; to preserve them from such dangers, by 1951 over a thousand transmitters were jamming western broadcasts round the clock.

Meanwhile, West German revanchism was depicted as the neo-Hitlerite spearhead of western operations, with particular reference to Poland and Czechoslovakia. This was combined with a general attempt to present the West as rotting in the last days of capitalism, and preparing at the same time, like Satan on his deathbed, to reinfest Eastern Europe with the evils of exploitation, class warfare and moral decay.

The next version of the enemy was the past, and every effort was made to isolate young East Europeans from it. Libraries were purged of all 'fascistic' and a good deal of 'bourgeois' material, which might include anything from Dostoyevsky to the East European peasant mysticists of the 1930s, and in the children's section, boy scout songs as well as Little Lord Fauntleroy. All school textbooks were entirely rewritten, and a number of them were actually supplanted with translations from

Russian. In addition to the expropriated sports clubs, restaurants and places of entertainment were also renamed, to eradicate the memory of their bourgeois past; thus the 'Moulin Rouge', say, became 'Moscow Heights', if not 'Enterprise 238'. Meanwhile, the national historical and literary heritage was wholly revised, and its interwar period was denounced as one of almost unrelieved darkness, in which only the Communist Party, leading the proletariat and the best elements of the rest, was worth remembering.

This combined quite naturally with writing off the parent and grandparent generations as full of 'remnants of the past', which could turn a number of them into open enemies. In Czechoslovakia, for instance, during the 1952 Slansky trials, the young son of one of the accused, Frejka, was held up as an example to all his peers for having written to the judge disowning his father as 'a creature who cannot be called a human being', and demanding 'the heaviest penalty, the penalty of death for my father'. (The State obliged.) Children were encouraged to denounce adult 'saboteurs' and 'kulaks' and 'rumour-mongers' and similar vermin. They were also to act as the Party's young guard not only in watching for enemies among their parents, but in convincing them and all older people of the Truth.

An even more obvious combination of the past and of the enemy was the Church, which was directly allied to the enemy abroad in the non-Orthodox countries. Apart from the closing of denominational schools and the exclusion of religious classes from the compulsory curriculum, everything was done to sever youth and children from the clergy. Parents who sent their children to religious instruction after school hours often found themselves interrogated on the subject at work, or were told that they were harming their children's future. Priests who organized outings for the young were lampooned as spiritual pederasts, and to prevent children from going to church on Sunday all kinds of functions from sports events to scrap-iron collecting parties were organized, with attendance as good as compulsory. Meanwhile, atheist propaganda that often combined viciousness with sheer idiocy* was being propagated in all schools at the State's expense.

* For example, it was advanced as proof of the non-existence of God that neither pilots nor even astronomers had ever come across him in the sky.

The last main enemy, never acknowledged but all the more fiercely fought, was plain truth, as opposed to the Truth. Here, however, the Party fought in two ways, one worthwhile, the other deplorable and in the end wholly counterproductive. The good fight consisted of the Party's essentially Aristotelian effort to change the economic and social facts surrounding the people for the better, and to bring the best out of the people itself. In the deplorable one, the Party tried not only to impose Platonic order on the people's spontaneity, but to suppress the world of plain facts and of the senses as hostile to the people and the cause, both manifest in itself as their Universal. And while the Party prided itself on fighting the first fight as the Champion of Progress, it never admitted being engaged in the second one, except in its martial command to those it pressed into service to hide plain truth beneath the Truth. Life, said the father of socialist realism and Stalin's cultural henchman, Zhdanov, at the First All-Union Congress of Soviet Writers in 1934, must be presented 'not simply as objective reality ... but rather as reality in its revolutionary development. The truthfulness and exactitude of the artistic image must be linked with the task of ideological transformation, of the education of the working people in the spirit of socialism.'[5]

It was to isolate the people from the plain truth about itself and the surrounding world that all newspapers, radio stations, publishing houses, theatres and film studios were brought under absolute Party control. In the media, descriptions of reality in the streets, in factories, in the countryside, in people's minds, in politics or abroad became treasonable. Human interest stories were banned as cheap trash and even small advertisements were wiped off the pages of newspapers. All the space available was filled with editorials and tales of Party miracles and enemy horrors, manufactured at the appropriate centres, while forced subscriptions boosted circulation figures beyond the wildest dreams of any prewar proprietor.

In literature, published in equally impressive print runs, and in the arts, made cheaply available to all, the same tales were expected to be retold, according to 'thematic plans' propounded at meetings of writers and others concerned. Lyric poetry, which

Platonists in politics (and Plato himself) had always found hard to accommodate, was replaced with virtual or actual marching songs. And stories about plain human emotions and problems, and plays and films treating everyday life in an everyday manner, were hardly ever allowed to reach the people, lest its heroic spirits should soften into plain humanity.

The propaganda effort directed at the young followed suit. Spontaneity, the liveliest version of the truth, was abjured unless it served some set purpose. Just as pioneers busied themselves with the fight against colorado beetles, which were said to have been dropped by American planes to destroy the potato crop, with political meetings about the Five-Year Plan, and with revolutionary sing-songs, so the Pioneer press was full of editorials on socialist patriotism, diligence and self-sacrifice, and stories, poems and drawings promoting the same. Just as the Youth League had become a clearing-house for Party cadres and for ranking members or plain card-carriers of monolithic and meaningless social organizations, so its press reproduced the themes of adult editorials, supplying features of its own in the same vein.

Most books and plays and films put out for the young also followed the 'thematic plan'. When, for example, the Party mounted a campaign for 'revolutionary vigilance', the Pioneer press was filled with stories of twelve-year-olds heroically unmasking espionage, and young lovers in films went to the woods only to discuss their problems in catching saboteurs. In line with other campaigns, there were pop songs detailing the benefits of motorized agriculture, deploring absenteeism and urging people to go easy on fuel.

The need to suppress spontaneity while trying to rally parts of it for heroic purposes was inherent in the Party's paradoxical position as both the Ideal Being and the Motor of Becoming. But it was also characteristic of the Hero's dialectical approach to each of its enemies. Indeed it became the chief source both of the Party's real propaganda triumphs and of the Platonic hubris with which it dismissed defeats as illusory until they proved to be disasters.

The Party envisaged all of its 'enemies', and indeed the whole of reality, as consisting of 'opposites'; and it declared itself (as the Ideal), to be the inalienable leader of one of the two resulting sets, in constant 'battle' with the other one. Beyond being a version of the ancient ruse of 'divide and rule', this dialectical manoeuvre was also perfectly consistent with the Party's view of itself as the Hero of Universal Progress. In terms of this, not only were all 'progressive' phenomena the Party's allies, and all things 'reactionary' its enemies, but nothing less than the inexorable march of time destined the first (and as their Hero, the Party) to conquer the second. The Party thus claimed for its inevitably triumphant vanguard one half of reality against the other, in the same manner as it claimed the young against the old.

In the West, the Party distinguished as its allies not only its brother Parties, said to be leading a starved proletariat towards imminent revolution, but also large numbers of 'fellow-travellers', 'friends of world peace', and other 'progressive elements'. These, together with their newspapers, books, plays and films, it presented to the home troops, and itself, as the vanguard of the best forces in the still capitalist half of the world. Meanwhile, it denounced western trade-unionists and social democrats as the rearguards of reaction among the proletariat, betraying it and mankind's revolutionary progress through mere wage negotiations and parliamentary politics.

The Party treated the past in the same dialectical way. While it denounced wholesale the regimes it had replaced, it also appropriated as much of each nation's historic heritage as legitimized its own position in command of the collective. It placed special emphasis on every State-building centralist period in each country's past, to which the nation itself usually looked back with pride, and of course claimed the national revival movements as, both culturally and politically, its own forerunners. Whenever possible, it took the heroic rather than the realistic view of national history, again so as to establish itself as the final reincarnation of all heroic élites. In Czechoslovakia, where realism had been the main tradition, the Party unleashed a vicious campaign against it, denouncing Masaryk as a traitor to the people, a sham humanist and a lackey of the West.

Of course where the heroic tradition was anti-Russian, as in Poland, the Party took care to emphasize that it was appropriating the heroism not of the upper-class 'nation', but of the people, which, as part of progressive mankind, had in turn fought not Russia, but only the reactionary forces of czarism. Beyond the Party's compulsory loyalty to the Vanguard Land of Socialism, the argument also reflected its view of itself as the Hero of all Mankind's Progress towards the Final Revolution.

It was in order to impart this heroic-dialectical view to the young that the Party laid emphasis on the teaching of national and world history as 'a powerful weapon of Communist education', in the words of the basic Soviet manual, translated throughout Eastern Europe.[6] 'Following the concrete facts of History and drawing conclusions from them, the student will think dialectically, and learn only later that he is thinking according to the laws of Materialist Dialectics.' This, the manual said, would 'wholly serve the cause of the struggle for Communism', by rallying youth around the Party, and creating in it a sense of invincibility, since 'if one is to be a consistent historian, one necessarily admits that the bourgeois order is necessarily doomed to destruction'.

This, of course, applied to history a version of Zhdanov's socialist realist rule concerning literature and the arts, which I have quoted earlier. The same rule was applied to the cultural heritage of each nation and of all mankind. Whatever seemed directly revolutionary, from songs of medieval peasant risings to twentieth-century anti-Fascist and truly Communist literature and art, was appropriated as a matter of course. Whatever else seemed worth rallying, from folk dances and Greek tragedy to, say, Thomas Mann, was embraced as 'progressive', either because it showed the evil passions which an unjust world of exploitation had bred in man to destroy him, or because it exalted in man the greatness and in life the joy both were to attain in perfection under Communism. And whereas progressive products were made cheaply available to the widest masses, whatever resisted the socialist realist treatment in modern western literature and art, from Joyce to Schoenberg and Klee, was denounced as corruption serving the enemy, against whom it was the Party's duty to defend mankind, and its heritage.*

* In much the same way Einstein's Theory of Relativity, Heisenberg's Uncertainty Principle and other modern departures in science were denounced

Among parents, too, while reactionaries were said to deserve
no mercy, 'honest progressives' were invited to join in the Party's
effort to bring up the young as the collective's vanguard. In fact,
the respectable and well-ordered family, and its virtues of fidelity
and fertility, were renamed 'socialistic', together with the kind of
children they had always tried to bring up, while all others were
denounced as wallowing, or at the very least knee-deep, in the
regrettable morass of the past.

In this the Party largely upheld the traditions dear to its national-
authoritarian predecessors in power and indeed those of the
Church. In much the same way the Party appropriated health,
joy, courage, self-confidence and moral rectitude as 'socialistic'
phenomena, and imputed disease, despondency, cowardice, self-
doubt and depravity to the enemy ranks. Thus while the Party
subsidized folk-dancing, classicist culture and sport, to further
Progress, the enemy manufactured jazz, prostituted art and
corrupted morals, to retard Mankind: 'Irresponsibility shown by
the young in the matters of love mirrors the harmful effect of
the remnants of the past,' wrote the Hungarian youth weekly in
1952.[7] 'And this is all too obviously nourished by the enemy. . . .
One of his methods is to exploit the already heightened sexuality
of adolescents by leading them into corruption and sexual
libertarianism. This is the aim of those erotic, immoral pictures
and drawings being circulated among the young.' It was for the
same hostile purpose that the West engaged in producing crime
novels and films, westerns and lewd art, and in the spreading of
the fashion for wild ties, tumultuous hair, drainpipe trousers and
slit skirts, all of which combined to cause juvenile delinquency.

Similarly dialectical was the campaign against the Church and
religion. While the Party tried to rally the minor churches against
the major one in each country, and 'progressive priests' against
'befrocked warmongers' in each church, it also called to itself
Christianity as originally a version of Communism stolen by the
clergy on behalf of the ruling classes. Reappropriating it on
behalf of the people, the Party affirmed all of its teachings on
unselfishness, brotherhood, equality under heaven and so on as

as enemy manoeuvres seeking to deny the absolute qualities of Matter, and thus
the absolute certainty of Progress, whose Vanguard was the Party.

72

'progressive', seeking only to perfect them through the introduction of dialectics. In particular, rather than simply loving thy neighbour as thyself, thou wert first to find out just who thy neighbour was. And if he was any kind of an enemy, then thou wert to hate him as much as thou lovest thy real self, the collective, manifest in the Party.

While so disposing of Charity, the Party incorporated Faith and Hope in its dialectical ideology and its vision of inexorable Progress towards Mankind's rebirth in Perfection. This is taught, much as the Church had all along been teaching its own brand of revivalism, with incantation, symbols and rituals for the masses, and high doctrine for the élite. To peasants and workers Dialectical Materialism was dispensed in slogans painted on walls and blared from loudspeakers, in rousing marches, in charts showing the inexorable progress of socialism, and in pictures of leaders and vicious cartoons of the enemy displayed everywhere and carried in huge demonstrations. Office workers, surrounded by the same world of incantation, symbols and ritual, in addition received the faith in seminars studying the Lives of Stalin and his local version, and the History of the Communist Party of the Soviet Union, on which yearly examinations were held. And at the highest level, actual works by Marx, Engels, Lenin and Stalin were also expounded in detail.

Imparting ideology to the young was equally stratified. The entire school curriculum was, of course, dialectical in its outlook – much more so than it had previously been religious or even national-revivalistic. Darwin's Theory of Evolution, for instance, was taught to have been dialectical not only as an act of rebellion against the dogmas of the Church, but also because as a theory it embodied the idea of Matter's inexorable progress towards its living perfection.

Apart from this general approach, reading primers carried excerpts from the Lives of the Fathers, and poems about them and tenets of the faith. Literature and history textbooks contained drawings and written descriptions of scenes supporting the dialectical argument, and algebra books had such problems as: 'If you know that between 1926–40 the production of pig iron increased 1·5 times in Germany, 9·1 times in the US, and 20 times in the Soviet Union, find out how many times faster the pig iron production of the Soviet Union had increased than that of Germany and the US.'

This much will have been offered even to those leaving school at about fourteen, to take their places as the next generation of peasants and workers. In secondary schools the argument was taken further, with quotations from Party classics and elucidation of some of their ideas; meanwhile, versions of civics lessons imparted a knowledge of ideology in practice. And finally, at all establishments of higher education, the next generation of the élite received courses in Marxism–Leninism, Politico-Economics, Scientific Socialism, and other versions of Dialectical Materialism, in a minimum of four weekly lectures throughout the academic year. Students of theology in several countries had further courses on how to reconcile the two versions of revivalism they were having to absorb.

The faith, whether dispensed as ritual or as dogma, had its promised land in the Soviet Union, 'the country of Realized Socialism', as propaganda put it. It was as the Language of Socialism that Russian began to be taught in mass courses to adults, and was made compulsory for all schoolchildren from the age of eleven. Meanwhile, everything Soviet acquired the incantatory attribute 'vanguard'. There were 'vanguard Soviet irrigation techniques', 'vanguard Soviet pedagogy', 'vanguard Soviet sport', and so on, the measure of a perfect irrigation technician, pedagogue or sportsman being his willingness to apply 'vanguard Soviet methods'.

Though repugnant to self-respecting East Europeans, in Party terms this was perfectly logical. If every aspect of human endeavour was subject to the same inexorable laws of development, then everything pertaining to the Country of Already Realized Socialism had to be the most advanced. It was stretching logic only a little to retroject the vanguard idea into history, and exalt not just Russian literature and music, already sufficiently recognized, but science and philosophy too. This was done by appropriating the invention of the steam engine, radio and a number of other things, the elaboration of non-Euclidean geometry, and even some of the basic ideas of Dialectical Materialism, as Russian achievements 'denied' by the West. From this it was barely a step to investing Russian folk dances with the same vanguard quality, and making them staple in the programmes of subsidized groups and school ensembles.

And of course it was as the Leader of the Vanguard of History, and the only living Apostle of the Faith, that Stalin was celebrated throughout the empire he had set up in Eastern Europe. Streets, factories, towns, mountain peaks and whole geographical regions were named after him, statues of him stood in squares and busts of him on office desks, pictures of him hung on walls and were carried in demonstrations, and his name was chanted at meetings for minutes on end. Authors and musicians sang his praises, some sincerely, school textbooks and scientific dissertations ended with lines from him, children penned poems in honour of his birthday, and folk artists wove his likeness into cushion covers. He was the embodiment of Dialectics, the Central Hero, the Greatest Whatever mankind possessed. He was deity on earth, in whose worship some Bulgarian kindergartens developed a whole ritual. Children were told to shut their eyes and pray to God; they did, and nothing happened. They were then told to shut their eyes and pray to Uncle Stalin; when they had, they could open their eyes and were given their sweets for the day.

As for the last enemy, plain truth and its aspects, Zhdanov's dialectical rule applied. Parts of objective reality were utilized to present reality as revolutionary development. Truthfulness and historical exactitude were subordinated to the task of ideological transformation, the education of the people in the spirit of socialism. Reports in the media worked bits of statistics, pictures of new housing developments and leaders' phrases into a rosy panorama, without ever questioning what the figures meant, whether the houses would last or why leaders preferred bloated metaphors to plain language. Spontaneity was similarly harnessed. Religious holidays, for instance, were reduced in number or altogether abolished, and instead non-working days were enlivened by demonstrations, entertainment, some free food and drink and firework-displays by night were given to the people on 1 May and special Party anniversaries. If Pioneers went camping, round the campfire they sang revolutionary songs, heard stories of heroic Russian partisans, and saw satire lampooning the enemy performed. If the Youth League put on a dance, this usually happened on the eve of Party days, and was preceded by speeches and various bits of instructive culture.

And often enough, if no facts at all had occurred spontaneously they were invented – not only in such traditional areas of fictitiousness as literature and the arts, but in science too. For instance, Lysenko's completely fake experiments, seeking to show that within a few harvests two ears of corn could be grown in place of one, became basic to the teaching of genetics, with doubters in both Russia and Eastern Europe banned from the profession and often sent to labour camps as enemies of the people's agriculture. This, proposing that under the Party's leadership the people could precipitate revolutionary developments in nature itself, was socialist realism in science.

It was also fully in line with Dialectical Materialism. For if the inexorable laws of Matter itself had destined the Party to be the Heroic Vanguard of Progress, then wherever the Party led, Matter was bound by its own laws inexorably to follow. The only logical explanation for its not doing so could be, for any believer, that it had fallen prey to enemy manoeuvres – which was just the explanation the Party offered for whatever seemed not to follow the laws it had discerned as inexorable in the World Process. In this, again, the Party was being religious. Rallying all usable facets of reality to confirm the faith and repelling all contrary evidence as the enemy's doing, it united the faithful and the beauty of the world as God's vanguard against whoever and whatever it said was still in the hands of Satan.

To be as supremely self-defensive as religion while claiming to be scientifically based on Matter was in fact the chief beauty of Dialectical Materialism. To outsiders its arguments might seem wholly circuitous, but to its believers it gave a prophetic rationale. On the one hand they could take justifiable pride in whatever the Party was actually achieving, from rises in steel production to the vast expansion of the school system down to nursery level; they could also take whatever pleased them in surrounding reality, from good summers and harvests to East Europeans' traditional hunger for books, as 'progressive' and so vindicating the Party.

On the other hand they could denounce whatever the Party seemed to find insuperable, from economic shortages to drunkenness in the streets and political opposition, as 'remnants of the past' still kept alive by 'enemy manoeuvres' but 'inexorably doomed'. Each believer who was willing enough could thus produce his own socialist realist vision of the world.

During Stalin's time the number of such willing socialist realists among Party members, non-Party sympathizers and in the youth organizations was relatively high, for two main reasons. One of these was that while the Party's economic policies were far more realistic and genuinely inspiring than those of the prewar élites had been, the Party not only professed to love the poor, but was also doing much more for them than any church ever had. The problems it was causing at the same time were at best only partially known to any one person or group, while many of its basic lies were so large that it alone could begin to dismantle them, as was to happen after Stalin's death.

The other reason was that in its propaganda about freedom, equality, brotherhood and future prosperity, the Party was indeed calling its faithful, its sympathizers and the young, on behalf of the most attractive dreams mankind had ever developed. Though the majority of each East European population tried to shut its ears in hatred to the Party's message, a significant minority of those who listened were bound to become millennially entranced. If many of the people who devised the Party's very complex strategies, and even some of those who executed the terror they entailed, could remain sincere, it was still easier for those of the faithful who could see only part of the pattern and know only some of the horrors at most to develop doubts or go through crises of conscience, but to accept the Party's behaviour as serving a beautiful purpose. In fact, central to what might be called sincere Stalinism was the dialectical ability of the faithful to see a hideously difficult and often wasteful and bloody process as the birth of another mankind.

Stalin's death in 1953, and the subsequent denunciation of him, had much the same effect on the ideological as on the political universe he had established around himself in Eastern Europe. The demise of the Central Hero led to decentralization in methods and rationalization in spirit, the extent of both depending in each country, first, on the fate of the local Stalinist leadership, and, second, on the course of the ensuing factional struggles inside the Party. But nowhere has the Party as Hero given up its prerogative to determine what kind of influences should reach the people and the young, whom it has continued to seek to command.

The spread of pragmatism since 1953 has amounted to phenomena that were previously rejected as hostile being admitted as at least harmless, if not directly 'progressive'. In other words, the Party has only extended grace, not granted universal pardon. It has retained both its heroic vision of itself as the Vanguard of World Progress, and the dialectical method of dividing all of reality into the direct allies and enemies of Progress (and hence the Party) and then dividing the enemy ranks into potential friends and irredeemable foes.

In some East European countries and within them in some spheres, the extension of grace has gone much further than in others. It has also varied from period to period in each country, as I shall explain presently. But throughout the region and at all times it has been limited by the fact that just as the Party can remain the Party only while it is Hero in central charge, so it cannot abandon its vision of itself as the embattled Vanguard of Progress without committing ideological suicide.

Given this limitation, the opposing fronts of heroic-centralists and pragmatic-decentralizers have formed in each country, in the spheres of culture and ideology, along lines similar to those observable in the economy and in politics. Convinced dogmatists, order-loving bureaucrats and those in posts for purely political reasons, plus people with a vested professional interest in the survival of heroic propaganda, have tended to take the centralist line in a radical or moderate manner. Meanwhile the creative intelligentsia, in culture and the media as much as in the sciences, has rather embraced versions of pragmatism and liberalism.

The alignment of fronts has, however, differed between the economic-political and cultural-ideological spheres, in two very important ways. One of these has had to do with the fact that whereas in the economy and in politics practice itself has taught large numbers of people pragmatism, to the same people culture as such may often be something of an alien phenomenon, and the more so the more authentic its manifestations are. Especially provoked by these, they emerge as philistines, ready to see firm policies imposed on intellectuals, artists and their ilk. The other difference is that whereas in the economy and in politics pragmatists are distinguished by their desire to stick to facts and rational argument, in culture and ideology they too can very often be rallied through the passions of nationalism and its variants. And though when nationalism first manifested itself in the rebellion against 'too-close imitation of Soviet models and methods' it was a liberalizing force, since about 1960 it has been ever more visibly embraced by the centralists, who denounce their opponents in the national-conservative manner known throughout the region since the nineteenth century.*

In one way or another the creative intelligentsia has in fact been the vanguard of de-Stalinization throughout Eastern Europe. It not only rejected Stalinism in its own fields far more violently than did members of the managerial class and of the political and state apparatuses, but also became instrumental in several East European countries in changing the whole of the heroic-centralist system established by the Central Hero before 1953.

Of course the intelligentsia, especially in the arts, the media and the academic world, represented the most volatile part of each people. It was also heir to a long tradition of regarding itself as the people's heroic élite against oppressive regimes. This indeed was the tradition out of which the Party itself had been born, only to betray it in power, and so provoke many of its formerly blindest supporters into democratic heroism against itself. But the most important reason for the contrast between the behaviour of the creative intelligentsia on the one hand, and the managerial class and even the best-intentioned apparatchiks

---

* This has been especially the case in Romania and Poland. Though many of the reasons have been peculiar to one country or the other, the main identical reason has been the need of a strongly centralist faction in the Party, ruling Romania and seeking power in Poland, to rally as much of the apparatus and of the people as it could.

on the other, was that the system imprisoning the people together with those trying to manage its affairs at any level could be changed only as it had been imposed – from the centre. Either the Party had to introduce sweeping reforms, or the people, prompted by the facts of reality and led by those able to see overall patterns and in positions to make themselves heard, had to sweep away Party centralism.

The unveiling of the Central Lie in 1953–6 was in fact followed – in measures and at speeds that have varied from country to country in Eastern Europe – by a combination of two revolts. In the first, Communist intellectuals threw themselves at the Party that had betrayed their life-ideals. Denouncing one Stalinist lie after another with the fury of duped heroes, they also extended their hands to the non-Communist majority of their colleagues, whom many of them had till then been denouncing as the enemies of Progress, condemned to silent death. In the second revolt, the front so born was joined, as soon as the crumbling of the Party's Platonic rule made this possible in any East European country, by the people.

The two revolts together amounted, in fact, to one vast demand for restitution by all those the Party had both claimed and often genuinely meant to lead and represent, but had been forced by the paradoxes of its position insanely to oppress, exploit and betray. They were versions of a revolt by reality, as manifest in the world of facts and of the senses, in the people surrounded by that world, and in the élite articulating what the world of facts had made the people feel and think, against the Party's Platonic attempt, since 1948, to impose total order and insane idealization, and suppress spontaneity and truth as the people's enemies.

Of course the Party itself made certain attempts to compromise with the people and the realities surrounding it after Stalin's death. Though it was only in Hungary that it introduced radical changes, throughout the region it granted some economic concessions, increasing the production and import of consumer goods, and trying to improve the agricultural situation and thus the supply of food to the towns. It also made noises about curbing the powers of the police, purged some of the worst-hated henchmen and released some political prisoners. But the demands articulated by the intellectuals on behalf of the people went much further. They aimed at nothing less than a reversal of the strategies and the dismantling of the machinery through which the Party had sought to isolate the people from the world around it, from its past, from its children, from its spiritual traditions and, more than anything, from the reality of its own experience.

In all these respects, the Party was at least to compromise, but preferably to give the people free choice. Travel to the West was to be allowed, and the jamming of western broadcasts to stop, and whatever the West had to offer in the sciences, the media and the arts, together with true descriptions of western life, were to be admitted without hindrance. The historical and cultural heritage of each nation was no longer to be insulted, distorted or suppressed, but rather made free for discussion, assessment and use by any part of the people. The fomenting of strife between children and parents on behalf of the Party was to stop. Religious worship was no longer to be an offence, and religious instruction in schools was to be made available to all those who wanted it. Ideology was not to be forced down the people's throat, and the mouthing of abject nonsense about Russia's superiority in everything, and about the immortality of living leaders, was to cease. And, most important, the truth rather than the Truth was to be told in the media and in literature and the arts as well as in the social and natural sciences, both to the people and to those in charge of any part of its environment, so that they could cope with the whole of it together as soon and as best they might.

To all these demands the young rallied with enthusiasm, led by their own conscious élite, the students. This, too, was natural, and very much in the East European tradition. Beyond that, it was also a reaction to the Party's betrayal of its own heroic claim on a group – in this case the young rather than the intellectuals – as a version of itself at the head of the people's march towards a better future. Altogether, in the revolt against the Party's heroic insanities to which reality was prompting the people under the leadership of its articulate élite, it was natural for the liveliest part of the people, and the one in the most spontaneous touch with reality, to form the genuine vanguard.

This they did. In fact they rose very much as the spontaneous storm-troops the Party had always made them out to be, but first of all against the order which the Party as Hero had sought to impose on their spontaneity. Long before the people attacked its monolithic mass organizations, let alone the Party in central charge, the young responded to the attack made at the top on 'one-man leadership' by turning on the youth and children's organizations which had held exclusive sway over their lives since 1948.

At the same time, meetings of young people and especially students began passing resolutions which, as liberalization widened in any one country, widened their scope to include every sphere ruled by the Party. Beyond youth policies, they attacked deficiencies in the pre-university and higher school system and the distortions and curtailment of the curricula for ideological reasons. They seconded the demands made by intellectuals for free access to the West and whatever it had to offer. They sought freedom for the media, and for research and publication in the social and natural sciences. And they demanded the rehabilitation of victims of Stalinist show trials, the curbing of the powers of the police, and the proper discussion of large numbers of problems created by the Party's policies since 1948 in the economy, in society and in political life. For some of these problems they also proposed practical solutions.

The Party's response to these demands, pressed under various forms and with varying intensity by the people's traditional élites throughout Eastern Europe since Stalin's death, has varied with the strength of its position as Hero in central charge of any East European country at any one time. Where external and internal factors and intra-Party strife had seriously weakened this position, or where centralists inside the Party had been suddenly routed, basic liberalization got under way and usually generated upheavals. Where at most moderate pragmatism prevailed inside the Party while its position in the country remained firm, the élites heading the movement for liberalization found themselves hopelessly beaten back – as the Party itself had been when, still a leftist intellectual élite, it had tried challenging the prewar establishment and its military.

As may be seen from the chronological table on pp. 52–5, the history of Eastern Europe since 1953 divides into two main periods, both of which began with a wave of liberalization. The first followed Stalin's death and the initial attack on him at the Twentieth Soviet Party Congress, which both brought changes at the top and raised popular hopes and demands until developments ended in the Hungarian and Polish upheavals of October 1956; the second started with the Twenty-Second Soviet Party Congress, at which Stalinism was denounced in terms not heard before (or since), producing a second wave of reforms from above and pressures from below throughout the region, and leading in Czechoslovakia to the Dubček months of 1968.

Of the two periods, though the first was more important in shaking the faith of many genuine Party members beyond recovery,* the second produced more basic and ultimately more durable changes. The first caught both the Party and the people largely unprepared, and in particular without any constructive ideas about a *modus vivendi* in the conditions forced on them by the unalterable fact of Russian domination and the Party's equally unalterable vision of itself as Hero or nothing. The result was a great upsurge of hope which in Poland very nearly and in Hungary actually ended in a violent clash between the people and the Russian-defended Party; this led not only to bloody repression in Hungary, but to a confirmation of hard-line policies throughout the region, eventually affecting Poland too.

By the time the second period began at the end of 1961, however, the situation was very different. Not only had the first shock of de-Stalinization worn off, but strong pragmatist factions within the Party were either waiting to assert themselves, as in Bulgaria and to a lesser extent in Czechoslovakia, or actually in the ascendant, as in Hungary; only Romania was still ruled by its Stalin, and only in Poland had botched policies of pragmatism (combined with Gomułka's increasingly autocratic style of

---

* I do not mean that they lost their faith, which many of them have not. But only very few among them could once again become the blind enthusiasts, or bear or even inflict the terror, of the 1950s; and their example and spoken advice has had an important influence on the Communists who have grown up in Eastern Europe since, as I shall try to show.

government) given a new chance to hard-liners. Krushchev's second, and more sweeping, denunciation of Stalinism thus allowed for non-violent but all the more effective purges of hard-liners in the top and middle-ranks of the Party, accompanied by a general airing of the country's worst memories of the Stalinist years, and followed by the introduction of important reforms, in Hungary and to some extent also in Bulgaria; in Czechoslovakia it combined with the effects of an economic crisis and of the rehabilitation of the victims of the Stalinist show trials to start the process leading to 1968. And though the events of that year in Czechoslovakia once again demonstrated the external and internal realities which have governed politics in Eastern Europe during the lifetime of the present generation, neither inside Czechoslovakia, nor in the rest of the region did they produce the reactions that October 1956 had produced in Hungary and elsewhere. In Czechoslovakia centralists came to power in politics, and ultra-conservatives in the cultural spheres, but Hungary held its liberal course, while in Bulgaria and Poland, where hard-liners had been asserting themselves since the mid-sixties, very few of them tried to use the example of Czechoslovakia as a bogey. Only the still largely unpurged Romanian apparatus exploited the August 1968 invasion to reverse the (anyhow timid) policies of liberalization instituted in the previous two years, so steering the Party on the course that led to the start of the vast ideological revival campaign in July 1971.

The situation now surrounding young East Europeans results from this chequered history. As in the economy and in politics, so in every sphere of culture and ideology every Party (including the Romanian one) is more pragmatic now than it was in the early fifties. But none has abandoned its prerogative as Hero in charge to determine what may be of use, and what may prove mortal danger, to the cause of which it still proposes itself to be the Vanguard.

Party policies concerning the Youth League provide perhaps the clearest and certainly the most pertinent example of how the situation in general has changed. Though the Party alone had established the Youth League of each country in the virtually impossible position of having to marshal the spontaneous energies of the young for specific purposes, as well as to let them have fun and transmit to them meanwhile its ideological message, in the period following Stalin's death it not only allowed but often prompted criticism and denunciation of the Leagues for their quixotic failures.

Both to the Party's permission and to its prompting the young responded with a vengeance, sometimes taking out on the Youth League what they could not take out on the Party. All the major periods of liberalization in Eastern Europe have seen the Youth League covered in shame, and in fact each time the Party's position has come near to being overturned in an East European country, its League was torn apart by the young.

In Poland, during the two-year thaw that led to the 'Spring in October' of 1956 independent youth clubs – literary, theatrical and finally political – sprang up in profusion. In Hungary, both the early periods of thaw (in 1953–4 and from early 1956 onwards) resounded with attacks on the League, and three days before the outbreak of the October Revolt students actually founded their own separate organization. And in Czechoslovakia, where between 1963 and 1968 the League lost some six hundred thousand members, students meanwhile began a campaign against its monopoly over the young, challenging it openly in December 1965 and virtually destroying it by late 1967. And in the upheavals that followed the Party let the Leagues die unlamented.

Only to revive each, however, and suppress its spontaneous rivals, as soon as it had re-established itself firmly enough in power in each country. The League was given a slightly different name, and allowed a more pragmatic outlook, but was put in the same basic position. Instead of the Don Quixote Youth League, fighting windmills until denounced by the Party and left to die, there is now the King Canute Youth League, fighting the waves.

Certainly the League's activities are much less tedious than they were under Stalin, but that makes its tasks even more difficult. It must be everything to everyone. Though at the time of its rebirth each League had visionaries who wanted an élite corps on the lines of the Leninist Komsomol and the East European Communist youth groups of the 1945–8 period, as the only available youth organization each has had to take all the members it could find, and cater for them in all the ways it might. This has meant vast masses in the League, depriving it both of mobility and of all storm-troop appeal, and a range of duties beyond the powers of any earthly organization in which membership may be advisable, but only a minimum of activity can be enforced.

In this position, the League has tried to marry political seminars with every kind of genuinely interesting pastime, from hobby and poetry circles to pop festivals and off-shore yachting, and the sponsorship of trips abroad. Even in Bulgaria and Romania where, because there have never been de-Stalinizing upheavals, the tragi-comic rebirth of Don Quixote as King Canute has been played out only in miniature (in Bulgaria in 1963–5 and in 1968–9, and in Romania in 1968–9) the Leagues now spend as much energy marshalling the vast 'voluntary' summer brigades to various 'labour fronts' as they do in running coffee-bars with juke boxes in youth clubs, and holding pancake-eating competitions. The Pioneers, too, have adopted throughout the region as much of plain scouting methods as they can politically afford, and no one now calls scavenger hunts and games in the forests 'fascistic'. Meanwhile, the youth media have come fully to reflect this diversification of interests by the youth organizations, and they often prove to be cheerleaders where the pop scene and its home-bred as well as foreign stars are concerned.

In the midst of all this, however, the League and to a lesser extent the Pioneers remain bodies through which the Party seeks to control the movements and inform the minds of the young. Though in Poland there are separate organizations for young peasants and for students, both of these are as much under the Party's supervision as the League itself, and elsewhere only the League and the Pioneers exist. Also, any activities that have been admitted as harmless or directly useful to the cause have all been so assessed by the Party alone and may at any time be reassessed by the Party, with summary effect. When, for example, Romania started its vast new ideological campaign in July 1971, the Youth League and its officials and activities were among the first to be affected. The League's pragmatist secretary, made Minister for Youth Affairs in December 1967 for the precise purpose of befriending the young on the Party's behalf, was removed from all his posts and had to suffer vitriolic attacks, while pragmatism was replaced with a combination of patriotism, puritanism and Party zeal.

In fact, being a Youth League official in Eastern Europe is a thankless enough task these days. Some functionaries seek to earn the genuine trust of their members by struggling to wring concessions from factory managements and university scholarship and disciplinary committees, and so get into trouble. But even apart from such rebels, pressures on those in charge are legion from every side.

Basic organizations, for example, may try anything from pop music to semi-political discussions to keep members interested. But should such interest become too lively, their functionaries could well find themselves dismissed for 'unprincipled liberalism' in their work. Similarly, while pragmatists inside each League leadership would like to keep everyone happy with the least wastage in money and words, and hard-liners strive for more political seminars and labour camps, both have a much harder time trying to put their ideas into practice than their equivalents in the Party have. They have infinitely less disciplined and more lively memberships swirling beneath them. They are under continuous pressure from the parent generations and educational establishments either for more fun to be offered to the young, or for harsher discipline and puritanism to be imposed on them. And they are invariably affected by the course of factional struggles within the Party, above their heads. King Canute, lucky man, only had the waves to worry about.

The same sort of situation prevails, *mutatis mutandis*, in every other sphere surrounding the young. In all of them the Party has admitted whatever it considers to be of practical use to itself and the cause, and continues at best to tolerate and at worst to reject everything else, with the execution of these policies dependent on the way those directly in charge, and those directly affected, deal with pressures on them from any relevant side.

In education, whose nature and organization tend to exclude sudden changes, some basic ones have nevertheless occurred. Centralism has been attenuated, at least at university level, in several countries, with institutions regaining a measure of their former autonomy and students a measure of freedom in attendance and choice of courses. At the same time, the system in every country has been opened as regards new teaching methods and factual information and, effectively, most worthwhile ideas, to the West. While indigenous experimentation has also been revived, curricula in both the sciences and the humanities have been considerably modernized, and now offer much broader horizons.

However, though no country is likely to go back to the isolationism of Stalinist days in education, nor to the ruining of the curricula, changes democratizing the educational system and life in its institutions have had political brakes applied to them at all times, and have proved reversible in times of crisis. In Hungary, for example, the 1961 reforms of higher education did not even begin to come into effect for about six years, while in Czechoslovakia the university reforms of 1966 were effectively annulled after the ultras' rise to cultural power in 1969.

As regards versions of the enemy, the Party has changed many of its attitudes and practices, but retained all of its basic suspicions and designs. And wherever it has felt itself to be, realistically or owing to the paranoiac disposition of those devising its strategies, still or once again in a war situation, its behaviour too has been warlike. This is why in certain East European countries attitudes towards the enemy have relaxed at certain times only to harden again at other times, and in certain others have never relaxed at all.

The changes in its attitude towards the most obvious enemy, the West, illustrate the point perfectly. There has been an easing of postures throughout the region, but only in so far as this accords with the Party's idea of peaceful coexistence: the replacement of vicious rhetoric and hatred of the enemy by waiting for him to be killed instead by Progress, assisted in every possible way by the Party.

Descriptions of life in the West offered to East Europeans in the media, for example, have grown much more realistic, but they always imply and on occasions directly state that they concern a civilization on its very last legs. Similarly, the jamming of western broadcasts stopped in Poland in 1956 and in the course of the

The Hero's Call

next eight years throughout the region, but the stations themselves (and all western media) continue to be seen as fair to the cause of Progress only by accident; and following the Czechoslovak crisis of 1968-9, jamming also began again in several East European countries. Products of the West which are of material value are readily admitted, whether they be straight cash, travel grants or know-how, but culture, especially in the hard-line countries, remains subject to definite rules of selection. These either aim at reinforcing the impression of a sick western civilization, or are in sheer conformity with middle-brow tastes, considered, quite rightly, to be the same the world over. And the designs of the West on Eastern Europe continue to be seen in essentially the same light as before, with crisis situations producing critically paranoid responses: 'The imperialist powers,' wrote the 1969 current affairs compendium issued to secondary-school leavers in Hungary, the least enthusiastic among Czechoslovakia's five invading powers the previous August, 'suited their policies to the [surreptitious] tactics of the internal forces of counter-revolution. During their talks in Rome in July 1968, the representatives of the USA, England, West Germany and Italy decided to refrain from all political moves in connection with Czechoslovakia, so as not to unmask themselves.'8

Meanwhile, policies on travel to the West have in fact constituted almost exact indicators of the outlook of the leadership in charge of any East European country at any one time. In Poland westward travel became virtually free in 1956, began to be restricted in 1959, and grew more and more difficult with every passing year of Gomułka's reign, to be made easier again only after Edward Gierek's rise to power in December 1970; in Hungary it began to be allowed as part of the policy of relaxation in 1959-60, and has been made gradually easier ever since; in Czechoslovakia westward travel became possible in the early sixties, to turn into a tourist stampede by 1968-9, but then was almost entirely stopped by legislation following the ultras' rise to power; and from the two southern countries no more than an infinitesimal number of people have been allowed to see the West at all since 1948.

Changes in attitudes and policies towards other forms of the

89

enemy have followed much the same pattern, with those enemies who are seen as presenting the least danger being most cordially embraced as 'progressive'.

With the past the Party has come to terms far more than it can, as the Vanguard of the Future, actually admit. In fact the paradox of its position as both the Ideal and therefore static Being and the Motor of inexorable Becoming has made the Party embrace as 'progressive' or at least harmless everything from each nation's past that might help to maintain the *status quo*, while it gets on with the work it considers important. This extension of its progressive grace has applied as much to nineteenth-century national anthems in which God is asked to bless the people now led by an atheistic Party, as to splendid royal castles now restored as part of the people's own heritage, and to nearly all the best and a good deal of the worst in the literary and artistic output of the interwar years. In history, though interpretations remain distorted in favour of the heroic view, there is little that cannot be discussed in at least learned publications, while many popular but formerly denounced figures from the prewar period have been rehabilitated, with special fervour in Romania and Poland, where nationalism has been most pronounced since the mid-sixties.

Towards the family the Party has adopted quite a different attitude. This is a direct result of its interpreting its own role in charge of the people in an ever more paternal manner, and is also in line with its having changed from an élite bristling with young storm-troopers of the revolution, to an irremovable body full of parents and grandparents.* In addition, with the employment of women becoming a problem in several countries, nursery accommodation still far from sufficient, and divorces and juvenile

---

* Indeed not only is the Party in charge as irremovably (and often as ineffectually) as any paterfamilias, but the men in charge of each Party are themselves less removable and more paternal than most countries of the region have ever seen. At the time of writing, Todor Zhivkov, First Secretary of the Bulgarian Party, is sixty, with seventeen years in power behind him, and Hungary's János Kádár sixty, looking back to fifteen years at the helm. Of the other countries, Czechoslovakia had had as First Secretary Antonín Novotný from 1953 until 1968, Poland had been led by Władysław Gomułka between 1956 and 1970, and in Romania Gheorghiu Gheorghiu-Dej had ruled in a Stalinesque manner right up to his death in 1965.

delinquency on the increase due mainly to the 'centrelessness' of families, the Party has changed from lionization of the working woman to courtship of the feminine housewife. From the early sixties onwards this has been manifest in propaganda as much as in policies on family allowances and the introduction of evening courses in cosmetics for ladies and housecraft classes in secondary schools for girls.

Peace with the Church has been established on terms which may appear very similar on the surface, but are very different underneath. Essentially, whereas the Party has accepted the family as stronger than itself and thus an indispensable ally, it has continued to see the Church as doomed by Progress, and hence as only a tolerated enemy. Tolerance is greatly increased at times of national crisis (such as occurred in the most strongly Catholic country, Poland, in 1956 and following the workers' riots in December 1970) which put the Party in a posture of supplication, while at normal times measures of tolerance by the Party may be traded for helpings of benediction by the Church. But on the whole the relationship as envisaged by the Party is a version of its peaceful coexistence with the West. That is, militancy has been abandoned in favour of waiting for Progress, with the Party's fullest possible help, to bring the enemy slow but certain death.

Meanwhile, instruction in the Party's own brand of religion, though less blatant in tone and generally less oppressive in method, has continued without much of a break. Following the reaction to Stalinism, slogans and pictures of the leader have become much less frequent even in the hardest-line country, Romania; ideological courses have been thinned out, propaganda is more realistic, and quotations from the classics are used more sparingly in school textbooks. However, the heroic-dialectical view of the world remains basic to both propaganda and general education, ideology continues to be taught as a major subject throughout everyone's university years, and in the second half of the sixties new courses propounding it in secondary schools were introduced in most countries of the region. And while every time a Party takes the road towards liberalization ideological education is allowed partially or wholly to lapse, every time hard-liners are in the ascendant, it is revived with new fervour. In Poland, for example, lectures in Marxism–Leninism were abolished in 1956, but began to be reintroduced in 1960–1 and were amplified in 1964–5, until by 1968 first-year students at university found themselves having to attend 'orientation courses' on daily politics too.

The Party's main, and in some ways ever worsening, problem remains its relationship with its most basic enemy, reality, against which it has only ever admitted struggling in the 'good' sense – that is, in the sense of fighting as the Champion of Progress to change for the better the facts surrounding the people, and the life that these facts govern. But while it has justly prided itself on every success achieved in this Aristotelian effort, the Party has continued to denounce as the work of the enemy all reminders of its concurrent struggle to impose Platonic order on the people's spontaneous life, and to isolate the people from knowledge of the facts which govern its own experience.

It is, however, inherent in the Party's paradoxical situation that every one of its successes in the 'good' struggle should render the 'bad' one that much more difficult to wage, by making facts and the life of the people more complex. Thus the Party's most basic enemy, reality, is proving the least tractable. Indeed it has not just humbled the Party in countless ways, but has often proved as dialectically treacherous about compromises that it has accepted from the Party, as the Party has been in offering them to its other enemies.

Not that the Party has abandoned the 'bad' struggle altogether. True, the lies of the Stalinist era, as monstrous as they proved in due course to be disastrous, have generally followed Stalin to the grave. Meanwhile, as the Party's transformatory work has progressed, so it has been able to afford more frankness in the media about general facts and the life of the people. It has also admitted the portrayal of spontaneous human emotions and problems, and even some peculiarities in the arts, as at least individually if not socially of therapeutic value, thus in the end helping the cause of Progress. At the same time, the Party has ceased to deny those in charge of managing the people's affairs a knowledge both of the facts and of whatever relevant ideas and methods have been generated in the rest of the world. Not only has it done away with all restrictions on research and foreign contacts, and virtually all ideological nonsense in the natural sciences, but even in the social sciences it has become a good deal more pragmatic. Sociology, for example, in which under Stalin no genuine field-work was done, nor any proper discussion allowed, lest truths about society contrary to the Truth should come to light, was rehabilitated as a discipline in Poland in 1956, and throughout the region in 1963-5, with even the hardest-line regimes now allowing research to stick to facts.

All this, however, has remained subject to the purposes which as Hero in central charge the Party claims to represent. As regards the media and the arts, for example, while liberalization instituted from above or developing from below always produces realism about the country and about people's genuine feelings and problems, when the Party reimposes itself as Hero in absolute charge, not only does it ban realism but it proceeds to make thoroughly treacherous use of cheap imitations of it. It does not merely allow, but encourages the airing of *past* problems, and the provision of middle-brow entertainment, as palliatives. Similarly, while research in the social sciences is pragmatic, the kind of studies commissioned, the form in which the results may appear and the conclusions that may be reached in public all remain within the Party's jurisdiction. In a country as consistently pragmatic as Hungary has been since the early sixties, sociological research ranges into every field including politics; most results and even half-way provocative conclusions may appear at least in learned magazines, and though a number of studies remain available, in cyclostyled form, only to top professional and Party personnel, no one in recent years has been punished for things they have written. By contrast, Poland saw a repressive clamp-down from the mid-sixties onwards, until the hard-liner purges following the March 1968 student riots took perhaps the heaviest toll among sociologists. And in Czechoslovakia the ultras who took cultural power after April 1969 not only suppressed all relevant publications, but disbanded all of the country's best sociological institutes and research teams, banning many of their members from the field.

In brief, it may be said that the Party is getting from reality only as good as it gives. Two things, however, are working to make the dynamics of the situation ever more treacherous for the Party, and more advantageous for its basic enemy.

One is that while it is difficult enough to rule the ebb and flow of the environment and the life of the people at the best of times, the Party is existentially obliged to make the job only harder for itself. It cannot cease being Hero in central charge without committing suicide. But its being Hero entails an excessive ambition to control the environment, and a need at the same time to isolate its facts from the people, which together present it with a managerial task beyond the powers of any human institution. And the more Platonic it remains in its view of the State and of itself as the Philosopher Hero at the centre, the less it can hope to satisfy its ambitions of controlling the dynamics by which it is surrounded, and the graver becomes its need to conceal them from the people. In due course disasters cathartic of its hubris must ensue.

The other is that the Party is engaged as Champion of Progress in making those dynamics only more dynamic and more complex. It is prompting the economic and social environment to move ever faster and in more sophisticated ways, and it is enriching the life and the mind of the people, so letting its choices in all spheres become more varied and self-confident. In fact, the more pragmatically fruitful the Party's policies, the richer and more complex and thus less amenable to Platonic rule spontaneous life around it becomes. In the course of its Aristotelian endeavour to improve the material world as well as its inhabitants, the Party is feeding from below the spontaneity that must in the end swell past the grid of its Platonic rule from above.

Nowhere is the movement of East European reality more spontaneously manifest than in the young generation. If during the last twenty-five years the Party has found its least tractable enemies in Matter and the People, whose Universal Hero it has always claimed to be, it has found its most cheerfully and dynamically treacherous allies in those it has seen as the Hero's Children and born vanguard.

Part III

The Hero's Children

Introduction

In what follows I shall try to describe the life of the young in Eastern Europe today, and their relationships with the Party above their heads and with the world which the Party has very considerably changed around them in the last twenty-five years.

The nine chapters are divided into groups of three, each group devoted to a major theme of the book, treated from three different angles.

The first group views the Party as Hero struggling with phenomena that it once thought it either could simply control (the influences reaching young East Europeans) or had on its side as a matter of course (the generational drift) or would be able to transform in a few years (the structure and behaviour of society).

The next group considers the Party's attempt to rally the people and especially the young as their Universal, for the purposes of collective coping. Three main factors have militated against the Party's succeeding in this attempt. One has lain in the nature of the political system that it must maintain as Hero in central charge, but which prevents the people and the young from accepting the Party as their true Universal in peacetime. The second, in the Forms of Order which shape young East Europeans from birth to adulthood (and of which the Party's centralist system is only the final embodiment) in such a manner as to make them largely unable to co-operate on terms of trust rather than coercion and reward. And the third, in the ways that East Europeans so formed choose for living together, and for coping with the circumstances the Party is meanwhile trying to change around them and with the Party's centralist order as the least changeable circumstance of their lives.

The last group explains the suicidal choices with which as a result both of its failures and of its successes the Party seems to be faced. It came on the scene as the Ultimate Hero of History,

Rationality Incarnate and the Sole Champion of Progress. Its failures, however, have discredited heroism, while its successes have so changed the East European environment as to make heroics useless; and in future the Party, as a body wedded to the *status quo*, is likely to induce heroism only against itself. Similarly, the Party's own practice has shown its ideology to be only a mixture of reason and myth, while its Platonic rule generates pressures that keep alive irrational hatreds, of which it must become in due course either the commanding hero or the central target. And finally, during the last twenty-five years the Party has transformed Eastern Europe in basic ways which make it ever less necessary as a motor of change, and, as a body by definition centralist in its methods of rule, ever more of an obstacle to further progress.

Each of the nine chapters starts with the part of its 'live' material that seems to me most characteristic of its theme. This is followed by a brief presentation of the chapter's framework of ideas, and then the development of these ideas in detail. As nearly all the effects I shall be discussing are due to more than one cause, the reader will find that I return to a number of phenomena in more than one chapter, until the circle of reasons I can adduce for them is complete.

1 Circles

On 10 March 1968 a crowd of several thousand people went to pay homage at the graves of Thomas and Jan Masaryk, in the grounds of the family's house some twenty miles outside Prague. Through sleet and strong winds hundreds of students had walked the distance in procession, to lay their wreaths and stand guard. The day was the twentieth anniversary of Jan Masaryk's death. Son of the founder of Czechoslovakia and Foreign Minister of the postwar Republic, he had been killed falling from the window of his office after the Communist *coup d'état* in 1948. According to the official version, he had committed suicide. According to rumours he had been murdered by the police on Russian orders, or even by Russian agents themselves. Now the Dubček leadership, ready to clear up the past, had reopened his case. To stand guard and pay homage at his grave expressed a demand for justice to be seen to be done.

This was not, however, only or even mainly on Jan Masaryk's behalf. He and his father had become symbols of what the Dubček leadership was now proposing to revive, the people's power to rule its own affairs. 'The question of how Jan Masaryk died does not seem to interest people so much as what he stood for,' wrote *The Times*'s correspondent on the scene. 'Students told me they wanted to show their respect to men who stood for democracy and freedom. Masaryk represented the best in Czechoslovak life, they said.'[1]

Some three months after the event I went to Czechoslovakia on the first of my trips to gather material for the present book. By then the Prague Spring had grown into full summer, and the mood was euphoric – too euphoric, as it subsequently became clear.

Among the people I interviewed were four young workers from a large factory on the outskirts of Prague. During the conversation, which lasted over two hours, I brought up the subject of the kind of political system they wanted to see emerge from the changes then taking place. They said they wanted a democracy like the pre-1939 First Republic. With social ownership of the means of production, but embodying T. G. Masaryk's ideas of humanism, of decency in public affairs, and of freedom for the individual.

'You were all born after 1945,' I said. 'In your schoolbooks you could read nothing good about Masaryk, and little that was good about the First Republic. How is it you all seem to know so much about both?'

'We have parents,' one of them said simply, as to a damned-fool question. 'We read other books. We talk to each other.'

Parents, other books, talking to friends. In a very large survey on the social life of secondary-school children in Budapest,[2] one of the questions concerned the adults in whom interviewees fully confided: 67·8 per cent named their mothers, 40·4 per cent their fathers, 16·4 per cent other relatives, 5·5 per cent teachers. Describing the results of a similar survey, conducted among sixteen-year-olds in secondary-general and technical schools in Prague, the city's evening paper wrote in 1965: '[In reply to the question] "Who has had the strongest influence on your life?" all girls put their mothers in first place and their fathers in second, while of the boys 80·67 per cent put their mothers first and 74·10 per cent put their fathers second. Third place is taken by a friend, a girl friend or boy friend, and so on. The column "official of the Czechoslovak Youth League" was invariably marked with a zero.'[3]

This does not, of course, mean that propaganda never got through to them at all. What it does mean is that all outside influences would have reached them in the midst of family relationships and friendships, both of which have remained very close. In the Budapest survey, for instance, to the question of how often fourteen to eighteen-year-olds talked things over with their parents, 36·8 per cent replied 'daily' and a further 29·4 per cent replied 'several times a week'. Of the kinds of friendships they maintained, 22·2 per cent could be called 'close' (limited to one to two friends) and another 49·7 per cent 'small group' (three to six friends). 'Out here friendships seem too loose,' a twenty-eight-year-old Polish girl on a visit to London told me, echoing many other young East Europeans I had occasion to interview in the West. 'People call everybody their friends. Even if they just meet in the pub, and lose them when they move. At home we make friends in school, and then we know them for a long time, maybe through life. We see them without any calling up, all the time, and we talk about everything in our lives. Perhaps it's too close, but it's what we call friendship.'

About the reasons for the closeness of the relationships surrounding young East Europeans I shall talk elsewhere. What matters here is that the influence of these close relationships over them has proved much stronger than either the Party as Hero or its enemies at home and abroad had expected. Both had greatly overestimated – the Party in hope and its enemies in fear – the powers of formal education and of propaganda from above. In fact, whenever East European parents themselves have blamed all insubordination in their children on the spirit of postwar schooling, or westerners have believed that the Party could bring up a generation of fanatical warriors, both have only subscribed to the Party's own heroic-dialectical argument, inexorably appropriating the young and the future for Communism.

The real dialectics of the process have proved much more complex. Parents, for example, may be accused by their children, in the heat of an argument, of 'living in the past'. But through the same arguments as much as through intimate conversations they nevertheless turn out to impart most of their patterns of thinking to their children.

The influence that, especially in the two less developed countries of the south, parents exercise over their children's choice of career, for instance steering most girls towards 'feminine' occupations, is something educationalists and propagandists have found very hard to combat. Almost every time I asked young East Europeans about religiosity, those who were religious explained this as due to the upbringing they had had at home, and often meant to give their own children. And even in less serious matters, and in the most developed part of the region, parents retain a strong say: 'Your hair seems rather short,' I remarked to a twenty-seven-year-old Czech pop star whom I was interviewing in June 1968. 'I tried letting it grow to my shoulders,' he laughed. 'But father couldn't stand it. So I had to cut it off again.'

As regards politics, the early attempts to capture the young as a vanguard against 'enemy' elders inevitably achieved some dire successes. 'I still carry a feeling of guilt about it,' a twenty-nine-year-old musician told me in Romania. 'My father was a priest. And he used to say, in about 1951 when I was twelve, that he believed in Communism, but that this wasn't Communism. Not with arrests and labour camps and the shooting of peasants who wouldn't enter collectives. And I thought, yes, he's a priest, an enemy of the people, that's why he's talking like that. I hated him. When much later I thought about it, you can imagine. . . .'

But even in the darkest fifties, most parents who tried to could retain the loyalty of their children. In Czechoslovakia I talked to the son of a victim of one of the major show trials. I asked him whether, at the age of only nine and with the huge propaganda machine working on the whole country, plus the victimization even by schoolfriends which he himself had just described, he too had not believed his father guilty.

'No, I didn't,' he said. 'I didn't because my mother didn't. She kept telling me she knew he was innocent, and I believed only her.'

'And what about young Frejka?' I asked.

'Frejka too. He wrote that letter to the judge asking for his father's death sincerely. He did believe his father had done those terrible things, because his mother believed it. Mrs Frejkova couldn't imagine that the Party would accuse her husband without reason. . . . But my mother didn't believe, so I didn't either.'

Such power over the thinking of their children, especially in the more dangerous years, put heavy responsibilities on East European parents. If they themselves were true believers there was little problem, until the young should begin to doubt, and ask questions of their own. But those in any kind of disagreement with the Party had to think hard about what they told their children and when.

'My husband and I used to argue about this,' a fifty-seven-year-old mother of two sons, now both grown men, told me in Warsaw. 'I thought we shouldn't enlighten them too soon. They would only be confused and then begin to doubt everything they're told, even things like twice two being four. But my husband thought we had to tell them the truth, or they'd be turned against us by propaganda, even kill us one day. In the end we agreed that whatever else they overheard, we would tell them only when we thought they were old enough to understand. And we kept to that, even when one of them, he must have been eight at the time, came home and told me he wanted to be a Russian soldier to protect me against the Americans, who everybody at the time was praying would come.'

Of course, silence could be telling enough, as a twenty-nine-year-old teacher in Bulgaria remembered. 'My parents never actually said anything about what I was hearing at school, not while I was young. But I still knew that they didn't care for it. Just from the way they listened to the news and read the papers, from the look on their faces and the way my father would shake his head, I could tell things weren't right between us and "them".'

Most parents, however, behaved and talked quite naturally before their children, only warning the latter not to repeat elsewhere what they heard at home. The results varied: 'I must have been about twelve when there were elections, and my parents made fun of the thing over dinner,' a thirty one year old electronics engineer in Hungary said. 'So two days later I put my hand up during History and asked the teacher why we ever had elections, there was only one candidate, it was all nonsense. She wanted to know who had told me these things and took me down to the head. But he was all right, so as I stood there thinking of what to say, he said hadn't I better shut up and behave in class instead of making trouble, and that was that. But when I got home and told my father how very smart I had been, he went red and gave me one of those huge right-hand wallops I can still remember around my ears. After that, I kept quiet about politics in school.'

As de-Stalinization began in any country, the tensions decreased. But a sense of constant political opposition between 'us' and 'them' has survived as part of the basic experience of the majority of young East Europeans. And though they may grow up to differ with their parents on any number of points, including political points, these differences fall far short of the dialectical pattern the Party once thought inexorably ordained: 'As far as conflicts between parents and children are concerned,' one of a number of sociologists in charge of a major survey on youth being done by the Polish Academy of Sciences told me in May 1970, 'we're finding that these may develop over the use of money or free time, the choice of friends and partners and life-styles, but almost never over attitudes to religion or politics.'

In fact the most serious political conflict between parents and children that I myself came across proved to be that between Communist parents and their young. Of this conflict there seemed to be three main kinds. One, most common in Hungary and Poland, the two countries with the longest histories of pragmatism since 1956, was the conflict between now pragmatic Party men and their neo-idealistic leftist children, about whom I shall have more to say. The other, to be found in all countries, was the conflict between hard-liner parents, and their simply disillusioned young: 'I was a believer till sixteen,' the twenty-one-year-old son of a ranking Party man told me in Bulgaria. 'Then I began to realize things. I tried arguing with my parents, but it was impossible. Always the same argument: every time I almost proved something to them they'd start on what it was like before the war and did I want that back. Now I don't argue any more, we talk about things like football, or nothing.' The third kind of conflict had developed between parents who were still idealistic Communists, and children to whom ideology itself was now something of a joke. 'Every household needs a dear eccentric,' the eighteen-year-old daughter of a sobered, but still convinced Romanian Communist said when, having coffee with the whole family, I brought up the question of his surviving belief. 'Daddy is ours.' Then she poured him a second cup of coffee, and put in the sugar.

Unlike parents, friends are a matter of choice. In this choice political opinions may already play a part. But this part, especially in the formative years, will be small compared with that played by shared hobbies and sports and personal traits and social circumstances and sheer luck. And even when politics enter, they may form a subject of discussion rather than a source of serious conflict for a long time, if not for ever.

I myself remember walking with two friends, in the summer of 1954 when we were fifteen and the atmosphere still far from liberal, for whole afternoons in the streets of Budapest, talking about whatever came into our heads. I would then have counted as something of an adolescent Communist, which my friends were not, but this made only so much difference. Over politics I might argue with them fiercely, repeating and defending the slogans and ideas in which I then believed. But when one of them drew a detailed verbal picture of our whole education system as a giant steamroller, designed to flatten our brains into bricks, I never thought he was being politically subversive, only that he was attacking school. Nor had I any political objections when from the other of these two friends I heard, for the first time in my life, about Freud, denounced though he might be as a 'bourgeois filthmonger, etc.' in the textbooks. As a matter of fact, I ended up reading *Moses and Monotheism* straight after *The Communist Manifesto*, to find the two, together, quite an experience.

Beyond taking up with my own friends almost where we had left off, entering the close, friendly circles of others also proved to be the main revelation of my three return journeys to Eastern Europe, to collect material for the present book. Especially in the countries where fear of the police was strong, once people had accepted me as a sudden friend their behaviour changed in a way that was both exhilarating to me personally, and appalling as a measure of the distance between the politic façade and the private reality of their lives. From then on, whatever we spoke about had a different depth, and the official propaganda and politics receded into the background. It was then that I heard people really talk, about true politics as much as anything else, that I heard them argue and wonder and laugh and sadden and bitch among themselves and with me, too. It was then that I was taken to meet others and yet others, and to the theatre and for drinks that lasted half the night or a whole day, that I was invited on fishing trips and to come and see the books and collections of earthenware people had at home, and made to promise to come back. It was then that I saw and heard and I hope understood much of what I am relating here.

Of course, whatever is discussed within even the closest family circle and among friends will reflect a number of outside influences. Most powerful among these in the life of any young East European will have been education, which to begin with the Party thought omnipotent: 'The People's Democratic State has entrusted to teachers an exalted mission,' Gheorghiu Gheorghiu-Dej, head of the Romanian Party, told a conference of educationalists in 1952.

> They are to mould the new man of our country, the builder of socialism, shape the new cadres of socialist construction . . . fight for the annihilation of obscurantism, liquidate ignorance and lack of culture, carry the torch of knowledge and advanced science among the broad masses . . . make of our youth people devoted body and soul to the working classes of our country and to the cause of peace, people raised in the spirit of the fraternity of mankind, in a spirit of infinite love for our great friend and liberator, the Soviet Union, and for the teacher of the workers of the entire world, the leading light of all science and culture, Comrade Stalin.[4]

This was some mission. True it only invoked that warrior-priest tradition of Eastern Europe, out of which the idea of the Party as Hero and Teacher had itself grown, and of which schoolteachers proper had long since become the willing and most humbly useful representatives. But what the Party had made out of this tradition now forced on teachers a new set of choices as to the actual aim of their missionary work in each classroom, and the methods they should employ.

Sincere Communists, especially in the first fervent years, tried to impart sincere Communism, and Communists who have since had doubts have tried to pass on the beliefs these doubts still left them. Aided by outside propaganda, by the dialectical drift of the whole curriculum, and by an ideological apparatus at the very least interesting, and in full cry formidable, they have throughout the period achieved some significant successes. But most teachers, irrespective of their views on Communism as a system of beliefs, have had no more sympathy with the actual propaganda it has hallmarked than parents have. And this has put them in the parents' own dilemma. Worse still, whereas parents have had to talk only to their own children, and could hardly be sacked by the Party, teachers have been having to face whole classfuls, and have seen waves of purges sweeping the school system in each period of repression.

Their ways of coping have varied. Large numbers have stuck to 'dutiful neutrality', repeating what had to be repeated, but no more. This, though close enough to the Party line, usually had a quite different effect from that achieved by convinced and often ideologically prepared Communists: 'A young teacher was telling the pupils how glass was made,' an article in the main Warsaw cultural weekly related in 1960. 'She began by saying glass was made from sand. There was an outburst of laughter in the classroom. . . . Finally, she asked one of the brighter boys why the children were laughing. He replied, "Because everybody knows that you have to say these things. . . . ".'[6]

Other teachers, especially in the sciences, have managed to preserve political neutrality altogether. They have taught their subjects as factually as possible, and simply communicated whatever moral attitudes they themselves possessed. A good many others, however, have tried 'positive' neutrality: exploiting the possibilities of the curriculum for putting over views of their own, even in the most difficult years: 'I remember my history teacher explaining about Fascism, must have been about 1952,' a twenty-nine-year-old poet in Hungary told me. 'He described to us what it had been like to stand on a street corner and watch the Fascists march by, shouting slogans and holding their hands high. It was a long and very vivid description, as if he were talking about things that had happened not years ago but only the previous week, and slowly we began to realize that he was talking about not just Fascism, but our own marches too. He spoke very quietly, but he was almost spitting the words when he said, "I'll have you know, boys, I'm an individual. I hate crowds marching and shouting in unison. And you, too, every one of you, are individuals. Not a mob." I can still see him, in front of a hushed class, saying those words. . . . '

A more open and sustained version of the same ruse has been the practice of either wholly ignoring official textbooks, or even using classtime for purposes different from those stated. In Czechoslovakia, from 1962–3 onwards students in some universities began gaining most of their detailed information on the sad state of the economy from their compulsory Political Economy lectures. Meanwhile, during not a few seminars supposedly engrossed in Marxism–Leninism, the works of Sartre, Karl Jaspers and whole schools of contemporary western philosophy were being studied and discussed at length. In Bulgaria in 1969, lecturers at Sofia University received a dressing-down from no less a person than the Chairman of the Writers' Association for directing students towards 'alien ideological meridians', such as the 'fashion of structuralism'. In Romania, where I found structuralism already as good as a pop fashion among students of literature in 1968, I was told by other students about ideology course for young priests turning quietly into parts of the theology course proper.

And quite a number of teachers have resisted in quite open ways, as complaints by Party spokesmen, and noisy dismissals for political insubordination have borne witness. Gheorghiu Dej himself spent a major part of the speech I have just quoted in denouncing 'certain elements in our teaching body who cling to retrograde bourgeois ideologies, and are entangled in the web of obscurantism and mysticism, of nationalism and cosmopolitanism etc.'.[6] Indeed, just as in new 'war situations' the Party has reverted to warlike behaviour, so the same situations have witnessed a stiffening of resistance among teachers. After the ultras had got into power in Czechoslovakia in 1969, for instance, while they proceeded to purge education and denounce in the shrillest tones 'sedition' in classrooms, teachers for their part joined the other side. 'We used to ask our teachers questions, just to see what they would say,' a twenty-six-year-old woman, now teaching in a Prague school, said in 1970. 'You know, questions about Masaryk, and why the Russians never announced failures with their moon rockets, and so on. There's nothing like that now. They know very well what we think, most of us make little secret of it. It's the same as what they think.'

The Church previously the State's most important ally in educating the young under God's blessing, became after 1948 the Party's staunchest enemy. As such it also became an important focus of resistance, especially in the Catholic countries. During the fifties large numbers of agnostics took up church-going as a form of protest, while for children the sense of defiance and danger involved meant an experience akin to shared martyrdom: 'We knew we were being watched every Sunday, and if we weren't, we imagined it,' a twenty-one-year-old girl, who must have been a very small child in the really dark days, told me in Poland. 'That was part of it. A feeling that you were doing something brave for God.'

Though priests could not openly denounce the godless State from the pulpit, their references to the 'forces of evil' and suchlike were meaningful enough. Combined with what they could say in private, over tea, and drinks at christenings and harvest times and pig-killing feasts, their words had an effect. When, for example, in 1956–7 in both Poland and Hungary religious instruction was once again allowed in schools, children not attending found themselves ostracized, beaten up and in some cases (carefully reported in the Party press), threatened with hanging by the rest.

With relatively more peaceful relations developing between the Party and the churches, the latter have lost much of their aura of resistance. But if at all times of both auspicious and threatening developments the Party has tried to keep well in with the churches, this is because at all such times religion has tended to become a rallying issue. During the 1968 liberalization process in Czechoslovakia, for instance, young people showed an interest in religion which even the clergy found amazing: 'We knew some of them believed,' a Catholic seminarist about to graduate told me in Bratislava in June 1968, 'but their campaigning for the freedom of worship, the numbers that come to mass, the letters of support they write to the Catholic paper, have all been surprises to us.'*

* Even much smaller events than country-wide repression or liberalization seem to have an appreciable effect on church attendance, as someone charged with cultural affairs in one of the working-class districts of Budapest explained.

Apart from religiosity proper, which I shall try to discuss later, the observance of religious rituals at all times has survived on an even more surprising scale. Churches have a good number of young people in them on Sundays, and are packed on such main holidays as Easter, as I myself observed in Bulgaria, Hungary and Poland, where of the crowds I saw at least two-fifths were under thirty. Marriages, and baptisms and funerals even more, remain overwhelmingly religious occasions. To replace them, 'socialist ceremonies' have been promoted for years, with richer town councils hiring unemployed actors to make splendid speeches, but so far without any great success. Even Party members tend to have their children baptized, if necessary in some other locality or in the arms of some obliging aunt, and themselves buried by priests, 'just to make doubly sure'. And it is common enough in early summer for children to be attending, the little boys in their best suits and white shirts and ties and the little girls in frilly dresses, their First Communion one Sunday and, in basic uniforms, their Pioneer initiation the next.

The two ceremonies may have an equal meaning for them at the time: indeed for a number of non-religious pioneers their initiation into the movement has the value of a First Communion. But then, while religiosity remains alive in many young people and may even intensify at university, whatever enthusiasm they once had for the youth organizations withers away. The Pioneers are now regarded, in most countries, as fun enough. But the Youth League, catering for the over-fourteens and much more of a 'transmission system' of Party propaganda, generates little loyalty: 'Ours is not a youth organization,' a boy in a class of sixteen-year-olds I was interviewing in a Prague school said in June 1968. 'It's an organization trying to force ideas on youth. I hope it'll die.' Which it soon did, to be artificially revived in 1970.

Towards the much larger machinery of general propaganda, the young's attitudes are, if more complex, basically the same.

'We make out reports about numbers attending church in the area, and every time there's any trouble, attendance rises. It rose after the bus and tram fares went up, then it evened out again, then it rose a lot after the invasion of Czechoslovakia. Now we're waiting for the effect of the increase in the price of shoes and clothing.'

Anything of genuine interest or entertainment that it offers is accepted, but what it tries to force on people provokes resistance, if not revolt. Almost every time I asked Polish students what they had wanted at the time of the March 1968 riots, their reply began with, 'Information. We want to be told the truth about what's going on in this country, and we're fed up with being treated as babies and idiots.' Whether or not such demands can be fulfilled has in fact become for many young East Europeans nothing less than a measure of dignified existence: 'I've met lots of Russians,' a twenty-four-year-old student of the language said in Prague in 1970. 'Mostly they've been intelligent people, generous, serious people. But I couldn't help feeling very sorry for them. They lacked information. And many of them didn't even know that.'

The boredom which the duty of Party-minded education forces on the media simply puts people off. In such periods of excitement as 1956 in Poland and Hungary and 1968 in Czechoslovakia newspapers have often sold out, but in the periods of repression that followed circulation figures fell, for some papers by as much as 45 per cent. And where Stalinism and its boredom have barely let up, young people's judgement on the media can be truly humiliating: 'Newspapers?' a lawyer of twenty-eight said to me in Romania. 'My friends and I look at them sometimes, mostly at the sports pages. But we only buy them regularly when there's a toilet paper crisis.'

On the whole, however, as all Parties of Eastern Europe are now more pragmatic than they used to be, at non-critical times the media everywhere also cater more for spontaneity, and concede more of the truth. They also enjoy correspondingly greater popularity. This is especially true of the press and the radio and TV programmes produced for the young. A good proportion of documentary material is now accepted as simply informative, while pop culture of one sort or another is staple, and in the more liberal countries debates on quite basic issues, from youth unemployment to the politics of university entry and the freedom of information itself, have taken place. It may in fact be said that, mixed with slanted news and direct propaganda, pure information and entertainment now try to do in the

East European media the kind of selling job for the Party line which in the Western commercial media they do for soap.

About the Party's measure of success with ideological propaganda in the wider sense I shall talk elsewhere. As regards daily coping, however, it has often proved much cleverer than its opponents in Eastern Europe or abroad would care to believe. It has not only replaced crude blatancy with the more subtly dialectical methods of western soap manufacturers, but on occasions it has also shown far fewer scruples about exploiting what it knew about the fears and hatreds harboured by its target audience, and with great success. Indeed, considering the very low esteem in which at times of crisis the Party's target public holds its media, its successes at just such times have been truly awesome.

In Poland in 1968, for instance, a twenty-two-year-old student of philology at the University of Wroclaw first described to me the local media's treatment of the March student riots in these terms: 'There we were, several hundreds of us, in the university on the second day of our sit-in strike, reading the Wroclaw paper which said that we had all rejected the enemy provocateurs and gone quietly home. We knew it wasn't true, they knew it wasn't true, the whole of Wroclaw knew it wasn't true. So who did they think they were kidding?' He could not have been more derisive. But within less than half an hour, as we got to the Street of the Heroes of the Warsaw Ghetto, to be found in many large Polish towns, I brought up the subject of the anti-Semitic campaign then raging in the same media. His reaction was wholly different (echoing, I must add, a good many other intelligent Poles I interviewed that year). 'The truth is,' he said, 'there are too many Jews in high places. At the university, I have good friends who are Jewish, but there really are very many of them. And our parents say it's because of the Jews that this country is where it is now.' I objected that this was not what the press was saying. It was saying Zionists were to blame for the March student riots. 'Of course it's saying that,' he laughed. 'But we know how to read between the lines. And they know that we know, they're Poles like us.'

In Hungary, in the spring of 1969, I met the mirror image of his reaction. I had a long talk with a twenty-three-year-old instruments technician, Jewish by birth though no longer practising. He was a very well-informed and profoundly thinking person who, among other things, explained to me in great detail why he thought that the invasion of Czechoslovakia had been a tragedy not just for a single country but for the whole of Eastern Europe, and for socialism itself. 'But you know,' he added finally, 'there were also some real fascists at work in Czechoslovakia. I myself have seen pictures of swastikas painted and chalked all over the place. And I must say, if there was a chance of these elements gaining the upper hand. . . . ' I then explained to him that the swastikas had been chalked, not in triumph but in anger, on Russian tanks, and that on the walls the painted signs had read 'SSSR = ⌗'. He was struck speechless, growing white with anger, then just swore terribly. There was nothing either of us could do about what he had believed some nine months earlier.

The propaganda machine has also achieved successes through inducing apathy and creating confusion. For instance, the basic cause of the lack of interest with which so many even of young East Europeans greeted liberalization in Czechoslovakia in 1968, and then the August invasion and what followed, was sheer ignorance of the issues and of the relevance of these to their own lives. Also, while the grapevine in each East European country has developed into a quite fantastically efficient means, for interested people, of getting past any degree of censorship, its sheer efficiency can also serve the Party's purposes. It was, for example, only through the grapevine that the Romanian regime ever whispered to its people, first the argument that too hasty liberalization would prejudice the country's independence, and after the invasion of Czechoslovakia in August 1968, that the reimposition of hard-line policies was due to Russian pressure. Yet on both occasions the argument got through. I myself heard the first version of it from countless young people during my stay in the country in May 1968, and the second version from almost as many a year later. In between, during Christmas, 1968, when a carol-singing procession of students in Bucharest developed into a sizeable march and political slogans began to be shouted, nobody could tell whether the citizens who were trying to persuade the crowd to dissolve, lest the Russians use the march to strengthen their case for bringing troops into the country, were plain-clothes police or just plain patriots.

It is thus not surprising if large numbers of East Europeans, especially at critical times, turn for information to the outside world. Indeed it was during the most critical period, at the beginning of the Stalinist years, that western radio stations intensified their broadcasts to the area and that the station now putting out daylong programmes in each of the area's five languages, Radio Free Europe (RFE), was set up. The task of western broadcasts, and particularly of those by RFE, was to counter the barrage of war propaganda then bombarding the peoples of Eastern Europe, and at the same time to keep alive in them the hope, traditional in the area since the nineteenth century, that the West would come to their aid.

This romantic idea was inherent in the then proclaimed American intention to 'roll the Soviets back'. But as nothing happened, the idea of the West as Saviour, and the lies and invective employed, especially by RFE, to maintain it, began to wear thin: 'When there was only one year left [to promised liberation] one ceased to touch on that subject. Faith changed into bitterness and suspicious vitality into apathy,' a Polish writer born in 1945 recalled in an autobiographical extract in a Warsaw daily in 1967.[7] 'One used to turn the knob in helpless impotence. Not believing in one side, one ceased to believe in the other. That was their [his parents'] school of bitterness, and my school of scepticism.' After the Hungarian and Polish events of 1956 talk about rolling the Soviets back never reappeared: by the time things began to move in Czechoslovakia in the spring of 1968 the unlikelihood of western participation was made amply clear in all broadcasts.

Meanwhile, as the war situation has relaxed in Eastern Europe, so the tone of western broadcasts has changed, on each station to the extent that this was felt necessary. The most radical change overtook RFE, whose rules now forbid putting out any news item concerned with Eastern Europe before it has been confirmed by at least two major western agencies, or one Communist source. And though listening to western broadcasts at normal times is now less intense, at critical times East Europeans tune from one foreign station to the next to catch as much news as possible. As RFE has hourly bulletins, people often keep their sets fixed on it and blaring away not only at home, but also in offices and hospitals and, in the more liberal countries, even on the beach.

Among the feature programmes broadcast by western stations, perhaps the most important have been those for the young. These were pioneered by RFE in the fifties, with hour-long afternoon music programmes which were an immediate success. As I myself remember, even in the darkest Stalinist times one could hear school bands at Youth League dances playing some recent RFE Tune of the Week. Rarely was there a political intention behind this on the part of the musicians. But it certainly made one aware that they too must have listened, as indeed any number of young Communists, including some of my own friends and myself, did at the time, also without any conscious political intentions.

This appears to have remained the usual practice since. The pop programmes of western stations have built up a huge following throughout Eastern Europe. While driving in Bulgaria in 1968 I was given the latest news concerning the BBC charts by local hitch-hikers; and all kinds of young people, from students of catering on the Romanian sea coast to seminarists in Slovakia, professed to be fans of RFE disc jockeys. The mail arriving in London and Munich has been equally huge, with its contents ranging from simple requests for records to love poems and even musings about escape. When the RFE Hungarian pop programme wondered aloud in a rare political feature about the phenomenon of children of Party high-ups rebelling against the Party in Hungary and Poland, it received some fifty letters in reply, not a few from children of Party cadres themselves. They not only put their views but also described the kinds of discussion which the programmes had occasioned in their circle of friends.

As regards physical access to the West, in the three countries where this has been allowed since 1956 the total of exit visas granted equals one-sixth to one-quarter of the population. Of course, a number of people will have travelled more than once, but then the impressions they brought back from the West would also have spread through their circles of friends as many times. I have been unable to find figures on the ages of travellers. But I can say that of the four young workers I quoted at the beginning of this chapter, one had spent a summer in Wales and another had been to West Germany. I have also seen busloads of Hungarian schoolchildren on day trips to Vienna, and among my Polish interviewees between twenty-three and thirty, those who had been to the West almost outnumbered those who had not.

In the two southern countries, whence travel to the West has remained virtually impossible, access to hundreds of thousands of westerners, also unknown under Stalin, opens each tourist season. Large numbers of young people actually migrate to resorts in the summer just to meet foreigners. The effect of the colourful holiday slice of life the latter bring with them is in fact proving more of a headache for the Party than if young people could see daily existence in the West for themselves. At the start of every tourist season Bulgaria mounts whole propaganda campaigns to warn the young about too much mixing with westerners, and 'unprincipled admiration' for their wares and ways. And though actual contact between locals and foreigners tends to be limited to the exchange of goods, kisses and easily understood ideas, for those who are able to overcome the language barrier it can also mean more.

'Last year I met a French family,' a twenty-one-year-old student of chemistry told me in Bucharest in 1969. 'The father was a mechanic, a Communist from Lille. We had big arguments. He wouldn't stop telling me how we owned the country here, and how free we were and happy, and so on. When I said to him, "Look, you're here in a car, from France, telling me these things, and I not only haven't a car, but even if I wanted to go on foot to visit you in Lille, I still couldn't get a passport," he said I was a reactionary. In the end he started shouting. I was afraid he'd go and report me to the police. I'd never have believed that people out there, where they can read all they want, could be so stupid.'

As regards 'reading all you want', and seeing and enjoying all you want, in literature and the arts, the Party's policies have never achieved more than partial successes. True, plays and films could be banned, and the publishing of new books could be wholly censored and vast indexes could be drawn up for libraries. But it was almost as impossible to force people actually to read what the State published in vast numbers as it was to stop them lending their own books, from thrillers to works on art and philosophy, and old magazines of all kinds, to each other. And to stop them thinking about what they found, in whatever way, was not possible at all:

'I was a sincere Communist and a believer in Stalin when I was about sixteen,' a Czech poet, twenty-seven at the time of speaking, remembered. 'Then I became interested in the *avant-garde* people of the thirties. Their work was not being published, but you could find it in magazines on people's shelves and even in some libraries. And in these magazines, next to the Surrealist poems and the *ars poetica*, I found long articles on Stalin's Great Trials, and arguments on whether these had represented the people's justice or sheer murder. I was very disturbed. Then I fell in love with a girl one of whose relatives had suffered during our own great trials, and I asked her about these things, and learnt a lot more. . . .'

Even in such public and therefore most strictly controlled arts as the theatre and the cinema, the Party has often found itself unable to control the actual experience of the public. It might, for example, licence the staunchest classics only to find that the performers played and the audience viewed every situation, from murderous intrigue to impossible farce, as mirroring its own. This has been especially the case at critical times. In Bucharest in May 1968 I myself saw a performance of *Macbeth*, played among sets and in costumes designed to look timeless, but in hushed whispers and with courtiers eavesdropping in a manner that the audience could not fail to recognize. The person with whom I was winked at me several times while the play went on, and in the interval we agreed that, with rehabilitations of major Party figures purged in Stalin's time having just begun, no performance could be more opportune.

Many such interpretations, whether of classics or of contemporary works, deserve of course to be called extraneous. In fact they only reverse the Party's own socialist realist approach from the fifties, seeing all art in terms of its immediate relevance. The resulting tensions, however, usually enhance rather than spoil the experience of those present by connecting that experience with the real tensions in each respective society. The same enhancement also very often turns courageous but otherwise not very good new plays and films into major successes in Eastern Europe, only to desert them when these works are exported to the West. In fact when these tensions relax in any East European country, often even locals cannot appreciate the same works in the same way: 'I had a funny experience with K's novel,' a thirty-year-old Czech photographer told me in Prague in 1969. 'When it first came out in 1967 and I read it, I thought it was great. Then in 1968, when the same kind of things could be talked about everywhere, I thought, well, really, this book was just compressed journalism. But now that censorship is being brought back again, I realize it is a very good book. I'm sorry to say, it's getting better and better all the time.'

It may be said that pop music has also seen a de-politicizing reappraisal of this kind since it became freely available in Eastern Europe. In the fifties, when the Party denounced it as a hostile phenomenon, thereby presenting the Devil with all the best tunes, there used to be an oppositional frisson just to hearing it played. This, and the fact that when it first began to be tolerated it was sung almost entirely in western languages (mainly English) remained for quite some time part of its thrill, replacing true quality. But then as the Party sanctioned attempts by the Youth Leagues and the media to popularize themselves with the aid of whatever music from East or West the young wanted to hear, audiences became much more discriminating, and groups and the songs they began to write for themselves in their own language became much better. By now only their generally poorer equipment and some unmistakably national strains in their music distinguish a good many of them from their western brothers and sisters.

Meanwhile, it is not only that pragmatists in each Party have realized the political harmlessness of pop music. Developments have actually reached the point where new leftists in such pragmatic countries as Hungary and Poland are accusing the Party of promoting pop so as to de-politicize the young altogether. In the most liberal country, Hungary, leftist protest-singing has in fact dissociated itself from ordinary pop, to some extent in spite: 'Why do you think it took them so long to let us enter the scene?' the song-writer of the best-known group, named the Guerrillas, said to me in Budapest. 'They'd been having pop music on TV and pop festivals for years, while we could only sing in cellars, and the record company thought we were too much of a risk. You can imagine what kind of a risk.' In other countries, such as Poland and to a much lesser extent Romania, oppositional protest-singing (as distinct from safe songs about American imperialism) works mostly through allusions but as part of the pop scene. In Czechoslovakia, where the shrill and brilliant protest-singers of the post-invasion period were all banned from appearing in public by the ultras after April 1969, it now exists only underground.

Realization of its political harmlessness has saved pop music proper from having to go back underground even at critical times. If the Party still rails against it on occasions, the reason is that pop music and pop sub-culture altogether are genuinely alien to the age-groups which both within and outside the Party now run and own the countries of Eastern Europe. It is on their behalf that every so often Party spokesmen denounce, with most conviction in the more conservative countries, pop music and fashion, along with loose morals and social selfishness, as foreign propagations to corrupt the collective's young guard. In other words, though it may still be presented politically, pop is now mostly a generational issue in Eastern Europe too. One of a number of the generational issues which I should like to discuss next.

2 Generations

'Leave us alone' is the title of the following poem by Tadeusz Rozewicz, the Polish poet born in 1921:

> Forget about us
> about our generation
> live like human beings
> forget about us
>
> we envied
> plants and stones
> we envied dogs
>
> I would like to be a rat
> I used to say to her
>
> I would like not to be
> I would like to fall asleep
> and wake up after the war
> she would say with her eyes shut
>
> forget about us
> don't ask about our youth
> leave us alone[1]

In any articulate society there are, I think, four active generations: the senior, the central, the recognized and the new. It takes about thirty years for the two older ones to be replaced by the younger set, itself being meanwhile replaced by the generations freshly born. In Eastern Europe, the thirty years in question have been momentous.

Those now senior were already adults when the war started. In the war they fought, lost relatives and friends, suffered and starved, some barely escaping with their lives. They saw the destruction of their countries and the death of altogether seven and a quarter million human beings. After the war they became witnesses, and some active participants, of the destruction of the world in which they had grown to adulthood.

Then central in the working force, this generation was the one most directly affected by the Party's policies of economic and social transformation. Working-class people brought into managerial positions could see themselves with proud pleasure as the proletariat rising into leadership in society. The same process, however, combined for members of the former middle classes political resistance with a struggle to save their own positions and often their sheer livelihoods. Of the working classes that remained, the industrial proletariat became ever more antagonized by the contrast between the Party's millennial propaganda and its own actual situation, socially improved, but economically much the same as before and politically worse off. The peasantry, which was made to pay the cost of each country's industrialization and was meanwhile being herded into collectives by an élite contemptuous of the peasant's mind and way of life, had no reason to see the regime as anything but a form of war on itself.

It was hardly surprising that the majority of this generation appeared all too ready to trust western rhetoric about 'rolling the Soviets back'. And even when no action had followed the rhetoric, though many such believers were disillusioned, not a few of the older ones retained their prime image of the West as Saviour: 'When my grandfather was dying,' a twenty-seven-year-old artist told me in Bulgaria, 'the priest was called. After the old man had confessed and it was all over, the priest asked him if he had anything more to say or ask. "Tell me, father," the old man said, "when do you think the Americans might be coming?"'

With Stalin's demise, and the effect of political as well as economic and social developments since, the generation growing senior achieved a degree of consolidation. Attitudes have remained largely what they were, and many basic hatreds unforgotten. Most non-Communists have continued to see the regime as essentially a Russian imposition, while many Communists have remained at heart the men they became under Stalin. But the sheer necessity of coping, which problems have forced on each East European country, often with a vengeance, has combined with nationalism, and with the authoritarian tradition and political system, leaving all essential responsibilities in the hands of the senior age-group, to reunite its opposed segments into a recognizable generation.

Where non-Party experts are acceptable, as in Hungary, those of senior age now hold about as many posts of importance from village headships to export management as their Party colleagues. Where they remain unacceptable many of them have entered the Party to gain good jobs, and frankly advise their children to do likewise. And in all East European countries their power remains far greater than in the pluralistic and more affluent societies of the West, because while the centralism of the economic and State machinery leaves the young little hope of promotion over the heads of their elders, children also become financially independent much later.

The next, now central, generation was still at school or just out of it when the war began. A part of it saw active service, making up each year more and more of the soldiery both on the open fronts and in the underground. The Polish resistance had whole Scout regiments, the seniors fighting, the juniors engaging in sabotage, reconnaissance and other auxiliary activities, while the youngest children joined the underground simply by going to school: 'I was nine then,' a thirty-eight-year-old doctor in Warsaw remembered, 'and we used to meet in small groups at a different person's house each day for our lessons. We knew we mustn't talk about what we did, because the whole school network had been organized by the resistance, and if the Germans found out they'd take away our teachers and perhaps us too.'

The war over, the generation then in its mid-teens to mid-twenties found itself facing not just the task of physically reconstructing each country, but the chance of effecting enormous changes throughout the region. Unlike its immediate elders, conditioned by a world the war had swept away, it had truly historic choices in politics. Almost inevitably it shifted towards the Left, its conservatives becoming centrists (often even in their directly religious organizations) and its Left reformers turning into revolutionaries.

Once the Party had acquired full power in each country, however, the generation went through a 'younger' version of the same Stalinist experience as was overtaking its parents. It profited, or suffered, from discrimination at universities, had its norms raised in factories and went on free holidays to workers' rest homes, saw its peasant elders being whipped into collectives or persecuted, and learnt from its own experience to dread and hate the police. Non-Communists saw in all this the confirmation of their worst fears, and more often than not turned back towards the Right. But many of the Communists of the same generation, even if they recognized terror as terror, remained faithful to their leftist visions for quite some time: 'Yes, I very much believed that here at last something good was happening,' a forty-two-year-old construction engineer told me in 1969 in Romania. 'In '47 I was at university, and we went in voluntary brigades to build a railway, and we were real volunteers, not like the students today who go because they have to. It was a joint project with the Yugoslavs, and even when at the time of the quarrel with Tito it was denounced and I think some of its organizers disappeared, I went on believing. . . . Perhaps it was that I very much wanted to believe, because I thought this country needed a revolution, and this seemed to be it.'

Once de-Stalinization set in, however, while it gave new strength to the non-Communists, it shook many of the true believers in terrible and often fruitful ways.

Meanwhile, the need for modernization in each East European country has created both the possibility of new alignments within this now central generation and the virtual certainty of a conflict developing between it as a whole and most seniors. This has been especially the case in the managerial strata, where many of the seniors are political appointees from earlier times, while most of their juniors have come up since, through education. Thus while the central generation may itself be divided into factions favouring different approaches to current problems, it is increasingly united in a vision of most seniors as sclerotic, fit only to be pensioned off at the first opportunity.

This is why the Partisan faction in Poland, for example, tried almost from its formation in the early sixties to present itself as the champion of, among others, the technically trained intelligentsia against the political fuddy-duddies – only to be outflanked when after the events of March 1968 and the Partisan bid for power, younger men began to be promoted in the Party and the managerial strata. 'Look at me, I'm thirty-eight and the man I replaced was sixty and the one billed to succeed him actually sixty-five,' the new editor of a Warsaw weekly, a none too likeable but basically realistic man, said to me in June 1970. 'What have I and people of my age to do with the Partisans? We can thank them for having stirred things up, and created a chance for us to come in. But as regards any ideas of what to do about Poland, they're still in the woods where they were in the days of the resistance, and on the platforms of 1945–8, demolishing the prewar regime. . . . That too was important, I myself fought and then made propaganda, but now we have quite different things to do.'

The main generation gap is usually considered to lie between the two older and the two younger active age groups. In Eastern Europe this gap is in some respects narrower and in many other respects much wider than in the West.

It is narrower, first of all, due to a sense of shared vicissitudes. 'We've had a terrible life,' a sixty-three-year-old stonemason whom I was interviewing with his grown-up son told me in Transylvania. 'But sometimes when I think about it, I think I'd like it even less if I were your age. Our life has been your childhood. And God knows what you may be seeing yet.' In debates about youth in the media, while nationalists of all shades may call for more vigour in socialist-patriotic education, members of the central generation of the Left tend rather to talk of their own duped heroism as a likely reason for present sobriety.

The young themselves have often been more aggressive, partly in self-defence. 'It may be true that there didn't use to be such dancing crowds as ours,' a student fan on a Hungarian TV programme about the pop craze said in 1968.[2] 'But it has happened that a pop singer named Adolf Hitler did his thing, nor even so long ago, and the people who are now adults went even crazier about him than we go about pop, and with much uglier results.'

They have also at times gone on the attack, more especially

at the start of major de-Stalinization in any country, when the lies and horrors of a whole period began suddenly to be revealed. In Czechoslovakia, for instance, a poet aged twenty-four in 1962 published a virtual manifesto entitled 'Poems for the Cat' (No-good Poems) in which he denounced all those who had subscribed to the cult of Stalin as undeserving of the trust of anyone, but especially of his own generation. Some young people demurred from his wholesale attack, but clearly he had expressed the thoughts of many others, as one of those attacked recounted in his long and earnest 'Attempt at a Reply' (published in the writers' weekly in 1964):[3]

> Once, late at night, two or three years ago, you asked me, with all the lack of consideration of your less than twenty years, 'What did you do at that time, what were you like; after all you were no longer children but adult people, you had your own responsibility, you were bound to know what was going on, and why and how?' . . . For a long time I have owed you a reply. Yes, everything was, and still is, in conflict with common sense, but the question we had to ask ourselves was whether our own sense, our healthy sense, could be a criterion, whether it could be placed above the sense of the movement, of the class, that sense which was interpreted so clearly through Stalin's mouth. From here it was only a short step to a blind, mystical faith in Stalin's infallibility and indispensability. When we arrived at this faith . . . it appeared to us as a liberation, for finally there was no difference between us and the masses.

The young have never quite understood the blind enthusiasm of their elders, but they have become much less aggressive. The shock of revelation has worn off. Just as important, the Party has since done further things to young and old, enthusiasts and sceptics alike. In fact the main reason why politics are unlikely to become the kind of generational issue they have at times been in the West is that no East European Party has a firmer mandate from one age-group than from any other.

The gap is also narrow enough as regards general standards of behaviour. I shall discuss these in detail elsewhere, but on the whole any western visitor would find the majority of young East Europeans, both in their looks and in many of their ideas, almost as conservative as their parents.

Where the gap between the generations is considerably wider than in the West, the difference has to do mostly with a concentration of effects. Many of the cultural and sub-cultural influences which have widened the traditional gap in the developed West have been spreading to Eastern Europe at the same time as rapid development has been changing life there. And this has coincided with a propaganda barrage aimed primarily at the young, and dialectically dismissing the old as doomed even while still alive.

The resulting cleavage has been deepest between peasant parents and their newly educated and now town-dwelling children. Bad enough if the young have become workers in distant factories whence they return only once in a while, it is even worse if they have risen further on the social scale and feel they have to reject their origins. This has been most common in Poland, where distances are among the largest in Eastern Europe, movement to the towns has been the most voluminous, and respect for social status always was and has remained the strongest. 'Peasant parents with children away at secondary schools and universities will quite literally kill themselves working so the young can have a carefree time to study and get ahead', a sociologist in Warsaw working on the problems of youth explained in 1970. 'When the children come back in the summer, if they just want to rest often even parents who badly need help in the fields won't dare to ask for it.' And the parents who do ask for help may get dirty looks from their town-educated children instead of help.

Though the separation is less formal, the conflict is only more continuous and often sadly more vicious in peasant families where parents and children have stayed together. This is true even if they have done so in the village environment, where the mass media and the spread of new occupations and of urban ways of living and behaviour have naturally affected the young much more than the old. But the conflict is graver still where the families have moved to the city, as very large numbers of them have. In the new environment, while parents are put on the defensive about their village and small-town ways often to the point of absurdity, the children are not only surrounded by many more urban influences, but find support in their city-bred friends, whom they may also try to 'out-urban' in behaviour and in arguments with parents. And even though the arguments usually effect a transference of patterns, making children of newcomers to town almost as different from their new friends as their parents are from theirs, inside the families tension remains high.

In all families, however, including those resident in cities for generations, the gap between parents and children has been widened by the fact that rapid development has combined in Eastern Europe with the still more rapid spread of education. In the majority of East European families today the grown-up children are likely to have had a minimum of four, but often eight or even twelve years' more schooling than their parents. Thus whatever the age has done to 'smarten' the young against the old the world over has been amplified in Eastern Europe by the effects of suddenly expanded education.

A similar concentration of effects has taken place to make the life-styles and general outlook of the young different from those of their parents. Largely rural societies have suddenly become at the very least half-urban, while starvation and poverty have given way to decent living and in some cases at least semi-affluence. This has affected people's existence as much as their attitudes, creating strong contrasts between those whom development overtook in an often traumatic way, and those who have grown up seeing it as simply the motion of surrounding reality. It is not only that many of the new trades and professions, from car-polishing to computer-science, belong by their 'feel' to the young, together with the new machines, furniture and gadgetry surrounding them at work, and increasingly at home too. Attitudes to money, to work, to free time, to household chores even, are sharply different: the woman who even a few years ago counted as a proper housewife now counts as an old-fashioned mother-in-law, grousing about the easy-lazy ways of her son's young wife a good deal more than her opposite number in the West does.

In addition, sudden development in the last twenty-five years has been seen by substantial parts of the peasantry and of the still semi-rural age groups in Eastern Europe as altogether an alien menace. In the early days, the memory of which is still unforgotten, this generated nationalist resistance to the Party as the agent of two very different phenomena: western industrialization and Soviet Communism. Now the same generation that in the 1950s hated Russian folk-songs on the radio hates pop music as equally foreign, and would often have it banned in favour of the national folk-songs it still knows.

It is in this general context that the Party's dialectical-futurist propaganda has helped to arm the young against their parents. Combined with the effects of rapid development, it has given the word 'old' not just a derogatory, but an almost denunciatory meaning. As a complement, it has given the word 'modern' the sense of 'unquestionably best', whether it is applied to electronic equipment, outdoor lavatories, hair-styles or human emotions. In arguments between young and old the terms are, of course, applied with a special force, and if the argument involves politics, then the dialectical rationale may come to be employed in the original sense, separating the young as the vanguard of the future from the old.

This, however, can be of little comfort to the Party. It too is often faced in arguments with the young with the rationale it has so often emphasized: 'We, the young people, are the owners of the present,' wrote an eighteen-year-old schoolboy in the Bulgarian Youth League paper in 1967.[4] 'The old times are passing into history, and you'll do us a favour by not reminding us of them over and over again. You do nothing but lose our confidence.'

In fact its membership statistics show a clear generational drift against the Party. In Hungary, for example, in 1968 only 1·1 per cent of the students of Budapest (two-fifths of the 1963 percentage) were Party members, while in Czechoslovakia in 1971, over two-fifths of the Party's working-class members were pensioners.[5] Were Lenin writing today, in all honesty he would have to begin with, 'We are the Party of the future which, however, seems to belong to the old.'

Of course, apart from boredom with its rhetoric, the main reason for the Party's ageing is that it is at the heart of a centralist system which, as I have already hinted, is hostile to the young: 'We hear it all the time,' a thirty-seven-year-old electrical engineer told me in Prague. 'From the twenty-eight-year-olds, but even more from the boys just out of university. "There you sit," they say, "in the jobs you got ten to fifteen years ago, with your arses getting bigger and bigger and blocking the way." And they're quite right, from their point of view. But there are even bigger arses blocking ours.'

The two younger generations I have called the 'recognized' and the 'new'. The first consists of people already involved in the business of their own lives, and recognized by themselves and the rest of society as the young adults of their time. The second is only emerging to independence, and to a sense of its own identity.

In Eastern Europe I found the pattern of contrasts between these two age groups much the most intriguing. It reflects the contrasting histories amidst which they have grown to consciousness.

Though this is fairly clear to me now, it was nothing like as clear when I set out on my initial journey to collect material for the present book, in 1968. In fact, finding the pattern and then the causes behind it formed one of my major discoveries during that first trip.

The pattern began to occur to me during the fourth week of my trip, in Romania. On my first Sunday in Bucharest I went to the University Club, and there I wandered into a circle of young people discussing literature. There were some twenty of them, sitting in a large room shaded from the May morning sun, reading out their own stories and poems and arguing about them fiercely.* I sat down and in whispers explained who I was to a gypsy-faced boy of about twenty-two. He turned out to be the chief critic of the circle, and he translated the goings on for me.

One of the stories read was called *Hegel in the Bar*. It seemed to have everything, an absurd situation, neo-Surrealist style, disillusionment, self-pity, digs at official parlance and philosophy, in short everything that could seem rebellious in Eastern Europe.

* As I later discovered, there are many such circles, formed of people of all ages and professions, meeting throughout Romania, true to long-established traditions. The next one I saw had some seventy members, mainly office workers, with some divinity students.

Yet it was torn to pieces. 'There's already an inflation of this sort of stuff, it's too easy, it's pseudo-literature,' one of the boys said. 'Unless it's done far better than a lot of people are already doing it, it's not worth doing it at all.'

This seemed to me, still fresh from the West, a cruel judgement. Hadn't the piece been a brave act of defiance against socialist realism? 'Oh, we're long past that,' the gypsy critic said. 'By now we're even fed up with the reaction against it. We want something really new. Different from both the vulgar sociology that used to be served here as literature, and the antidote which so many people are writing now.' Cruelty, it seemed, had been a matter of sophistication.

'Yet they're also more tolerant than we used to be,' a thirty-one-year-old teacher to whom I related the story in Poland said. 'I see them sometimes watching an improvised play or an amateur pop group. I know we'd have hooted the same people off the stage. But not them. If it's not professional, that doesn't matter, what matters is that somebody is trying to do what he wants to do, without posing. I think, basically, they're much less self-conscious than we were.' This must cut both ways, making them both more cruel towards what is sham, even if it appears rebellious, and more tolerant of the unrehearsed, providing it is authentic.

'I think it's that they have many fewer fears, in general,' a twenty-nine-year-old raw materials buyer said in Hungary. 'We've nervousness in our bones. Often we're much more afraid now than we need to be. If we were given power tomorrow, I doubt if many of us would know what to do with it. I think they would – or at least they would try.' This again would be an aspect of being less self-conscious, less cowed by precedents and possible consequences.

'They have a much closer contact with life,' a thirty-four-year-old artist said in Romania. 'They believe, or at least some of them, in action, much more than we can. It's not just a matter of nerves that are still fresh. They'll look at a situation just as it's there, in front of them. And then find ways to go to work on it, ways we might never think of trying. That's courage.'

'I rather think they're more factual, less melodramatic about things,' a thirty-one-year-old sociologist said in Slovakia in 1969. 'They have many fewer problems about religion, for instance. I don't mean there aren't any who're religious among them. But just as the business between the Church and the State is different from what it was in the fifties, so inside them too there's not the same intense struggle between Communism and religion, nor between sexuality and religion, that there was in quite a few among us.' Less than a year later, a survey published in the quarterly of the Sociological Institute of the Slovak Academy of Sciences showed that the percentage of conscious atheists was in fact much higher in the twenty-five to thirty-nine age group, who had been through those more 'melodramatic' experiences with religion and Communism, than in the eighteen to twenty-four age group, that is, the new generation, among whom agnosticism was most widespread.[6]

'Their concerns are just very different from those we had,' a twenty-eight-year-old woman, a member of the Party, said in Budapest. 'The other night I went up to the Youth Park.* I was amazed. It's not just the crowd that used to go to Saturday dances when I was sixteen that go there. Perhaps if I were sixteen now I too would be interested not in ideology and books but the Rolling Stones. Or at least both.'

The differences between the two age groups are less clear to the new generation, partly, no doubt, because it is as yet less conscious of its own identity. But its admission of this is in itself important. In Hungary I saw a film based on stories of pure fantasy which an eighteen-year-old, trapped in a half-built house for a night, might be telling himself and two hitch-hiker friends. In an episode shot as *cinéma vérité*, the three of them could be seen wandering down a busy street in Budapest, shouldering boards on which nothing at all was written.

'Are they fed up with all the slogans they and their parents have had to carry?' I asked the director, who had been twenty-four at the time of starting on the film.

'That too, perhaps,' he said. 'But even more I was trying to suggest that anything could be written on those boards. There's

* This is a huge dance-garden, overlooking the city from the hilly side of the Danube.

131

an early time in every man's life and in the life of every society when they just can't tell what their experience means. And then you want to be honest and not cover it up with false confidence and brash slogans.'

The part of the new generation prepared to be involved in political or social action also tends to see its preparedness as a basic difference between itself and its elders. 'He's very honest and he's a good person,' a twenty-two-year-old said about a writer of thirty-four specializing in youth affairs in one of the East European countries. 'I regard him as a good friend, too. But he shouldn't be writing about us. He's a broken man. I mean, he's seen too much trouble, as they all have. He's accepted the system and doesn't want to push it. Which is all right as far as he's concerned, but when he imputes the same feelings to us, that's bad. It's not true, and it's not helping anybody. Not us, not him or his generation, nor even the people at the top.'

But irrespective of how far the two halves of the younger generation recognize the differences between their characters, these are abundantly clear in their behaviour, as I discovered in Poland, where I arrived at a critical time in 1968. Repression after the March student riots was just reaching its climax. Stories of beatings by the police, long interrogations, listening devices openly installed in students' rooms, new police agents put in strategic rooms in hostels and so on cropped up in countless conversations. Yet it was the students who were least afraid to talk, even if I just accosted them in the street. By contrast, people about thirty and older very often refused to talk to me 'in such bad weather', as one of them put it, when a good friend of his and mine was trying to introduce us. More than once, people to whom I was bringing news from friends abroad subjected me to a painful period of interrogation before they believed that I was not a secret policeman posing as the friend of a friend.

The new generation, having grown up since 1956, quite simply had not the reflexes that earlier times of terror had bred in the older one, and which the new terror revived. The idea of such a revival itself appeared alien to most of its members. 'This can't last,' a twenty-one-year-old student of geology said in Cracow. 'Unless it is part of a much bigger pattern. But that it can't be.

They can't turn the clock back, that's impossible.'

The period to which there can hardly be a full return, however, left indelible marks on what is today's recognized generation in Eastern Europe. Its members, irrespective of their current political views, are Stalin's children. They were born just before or during the war, in which they lost relatives and not a few their fathers or even both parents. An important part of their childhood experience had been the physical deprivations and mental shocks that had prepared the way for what happened after 1945 and also marked the psyche of their parents. Following 1948, they found themselves, still as children, in yet another war situation. This time it was internal, but that made its effects only more pervasive, surrounding each family and each individual. Indeed this war situation, with its special atmosphere, its shortages, its amorality, its terror, its insane propaganda seemed to be normality, and was proposing to endure and to centre for ever on Stalin the Father.

That central proposition is still remembered by not a few of his children: 'One day in my third year at school,' a twenty-nine-year-old agricultural technician in Romania remembered, 'I made my mother very angry. 'You'll be the death of me," she said. "Never mind," I said. "If you die, I'll go to Comrade Stalin, and be his son." She slapped me, and then she just cried.'

'When Stalin died, I was a little enthusiast, and secretary of my form at school,' a twenty-seven-year-old woman in Poland recalled. 'I was stunned. What's going to happen to us now, I thought. On the radio all you could hear the whole day was the announcement, and slow music. But the children in the class seemed very happy. Their parents must have told them this was good news. But I didn't understand that at the time. I could only think they must have gone mad, and it frightened me. They'd gone mad, and Stalin was no longer there to look after us.'

And though Stalin himself has since been removed from the Moscow mausoleum, and almost expunged from the history books that he once dominated, his children have hardly been able to forget the debt they owe him, in both love and hatred. 'When Stalin died I wrote a poem that was full of sincere sadness,' said a thirty-three-year-old Bulgarian poet. One of the best of his generation, he had become a Communist at the age of fifteen and has remained a Party member to this day. 'And I wouldn't take back a single word of it. Because if I did, I'd also have to take back the anger I felt when I found out what kind of a man Stalin had really been. I never mention his name now, but everything I write in a way expresses my feelings about his epoch.'

'Miserable Stalin,' the twenty-seven-year-old Czech poet I quoted in the previous chapter had written in 1962, following the Party decision to take down the tyrant's enormous statue overlooking his city

> So now at last it is to melt
> this extravagant iceberg in the midst of Prague,
> one-tenth of which
> floats on the city's rooftops
> and nine-tenths
> are within us
>
> Slowly
> without cease
> the heavy turbid water
> snakes forward
>
> In the moraine underneath
> each of us can find
> his foundation stone[7]

To the new generation, the Stalinist epoch is history, and Stalin the name of a man whose picture the generation was told by its teachers to tear out or paste over in its history books, until new books could be printed. Of course aspects of Stalinism have survived, and where they have been abolished they can be revived, often with the same effect. In Poland itself, whereas in 1968 even students who suspected their own room-mates of working for the police were open with me, by 1970 I found many of them worried about meeting a foreign writer, and not a few refusing to do so.

But this, I think, is a matter of outward behaviour, and not, as it was for many people in the fifties, of inner psychology. Both enthusiasms and fears now reach only so far down. The same foundation stones cannot be laid again. In the economy and in politics versions of Stalinism may appeal to smaller or larger groups in the Party. But the demiurgic aura of a Stalin and the passions of his world are unlikely to be reborn in the lifetime of the new generation of East Europeans.

Of the two main reasons for this, one is that Stalin's abuse of heroic passions and authority has deprived the Parties he put in power and left behind of any further rights to the same. 'I want to ask what comrades in the highest positions did to prevent the development of the personality cult,' a Youth League member who had obviously been a sincere Communist said in a long letter published in *Po Prostu*, the famous Warsaw student weekly in March 1956

> It was not my fault if Stalin exalted himself above the Party . . . even if I had known the true state of affairs, I would not have been able to say anything. I would like to know why. . . . I know this is a chaotic letter, but it cannot be otherwise because there is chaos in my mind. However, I can see a certain fact emerging from that chaos. You see it also: All along the line, from the basic Party organizations up to the Secretary of the Central Committee, there are no authorities.[8]

The effects of the shock also remain ineradicable: 'I'll tell you why I don't think there'll be great trials here,' a twenty-seven-year-old Prague journalist said to me in 1970. 'One of the reasons is, of course, that whether or not the people at the top know what it means to be involved in such trials from personal experience, they know that once they start real terror they can never stop it before they themselves have been destroyed. But the other reason is that show trials would be pointless. In the fifties a lot of people really did believe that Slansky and the others had been guilty. My own father believed it. But today, even if they could prove that Dubček had been selling the country to the Americans, bit by bit, and show receipts with his signature for every dollar he got, people would say, thanks very much, we've heard and seen all that before.'

The second main reason why Stalinism could not again inspire the same heroic passions has to do with a change from a continuous emergency situation to peacetime and a generally much richer life. The new generation has grown up amidst increasing prosperity and has acquired ambitions and concerns very different from those of its elders. 'I think one of the reasons we cared more about books and ideology and religion,' reflected the twenty-eight-year-old Budapest woman I quoted earlier, 'was that we were poor. Little Communists or reactionaries, all of us. We had little else to play with, you might say. My parents were both teaching at university, so we lived well enough, still, when I was thirteen my pocket money for the week would have bought me a bar and a half of chocolate. I don't think I knew anybody my age who had a radio of his own, never mind tape-recorders.'

Nor has enrichment been just material. With the passing of heroic isolationism have gone its hysterically simplified images of the world, while the school curricula as much as the scope of what the young can read and hear and see have widened enormously. 'What do you envy them most?' I asked the thirty-three-year-old Bulgarian poet about the boys who now brought their poems to him for an opinion. 'Their greater knowledge,' he said. 'Their much wider horizons.' Knowledge which, less enclosed by any rigid framework, has been kept in fertile motion by doubt. 'Do you think an intelligent man should be always sure of what he is saying?' I asked a Prague class of sixteen-year-olds. 'No, no,' they said immediately. 'A man who is always sure of what he is saying can't be intelligent. An intelligent man knows he doesn't know everything.' Socrates had not been wasted on them.

Of course Party propaganda still has a genuine effect on what may be called the 'fifth generation'. 'When Czechoslovakia was invaded,' a sixty-six-year-old Party member told me in Budapest in 1970, 'my grand-daughter and I were watching the news on TV together. She's only seven, but of course she wanted to know what all this was about. What could I say? I said there had been some problems in Czechoslovakia, but now the Russians were going in and things would be quiet. She wanted to know if the Russians were good people. I said they were people, there were good and bad people among them, like in every other country. Next morning we went down shopping together. As we stood there in the queue, she heard others talking about Czechoslovakia. And she started telling them not to worry, there had been some problems there, but things would be quiet now, the Russians were good people and they'd take care of everything.'

'It can also be quite frightening,' said the thirty-eight-year-old Polish doctor quoted earlier. 'As you know, for about two years now we've been having these terrible war films, and war serials and propaganda on TV and radio. All the time, Polish heroism, and the crimes of the Germans. We know it has to do with the Partisans whipping up nationalism, but you should see the children playing in the street. "Shot you, bloody German, down, bang, bang, German swine, you dead." I'm really afraid what will happen when these children grow up.'

My own view is, they'll have forgotten most of it as games, unless the Germans meanwhile oblige by living up to their Partisan image. Judging by all my interviews, whatever East European children may or may not believe now, there is much less chance of even a minority of them turning into adult fanatics than there was in the fifties. To compare beliefs with reality is an essential part of growing up, and young people in Eastern Europe today have far more access to reality at large than their counterparts did in the Stalinist years.

Equally significant, those of my interviewees in the new generation who had come through belief to scepticism almost invariably put the birth of the latter at the age of sixteen to seventeen. That is, it had been part of their becoming aware of the world during adolescence, rather than the mature crisis the same awakening meant for many Communists in the older generations. 'If I quote Lenin to a class of fourteen-year-olds,' a language teacher of twenty-nine said in Bulgaria, 'they'll accept it as a matter of course. But if I quote the same kind of thing to the boys who're seventeen or eighteen, they'll look up at me as if to say "What's the matter with him, he was all right a minute ago".'

It must be said that while the effect of the Party's propaganda on the young has been declining, the Party too has learnt to give up some of its romantic illusions about its identity with the young. In the old days, Party spokesmen used to state categorically on the one hand that under socialism, which resolved all contradictions in society, there could be no such thing as a conflict of generations, and on the other that in the conflict of generations the Party and the young together formed the vanguard of the future against the rest. These categoric statements not only made nonsense of each other, they also completely failed to affect reality. Then as realities began to be admitted, the Party began acknowledging that it was puzzled by the young. In fact when sociology first became respectable in each East European country, youth was made its prime target of research. During the late fifties surveys on the attitudes of the young crowded each other in the general and specialist media in Poland, and the first opinion poll published as part of the new wave in Romania, in early 1965, was also about youth.

The results of a number of detailed surveys on the young have been found so depressing by the Party that it has never allowed them to become known except to trusted personnel. But it has certainly acknowledged the existence of a 'youth problem' throughout Eastern Europe, and has also established ministries or committees with ministry rank to deal with it. How realistically these bodies cope with the problems facing them depends, as always, on how pragmatic is the faction that rules the Party, and what kind of men it appoints to rule the youth scene. But at least they can have access to proper information. In every East European country whole research centres and institutes have been set up to specialize in the sociology of youth; the institute attached to the Polish Central Committee was in fact charged in July 1970 with the task of producing an annual report 'on the situation among young people'. As will become clear in the course of this book, I myself am very much indebted to East European sociologists who have done research in this field and have been most generous both in letting me see their results and in discussing with me their personal experiences and current ideas on the subject.

From the point of view both of the Party and of the present book, one fact emerging from all research and interviewing done by others and by myself among the youth of Eastern Europe is of cardinal importance. This is the fact that while Party propaganda in the last twenty-five years has been able to score some successes of its own, its real influence has depended all along on whether it coincided with, or tried in vain to hide or contradict, the much more powerful effect of true social and political developments. The resulting social and political attitudes of the young will be the subjects of my next two chapters.

3   Classes

'Why is it you all so badly want to go to university?' I asked a group of fifteen- to eighteen-year-olds I was interviewing in the English-Language Secondary School in Plovdiv, in Bulgaria.

'Because otherwise you can only be a worker,' said a poker-faced boy who had all along been giving the fastest replies. There was a hush. Then another boy coughed.

'No,' a girl said. 'It's because we want to have a good education. . . . ' Then she too fell silent. Given the advantages of the educated, especially in a centralist system, hers was only another way of saying the same thing.

The school, teaching nearly all of its curriculum in English, is one of a small number of foreign-language schools maintained by Bulgaria. According to the principal, selection to these prestige institutions, providing a virtual passport to university, is based only on ability. According to everyone else I asked, including people who had been through such schools, ability counted, but not more than good connections and often less. 'It's where the élite sent their children,' a thirty-four-year-old woman said, as a matter of course.

The social revolution begun by the Party as Hero in 1948 had two main aims. One was to make the industrial working class the material and spiritual leader of society. The second was to produce full social equality and egalitarian attitudes in every human being. The Revolution which the people was to execute under the leadership of the proletariat and its conscious élite was meant to end in the incorporation of the élite and of all classes in each other.

At first sight it may appear that the Party has completely failed in this revolutionary aim. But I think it would be fairer to say that it has achieved a good deal, while finding East European society less transformable than it had expected. In fact both the social situation in the area today and the Party's own outlook are very different from what they were in 1948, due on the one hand to the Party's radical work, and on the other to the influence of factors the Party either had not seen, or dialectically assumed to be moribund – only to find itself enmeshed in dialectics for which it had not bargained, and which have both changed East European society and taught the Party a few humble lessons.

The original situation facing the Party had merited violent reshaping in every country of Eastern Europe, except Czechoslovakia. Prewar economic and social inequalities had been glaring, and educational opportunities virtually limited to children of the middle and upper classes. In the attitudes of the ruling castes towards the lower orders, arrogance, selfishness and sheer ignorance had formed a revolting mixture. Most members of the middle classes had not only shared these views but, being less established, were often more vicious about them than the landed aristocracy and its industrial and commercial equivalents. And while economic underdevelopment had allowed only so much upward mobility, the attitudes of the lower classes had sadly complemented the attitudes of the people above them. Those who worked and starved admired those who worked and starved less, and hated themselves for working and starving.

On this situation, the Party went to work with zest. Its nationalization of the economy was meant not only to serve the purposes of centralized planning, but also to deprive the former ruling classes of the remaining bases of their power. At the same time, members of these classes began systematically to be driven out of all property, and all professional and social positions they might still possess. Their way of life and attitudes and manners, from their habit of kissing ladies' hands to their contempt for the 'proles' came under propaganda fire. Members of the former middle classes, industrial, commercial and professional, found themselves denounced for having been the lackeys and poor imitations of those above them, and often treated in a similar way. The term 'working intelligentsia' was coined so as not to exclude administrators and experts from the 'working people's front' altogether, but the main elements of this front were understood to be the industrial proletariat and the 'working peasantry'.

These received the privileges withdrawn from the former

ruling and middle classes. Their incomes were raised and they were given priority in housing and welfare. Workers, and some peasants, were made into managers, with high-pressure courses instituted to train them if possible. The Party, as the élite body in the State, took care to ensure that the majority of its members also derived from the manual-working strata. In education, beyond enormous efforts to extend basic schooling to the masses and their children, the children also had the majority of places reserved for them throughout the secondary and higher school system.

Meanwhile, there were not only special propaganda campaigns to make labour-hungry occupations, such as mining, attractive, but a whole vast effort began that was intended to raise the prestige of physical work:

> Manual labour [wrote a Czechoslovak paper in 1950] was once a punishment and a threat to children of the so-called better classes. . . . 'He who will not study, will have to be a factory worker' [they used to say]. . . . Our schools are educating children in another way. Textbooks contain this type of teaching: 'What will I be? From the time I was a little girl, I kept telling my mother that I would be a gardener. I will grow not only flowers and vegetables but also trees. . . . If Peter wants to be a tractor driver, then I will not only be a tractor driver, but will drive a combine harvester too. What's more, I'll go to the factory where they make these wonderful machines, and then Peter will see.'[1]

Beyond this, though demands for absolute equality were rejected as 'infantile' for the moment, every effort was made to develop an egalitarian–collectivist outlook.

Combined with the effects of rapid development, also championed by the Party, the policies of social transformation since 1948 have achieved some indubitable results. Of these, the three most important have been as follows. One has been the movement of large numbers of peasants and peasants' children into industry and various trades. The second, the movement of a number of industrial workers, a smaller number of peasants and a very much larger number of their children into the 'intelligentsia' (this term is applied in several East European countries to all those not doing manual work, and I shall be using it in the same way). And the third, the equalization of incomes which, as a complement to the opening of the avenues of social mobility and the direct elevation of members of the manual working classes into the intelligentsia, has greatly contributed to homogenization.

The first of these changes has mostly had to do with industrial development, and with the concurrent urbanization of village life. In several countries of Eastern Europe today 65 per cent to 80 per cent of the industrial labour force consists of former peasants and peasants' children, for whom their new occupations have meant a change both in ways of life and in social outlook: 'Lots of people have moved, of course,' a thirty-four-year-old teacher in eastern Hungary said. 'But even among those who've stayed, different things matter. In the old days, when it came to marriage what used to be important was how much land a man tilled, or a girl could expect from her father. I won't say that now it's all romance. But when a girl looks at a man now, she won't be thinking of how much land he or his father has; most of the land will have gone into the collective anyway. But quite apart from that, what she'll be interested in is what he's learnt to do. An animal-keeper is better than a mere peasant, a tractor-driver is better than an animal-keeper, a shoe-maker is better than a tractor-driver, and if he's learnt a town trade and will be moving there, that's best of all.'

The movement of adult workers, and to a smaller extent peasants, into the intelligentsia, has also owed something to industrialization and the sudden growth of the administrative and managerial strata. Still the major motive force behind it has been political: the Party's revolutionary drive to elevate the formerly oppressed, and to replace as many members of the former middle classes as it could with people it thought politically reliable. Throughout Eastern Europe the managerial class that is now senior and retiring is studded with men who began their working lives on the shop-floor, down mines or on the land. And a very much larger percentage of the new intelligentsia in every sphere has been recruited from children of workers and peasants.

The levelling of incomes, again due partly to development but mainly to deliberate Party policies, has produced a measure of homogeneity striking by comparison not just with the prewar situation in Eastern Europe, but also with that visible in even the most developed countries of the West. In Hungary, for example, in 1970 the earnings of semi-skilled and skilled workers were only 22 per cent, those of technicians 39 per cent and those of university-trained personnel 70 per cent more than those of the unskilled labour force.[2]

All this has replaced the former structure of rigid castes separated by wide gaps with a much more fluid system consisting of three main sectors, themselves much nearer to each other. These three main sectors I shall name the upper crust, the middle mass and the people.

The upper crust is thin and chequered. In addition to people high in the apparatus of the Party, the State and the economy (including some members of the former upper and middle classes, as I shall later explain) it contains established free professionals and, where allowed, private shopkeepers and small tradesmen in cities. The incomes of these various elements may range between three and seven times the national average. With these earnings, the upper crust is the first buyer of whatever comes on the market, from expensive fruit to cars, is best able to travel abroad, to build itself bungalows in the suburbs and in resorts, and generally to furnish its life with all available comforts and – given the flair – to constitute fashionable society.

The middle mass is vast, and now dominant in every East European country. It includes all kinds of people from middle management to skilled workers, employed professionals and the intelligentsia, rural administrators and technicians, and substantial parts of the peasantry. Its spectrum of earnings spreads from about two-thirds of the national average to two-and-a-half times that average. Its material aspirations seem to embrace what the middle classes alone used to have, and the lower classes used to want, plus what has since become fashionable and in part available. In other words, they form a dilution, according to possibilities, of the wants of the upper crust, with their tastes similarly diluted both in culture and in their way of life.

Below the upper crust and the middle mass, now constituting

recognized society in Eastern Europe, there is the people. It is smallest in Czechoslovakia, the most industrialized and prosperous country, and largest in Romania, where the peasantry still accounts for well over half the population and has remained the worst-off in Eastern Europe. Beyond the poor peasantry and the seasonal labour force in various backward areas of each country, the people embraces the barely-skilled and unskilled urban workers, usually fresh arrivals in town living in still extant or new slums and in dwellings that may house four or five families in as many rooms, and several grown men to each bed.

Though some of the people earn, by official assessment, only enough to subsist, this is not universally the case. More important is the people's continuing separation from East European society:

> Room 34 is inhabited by the oldest residents of the hostel [wrote a report on life in the largest Warsaw workers' hostel, housing 2,400 men, in 1965]. There are eight men, who have eight tin mugs, forks, two toothbrushes and four kilos of smoked pork belly per day. They take one bath a month, but only in the summer – 'in winter it just softens you up'. . . . After work, they sit in their rooms, eat smoked pork, and the one who finished fourth grade reads *Express Wieczorny* [the evening paper] out loud. . . . On Saturday, they take their pay envelopes and go home to the country. It takes four hours on the bus. They come back Sunday night and start working again Monday morning. And this is the way it has been for eight years now. . . .[3]

Of course, even in the life of the people significant changes have taken place. Quite apart from welfare measures and the possibilities for further education, the same labourers who now eat half a kilo of smoked pork belly a day might have eaten nothing but bread and onions from one wedding to the next before the war, and walked home for the main holidays instead of taking the weekend bus.

The same sort of thing may, indeed, be said about a very large number of social phenomena that the Party has found stronger than itself. They have all been affected by its effort, while some of those that the Party would now wish away actually live on in forms they owe to the Party itself.

The new upper crust, for example, is not a thing the Party has gone out of its way to advertise. Yet its composition and ways of recruitment are both very different from those of its predecessors, and generally much healthier. Nothing illustrates this better than the terms on which it has readmitted members of the former upper and middle classes and changed them in the process of reintegration – the same process also representing a sane compromise with realities by the Party.

Under Stalin the formerly rich, irrespective of their talents and previous political attitudes, had either to take jobs as labourers or to live off the credit and personal possessions they had left. But then, as pragmatism gained ground, quite a few of them began to be accepted, and duly rewarded, for whatever they had to offer the State in the way of skills or sheer flair. This has been especially the case in Poland, where the landowning class had been the largest and best established in the region and where 1956 also brought the most complete break with Stalinist practice.

The results have cut both ways. 'After '48, five families were put in this house, which once belonged to us,' the twenty-two-year-old son of a former Polish aristocrat, now director of a publishing house, explained to me while we were having tea on their verandah in 1968. 'Then, as things became easier, we began to reoccupy the place. It's a slow process. We have to find and buy each new tenant a flat elsewhere, which takes time and money. But we only have two more to go now.' Taking tea with us, the father, however, talked of himself as having meanwhile 'become rather a good socialist. I'm not a Party member, of course, but I think the main things they did were right, and nowadays I may even be a purer socialist than some of the Party members I know.'

Whatever may or may not have happened to their convictions, members of the former middle classes have survived in their social positions on an even larger scale. Their reserves had been generally easier to save, while their skills and knowledge made many of them indispensable even under Stalin. In Romania stories still survive of former capitalists and managers hiring themselves out in the fifties as 'black consultants' – people who came and expertly sorted out the problems of an enterprise they had once run or owned, for a large fee which the new management never, of course, entered on the books. The onset of pragmatism merely legalized this process: unless the Party could find a host of expert angels, it had to use the humans available.

'Your family used to be rich, and I understand your father was in the Legion,* yet he seems to have a good enough job now,' I remarked to a Bucharest student whom I had got to know well enough to broach such uncomfortable topics. 'Yes, my father's people used to own land,' he said, 'and it's true he was in the Legion, commanded a unit in 1940. But he was very young, had just finished law, and when the Legion was being smashed, he gave up without much fighting. After the war, he was in some trouble, but then he turned himself into an economist, and he was needed, and he also joined the Party. He's been all right for some time now.' The family had most of the house in which they lived to themselves, and he had his own room, with old photographs, and some relics, and lots of old as well as new books. We were drinking wine brought back from the village where his grandfather still lived, and where the family went in the summer holidays, and in the winter to go shooting.

At the same time, some of the elements which have newly joined the upper crust would be a surprise to most westerners. Party and other high-ups may be considered to belong there by right. Next to them, however, are not just independent professionals, ranging from poets to dentists, but also small private tradesmen in the cities, from grocers to plumbers and tailors, generally earning more than ministers and certainly sporting the mixture of styles now proper to their stratum. 'We have to admit that some people will always be well off, whatever regime comes,' a twenty-eight-year-old university lecturer, daughter of a ranking Party man, told me in Budapest. 'Gynaecologists and

* The Legion of Archangel Michael, the main Romanian Fascist organization, founded in 1927 and surviving into the forties. After King Carol's abdication in September 1940 the Fascists and General Antonescu formed a government to rule what the Fascists called the 'National Legionary State'. Disagreements, however, soon led to violence by the Fascists and in January 1941 to a Fascist insurrection, which Antonescu used the army to suppress, taking power alone. It is to this struggle that my interviewee is referring.

better shoe-makers and so on, they can be sure that people will always pay extra for their services. They're now the cream of our bourgeoisie – I suppose I too belong to it, but further down the scale. I have some of their children for private tutorials. The children get a salary to study and a bonus for passing exams, about equal to the wages of a good typist. And they live well. They go to places, have swish parties, wear clothes I could not afford, and make little secret of knowing more about these things than I do. The other day one of the girls, just twenty, warned me, nicely but firmly, that to wear a silver brooch with a gold bracelet was just not done.'

Their being mixed, and in many ways much closer to the rest of the people than their predecessors, has not, however, made today's East Europeans upper crust any more popular, as may be seen from the names it has earnt. In Romania, where private entrepreneurs are rare, the term 'new boyars' is applied to the Party and administrative élite, living in appreciably different style from the rest. In Hungary there seems to be no generic term for the upper crust, but children of the Party élite are known as 'cadre-kids'. In Poland the same children have been named 'young dignitaires', but a more general term in use since the late fifties for children of the whole upper crust has been 'banana-eaters'. Originally this meant the offspring of families rich enough to afford bananas for their children to take to school, and later western clothes for them to wear and gadgets for them to play with and even the occasional car for them to drive, until some grew up into conspicuous *fainéants* of Warsaw café society. But then, although their lack of intelligent interests separated the 'banana-eaters' even from other children of the upper crust, for the ordinary man in the street they came to represent all better-off young people and students. This produced ugly results at the time of the March 1968 student riots, as I shall later explain.

Many other aspects of social alienation have survived, or reappeared in forms that are new but as acute as ever, though the pattern of divisions between the strata has greatly changed. In fact the most important division today does not coincide at all with the pattern of income levels, but is the one between manual workers on the one hand and the intelligentsia on the other.

Basically, respect for manual work has risen to nowhere near the level the Party's propaganda once envisaged and still makes efforts to achieve, nor even to that prevailing in the West. The idea of working with one's hands unselfconsciously out of sheer domestic need, let alone for pleasure, is itself almost unknown. For example, despite the phenomenal shortage of handymen, few people think of decorating their own rooms or repairing taps that drip away for ages: when I mentioned that I normally did such things myself, I seemed to arouse in them the gravest doubts about my being a writer at all. The Party, too, is self-conscious enough in its practice. East European countries which now give passports to the West specifically refuse them to girls who state that they want to work as au pairs while learning a foreign language.

'Nor do most of us want to work as au pairs,' a nineteen-year-old Polish girl, from an old-established family, said in Cracow. 'Why should people in the West think they can use us as char-women?' A girl with her, the daughter of Party people who had once been working class, fully agreed. I tried to explain that the daughters of Swiss millionaires or Danish pig-farmers didn't seem to mind so much, but made no impression. 'It's different in the West,' a twenty-three-year-old student of English commented. 'There, students work in their holidays, some even through the university year, to earn money, and that's that. Not here. I myself have worked as a gardener, and a few others do jobs of this kind, but most people wouldn't dream of it. The idea is that you rise in society by rising into the classes which never have to work with their hands at all. So once you're there or on your way, you hate to fall back.' The same kind of attitudes have also doomed to failure any attempt at mixing the strata through mixed housing settlements: children who play together separate as they grow up to have different jobs, and with them different interests and *mores*.

Nor is this confined to such strongly stratified and perhaps socially over-conscious countries as Poland and Hungary. Even in the Czech lands, where history has produced the most homo-geneous society in the region, the distance between the manual and non-manual working strata is felt on both sides: 'At secondary school, one day a week we had to go and do factory work,' the twenty-two-year-old daughter of an insurance executive said in Prague. 'Some of the workers were nice and told us to go and sit in a corner and get on with some reading. But quite a few of them, especially the younger ones, said, "Now at last you'll see what work is like." They were jealous, but it's also quite true, I'm going to have a degree in psychology, and I don't really know how workers think, and they're the majority of the people in this country.'

'How much do you know about young workers and what they think?' I asked a twenty-four-year-old Romanian writer. 'Nothing, really,' he said. 'That's always been a problem here, the separation of the intelligentsia from the people, which censorship only makes worse. Some people go and work in factories and find out and write about it as much as they can, and there are a few who were workers before they started writing. But otherwise, even those who think it's their business to know mostly rely on hearsay. We know more about the peasantry, because that's a tradition and many of us come from the countryside, but even there I'm not sure how much we really know about young peasants now.'

(The present book, by the way, also suffers from a defect of this kind. Most of the people I am able to quote, whatever their origins, now belong to the higher-educated classes. My only excuse is that, coming from abroad, I had to concentrate on those with whom I could best surmount linguistic and cultural differences and establish the fullest contact. For the rest, I have tried to find as much evidence as is available in surveys, to complement my actual interviews.)

Both direct and indirect evidence, however, strongly confirms the survival of the division between manual and non-manual workers, not just in their minds and their ways of life, but also in their basic circumstances. For example, despite the enormous efforts made to extend education to the people, as much as one-fifth to a quarter even of the youngest age groups of peasants and workers in several East European countries have not finished their compulsory schooling. And whatever this percentage in any country, the cultural gap between young manual and non-manual workers not only remains wide but promises to widen further as they grow older. Surveys have in fact shown that while among technicians in factories 45–50 per cent may be studying for higher qualifications, once workers, especially the unskilled, have taken up jobs, both their cultural and further-educational interests decline.

'These are the people for whom our cultural revolution should have done something,' the twenty-eight-year-old Party member quoted in the previous chapter had said in Budapest. 'Well, we've taught the young ones to read and write, but not much more. So most of them read trash, and old magazines, and listen to the worst kind of music, not folk music or good pop or jazz, but the rubbish in between. And the cultural revolution is being abandoned, what with the kind of films and entertainment we have now, and book prices raised to meet costs. . . . Maybe the cultural revolution never was the way to go about these things. But something must be done, because it's not good for people to be living like that, and it's also the way city mobs are born.'

Quite apart from such extreme aspects of the problem, however, life-norms and aspirations also remain divided. Studies that I shall discuss later in greater detail show that a life of ambition, some adventure, social and even to a certain extent political involvement has many more aspirants among the young intelligentsia and students. A quiet life of family happiness and immediately achievable goals, though favoured by the majority in each stratum, is particularly favoured by young workers and peasants.

The division is, in fact, noticeable even where, as a result of the most crucial and still continuing aspect of the Party's revolution, worker–peasant children are enabled to cross into the intelligentsia. In each country it has been found that as applicants for further education they tend overwhelmingly to choose courses that promise immediate and tangible results and security for the future, rather than fame and more abstract rewards. They become technicians and engineers much more willingly than research scientists or linguists. Part of the reason for this is, of course, that with middle-class preferences for the arts as marked as ever, technical courses are less hard to enter. But that is only part of the

reason. 'My father is a metalworker,' a twenty-seven-year-old
social scientist said in Slovakia. 'The family wanted me to go to
the engineering faculty, and I did. But once there, I realized I
had more of a head for history and philosophy after all, and with
a lot of trouble I managed to change over. It meant almost a break
with my family. I'm not talking about the intellectual part, but
generally. They've never been able to understand, they think I've
thrown up a perfectly good profession for some nonsense. And
I can tell you, I think few people with my background would
have done it, the faculty was full of intelligentsia children.'

The political aspect of the same thing was strikingly illustrated
at the time of the March 1968 student riots in Poland. The
minority of students who had been active in previous years,
getting together for political drinking-parties, provoking discussions at open meetings, distributing leaflets and manifestos
and organizing virtual conspiracies, and who then emerged as
the activist kernel of the riots, consisted almost entirely of
children of the professional intelligentsia.

One of the main reasons for this was that students from worker-
peasant families had brought with them as part of their down-to-
earth ethos a lack of interest in apparently useless politics. The
other was that children of established families could far better
afford the courage it took to participate in action against a
system likely to defend itself in summary ways. 'This was one of
the things over which my boy friend and I broke up,' a twenty-
four-year-old girl, who had earlier described herself as being
'of the red bourgeoisie', told me in Warsaw in 1968. 'I was going
to meetings, typing leaflets, passing messages, everything. But
he wouldn't, and he didn't want me to either. He was afraid. He
came from a miner's family, he'd worked very hard to get to
university and then to stay there, he'd just got his first job, and
he didn't want to risk all this. Partly, I could understand: we'd
been going together for two years, and this was just one of the
many things, the different books we liked, the different people
we could talk to, the different aims we had in life, in which
the difference in our backgrounds showed. But it also made all
the other differences stand out more clearly. Not much later we
broke up.'

Divisions within the two occupational halves may be equally clear. Among young workers, for example, not only are there exact scales of job preferences according to qualifications and the 'modernity' of the work but, factories being microsocieties, patterns of association have also been shown to form along such lines.[4] And even stronger is the sense of alienation between the two manual-working classes. 'I come from the country,' a twenty-eight-year-old merchant seaman said in the Bulgarian port of Varna. 'I wouldn't want to be a peasant again, I know them. They're dirty. They can't talk, they don't know anything. When they come to town, you can see them a long way off, it shows. . . . '

In the upper occupational half the lines may be more subtle, but the minds perceiving them are sharper too. 'How about mixed marriages, whose language will be spoken first?' I asked a Hungarian linguist in Transylvania. 'In the chiefly Romanian areas,' he said, 'Hungarians will tend to assimilate. But otherwise, if often depends on whose family is higher in the social scale. If, say, a doctor from a family of doctors marries his assistant, it's his relatives they'll be seeing much more, and the woman will know that there's no better way of pleasing them than by showing that his language is spoken at home and taught to the children. If the doctor is Hungarian, it'll most likely remain a Hungarian family. If not, we can say goodbye to them.'

Of course, acute as the divisions may have remained, their visibility is itself often the result of changes in the last twenty-five years, both allowing people to escape from their former conditions and bringing them into daily contact with new and difficult milieus. 'Since time immemorial, people here have dreamt of moving to town as their way up in the world,' a twenty-year-old student of sociology, himself a son of peasants, said in Poland. 'Expressions like "works like a peasant" and "has hands like a peasant" have always been used in contempt. But it's even more the case now that they've had a chance to get away and realize the dream. They may not earn more in a factory. They may be still afraid of town life, and be very lonely because town workers won't associate with them. Still, you couldn't drag them back, even though farms are becoming depopulated.'

A version of the same sort of thing has in fact been brought to the villages themselves by urbanization, and whatever degree of prosperity has been created. In Hungary, where the peasantry's living standards have shown the most marked improvement in the region, in 1967 a daily paper described some of the effects on the rural young thus:

> One of the signs of the 'new top-end' in the village is that in dramatic-society productions secondary-school children and people in administrative jobs refuse to take 'lowly' parts – such as those of peasants and workers – and insist on being doctors and engineers and other such 'better sort' of people. At dances, secondary-school girls turn down boys from the collective farm with, 'I beg your pardon, but I'm not for *kolkhoz* yokels'.

This is, of course, a diluted version of the upper-class airs the Party set out to destroy. But instead of being a straight dilution, it rather reflects a paradoxical development in a paradoxical way. What has essentially happened since 1948 is that while the former ruling and middle classes have disappeared or been absorbed by their successors, many of their attitudes have spread far and wide among the masses that have risen from the ranks of the people into those of recognized society. The result is that a number of phenomena that appear to signal the survival of former structures actually show the extent to which these have been democratized by the Party – and in some cases the extent to which the Party meanwhile has allowed a dilution of its own former attitudes.

To take a simple example, in the Stalinist years the Party insisted on everybody calling everybody 'Comrade', and greeting each other in an ideologically suitable way.* Nowadays, 'Comrade' is on the way out – I myself heard it used between ordinary people only in Bulgaria – while 'Sir' and 'Madam' have come back, with professional titles where possible (producing 'Sir Engineer', 'Sir Dentist' and so on). But the basic forms are now addressed to much greater numbers of people than once seemed to merit them, while much greater numbers are also

* In Hungarian, for instance, the formula was '*Szabadság, Elvtárs!*' ('Liberty, Comrade!') whether one was meeting the local Party secretary or entering a barber's shop.

Classes

entitled to the professional formulae. In other words, a convention which, whatever outsiders may think of it, is germane to Eastern Europe has been greatly democratized.

The same sort of thing has happened to another such convention, the habit of kissing ladies' hands. It has both survived – in Romania, Hungary and especially Poland – and spread much wider. In Cracow I saw it accorded not only to matrons at tea-parties, but also to young girls who were dressed in jeans (as were the boys who kissed their hands on meeting them in front of a cinema). In a night-club I noted men in their early thirties, and rather obviously newcomers to the intelligentsia, kiss their partners' hands before starting each dance. 'That, of course, is vulgar,' I was warned by the thirty-two-year-old wife of a Warsaw musician. 'Or at least provincial, shows they're trying too hard.'

The habit of hiding one's social origins has spread in the same, to my mind paradoxically encouraging, way. 'If people are proud of their origins, it's usually that they're proud of how far they've come in society,' said the twenty-seven-year-old Slovak social scientist I quoted earlier. 'But mostly, they try to hide it. On my university course there was a girl whose mother was a cook, but the daughter claimed her to be an accountant. We laughed behind her back, but I knew many others who told such lies.' A sad thing to see, no doubt, but still better than if the people who now try to conceal their origins had never had a chance to rise above them.

Similarly democratized has been a social habit older in Eastern Europe than anyone can remember, and as pernicious as it can be genuinely useful. This is the practice of getting things done through connections, known as *protektsio* in all of the area's languages.* String-pulling is, of course, useful in any part of the world, but in Eastern Europe its power has long been quite extraordinary. And with society having become more mobile, this power has both spread and acquired still greater significance. 'In my view,' a university lecturer said to me in Budapest,

* As Hugh Seton-Watson remarked in his *Eastern Europe Between the Wars* (London 1945). My spelling is a phonetic approximation – the actual spelling differs from language to language.

'any parent who has a child about to apply to university, and does not make sure of the maximum *protektsio* is just being irresponsible.'

In fact, throughout my interviewing I found that the overwhelming majority of those young East Europeans who resented *protektsio* resented the fact that in some particular case they had been unable to secure enough of it. But mostly it was accepted as a live convention. 'Why doesn't your paper start a campaign against *protektsio*?' I asked one of the editors of the Bulgarian students' weekly in Sofia in 1968. He said it was beyond the paper's competence, and mentioned a few other reasons. 'What he couldn't tell you,' a twenty-one-year-old engineering student commented, 'was that if such a campaign were a success, Bulgarian society would just collapse.'

If divisions between new strata have often affected family life much more than differences over politics, the main reason for this too seems to be the great increase in mobility. A Romanian sociologist whom I interviewed in 1969, for example, had found in a study on the patterns of communication between generations that adolescents from no matter what class were keenest and best able to make contact with adults in the intelligentsia, especially professional people.[5]

'Is this because these are the people who can best talk to the young?' I asked him. 'No, it makes little difference whether they're talking, sharing a hobby or playing football,' he said. 'Invariably, fullest communication exists between intelligentsia adults and children of the intelligentsia, then between the same sort of adults and workers' children, and then between the same sort of adults and peasant children. And the reason seems to be that these are the adults who have the qualifications and jobs the children want to have too.' This was also why skilled workers emerged as the next most popular.

Where past phenomena have proved altogether much more stubborn, this has largely been a matter of the Party being too romantic to take realities into account at the start – to some extent because it knew little more about the actual life of the people than the rest of the intelligentsia, from which it derived as a revolutionary élite. A prime example of such romanticism has been the

Party's cultural revolution. It has failed mostly because, while making enormous efforts to spread high culture to the people, the Party has never stopped to think how far the people was, even physically, in a condition to take any such thing. Perhaps an élite derived from the manual-working classes will be wiser. 'For a year before going to university, I worked in a shoe-factory,' a twenty-five-year-old girl who had since finished studying languages told me in Prague. 'That year taught me a few things. I now know why workers read so much less and why they just want to be entertained in the cinema and by TV. After standing a whole day by the machines and hearing all that noise, there's little left in you for anything else. I'd been used to reading all my life, and I knew I had to read things for my courses, still, often I took up a book and in half an hour I was asleep.'

Equally sobering has been the Party's experience with positive discrimination in secondary and higher schools. Only here its problems have remained far more serious. Not only has positive discrimination been the central feature of the Party's effort to democratize East European society, but its success or otherwise is bound also to affect the economy and is an issue of vital importance to most families.

As regards the economy, having once filled a number of administrative and managerial jobs on a purely political basis, the Party could have carried on with this form of the revolution only by replacing wave after wave of at best half-experienced people with fresh workers and peasants. This would have been madness, especially as no East European country has ever quite got over the problems caused by its first wave of crude replacements. The number of these, in fact, soon began to decline, and by now workers and peasants can rise into the intelligentsia only through night school.

This, however, has put a stop to counterproductive policies only in respect of the adult generations – while the same crude polices in the selection of the young have had even worse consequences. During Stalin's time, when 30–65 per cent of all places in higher education and a corresponding number in secondary education were simply reserved for children of the manual-working classes, failure rates among them ranged to 60 per cent of the intake, despite the prodigious efforts they often made to keep up with the rest. This not only wasted everybody's time and money, but also discouraged other working-class children from trying to continue their education. And where positive discrimination was applied instead in examining, it allowed hosts of unqualified people to emerge from the schools and cause havoc in economies where enforced development would have needed the most brilliant experts as managers.

Unfortunately, the conclusions have been drawn by each East European Party only as and when it became pragmatic, with partial or full madness often redescending in centralist periods. For instance, Hungary began restoring the importance of academic ability for university entry, and Poland made it the sole criteria, in 1956. Following the 1956 revolt in Hungary, however, the country reimposed a 'points system' greatly favouring the children of manual workers, and in the area-wide climate of repression Czechoslovakia and Romania actually raised their working-class quotas, Romania to 75–80 per cent of the student intake. Similarly, though policies became more and more pragmatic during the sixties everywhere except in Poland, after the ousting of the Dubček leadership in Czechoslovakia in April 1969 a points system was reintroduced, boosting the percentage of working-class children among first-year students by 1970 to what it had been in 1952, as articles in the press proudly emphasized.

The truth is, however, that no Party can be truly pragmatic about the problem. Not only because this would amount to ideological suicide in an important sphere, but also because without positive discrimination working-class percentages would indeed fall below what is socially efficient for selection, and genuinely popular. As it is, even though various overt and covert forms of discrimination keep these percentages much higher than they are in the West, throughout Eastern Europe they are declining: by 1969 in Romania, for example, the percentage was down to 53, and among first-year students in Hungary to 39·2.[6] Altogether, as a leading Polish sociologist noted just before the reintroduction of working-class quotas in the country's universities in 1964, without such quotas 'the chances that a youth from a worker's family will become a university student are something like 25 times smaller than the chances of a youth from a family belonging to the intelligentsia.'[7]

Further decline in working-class percentages would not only waste talent (in countries which badly need it) but also generate grave political resentment (in countries where there is enough of it anyway, and all centred on the Party as Hero in charge). As I found throughout my interviewing, and as debates in the East European media reveal, the issue of positive discrimination is among the most sensitive as far as the young are concerned. But the debates themselves show the complexity of the issue, and in the more pragmatic countries also get down to some of its basic facts. 'Do workers and peasants really want their children to go on with their education?' journalists doing a comprehensive article on the topic for the Hungarian youth monthly asked a meeting assembled in a mining town.

> A well-dressed girl rises to speak [the article went on]. She's in the final year [of the town's secondary school], her father is a carpenter in the mine.
>
> 'They don't,' she says determinedly, then after some thinking, she adds, 'or rather, they're satisfied if their children just learn a trade. In my form, as usual, there are many more intelligentsia children. I think this is because even today most working-class parents think, "I'm a working man, why shouldn't my son be a working man too?" So if the children go on with their education, they're left to themselves, at times even come into conflict with their parents. . . .'
>
> 'The children of professionals and of white-collar employees' [the deputy head of the school said], 'want to go on to university with only rare exceptions. Their upbringing has been such that they consider it almost a tragedy if they can't get a place. But working-class parents would much rather send their children to apprentice schools or lower technical colleges. Enormous, at times unreasonable, ambitions on the one hand, the loss of many talented children on the other. . . .'

And, on occasions, the causes of the problem lay not even in attitudes, but in basic circumstances:

> 'There are seven of us children at home' [said a girl who had top marks and a high post in the school's Youth League organization

and would have been bound to get a university place], 'my brother is just going off to the army, my father is a labourer. I can hardly wait to start working. The family wouldn't mind if I went on studying, but I can't do that to them. Perhaps an external course. . . .'[8]

The article provoked letters that filled a special column of the magazine for months. Arguments were as often emotional as factual, but there could be no question about the importance of the issue. Middle-class children demanded to know why they should be penalized for having been born into certain families. They pointed out that their parents' incomes were often no higher than those of skilled workers; only their priorities were different, and that was no crime. They could not accept that in a socialist system, whose children they were, they should be denied equal rights. Workers' and peasants' children talked of teachers who had given up with them from the start. They described how much better and calmer the homes of middle-class children were, how much more encouragement middle-class parents gave, and the private tutors they engaged and the connections they had.

Judging by the tone of the letters published, a good many must have been found unprintable. In my experience, it is very rare for young East Europeans, especially in the countries where positive discrimination exists in crude forms, to talk about it as objectively as the twenty-three-year-old student of English I quoted earlier did in Cracow in May 1970: 'I think it's right that workers' and peasants' children who have a harder time studying, and people who come from country schools, where the standard of teaching is lower, should be helped over university entry,' he said. 'But look at me. My father is a railway clerk, so even though we aren't rich, I had no points for social origin. I come from a town that's small but not small enough, so even though the language teaching I got was useless, I had no compensatory points for that either. And it's still worse for people whose parents have just come into the intelligentsia, and can't even give their children the kind of support I had from mine. . . . So whatever the ideology is, who can sort all this out?'

While faced with equally complex problems in many other spheres, the Party as Hero has also found itself achieving results which, though worthwhile in themselves, might have put its founders and early enthusiasts off revolution for good. The most important of these results has, in fact, been the Party's main achievement in Eastern Europe during the last twenty-five years, namely, the enormous growth of the middle mass and its rise to a dominant position in society.* And though any realist would consider the abolition of the former social structure, the raising of popular living standards and the democratization of opportunities to be good things, the inevitable outcome of the whole gigantic effort has been the birth of a new *petite bourgeoisie*:

'We call it the socialist petite bourgeoisie, but only because this is a socialist country,' an embittered new leftist of twenty-six said in Hungary. 'A socialist petit-bourgeois is a man who has long forgotten about any revolution. He'd scream if he saw one coming. He complains, and when things turn bad, he may demonstrate, but that's all. For the rest, what he wants is a flat, and even before that, the way things are with us, he'll buy gadgets and if he can, a car, which he'll wash and polish every Sunday. He collects matchboxes and miniature bottles of western spirits, and things like that. If he's given a passport to the West, he'll not eat for six months so he can have three weeks abroad, where he'll rush through the programme of the guide-book, and spend most of his time looking for bargain sweaters. He's petty and jealous and gossipy, and as narrow-minded as any petit-bourgeois in the world. I'm not sure what he thinks his class identity is, but you can see it growing thicker every day, like his midriff.'

Judging by my own knowledge of a fair number of socialist petit-bourgeois, both young and old, though materially they may not all be so well off, as far as their attitudes are concerned the description largely fits. Where it exaggerates, this is due to a special animosity, about which I shall have more to say in a moment.

As far as the Party is concerned, however, abhorrent as the idea of producing such a class might have been to its early faithful, the result of its heroic effort was bound to be just this. The material

* In the Czech lands of Czechoslovakia the middle mass had long been significant; but even there it has grown a good deal, and elsewhere in the region it owes its birth as a dominant social phenomenon to the Party.

purpose of the Revolution had always been to distribute as far as possible what the upper and middle classes had till then had to themselves. With the material conditions has, predictably enough, gone the kind of consciousness these had helped to generate. Indeed as regards bourgeois aspirations, culture, tastes and manners, only hotheads inside the Party had ever believed that there might be something with which to replace them.

And while the birth of the new petit-bourgeoisie as a result of the Party's own good work is now irreversible, certain other results of its work seem, by themselves, to have begun reversing its own earlier policies. One of the most important of these is the ever graver need for fresh incentives in the economy, and hence for at least some de-levelling of incomes, as I shall presently explain. The other is the rise of an élite, meritocratic to begin with, but likely to prove, even if for the best of reasons, self-perpetuating. 'Clearly we must study this problem,' said the Romanian sociologist I quoted earlier. 'If the closest communication exists between intelligentsia adults and all children, then their own children will have known such communication longest, and benefited from it most. They will start with advantages over everybody else, and keep ahead for ever, and hand the same advantages on to their children, which means the rise of an élite.'

This is a problem that the Party has begun to find bad enough as it is. 'You may say I'm the kind of person for whom everything in the last twenty-five years here has happened,' a thirty-three-year-old research scientist told me in Poland. 'My father was a worker, my mother a daughter of peasants. It was on that double qualification that I got to university. But having educated me into a member of the professional intelligentsia, the Party doesn't know what to do about me and my children. Are we working class? If so, who isn't? Should our children be discriminated against? If not, what's happened to the leadership of the working class in society, and the whole socialist revolution?'

Paradoxically enough, it is also from the élite that the young enthusiasts come who ask such questions with most conviction, criticizing the Party on behalf of its own prime heroic aims. Everywhere it has appeared, and particularly in those East

European countries where the Party's own founding cadres had derived from the professional and commercial upper classes, the New Left has found its adherents especially among children of the Party élite. In Poland, prominent among the leftist students and lecturers purged and tried following the March 1968 student riots were the son of the country's Minister of Foreign Affairs between 1947 and 1951, the son of a leading member of the pre-1956 Politburo, purged in the sixties as a revisionist, the son of a prewar Communist who was made editor of the country's Yiddish paper in 1968, and the son of the Polish translator of *Das Kapital*. Among the students tried as Maoist conspirators in the summer of 1968 in Budapest, one of the two given prison sentences was the son of the Party's one-time cultural arbitrator, a learned and altogether brilliant Stalinist, now dead. And in both Poland and Hungary the circles surrounding these young leftist leaders have consisted overwhelmingly of children of Party people.

In their social origins, most new leftists of Eastern Europe have in fact remained true followers not just of the Party's prime cadres, but also of the fathers of the whole Communist movement, Marx, Engels and Lenin themselves. One wonders if the fathers are turning in their graves, or smiling into their ghostly beards, at the sight of their ideas being turned against the Party which swears by their heritage. For the new leftists of Eastern Europe have not only assimilated Marx's ideas on alienation and class warfare; they have also studied with great care Lenin's conspiratorial and political tactics in the face of an oppressive regime. 'But of course,' one of them said when I pointed out the resemblance. 'Naturally we use Leninist tactics. They're the best.'

Most important, however, in their critique of society they reproduce the Party's own critique from the earliest days. Indeed in precisely the two heroic countries of the region, Poland and Hungary, central to this critique has been the paradox characteristic of the Party's own prime vision, in which a Platonic contempt for the real-life concerns of the people was combined with realistic assessments of the system under which it lived. In the new-leftist critique, the contempt is manifest in a rejection of the socialist petit-bourgeoisie for wanting peace, and of consumer goods the like of which most of its members had never before had a chance to touch. Two of the most important new-leftist ideas may serve as examples of the realism. One of these concerns the grave and growing bureaucratization of the Party, to balance which the leftists would have either workers' councils or a whole workers' party; the other concerns the non-egalitarianism inherent in the wage policies of the economic reforms of the sixties, which the leftists reject for giving managements more than they deserve.

The bureaucratization of the Party is basically due to versions of the same causes that have increased the proportion of middle-aged and older people in its membership. Namely the decline of its political appeal – in this case to manual workers rather than to the young – and the existential need to be card-carriers of those intent on a career in any of the apparatuses the Party rules as Hero in central charge. Some parties have tried to counter the inevitable effect through 'positive discrimination' in their membership policies. Or they simply count as workers all those who have ever been workers, or combine the two equally tragicomic policies.

Where the Party has let developments take their own course, however, worker-peasant percentages have seriously declined. By 1970, in Poland they were down to 51·5[9] (from 79·4 in 1948)[10] and in Hungary to 38·0[11] (from 83·8 in 1947). In Czecho-slovakia, where in 1948 industrial workers alone had constituted 57 per cent of Party membership, twenty years later their share was 30·4 per cent.[12] Even worse is the fact that, meanwhile, within the intelligentsia groups that have come to dominate the Party, the politically elevated and hence least expert segments have become the most important, and the most blindly zealous. Combining conservatism, lack of expertise and political weight, these now constitute in several countries the bureaucratic core of the whole centralist system, which better-intentioned Party leaderships themselves have found very difficult, if not impossible, to fight.

As for the economic reforms, these contain incentive schemes which offer productivity bonuses for all. But at the same time some of them extend the maxim 'to each according to his deserts' to prize most highly the responsibilities taken by manage-ment. In the original blueprint of the Hungarian reforms of

1966-8, for example, an enterprise showing a profit at the end of the year was authorized to give bonuses of up to 15 per cent of yearly earnings to its lowest-paid employees, but up to 80 per cent to its highest-paid employees. True, the lowest-paid had their incomes guaranteed while the highest-paid could also lose money if the enterprise showed a loss. All the same the over-all effect of the scheme, combined with the raising of prices of essential goods in the interests of profitability, was bound to be an increase in real-wage differentials, and hence in the distance between the strata. Following protests by the trade-union movement the percentages were contracted, but de-levelling nevertheless took place, and in some form or another it is inherent in all the other reforms in Eastern Europe.

Thus the new leftists have been criticizing the Party's present position on behalf of the most genuine of its own former ideas. But everywhere outside Czechoslovakia the leftists have found themselves carried away by their romanticism – to a large extent, as was the case with the Party itself in the early days, because of their social isolation from the people. This isolation was thus made worse. 'Everybody knows they are rich kids, without contact with the workers,' a thirty-nine-year-old Party member, himself sympathetic enough to the New Left's social critique, said to me in Budapest. 'But even when they're right, the workers wouldn't listen, because they use rich kids' terms, and have rich kids' ideas. Also, they sound like Stalinist terms and ideas here, as I tried, in vain, to explain to new leftists in the West. The workers want more consumer goods, not revolution for its own sake instead.'

In Poland, though some of the leading young leftists deliberately frequented Warsaw workers' cafés and managed to establish personal contacts with people there, when the students rose in March 1968 they found the workers unresponsive to their heroic call. Nor was this without reason. The resentments that had long been building up against 'banana-eaters' were only aggravated when one after another student resolutions demanded political and intellectual freedoms but ignored economic matters and with these the workers' interests. The media's descriptions of the student leaders as spoilt children, wafted from their upper-class homes to their exclusive schools in large cars with curtained windows, out of which they had only seen 'the life of the working people from a distance', thus went to the heart of the people at whom they were aimed.

At the same time, having substituted itself for the prewar bureaucratic-military regimes, the Party has also been reacting to the new leftists rather as these regimes had reacted to the Party itself, when it had still been only a leftist intellectual grouping – by combining repression with anti-intellectualism and versions of nationalism in propaganda. This has been much the most apparent in Poland where, instead of a pragmatic and secure enough leadership keeping the leftists at arm's length in a paternal way (as has been the case in Hungary), a Party faction rooted in the hard-liner segments of the bureaucracy, the economic apparatus and the armed forces, and trying to hoist itself into power, used the new leftists as 'the enemy'. This was why the March 1968 student riots – generally agreed to have been provoked by the police for the purpose – were followed not just by repression, but by a wave of anti-Semitic, anti-intellectual and anti-liberal propaganda in the Nazi manner, with ugly results both in the streets of Warsaw and in the more competitive occupations.

Beating off the new leftists has not, of course, solved the problems that in any case they were only one of several groups to point out. In particular, each East European Party is faced with having to decide not whether but how far to de-level incomes, within its attempt to reform the centralist economic system that was originally established throughout the region by Stalin and has remained basically the same since his day. It may even be said that de-levelling constitutes the pragmatic-gradualist solution to the reign of the bureaucracy, which the new leftists would overturn in a revolutionary-romantic way: to prize expertise over political conformism inevitably eases the worst bureaucrats out of the posts that matter.

There is, however, a far more important reason for the need to de-level, to which the new leftist reply is as beautifully unreal as the Party's own once was. This reason was put to me not by Party people, but by two planners in their late twenties whom I interviewed in Prague in June 1968. I asked them how far they thought the new schemes of graduated incentives, which aimed in effect to enhance individual drive through rewards in cash and social elevation above the rest, accorded with the ideals of socialism.

'But socialism is lost without incentives,' they said, meaning by socialism the system in which they had grown to adulthood. 'For years here the problem has been apathy. Nobody worked hard, nobody cared for quality, nobody wanted to be responsible, let alone take risks. They all knew that whatever they did, they could get neither much less nor much more than they were getting. People stopped trying, they even stopped bothering about a better education. Well, that's stupid. If you want people to work harder, to be really interested in their jobs, you have to give them incentives. You can't expect them to do it just for love.'

Originally, the Party thought you could. It was said, and was believed by a number of sincere and intelligent enthusiasts as much as it is by the new leftists now, that while in exploitative systems each man worked only for himself and his own, once exploitation had ceased each would be incorporated into his larger self, the collective, for which he would cheerfully work and live.

This was the essence of the socialist idea. Nor was it an idea that was alien to Eastern Europe. On the contrary, for an élite to pose as the collective's super-ego and claim all individuals for the purpose of their rebirth together to a new golden age was part of the area's main tradition. The Party's proposals for collective rebirth were also economically more realistic and socially more democratic than those of any heroic élites in the past. And yet the idea has remained in some ways more of a dream than ever.

For this I can see three main reasons, which I will discuss in the next three chapters. The first of these has to do with the way in which the heroic-collectivist idea relates to the political system maintained on its behalf in Eastern Europe, and to the changes which the Party as Hero has actually helped to bring about. The second has to do with the type of individuals whom the environment born of the same history as brought the Party to power has been breeding, and with the manner in which changes in the environment have affected the type and its approach to heroic collectivism. And the third has to do with the ways that East Europeans bred by such an environment tend to choose for living as best they can within it.

In other words, the reasons lie in the three main factors that shape the relationships of every young person to society in Eastern Europe today. Of these, I shall discuss politics first.

4   Self and Politics

'My nine kids would drive you mad,' a twenty-nine-year-old woman, in charge of nine junior clerks at her office, said to me in Hungary. 'They'll work if I'm there, they won't even stop if I'm out of the room. We're good friends, I think they respect me, and if there's a rush and we have to get a shipment out, they'll stay on with me late into the night. But they'll never do anything on their own, not a thing more than they have to. And I can't tell them about Stalin to make them enthusiastic, as they could twenty years ago. Maybe it wouldn't have made them enthusiastic even then, or just scared, I don't know, I wasn't old enough. My problem is, what do I tell them now, how do I explain to them that we're in this together?'

From the drift of our conversation till then, it was clear that she herself very much believed that she and the rest were 'in it together'. To spread her kind of belief, however, has long been not only her problem, but the Party's own problem throughout Eastern Europe. It is, in fact, the gravest problem facing the Party. As self-advertised Hero in complete charge of each country, it must either involve the people in its projects, whatever their value, or take all the blame not only for its own mistakes but also for every disaster that the people remain too uninvolved to try to avert.

The paradox about this is that in effect the Party and the people are 'in it together'. Besides them, there is simply nobody else to cope with their circumstances. As a result of the Party's total identification with the heroic-collectivist idea, it alone rules everything from the economy to the machinery comprising the police, the bureaucracy and the media, with which the people may be involved at any level. But this is also what makes the two antagonists in almost as many situations as there are between them. And in the all-round struggle that ensues they become alienated not only from each other, but also to some extent from reality itself.

Not surprisingly, their alienation from reality is most acute as regards their own relationship. In fact concerning the extant, necessary and possible forms of collectivism, especially among the young, who are newcomers both to the present situation in Eastern Europe and to its background, there are only beliefs, which for a number of people in the region count as truths. These seem to me to coalesce in four main planes, each self-consistent but at a greater or lesser remove from basic facts: the crimson plane of rhetoric; the black plane of despair; the plane of realism which hope has coloured green; and the plane of realism without any special hope, as grey as earth.

Common to the first two planes is perfectionism. That is, an attachment not only to the traditional virtues of honesty, diligence, self-respect, respect for others and preparedness for social involvement, but to the heroic tradition of being able to recognize these only in spectacular forms. People on the rhetorical plane tend to believe either that certain signs show that these ideals are actively accepted among the young or that the generating of such signs equals the generating of such acceptance, whereas the desperate see only signs of their ideals being rejected.

The crimson image of the young conjured up on the rhetorical plane has often enough been presented by the East European propaganda machine both at home and abroad. It shows young East Europeans as, 'with rare exceptions', collectivistic-patriotic at school, at work and in their social activities, and politically convinced of the rightness of the Communist cause, as manifest in the Party and its youth organizations. An almost equally rhetorical counter-image of the youth of Eastern Europe used to be presented by parts of the western media during the Cold War, and has continued to struggle with the Communist propaganda image in the minds of average westerners ever since.

As a writer with no kind of reputation in these matters, and a generally patient face, I myself was often enough shown the crimson image, especially during my first trip through Eastern Europe in 1968. In the course of more than one interview with Youth League officials I was shown statistics on participation in summer work-brigades and political education courses, and brochures that featured joyous pioneers marching and League members doing gymnastics in formation on May Day. They were spread out before me in all seriousness as illustrating the life of East European youth. On many other occasions I was treated to children reciting with passion patriotic and socialist poetry as their favourites. And if I asked officials or teachers or a school class stock questions about politics, in every country except Czechoslovakia in 1968 (then euphoric with liberalization) I got stock replies.

The kind of impression I was expected to take away from such occasions seems to be taken away not only by naive westerners, but also by a number of older East Europeans themselves. 'I don't know why you should think that the youth organizations and politics are of little importance to our young people,' a Bulgarian university lecturer in her forties, whom I was seeing in private, said to me with real anger. 'My youngest daughter has just been accepted in the Pioneers, and the initiation ceremony was clearly the greatest experience of her life.'

The inference that therefore politics would also remain one of the most important things in the little girl's life seems equally to be drawn by many of those whose job it is to cope with young people every day. Propagandists holding courses are notorious for believing that the meek silence and stock responses of their listeners signal success, that is, profound changes in the outlook of the next generation. Many of the Youth League officials, putting the brochures and statistics before me, also appeared to believe that these indeed meant something beyond printer's ink on paper which they were paid to dispense. When officials and Party men make speeches about problematic attitudes and ways of life prevalent 'among certain sectors of our youth', and propose to deal with these problems through renewed efforts to 'raise the level of ideological awareness of our young people', they too appear very often to believe in the validity of their own proposals. If they did not, presumably they would not try so hard to have them implemented, spending vast sums on propaganda, and everyone's time on political study sessions in schools, Youth League seminars and ideological courses at universities.

Nor would so many young people respond to the inherent expectations not only by giving stock replies to stock questions, but also by writing poems and compositions which I myself have seen or heard their teachers describe, in which postures and Party rhetoric had overwhelmed all live thought and feeling. There would not be a number of children in each school class producing these vacuous pieces if there were not a number of adults, in and out of school, expecting, accepting and rewarding them as truth – which they thus become for many of the children themselves, who from then on treat the rhetorical effort as 'politics' and their own response to it as required participation.

What makes the exercise especially futile, however, is not that so much of the response to it is vacuous. It is that even if all of the response were sincere, the resulting enthusiasm would only be of limited use. Ideological fervour and readiness for heroism may be of supreme value to the collective in battle situations, but the peacetime that now prevails in Eastern Europe necessitates entirely different forms of involvement. Not being able to understand this is what makes those moving on the rhetorical plane, however sincere they themselves may be in their beliefs, so sadly quixotic. Most vocal in the hard-line faction of each Party, they are in fact the people whom the situation of the Party as besieged Hero has alienated most strongly from reality.

The second plane of truth is, by contrast, that of black despair. To this plane the Party itself descends only by implication. In its periodic outbursts about 'unprincipled admiration for the West and indifference to our country and its history', or 'contempt for hard work and taking things for granted', or 'insufficient ideological preparedness and political lack of interest' or '*carpe diem* attitudes and bourgeois nihilism', it always states that these exist only 'among certain small sectors of our youth'. However, by now the Party's dialectical mannerisms are so well known in Eastern Europe that when it talks of dislikeable behaviour that it has noted among 'a minority', everyone actually listening knows that it means a mass phenomenon, about which it is seriously disturbed.

This is the more so as in deploring such phenomena the Party is only articulating the sentiments of many older people, almost regardless of political allegiances. If there are members of the central and senior generations who see the young in the crimson terms of rhetoric, there are a good many more who give up with them in black despair. 'I sometimes think they weren't worth it,' said a retired Party functionary on a trip to the West. 'For instance now, looking at young people here. Ours are just like them, more or less. Nothing interests them, only music and clothes and themselves. What difference have we made, and all the things we went through?' Many older-style nationalists are just as unhappy. 'They don't care,' a forty-eight-year-old resistance veteran said in Warsaw in May 1970, when I asked him why he thought the young were not going to the war films poured forth by the Polish film industry under Partisan domination. 'The things that were sacred to us mean nothing to them. What matters is that the Germans make good cars and have money. Mind you, I think they're learning from the regime, there are many people up there to whom nothing else matters either.'

Despair may also be caused by the political apathy of the young. 'Not long ago, I went to a provincial school for a "writers'-readers' meeting",' a forty-four-year-old Hungarian poet told me. 'The boys were nice, there was quite a discussion, first about my work, then about literature and films and so on. Then one of them brought up a sort of unsafe question. "Leave that," somebody else in the hall said, as if "that" would spoil the evening. I got mad. I answered the question, and then insisted that we talk politics. After a lot of prodding, some did, but only just. To think that in another ten to fifteen years we shall be handing the country over to these people. . . . 'Or it may derive from simpler, down-to-earth concerns. 'When I look at them at work, I could cry sometimes,' a fifty-three-year-old woman said in Bulgaria. 'In the office, they're making coffee, telephoning their friends, the girls filing their nails, the boys doing I don't know what, everything but work. It's not even as if they had to rest, the younger ones, because they've a second job or are digging the vegetable garden at home. . . . Down at the plant, wastage everywhere. The other day they brought in some bricks in lorries, to rebuild something. You should have seen the way they threw them down,

I bet half of them broke and couldn't be used. How can a country live like this?'

There are also not a few young East Europeans who see their own age groups in a desperate light. 'There's no reason to pity our lot,' a twenty-one-year-old Hungarian writer said, echoing his older colleague. 'It's not so much that we're muzzled as that we aren't interested. At the university, it doesn't matter if the lectures are compulsory or not, people come in for the company and sit there and talk through the thing, the lecturer can be as brilliant as he likes. And it's the same with everything else.'

'Really, we have no ideals,' a twenty-eight-year-old engineer said on the Bulgarian sea coast. 'A true ideal is something you can't have but you feel sure your children will. And you work for it. But we have none. We dream about a job, then a flat, then a car. These things don't come easily, but still, once we have them, what? Disorientation. . . . '

The plane of despair is, of course, closer to the facts than the plane of rhetoric. The unreality of its black image derives only from a comparison of how young people actually behave with ideals which have either been made unreal by the age, or have never been real at all. But this is damning enough. A proclivity for making such comparisons is in fact one of the things that has doomed the New Left to failure in the two traditionally heroic countries of Eastern Europe, where it has been most discernible. Despite its idealism, about which there could be little doubt, 'If there's ever a real attack on the Youth League,' a university official in Budapest said, 'it comes from the Left. The apathetic majority and the vague rightists don't care. To them the League is an organization they've entered to get into university and get jobs. If otherwise it does nothing, or just puts on dances, they won't shed tears. It's the leftists who'd like to make something of it, on the shock-troop lines of the Leninist Komsomol, and the Communist youth groups of the 1945-8 period. But these are not Lenin's days, nor the 1945-8 period, nor, thank God, the years of Stalinism. Nobody wants shock-troops now.' In fact, by growing shrill about political involvement in the all-or-nothing fashion of bygone days, the New Left has become associated in the eyes of the young with just those hard-liners in the East European political spectrum, whose bureaucratic rule it so vehemently rejects.

Below the twin planes of crimson rhetoric and black despair lies the plane of realism, which hope colours green. Central to this are two things. One is, precisely, a recognition of the value of other than spectacular forms of involvement. 'I suppose my grandfather would say I don't love Poland,' a thirty-one-year-old naval engineer said in Gdansk. 'To him, and to my father's generation too, patriotism meant a glorious rushing about on horses. Fighting for the country, and dreaming about it, and going off to fight for the freedom of every other country on earth. One of our great poets in the last century called the Poles "Christ among the nations". Well, it's true that sort of thing doesn't mean much to me. But I design ships. We export most of them. And when I think of people travelling in one of our ships, I know that if they like it, they'll say it's a nice Polish ship, and if they don't like it they'll say it's a rotten Polish ship. And I think of that, not all the time, but it's there somewhere in my mind. I don't know if it's the same with people who design ships in Germany or England or America, maybe not. But we're a small country, so we do think like that.'

This consciousness of being the son of a small country, with special claims to the loyalty or at least attention of its people, I met again and again while interviewing young East Europeans, often even in those who might, in reply to a direct question, have denied it. 'I think everybody should be allowed to go where they like,' an engineering student about to get his degree told me in Bucharest. 'Wherever they can find the best life for themselves. This idea that we must be patriotic is just an excuse to keep the borders closed, with us inside.' But only a few minutes later he was already telling me about the row of new hotels put up along the Romanian seacoast, with the kind of pride and sense of ownership which I found widespread about similar novelties in each East European country, but which I doubt they would excite in many students in the West.

The same sense of ownership may also on occasions override political issues. It manifests itself in an attitude of 'my country, right or wrong' among quite a number of those without sufficiently developed ideas about democracy. 'And even if we don't look on Poland as our fathers did,' a twenty-two-year-old laboratory technician said in Warsaw, 'if the country were in danger, of course we would fight. But it's not, not in that kind of danger. And the reason we don't go to see these war films is because we've seen too many, and these are bad films.'

As regards social apathy, survey after survey on the life-aspirations of young East Europeans has in fact shown that while personal goals are always thought to be of the first importance, a good many young people were looking next for social involve-ment. Naturally enough, it is much easier for people in the managerial strata to realize such aspirations while doing their jobs than it is for junior clerks, sales-girls in shops or semi-skilled labourers. But at least the willingness seems to be there. Mean-while, the kind of criticism young East Europeans level at the society that surrounds them also shows more care than selfishness. Concerning apathy at work, for instance, again and again I found them not revelling in it but criticizing the system for having given it birth, and allowing it to live on. 'It's different in the West,' one of the four young workers I quoted at the start of Chapter 1 said in Prague. 'That was one of the things I liked out there, people taking care over their work.'

'Because if they don't, they get kicked out,' another of the four said. 'Not here. Or if they are, they go somewhere else and do the same thing, and it still comes out of our pockets.' In both Czechoslovakia and Poland surveys among students found that when asked to compare capitalism and socialism, even those who gave socialism its due mentioned as one of its disadvantages that it killed people's interest in their work.

The same kind of caring is often manifest in their socio-political criticism, even though they themselves may think they are apathetic. 'Politics don't interest me at all,' a twenty-three-year-old travelling salesman said in Hungary. In no time and without any special prompting from me, however, he was talking about the kind of life he had been seeing in the country and on his journeys to and fro. 'People in Budapest don't know. About the areas in the east, and other places too, and the poverty there is. And about the labourers, tens of thousands of them, travelling half-way across the country so as to bring home a living wage at the end of the week. They're de-levelling wages now, but if you travelled on those trains with those people, you'd go careful about that. There's the crowd of a revolution travelling on those trains, every Monday to work, home every Saturday afternoon.'

Nor are actual politics very much less of an obsessive pastime for an intellectual minority than they have traditionally been. 'In the last century, there were freemasons' lodges,' a twenty-one-year-old student said in Cracow. 'Well, the fact is, we too have our freemasons' lodges, circles of five to eight people who get together to discuss things, among them politics. One thing leads to another, people may start off talking about the moon-shot, and end on politics. I couldn't tell you how many plans for doing something about this country are formulated in just this one city in one night.' Admittedly, this appears to be more the case in the three northern countries than in the two southern ones, whose political traditions are less developed and whose history since Stalin's death has seen no real upheavals. 'We're not like the Poles or the Czechs,' I heard again and again in Romania and Bulgaria during my 1968 trip, when there were student riots in Poland and liberalization in Czechoslovakia. 'There'll never be such things here,' a twenty-six-year-old Bucharest woman said. 'People here will just put up with what is, until it changes. They're not used to getting worked up about politics, there have never been any real revolutions.'

Even on this point, however, appearances can be deceptive. In Poland itself, the swift progress of the March 1968 riots from Warsaw to other university towns took many people by surprise. 'When I heard what was going on in Warsaw,' a twenty-one-year-old girl studying psychology in Cracow said, 'I thought to myself, it would be fifty years before anything like that would start here, the way people are about politics. There'd hardly ever been any discussions like the ones I knew had often broken out when politicians went to speak at students' meetings in Warsaw. But I was wrong. In two days the whole university was in motion. People I'd always known as completely apolitical and interested only in their work suddenly started to talk, and write poems and draw political cartoons, and circulate leaflets and stick them on walls. And they knew what they were talking about, it wasn't as if they'd never thought about politics.'

In Czechoslovakia, too, and at much the same time, the participatory zeal and political acumen of the young took even their immediate elders by surprise. 'We always thought they just weren't interested,' said a thirty-six-year-old editor of youth programmes on TV in Bratislava. 'Judging by the conferences we'd held, and the thousands of letters we got every week, they'd seemed to care only about pop music and pop stars, and fashion and travel, and their careers, and that sort of thing. Then all of a sudden, when things began to move, they not only wanted to partake, but often knew better just what had to be done than people in my generation did.'

However, the second element central to the plane of realism with hope is precisely an awareness of what makes large-scale and genuine involvement at times when things are not 'on the move' impossible in Eastern Europe. This is true in the economy as much as in politics. 'Most people don't care a damn, and if you had a job here you'd soon realize why. It's impossible to care,' a twenty-four-year-old construction engineer, in his second working year with a building firm, said in Poland in 1968. 'What happens at my place is that the plan says we have to spend so much money in so many months. In the winter, too, when you can do very little building; concrete laid in our winter won't set properly. But the manager can't not fulfil the plan, so he makes the workers work, construct staircases and so on, which we all know will have to be knocked down in the spring, and done again. . . . It all becomes useless. Why do you think there's this saying in Poland: "Whether I sit or lie, I get my two thousand* . . ."? Because people are rotting in their jobs, and they don't care.'

It is in fact on such conclusions that most of the pragmatic reforms of the economy in Eastern Europe have been based, as even those affected by the most timid of these reforms soon realized. 'They know what they're doing,' a twenty-nine-year-old metal-founder said to me in 1968 in Bulgaria, where a system of

* 2,000 *zloty*, the average salary.

'private brigades' was then being tried. He and two friends had recently formed such a brigade. 'If we contract for something, they know we'll try to be on time, not like the state firms. Better stuff, too, they won't buy it from us unless it's all perfect. And we get more money, even though our taxes are higher. We don't waste things. We work in our own time, with nobody standing behind us; still we work much harder. It's for ourselves.'

Indeed, working not for some impersonal 'them' but recognizably for 'ourselves' has often proved more important than the money to be earned. In a Polish survey conducted in 1965, to the question 'Do you think you can contribute to the welfare of the people?' much the highest percentage of positive answers came from children of peasants.[1] 'The main reason seems to be,' the sociologist in charge of the survey told me, 'that to them doing things for the rest is an immediate matter. They nearly all live on farms which their families own, and also when they partake in community projects it's for their own village, building a road or a schoolhouse, and they can see its use.'

In politics, too, what dooms the Party's effort to failure is that it isolates 'them' from 'us', whether we are interested in actual politics or not. In response to 'their' rhetorical effort, young East Europeans have in fact developed the regurgitation of rubbish with an air of conviction into a whole art form. Tragicomic in nature, it has even been analysed by the Party press itself in periods of pragmatism, and I may claim to have seen some perfect and even bewildering performances. Not only did young East Europeans often give me, in the presence of some unreliable person, wholly consistent exposés of what, on a subsequent private meeting, they dismissed as absolute nonsense, but more than once they even reversed the process.

In Romania, for instance, three young people I met during my initial visit to the country in 1968 talked frankly on first meeting me and then changed, for our second encounter, to the propaganda line. This they expounded with the same air of frankness, despite my ever more incredulous questions, and attempts to revert to the tone established earlier. I found out what had come over them only during my return visit, in the following year. 'When we'd left you after the first meeting,' one of them explained, 'we suddenly looked at each other and said, good God, what have we been saying to this man? It's bad enough if he goes and writes about it with our names, but what if he's from the police posing as a western journalist? . . . So we decided to be careful. And then your questions also became more probing, which made us really afraid. It was only when you sent us a postcard from out there that we thought, he can't be police, we aren't important enough for them to go to such lengths. You don't know how pleased we were!'

In Poland, too, despite long periods of pragmatism since 1956, the tragicomic art remains part of every young person's prime skills, and the performance is put on with a sure instinct. 'You should have seem them at meetings after the March riots,' a Warsaw lecturer related in 1968 with some glee. 'Party speakers tried their best to provoke them, so the leaders who stood up to argue could be picked off. But the only ones who spoke made approving noises, and the rest listened sagely, letting the speakers go on and on, until they had to give up.'

In pragmatic Hungary, the propaganda machine itself has entered the tragicomedy with honest panache by now. The 1969 current affairs compendium for secondary-school leavers to which I referred on page 89 introduces itself thus: 'What non-academic questions may come up in the finals? And what sort of things will they ask during the university entrance exams about Czechoslovakia, Vietnam? What literary debates have there been in the past year? How's the entrance exam actually conducted? These are the questions our book answers. . . . It gives a résumé of all that is not in the textbooks, nor could be as it is so recent; but it must nevertheless be known, because it is on the basis of such knowledge that students' general acquaintance with affairs will be judged.'[2]

It would be difficult to be much nicer about compulsory verbiage. But the inherent approach also goes some way towards explaining young East Europeans' cynicism about Vietnam, as well as the unwillingness of schoolboys to spoil a good evening's talk with a poet about literature with chit-chat about politics. Literature is 'ours', politics generally 'theirs', so let 'them' worry about it.

'And here we come to the root of the matter,' wrote a student of mathematics in an article in the Slovak writers' weekly, responding to the campaign 'The Party Talks to Youth' in 1966.

> Students are keenly aware of the fact that, unfortunately, the follow-ing words of Lenin are not always abided by in our country: 'God forbid that our Party should get to the state where politics are made secretly, somewhere at the top, behind locked doors, saying to our-selves: we are the ones who know what is best, we are able to recog-nize the whole truth and we shall tell the people half, a quarter, an eighth of the truth. . . . Every citizen must be given the opportunity of participating in the deliberation and in the execution of measures taken by the state'. . . . [As this has long been otherwise], no one wants to burn his fingers any more or poke his nose into things that don't concern him; it is much easier to agree with those who are 'older and more experienced'.[3]

This was also, he explained, why young people were interested only in their own careers and lives, and whatever pleasures they could find.

For the Party to have to be reminded of Lenin's words is paradoxical enough. But worse is the fact that hard-liners, while they grow hoarse in calling for mass enthusiasm, also regularly and deliberately kill youth's desire to participate, rejecting as subversive everything but the vacuous and in practice useless responses to their own rhetorical effort: 'March '68 taught us a lesson for meddling in politics,' the twenty-one-year-old student of psychology I quoted earlier said in Cracow in 1970. 'Demon-strators were badly beaten, girls were kicked in the stomach, one I know carried bruises on her back for months. Then there were interrogations, much stricter surveillance, then the trials of stu-dents which we all knew they put on to frighten us. They also increased the work-load. More political seminars, much more work in other courses, and a whole month of factory work in the summer. They want students to be too busy to think of politics, and too scared to take part in anything. And the lesson sinks in. People aren't meddling in politics now, it's not worth the trouble. Once again, they get on with their work, and are interested only in their careers and themselves.'

In fact, when some eight months after this conversation took place the workers rioted in December 1970, social and political reasons combined to keep the students aloof. 'They didn't help us in '68, so why should we have helped them now?' said a Polish student visiting London in early 1971. 'Also, we tried and only got into trouble, so this time, let them have a go.'

What makes the paradox even more poignant, however, is that even at its most pragmatic and humane, the Party must remain Hero in total charge. This alienates it from the people in as many situations as exist between them, rendering plain speech, trust and spontaneous interaction at best exceptional.

For example, despite any amount of decentralization in the economy, the Party has retained the right to prescribe and intervene at all levels. Even where factory councils have been allowed, decisions rest with the manager, appointed from above. In the same way the police may have been chastised for their 'excesses' and become altogether tamer, but they still constitute the Hero's private army and intelligence corps. If thugs no longer drag people from their beds, it is enough for well-spoken and occasionally university-trained men to invite citizens for chats, and acquaint them with details of all they have said and done in the circle of even their closest friends, to chill the atmosphere. It can be no surprise if people feel little involved in their work, and if feelings about the police emerge even in the most liberal countries at the most peaceful times in such quibbles as: 'Q.: Why do policemen always walk round in threes? A.: Because one can read, one can write and the third one is needed to make sure these two intellectuals won't get up to any mischief.' And when times turn critical, police behaviour itself becomes vicious primarily because the force fears the people – whom it thus provokes still more. It is generally agreed, for instance, that the Polish workers' demonstrations of December 1970 would not have developed into full-scale riots had the police not charged and shot into the crowd, eventually killing an estimated minimum of two hundred people.

And however many elected bodies may have been allowed or created by the Party, it remains in control at the very least through the statutory number of card-carriers they contain.

'What used to happen,' a twenty-six-year-old Party member, who in his university days had been on his faculty's student committee, explained in Prague in 1969, 'what used to happen was that though we had all been genuinely enough elected by the students, before each meeting of the committee the Party members would hold a separate meeting. At this they would be told what the Party line was on all issues to be debated, and when the actual meeting came, they would all stick to this line. That decided everything. Not only because they formed a determined caucus against the rest, but perhaps even more because the rest knew that the line the Party members took had backing from above, so there was no point in voting against it. When I once voted in the open meeting otherwise than I had been told to vote, I was threatened with expulsion from the Party for a major breach of discipline.' In other words, representatives of the people may be elected, but only if they agree to become part of the tragicomedy, which will inevitably alienate them from their electorate.

It is this permanently tragicomic situation that abnormalizes both the Party's and the people's views of politics. The tensions, which, derived from the same situation, so enliven East Europeans' experiences when seeing a play or reading a book 'craze' their appreciation of civic reality even more naturally. In fact, just as brave but otherwise not very good books and plays to which extraneous tensions had lent power emerge as really not very good when these tensions relax, so issues which only the permanently tragicomic situation makes political may disappear altogether once the situation has been abolished.

The parallel is precise, and its political side was illustrated for me where its literary side (as quoted on page 118) had been, in Prague. 'The main reason why students' political interest began to lapse in the summer of 1968,' a twenty-four-year-old graduate in English recalled the following year, 'was not just their natural apathy. It was more that they had lost their aim. When the campaign for founding a spontaneous students' organization had started back in 1965, the aim had counted as political, and the campaign as a political act. Several of its leaders were kicked out of the university or called up for army service, which was really what stirred up the students and grouped them into a political movement. But by the time the aim was achieved and the organization was founded, in April 1968, spontaneity was no longer a political issue, everybody could have it. So the movement fell apart.'

The arch-paradox is thus that the Party is obliged to force spontaneity into movements opposed to itself, because without such a circle of opposition it too would fall apart. Though claiming to be the essence of the people, the last thing it can afford is to be spontaneously popular. In fact, the few occasions on which it has become even half-way so have only proved the point, teaching both the Parties and the peoples of Eastern Europe their truest-seeming lessons in politics.

Each time the process began with a revival of sincerity. It is the quality most patently banished by the system, and most sincerely missed by the young. For years, in survey after survey, sincerity has been named as among the most important of human qualities, and in politics its absence has made it seem almost a panacea. 'There might be a way of getting through to them,' said the twenty-nine-year-old woman whom I quoted at the beginning of this chapter, attempting to answer her own question towards the end of our interview. 'Not just my kids, but the whole country. If they could turn round and say to the people "Now look here. We're in the shit. For these and these and these and these reasons that we know, and you tell us some more. Now, if you do this and this and this and this, and we do that and that and that and that, then there's a chance that we might be able to climb out of this shit." I'm sure people would at least give it a try.'

'Yes, I think they would try,' the twenty-three-year-old Cracow student of English whom I have quoted several times in the previous chapter said in 1970. 'Even now, after everything that's happened, they would. You don't know how much people would like to believe in something here. And they could believe even in socialism, a lot of us think something could be done with it. If there was someone who could make it credible. Like Dubček. People would try, they would do fantastic things if they could really believe it mattered.'

Like Dubček. . . . What had most clearly distinguished him had been his sincerity. 'There's not the falseness we've been seeing for years, none of that about Dubček,' I heard again and again in Czechoslovakia in the summer of 1968. 'If he went on TV and told people that first of all we had to tighten our belts, all of us,' said a twenty-two-year-old student of economics in Bratislava who thought reforms had to begin with austerity, 'from him people would take it.' 'Yes they would,' one of the four young workers I quoted earlier said in Prague. 'Even if people don't have more to start with, they'll work harder if they know they're not just being manipulated. And if he said so, they'd believe it.' In a documentary film made at about the same time, a char-woman interviewed said, 'It's so nice to be doing the floors now. . . .' 'Yes, that was it,' said a twenty-seven-year-old cameraman, recalling that scene in Slovakia in March 1969, 'she was right. It became nice to work. Whatever you did, it felt good to be doing it.'

Beyond the sheer exhilaration of surprise, sincerity from an East European Party leader, in the form of revelations about the past and straight talk about the present and the future, will politi-cize the people and especially the young in at least five important ways. Cutting through the maze of dead propaganda, it makes even complex issues seem immediate. Disarming former stock responses, it releases people from their tragicomic state of isola-tion. Generating a sense of purpose, it offers everyone a chance of doing some good, and so of being their best selves. Arousing excitement throughout the country, it touches the heart of patriotism. And establishing trust between the people and a visible leadership, it creates unity and hopes of worthwhile progress. In short, it provides for that identification of the individual ego with the collective super-ego manifest in a true élite, whose historic heritage in Eastern Europe the Party has been trying to appropriate and activate all along.

I know from personal experience the ease with which develop-ments such as occurred in 1968 in Czechoslovakia can activate it in young East Europeans. In the spring of 1956, when I was still at secondary school in Budapest, the Danube flooded southern areas of Hungary. A few weeks later schools began to recruit volunteers to help with reconstruction during the summer holidays. Our form-master, a well-meaning but none too brilliant Party promotee, came in one morning, made a speech full of the usual jargon and then said 'Well?' with the air of someone sure of losing yet another battle. In a proverbially apathetic form, about a dozen out of the thirty-seven boys stood up, myself among them.

The floods represented, of course, a real emergency, and reconstruction a visible purpose. But quite apart from that, the political excitement in the country had created in all of us a desire to participate. It had given people a sense of belonging to their country and of it belonging to them. As such it had lent our form-master's rhetoric about the call of the collective a power he had never suspected. He received our standing up in such numbers literally with his mouth agape. And when we went off to our volunteer camps newspaper reports about our work and general spirit there also very often reflected his kind of amazement. The Party was not used to having its call answered in such a way.

'Well, I'm glad there's no comparable spirit among our young people now,' said the thirty-nine-year-old Hungarian Party member whom I quoted in the previous chapter, and with whom I had reminisced about this in Budapest in 1970. 'I've yet to see an older generation or a government who know what to do with the enthusiasm of the young. Maybe it's not even people, just the way things go here. In 1945-8 we were enthusiastic, and there followed Stalinism, and the enthusiasts became part of the machinery, or remained enthusiasts, or were being persecuted. And then in 1956, there was enthusiasm, and I don't have to tell you what followed.'

What had followed enthusiasm, both in Poland and in Hungary in 1956, and in Czechoslovakia in 1968, was more enthusiasm, and generally more participation. Newspapers began to be read and to sell out, people found their voices and gathered for discussions, grievances as well as plans for something better came to the surface, action committees were formed and resolutions passed and hopes rose. And an important feature of all these developments was that the Communists who put themselves in the front line of the people's hopeful march were accepted as the heroes the Party had always described them as and wished them to be. Only now wishes and reality coincided: in Czechoslovakia in the summer of 1968 even young lovers out for walks on Sunday afternoons remembered to send Dubček postcards to assure him of their support.

Unfortunately, the Party as Hero cannot afford to arouse such real involvement. Rising out of its apathy, the people may first rally round those who alone have made its participation in the country's affairs possible. But things cannot stop at this optimal moment. If they are stopped, the state of affairs so created itself becomes an imposition, alienating support. If they go on, inevitably the Party becomes absorbed in the people. It ceases to be the Party as founded by Lenin, and becomes a party, next to which other parties are bound to appear. That is, democracy will have overwhelmed its centralism. By rallying true popularity, the Party commits suicide.

It was to preserve the Party as Hero (and thus the region as their own) that the Russians intervened in Hungary in 1956 and in Czechoslovakia in 1968, and let Gomułka in early 1957 invoke Poland's 'geographic realities' to keep his Party in power. And of course reimposition of the Party as Hero has each time entailed reimposition of its devices of control, which also inevitably alienate it from the people. To an extent this serves the Russians, on whom the Party must rely all the more to survive in power, but it also serves the hard-liners within each reimposed Party. They regularly set out to recreate in the people hatred of the Party and its agents, so as to create a fear of the people especially in the Party's agents, and to be able to exploit the alienation between them.

And while pragmatists in both Moscow and within the East European Parties have realized that absolute Party rule also makes the Party's heroic burden and isolation absolute, East Europeans have largely realized that, given geography and the Party's egocentric vision of the world, democratization cannot go too far without provoking disasters. In Hungary, the first country to be taught the bitter lesson, the thirty-nine-year-old Party member I have twice quoted summed up his feelings thus in 1970: 'I just hope things won't get much better much faster. If they do, the vast divisions will start moving, and we'll be back where we were in 1957.' In Poland, though Gomułka abused the 'geographic realities' to force his own brand of autocracy on the country, after his fall in the midst of riots in December 1970 these realities were invoked again by all those advising caution, including the Polish episcopate in a letter read in all churches. And in Czechoslovakia, where political realism had in any case the strongest traditions in Eastern Europe, August 1968 only revived these, not least among the young. 'When western students come here and see how desperate we are,' a twenty-three-year-old girl said in Prague in May 1970, 'some say it's our fault. Why do we just sit around, why don't we organize, demonstrate, set fire to the Party headquarters; they would. They just won't understand that we have to think of what will happen after that. Not only to us, but to everybody else. One of them even suggested we should kidnap the Russian ambassador. . . . '

In such conditions, however, for the Party to involve rather than just rule the people becomes as difficult as to give up its heroic position altogether would be suicidal. Yet to retain this position means generating apathy, which makes response to even the Hero's most genuine calls for help at best half-hearted; and thus the Party's heroic burden and isolation becomes ever worse, until tragedies ensue.

The last plane of truth is visible to only a very few people in Eastern Europe, living as they do in a situation of permanent abnormality. It lies beneath the plane of realism which is coloured green precisely by the hope that if only possibilities opened up, large-scale and permanent involvement would follow. It is the plane of realism without such a hope, as grey as earth, but in my view just as fertile. Among other things, it is from an understanding of its complexities that some of the most useful political ideas in the minds of young East Europeans have also grown, as I shall explain more fully in another chapter.

Basic to these ideas, however, is a rejection of undue hope, and a recognition of where the work of creating useful involvement in Eastern Europe needs to begin. Viewed on this last, grey plane, political involvement depends only partly on immediate possibilities and much more on the material security and sheer leisure, and the level of general and political education and sophistication, of those concerned. For a start, people have their own sufficiently complex lives to manage and if possible enjoy. They may become involved in public affairs when the issues themselves become simple and immediate enough, such as during a war or a major social or political upheaval, perhaps a truly decisive election. In the period of normality between, however, very few possess what it takes to be politically involved.

Just as important, while extraordinary moments may produce the kind of involvement envisaged by the Party as Hero, and also by much of its present opposition, what is actually needed in Eastern Europe is a far more complex and durable kind of readiness. That is, not a heroic state of mind, simplifying the responses of the individual and recruiting him as part of a self-defensive horde equally capable of major feats and follies, but a peacetime attitude that is more fruitful, but is also dependent for its growth or otherwise on countless choices that the individual remains free to make or reverse. It is dependent, in other words, not so much on the possibilities for sudden participation as on the kinds of individuals present to participate, and on the kinds of lives they choose, or find it possible, to lead.

Basic to the whole complex phenomenon is the conflict between spontaneity and order. Both are necessary to the recognizable functioning of both the individual and society, and the more so to their functioning well together. The order (structure) which his environment fashions out of the spontaneity of each newborn child is what gives him his individuality, just as it is the order (organization) in which society gathers the spontaneous activity of its individuals that makes it at all a society. The more order within and round themselves they consider essential for their existence, the more authoritarian they are, while the more spontaneity they can admit without fearing it as mortal chaos, the freer their relationship with the rest of the world will be.

Now the kind of battle-enthusiasm traditional in Eastern Europe may fruitfully coexist with maximum order imposed from above. But peacetime working involvement can grow only in combination with trust, that is, a decrease of self-defensive egotism all round; this alone makes it possible for people to give and receive not on terms of command and obedience, but on those of free and equally rewarding compromise. This, however, also entails the admission of ever greater amounts of spontaneous interaction in their lives. And the problem is that at some point either society or individuals within it are bound to find that spontaneity has grown beyond what their existential egos can bear and to react oppressively in self-defence.

The other problem is that spontaneity, though essential to involvement, will not necessarily result in it, even though it may not degenerate into chaos. It has countless other ways of manifesting itself, each less difficult than the first and less threatening to the individual than the second. Some of these ways may be indirectly social or political, but many others will have such names at best only imposed on them. They constitute what most people regard as, quite simply, life. And the more society provides for people's spontaneous needs, the more each individual may feel inclined to equate his aims with sheer living in self-absorption – at most extending his defensive egotism to embrace those he accepts for his own.

Thus anyone in Eastern Europe wishing to generate true involvement rather than purely tragicomic enthusiasm will have to descend to the fourth plane, that of sheer realism. The forms of order which on that plane surround and shape young East Europeans, and the ways in which as formed human beings they shape their lives, will be the subjects of my next two chapters.

5 Forms of Order

In Romania in 1969 I saw a beautiful play by a thirty-four-year-old poet. In an almost naturalistic setting it presented the story of Jonah. The only person ever on stage and talking throughout, he was fighting his way out of the whale, cutting through one layer of rubbery white fat and muscle only to find himself embedded in the next. Finally reaching freedom on an empty shore, he committed suicide.

The play over, I went backstage to congratulate the actor on a brilliantly compulsive performance. To my surprise I found that both he and the director there with him received my words with just a polite smile and thanks. They had none of the eagerness to talk that a foreigner usually meets in Romania.

Only the following day did I discover the reason for this. The censor had deemed the play 'too tragic', and was having it taken off. It had been on for only a few nights, but the performance I had seen was probably to remain its last. The author, the director and the actor had worked in vain. Jonah was not to reach the vacant shore, the spectators were not to find catharsis and relief through recognizing in another human's fate their own predicament.

Yet if only the Bucharest censor had realized it, the main fact about the predicament shown by such a play is precisely its being only to some extent political. It comes to seem more wholly political through censorship banning its presentation as human tragedy. But long before a thirty-four-year-old East European comes up against such reminders of the political order around him he will have come to know life as a struggle against forms of order closely enveloping him since birth. It is in this struggle against order, which is often as protective and productive as it is oppressive, that he will have grown into the individual he is, ordered and part of the order surrounding others in more or less protective, productive and oppressive ways, some of which he will even have come to love. For him to reach the vacant shore would mean a crisis of identity amounting to inner suicide,* almost as much as it would be suicidal for the Party to immerse itself in the free spontaneity of the people. If only the censor could see the Party in sufficiently human terms. . . .

Of course the Party's heroic-centralist rule does influence many of even the most intimate forms of order surrounding young East Europeans, in the direction of authoritarianism. But far more important is the effect of the East European environment and its native traditions on each of these forms, and indeed on the egotistic visions and behaviour of the Party itself.

The world over, all forms of order surrounding a person are by nature authoritarian. They all exist to shape his attitudes and behaviour in ways that are foreign to him at the outset, and in some cases remain so for ever. The family, for example, beyond physically taking care of humans who cannot as yet do so for themselves, is also society's agent for imposing on the spontaneous nature of every new-born child the order that will enable him to survive as a recognizable individual among the rest. For this reason, there are no completely 'democratic' families in the world, only families that are less or more authoritarian, depending on how long parents continue to distrust each new-born child's own skills and judgement, and how aggressively they teach their own. The same is true, *mutatis mutandis*, of every other form of order shaping the mind and actions of a person, from his circle of friends and his school and neighbourhood to his place of work as an adult, and the social environment of which he becomes a part.

In Eastern Europe, however, nearly all of these forms of order are more authoritarian than they are in the West. The reasons for this have to do mainly with traditions surviving in strength, some recent events I shall later explain, and to a very much smaller extent – especially during anyone's formative years – with politics. True, the Party's heroic-centralist system is the form of order

---

* As I know from the experience of many *émigré* friends, and from my own. With luck, and much difficulty, one may be reborn later.

which surrounds all East Europeans throughout their lives, but by the time they come in active contact with it they are as good as grown individuals, with reactions at the ready to cope with any version of authoritarianism imposed upon them. Essentially, being the final embodiment of the authoritarian traditions of the area, the Party comes to young East Europeans reaching adulthood as no surprise.

In the average East European family, for example, the authoritarian period is still a good deal longer than it is in the West, and the manner of treating the children, though affectionate, aggressive. 'Some time ago I had a colleague here from Denmark,' an eminent Hungarian child-psychologist recounted. 'One Sunday I took him down to an open-air pool, and he was amazed at the way people behaved with their children. He said that if Danish children had to put up with as much aggression from their parents, they'd probably go mad. The reason they don't go mad here, at least not visibly, is because they see everybody treating their children in this way, so they accept it as loving care, and then they grow up to face an aggressive environment, where what they've learnt comes in useful.'

Aggression may be physical, mental or both. Beating children in pure anger, often not even at them but just at life, looks back to long traditions, especially among poorer East European parents, and is still accepted practice in a number of families. But beating children 'for a pedagogical purpose' has also survived, up and down the social scale. 'Whether we feel like slapping the children or not,' a twenty-nine-year-old teacher said in Poland, 'a lot of parents will come to us and ask that we should beat their children hard, it's what's good for them.' In a Budapest school, a survey conducted by teachers in the mid-sixties found that four-fifths of the children were being beaten at home, some severely.[1] 'Things mount up,' a thirty-one-year-old lawyer, with sons aged six and eight, explained in Slovakia. 'Then when the list is full, I take off my belt and give them a good hiding. That clears the account, and there's peace, and later they can watch TV. I don't think they mind, I'm sure they know it's good for them, hardens them for life.'

Mental aggression is more a matter of seeing children as 'mere children', often well into their adulthood. It may or may not be combined with physical punishment, but underlying it is the assumption that the young cannot understand grown-up reasoning or work out things for themselves, and so need peremptory guidance from their elders. At the same time, whereas beating is more often doled out by fathers, psychological domination of the children has always been the mothers' role (combined, even in many seemingly patriarchal families in Eastern Europe, with domination of the fathers themselves). Mothers have also tended, to be, especially in middle-class and lower middle-class families, the more 'productionistic' of the two parents, more interested in the family's daily bread and security, and in the children's schooling and material future. Perhaps the best indication of how things have long stood in Eastern Europe is the fact that though Jewish jokes are legion, the joke about the Jewish momma is virtually unknown. An odd transplant in the Anglo-Saxon countries, in Eastern Europe she represents in many ways the norm.

In addition to parents as affectionate as they are aggressive, young East Europeans are surrounded by families that are on the whole much more close-knit than they are in the West. Not only are distances inside each country rather small (while emigration is virtually nil) but rural families have tended to move to cities together, while the cities themselves have remained fairly small and thus manageable. At the end of the sixties the average population of even the five capitals amounted to no more than 1·3 million. In the whole region there were only four provincial cities (all in Poland, the most populous country) with more than 400,000 inhabitants, and only another ten (of which none was in Romania or Hungary) with between 200,000 and 400,000[2].

This has, among other things, allowed many extended families to survive for generations. At the same time, an even larger number of families have remained three-generational. This is due partly to housing conditions which offer the majority of newly-weds the choice of either staying with parents (most often the wife's), or moving in with total strangers, and partly to the fact that, with the majority of women working and nursery places still far from sufficient, grandparents take care of the children even in many urban families. 'Whether it's psychologically better or worse for the children, it's the only solution,' said a Prague sociologist. 'Women not only want to go out to work, but they're also needed. It's even been said that success in the building of socialism depends not on the completion of heavy industrial targets, but on the availability of grandmothers.'

The closeness of families, combined with the proximity of the rural past – and, indeed, present, as in several countries of the region over half the children still grow up in the countryside – naturally tends to keep older traditions of upbringing alive. At the same time, the physical and often psychological shocks that the years since the start of the Second World War have administered to today's parent generations in Eastern Europe have also helped to make their members more aggressive towards their children, in both their loving and their magisterial ways. If they often over-protect and over-guide their young, this is in no small measure because they fear for the latter in an environment they themselves have known as deadly dangerous. And the shocks of their lives have only increased their own need to find security in the obedience of their young, in whom they will survive.

But even when all the reasons for the survival of family authoritarianism are known, the results can be saddening. 'In London, I often watched people playing with their children in the parks on Sundays,' another Hungarian child-psychologist told me. 'What struck me most was how much less condescension there was about the whole thing than we're used to here. They were treating the children much more as potential adults. Here, the idea of talking a nonsense language to children, or talking only about "childish" things, or just telling them what to do "because I say so", is still more or less the norm.'

Condescension allows, of course, for a good deal of cosseting, which has been made all the more possible by increased prosperity. What it often prevents, however, is the evolution of certain more participatory 'games' among parents and children, which might help the latter to mature earlier and to develop the habit of genuinely giving of themselves, rather than performing roles on command or under pressure. In other words, it banishes sincerity. Instead, it maintains an atmosphere in which independence from below goes on being regarded by both sides as revolt, bound to provoke aggression from above or at least to produce hostility in between.

This is in fact the basic form of the order-situation young Jonah will meet again and again, until he grows up to find that it prevails in its most acute form between himself and the Party. And though his parents are much the most loving versions of 'them' he will ever know, Jonah will learn to see 'their' alienation from 'us', and the tragicomic performance the two sides put on for each other, as perfectly natural in the home.

The behaviour of the next major form of order he meets, namely school, will have been shaped by the same traditions and present factors as those that have influenced that of his family. Teachers have been through the same upbringing and experiences as parents. Even if they are not yet parents themselves, they are *in loco parentis* during the school day, and if they have more pedagogical training – itself very much within the local tradition – they also have many more children to manage. In fact their sense of responsibility often reinforces their authoritarianism very simply because holding children down and putting into their heads all that will get in is what teachers know as the ideal.

I found the power of tradition most clearly illustrated in the attitudes of a Romanian science master in his forties, whom I interviewed in 1969. Parents of children he taught, and several of the children themselves, had described him as both conscientious and very popular, and during our interview I myself got the impression of a devoted and at the same time enterprising pedagogue. Still, many of his basic reflexes were rooted in the magisterial tradition beyond much hope of change.

For example, I mentioned that for some time I too had taught in London schools, and described to him the kind of debates we used to have in class, with a motion, speakers for and against, then a discussion, then a vote. When I had finished, his immediate question was, 'But then you told them the answers, didn't you?' I said I might have taken part in the discussion, and after the vote pointed out who I thought had argued well, but the issues were for the class to decide, that had been the object of the exercise. 'And you just left it at that?' he asked, laughing, but with as much surprise as anxiety in his voice. He seemed to think that this was bad teaching: it gave the children no certain knowledge or standards, and could undermine the teacher's authority. When we got round to talking about more participatory teaching methods, of which he appeared to have tried many more than most of his colleagues, the fear of losing traditional authority came once again to the surface: 'One of the problems with these newer methods is,' he said, 'that you'll be challenged by the children all the time. So you need much more self-confidence than a young teacher would generally have to retain your hold over the class, and have to be much better prepared than most of us are, otherwise the children will catch you out.'

Of course all schools are by nature authoritarian institutions, for the same sort of reasons and in the same sort of ways as families are. If they offer Jonah freedom from close parental supervision, and a whole new 'underground' to give him support, they also impose on him more difficult forms of discipline, and novel hierarchies, slotting him into a place according to his abilities to conform and perform. In East European schools, however, authoritarianism has long been more pronounced, mainly because education has aimed much less at encouraging self-realization and self-improvement in its charges, and much more at acquainting them with high culture, which meant regular habits, ready knowledge and respect for visible performance.

This has always put an enormous burden on teachers. The average ones can only try to impose discipline on classfuls of children, who are being overloaded with curricula which most of them can learn by rote but not creatively understand. But even the majority of the most conscientious and brilliant East European teachers have tended to see a position of unchallenged mastery over their classes as best for all concerned. 'We had a wonderful woman teaching us literature,' a twenty-seven-year-old Warsaw girl recalled. 'Her lessons were interesting, she brought writers and poets to talk to us, she taught many of us our love of reading. But if anybody's opinion differed from hers, or if somebody thought they knew something better than she did, she'd suppress them. . . .'*

* I myself, though taught literature in a Budapest secondary school by a man to whom my classmates and I listened with rapt silence, and whom we still

The spirit and practice of the Party's own magisterial rule since 1948 has reinforced aspects of authoritarianism in East European schools, but has not been the main cause behind them. For example, the politically blessed formulae which teachers and pupils alike have been under pressure to mouth only enlarged the repertoire of performances which the two sides would have been putting on for each other in any case. Similarly when, following the climactic period of the 1950s, Party centralism became less pronounced, the standards to which education reverted proved to be still authoritarian enough.

In 1969 in Prague, the most westernized capital, I was taken to visit a nursery school, and found the regime there much too orderly for three- to five-year-olds. The children had a weekly timetable, with regular pre-school lessons, they wore uniforms, they sat for their meals and all sedentary activities in their allotted places, hung their street clothes on allotted pegs and put their shoes beneath them. While I was being shown round they sat there in dead silence, and then performed some of the songs and dances they had learnt.

The woman who had arranged my visit, on a friendly basis, was the young mother of two children there, and an educationalist with liberal views, while the head teacher, in her late forties, had been working with young children since before the war. Yet both women seemed to take sincere pride in the way the establishment was being run. 'In the fifties, it was terrible,' the head teacher recalled. 'Especially the work-load on the children was very heavy. This was because we were copying Soviet models which had been designed for a backward country having to educate a modern generation from scratch. Now, I think the balance between work and play is about right.'

In another nursery school, in Bulgaria, the children were playing outside when I called, but the regime was much the same. It was also explained to me by the head teacher, another woman in her forties (and a graduate in philosophy),* with the

remember with loving awe, cannot recall a single occasion on which he gave me an unsigned piece of writing for independent analysis.

* When I heard this, in the course of an interview in which we had somehow got down to discussing how far society itself should be run on nursery lines,

same sincere pride: 'It's always found that children who've been through nurseries are much better prepared for school. They're healthier, easier to discipline, do better in their subjects. And they'll have learnt about life in a collective: when somebody misbehaves, we get the children together and talk about why such and such a thing is bad and what should happen to who had done it.'

Apart from the force of traditions and the pressure of circumstances, change is also made more difficult by parents' views on what their children's schooling should be like. 'The idea that children will be finding things out for themselves still seems too strange for most people to take,' I was told by researchers working on participatory methods at the Pedagogical Institute of the Czechoslovak Academy of Sciences. 'Apart from devising new methods to teach the children, and re-educating the teachers, we've also had to work out courses for parents who insist that their children should have the kind of schooling they themselves had, and whom we have to persuade that the children won't be ruined by new methods.' The Romanian science master quoted a few pages back had met the same problem in a still more basic form: 'If you start experimenting and trying to get the children to teach themselves, parents often accuse you of making the children do the job for which you're being paid. I've actually heard them put it that way.'

Perhaps the clearest example of how traditions, current pressures and parents' wishes combine to maintain magisterial practices in force is to be seen in the importance attached to marks and examination results. 'Many of us would like to replace the whole business of constant marking and exams with something much less formal,' a forty-eight-year-old deputy headmaster in Hungary said. 'It's cumbersome to us, nerve-racking for the children and often counterproductive. Some boys learn up whole pages by heart when they think they'll be called on, after which they feel they've done with the subject until the next reckoning. But even if the ministry abolished the rules prescribing so many marks for

I asked her if among philosophers she preferred Plato or Aristotle. 'Definitely Aristotle', she said, without too much doubt about the relevance of the point.

each child each term, parents would still want to know how their children are doing, all the time. And at the end of the year, all hell would break loose when they started disputing whether or not their children had been properly assessed.'

And although parents going to see teachers and trying to better their children's marks, making use of all methods from emotional blackmail to political threats, turns the whole thing into rather a tragicomedy, it continues unreformed. Heavy stress is put on marks for essays, and even more on the verbal 'testing' that each child must undergo every so often in front of the whole class, by way of keeping the lot on their toes. This clearly rewards performance in surface communication with authority much more highly than creative involvement in the subject. Encyclopedic curricula, also rooted in the tradition, make the effect still worse. As the pressure for performing well grows with every year, what comes to matter less and less, especially in the humanities, is how interesting or profound anyone's reactions may be; what will matter increasingly is how well anyone can repeat what the teacher has said on any topic.

The final performance is put on at the end of Jonah's secondary-school years. A board of austere figures descends to examine everyone, mostly *viva voce*, on virtually all the material they have ever absorbed. Effected in a few days, this is bound to prize fast showmanship to a far greater extent than any previous 'testing', while, fearsome as the examination is made to appear, only an infinitesimal number of people fail to pass it. The reason is that its main purpose is to set the seal of final approval on each generation of eighteen-year-olds as now mature (which is why the examination is called the *Maturita* or its equivalent) and to issue them with a piece of paper to this effect.

Understood in this way, the *Maturita* becomes more than anything a ritual. As such, it is a moving experience for its participants, and, especially in the smaller cities and rural areas, a major social occasion. The *maturandis* go singing through the school corridors lined with younger pupils as a guard of honour, they walk ceremonially through the nearby streets, they have their pictures in tableaux displayed in local shop-windows, and when their examination is over, they wash it down with a banquet which Jonah will remember as a unique affair, perhaps to the end of his life.

Sadly, the celebration of freedom proves premature. In fact, reaching essential independence is what brings Jonah face to face with a form of order harsher than any he has known, and destined to surround him for ever. This form of order is the adult world, with the Party as Hero at its centre. Jonah's most important experience of emerging from one form of order only to have to start struggling that much harder with the next is, exactly, that of leaving school and seeing all the major pressures of his child-hood disintegrate, and then finding himself surrounded by a system from whose mastery he cannot hope to escape. Since the idea of the Party as an élite in complete charge of the people and its environment is the final result of the magisterial tradition of Eastern Europe, in a sense Jonah may be said never to leave school at all.

What he actually does as a member of the new generation makes only so much difference. If he goes to do his two-year national service he will be freed both from parental pressures and from the responsibilities of keeping himself, but at the price of having to endure total command from above, physical and (as far as this is possible) political too. If he becomes a manual worker or takes an office job, he will leave behind school-type discipline and gain a measure of financial and personal inde-pendence, only to be so much more responsible for himself and in due course for a family; and while he is all too likely to see the school hierarchies reappear in the structure of prestige and social-status levels, and be reinforced by the centralist system, the more exposed his job is, the more vitally he will be bound to remain an actor in the tragicomedy of politics. And if he goes on to university, so realizing his parents' and his own chief ambitions for his future, and gaining what seems the most freedom, he will be the first to find that he has only entered another school. 'I won, I was admitted to university,' the young hero of a short story published in the Romanian writers' weekly in 1971 recalled. 'One month later I realized this was just another secondary school, with backward teachers, anachronistic courses, incom-petence, meetings, speeches, sneaks, sons of big shots getting by rights the highest marks, after all, everything according to ritual. . . . '[3] For absence from more than three lectures in a half-year, Romanian students may be condemned to repeating the half-year, or expelled, while throughout Eastern Europe students have their scholarships as closely geared to their performance in examinations as their pocket-money bonuses may have been at the age of twelve.

Of course by the time Jonah really comes to grips with his environment, and with the Party as the essential 'them' in every situation, he will have developed considerable skills for the struggle. Apart from having had to cope with the Party's media, and occasionally its machinery of power, and the influence of politics on the atmosphere of his school and also to some extent that of his family, he will have had direct experience of those versions and agents of the Party, the youth organizations.

It may even be said that the Pioneers and the Youth League combine for a young East European the versions of 'them' he has known since birth with those he will know until he dies. Though the Pioneers in particular provide a good deal of entertainment nowadays, both organizations reinforce parental pressures on the young to conform and perform, while they actually duplicate the structure of the schools to which they belong, and further accentuate the hierarchies. Each school form has its basic organizations, usually run by the star pupils in conjunction with the form master, as part of the school organization, itself run by the top performers and a teacher or adult functionary. If members misbehave or get bad marks, instead of finding consolation in what is supposedly their own coterie, they find that coterie joining their parents and teachers in censuring them, and so closing the circle of productionist pressure above their heads.

In exchange, while the organizations dispense Party propaganda, they find that parents and teachers often act as their allies, if not their recruiting corps. 'By the time I had finished basic school, I was as bored as hell with the Pioneers,' a twenty-two-year-old Czech girl who had just interpreted for me in an interview with a Pioneer leader said in 1970. 'Still, when I got to secondary school my parents said, "If you want to get yourself to university, you go and be something in the Youth League."

I wouldn't, but they forced me, and I went. In '68, this was one of the things I hoped I wouldn't have to do to my own children. But the way things are going now. . . . '

This is, of course, another tragicomic situation, about which teachers may in fact be as open in the classroom as parents are at home. 'My joining the Youth League came about,' an enthusiastic activist wishing to make more of the organization complained in the Hungarian youth monthly in 1970, 'by our form master just lining up the form, picking out ten boys about the same height, and saying to them, "You'll be the League members". Perhaps so we'd look good at the initiation ceremony.'[4] Similarly, Youth League leaders themselves have more than once remarked on the fact that while the League tends to be able to enrol no more (and often a good deal less) than about two-fifths of any country's young peasants and workers, the percentage of its members among students in secondary and higher schools ranges to 95, and is always the most impressive in the last, pre-university year of the secondary school.

Pragmatists in the Party, too, are aware of the situation. Nevertheless, the Youth League continues to be taken very seriously as a source of references, especially for university entry, which in turn maintains its present membership structure. To uphold the Don Quixote–King Canute League through such administrative means, is quite simply inherent in the Party's own magisterial position throughout Eastern Europe.

This is also why versions of the same tragicomedy will await Jonah as he goes through life. But the situations are likely to become ever less comic, and make ever worse demands on his skills and resourcefulness. And while all too often he will find that he has fought in vain, on every occasion he will have cause to believe that to some extent he is facing the Party, as Hero in central charge.

This is so in three main ways, all three of which inevitably derive from the Party's existential position. One has to do with the fact that heroic centralism gives scope to the dictatorial tendencies of all those in any position of power, from traffic policemen to university professors. In the economy, for example, the 'principle of one-man management' is the Party's device (as I tried to explain in the previous chapter) for ensuring that, by retaining the right to appoint all managers and consolidating all real power within an enterprise in their hands, it remains in effective control. But the same principle also suits bosses disinclined to waste their time on democratic discussion with workers and staff. Much the same is true of any number of other centralist measures, however refined they may have become in recent years, which the Party cannot see itself abolishing without entering on the road to suicide.

The second reason has to do with the totalistic behaviour of the Party's system, placing Jonah in a state of almost helpless isolation. There is little chance of his successfully appealing against the police to the bureaucracy or the media, and only slightly more chance of the media helping him against (usually single tyrants within) the bureaucracy. And when the whole of 'their' order acts against him for a deliberate purpose, he has no chance of appealing to any part of it at all. If he is kicked out of university, for instance, he will be barred from all universities in the country and thus (since he will not at the same time get a passport) from every university there is. Sacked from a job for political reasons, he will find himself excluded from all jobs of the same type, and often all jobs above the level of unskilled labour, throughout the country, and, again, effectively, the world.

The third, and probably most depressing, aspect of Jonah's captivity within the Party's system has to do with the way in which heroic centralism both magnifies and locks into a complete circle round him the problems which he would find difficult enough even in a single organization of any size. 'It's almost impossible to make a killing here, or in any way jump ahead of the rest,' a thirty-year-old company economist said in Poland. 'Changing your career is almost unheard of. You can try changing your job, but often you lose all the effort you put into getting ahead in the previous one, and you may also get yourself a bad name, if they think you've done it too often. And that's what you want to avoid most, to spoil your record in any way. So most people put themselves into some groove, very early on, and stick to it, going on and on and taking every care never to put a foot wrong, politically or otherwise. If you do, you get no second chance – that's the worst thing about the whole place, the lack of a second chance.'

Similarly, while the favouring of conformity inherent in all organizations is bound to frustrate many talented individuals, the effect is much worse, both psychologically and economically, where counter-selection rules a system ruling a whole country. 'I'm very glad, of course, that we're working ourselves free of the Russians,' a thirty-one-year-old Romanian journalist said to me in 1969. 'But our real problem is not that the Russians want to sit on us. It's that we have sitting on us a vast outdated machine, preserving itself through counter-selection. It's not the Russians, it's counter-selection that'll do us in.'

Of course counter-selection as well as many other results of the Party's centralist rule hold it, as Hero in charge, Jonah's captive companion. Heirs to the same traditions and environment and facing the same circumstances, they are 'in it together'.

At the same time, as Champion of Progress the Party is engaged in, precisely, changing Eastern Europe. This is bound to undermine the power of the area's traditions, and to affect not least the forms of order on which the situation there is structured. In due course, the results must come into conflict with the Party's centralism, until it is completely surrounded by them as Hero at the centre. But even now the Party is fast becoming imprisoned by a situation it has helped to create. Long before it has worked itself and the countries it rules free of the grip of the past, it has to face the popular pressures and demands which rapid development in the last twenty-five years has greatly heightened, and the still more complex problems of an impending future. If the Party as Hero is captive inside the traditional-authoritarian system it rules, as Champion of Progress it is even more inextricably a captive of the circumstances its own good work has brought about.

But as regards this version of the predicament, too, the Party and Jonah are 'in it together'. The forms of order surrounding and shaping him have also been changed by development in such a way as merely to replace many traditional aspects of authoritarianism with new and less escapable demands and pressures. Helped out of one layer of white fat and muscle by the Party as

Champion of Progress, Jonah has been finding himself all the more firmly embedded in the next.

Within family life, for example, urbanization and the spread of education and new ideas have brought a redistribution of roles and a democratization of the atmosphere. With women going out to work and still retaining their central position in each home, large numbers of families have become much more openly maternal. Combined with changes in views on child-rearing, this has furthered the slow change from physical to psychological methods of trying to cope with the young. Greater prosperity has allowed parents to give their children a better life, and more financial latitude in the choice of pastimes. And the fact that the whole environment has become more mobile gives both parents and children more scope for finding diversions of their own at critical times.

However, sudden urbanization has all too often meant the transference of village ways to town, and in some cases their survival in more acute forms. It has, for example, made anxieties about 'what everyone will say' almost neurotic in some people, while many parents have become all the more fierce in defence of their own standards. Even more important has been the effect of the redistribution of parental roles, and of the maternalization of family power. It has united parents to a much greater extent than before in putting productionist pressures on their children, while psychological methods of discipline often not only prove to be as effective as physical punishment, but leave much deeper marks. 'I was never beaten at home,' said the twenty-seven-year-old Warsaw girl I quoted earlier in this chapter. 'It was enough for my mother to call my name in a certain way to make me feel awful inside. What she wanted most of all was for my brother and I to get through university, and I remember if I went out even once in the weeks before my exams I never dared tell her, I felt so guilty.' She ended up having two nervous breakdowns, both mainly over her educational performance, and seemed to have remained altogether a warm but sadly defensive-aggressive person.

Increased prosperity, too, has often affected parent–child relationships adversely. As parents devote more of their time to making and spending money, their children get more from them

Forms of Order

materially, but see less of them as human beings. In due course
there develops a vicious circle of parents expressing their love of
their children ever more in material terms, and ever more
expecting visible performance from their children as recompense
for love received, while each side comes to feel that the other is
failing it. Parents complain of their children's ingratitude, while
children come to regard material generosity as the most important
attribute of good parents, as surveys among urban children in
Eastern Europe have shown.[5]

All this has combined with the effect of the Party's social
revolution. On the one hand, it has extended to the new middle
mass, and in particular the industrial working class, many
previously middle-class modes of behaviour and attitudes. For
example, working-class children who used to go out to work,
and thus become self-supporting, as adolescents now stay on at
school for several more years, and thus remain in need of support
and under much closer supervision. On the other hand, the Party
has opened wide the roads of upward mobility before children
of the manual-working classes, making even worker–peasant
fathers (in addition to mothers) interested in seeing their children
through at least secondary school. This, in turn, has transformed
traditional eagerness among intelligentsia parents into chronic
anxiety. 'There's always been a kind of fetishism here about the
notion of a "trousered man",* but now the thing has reached
insane proportions,' said the forty-eight-year-old Hungarian
deputy headmaster quoted earlier in this chapter. 'Intelligentsia
parents, and also some working-class parents, bring up their
children to think it's the end of the world if they can't get into
university. Parents start invoking this as a threat when the
children are still in the first years of primary school, but they
themselves are at least as worried about it as they make the
children feel.'

Altogether, parents' traditional awe of what everyone will say,
and their existential fear for their children in a dangerous environment, now combine with the much heavier responsibility
they feel for their children's success in a newly mobile world to

* 'Nadrágos ember' – the traditional Hungarian term for all those privileged
or educated enough not to have to work with their hands.

207

emerge in the productionist pressures put on the young. 'My father, too, always said life was not for just living but for achieving something people could recognize,' said the twenty-seven-year-old Warsaw girl I have twice quoted. 'But it was really mother who pushed us hard: father had at least achieved something, while she'd never been able to have his kind of education. So it was always she who kept telling us we had chances she'd never had, and if we failed, it would be the shame of our lives.' And developments reducing the size of East European families, and thus the number of children among whom pressure from above might be shared, has made such pressure even more difficult to bear.

Education has been affected in rather similar ways. Many more and much better fed and clothed children are going for much longer periods to more and better-equipped schools. The striking feminization of the teaching staff, paralleling the maternalization of family power and due basically to the same causes, has combined with the spread of newer ideas to change the approach to discipline and even to some extent the styles of instruction. Meanwhile the mass media have begun to provide children with more knowledge much earlier, and in forms more interesting than almost any school can generate, so helping to undermine unquestioning respect for teachers as much as unquestioning obedience to parents.

However, the democratization of the school system has put teachers in charge of still larger and more uneven classfuls, to whom they are having to teach material once reserved for middle-class schools. At the same time, the needs of rapid development have dictated that if reforms thin out curricula in one direction, they must be broadened in another. These are, in fact, two of the main reasons why more participatory methods make so little headway. 'Quite apart from the need to change your own habits', the Romanian science master said, 'you'd have to have much smaller classes than ours are, and you'd need much more equipment, maybe ten times the microscopes a biology man has. Also, with the masses of homework we have to supervise, and the extra teaching we have to do, just where would we find the time and energy to retrain?'

In addition, the democratization of society has diminished

general respect for teachers, known to be 'the proletariat of the intelligentsia', while in the new urban communities the problems of barely settled populations, which show most severely in their children, often bring out the worst in teachers who are merely trying to do their best. 'As soon as I arrived at the school,' a twenty-six-year-old woman teacher from a new Hungarian mining town related, 'I was told by my colleagues there that they all, except the oldest and most experienced men, had to beat some children. One of the men in fact offered that if I had problem boys, I should send them to him. I did, too, until one day I saw what he did to them and then, though I hated doing it, I decided I'd rather slap them hard myself. I try everything else first – the life stories I hear are at times sheer nightmare – but with some of them only beating works, and that not for long.'

Finally, the widening of opportunities has made the pressures many children have to bear debilitating, if not deadly. In Bulgaria, a survey on secondary-school children published in 1969 had found that average sixteen- to nineteen-year-olds spent ten hours a day on schoolwork, and if they took private lessons, which many of them did, and participated in Youth League activities, which most would find advisable, their work-day lasted thirteen hours. Spinal malformations had been discovered in 36 per cent of the sample, eye troubles in 23 per cent, and psychoneurotic symptoms in 18 per cent, all the figures showing steep increases compared to those of previous years.[6] In Hungary, research into the causes of the country's appalling suicide rates has shown that among fifteen- to nineteen-year-olds, more of whom died by suicide than in any other way, 'bad progress in studies' had been a significant motive.[7]

Of course the manner in which the 'traditional' and 'developmental' aspects of order combine to weigh on young East Europeans varies considerably from country to country, from class to class, and from generation to generation. As a general rule, it may be said that those 'in the middle' from the point of view of development have fared worst. Among countries, this would mean Poland and Hungary. The Czech lands have possessed an urban-industrial culture and a homogeneous society for generations, and though the ethos of the latter has always included a respect for efficiency, social conformity and small creature comforts, development in the last twenty-five years has not, at least, come to it as a shock, nor as a source of fresh neuroses. In Bulgaria and Romania, by contrast, industrialization and urbanization have been virtual novelties. But the young will have profited from this in a different way, namely, by continuing to receive a good deal in the way of traditional-type support from their parents. Not only does the peasantry still constitute well over half the population in these two countries, but in urban families, too, there is the warmest atmosphere and the strongest sense of natural cohesion to be seen anywhere in Eastern Europe.

In Hungary and Poland, however, industrialization has been a stop-go process since the late nineteenth century. While it has loosened the fabric of rural society, it has never quite allowed an urban civilization to develop, and most people could only dream of reaching the social goals it set. (It is hardly an accident that emigration since the 1880s has been by far the heaviest from these two countries.) Altogether, the neuroses which rapid development in the last twenty-five years has been bound to bring cruelly into play had long been there under the surface. Added to this has been the influence of a cultural heritage that is mostly romantic (that is, egotistic in both the self-liberating and the self-imposing sense, and very much bound up with the heroic tradition) and of the perfectionistic moral doctrines and family visions of the Catholic Church. The shock which the last war administered to parent generations throughout Eastern Europe was also much the worst in Poland, which was wiped off the map as a country and saw close to one-fifth of its population destroyed; it was probably the next worse in Hungary.

As regards classes, again the least bearable combination of old-style authoritarianism and modern pressures has weighed on children of families which have just arrived in higher strata, or are making their way into them. At one extreme of the social scale, peasant homes have remained closest to the traditional producing units in which children grew up as little workers subordinate to all those stronger than themselves, but also able to rely on a strong framework of standards and protection. In established working-class families, too, firm enough conventions and a certain pride in belonging to a skilled stratum might compensate for the amount of physical punishment doled out, and the possible lack of a cultural background necessary for making the best use of educational opportunities. At the other end of the spectrum, parents among the professional intelligentsia would usually have the subtlest ways of dealing with their children, as well as being able to give them the fullest cultural background, and the best conditions in the home. Parents belonging to the strata in between, and especially to the new non-professional intelligentsia, however, are likely to be putting the heaviest pressure on their children to succeed, without at the same time being able to apply pressure in the manner of the already well-educated. Nor can they provide anything like the same background, while very often they are too busy securing their own new places in society even to be able to offer their children enough human care.

As regards generations, parents now senior will be much closer to old-style authoritarianism in their behaviour and outlook than parents in the central age group. The latter have been affected not only by changes in conditions and in the general atmosphere, but also by newer ideas on child-rearing, at times to the extent of losing their self-confidence. In fact the central generation of parents, 'in the middle' from almost every point of view, deserves all human sympathy. It grew up under firmly authoritarian family rule in the destitute twenties and thirties, went through the war as the most dispensable part of the soldiery, and spent what should have been the best years of its life first under Stalinism and in trying to make ends meet since. Now it only finds itself blamed for allowing or actually perpetrating the horrors it mostly suffered, with its children rebelling against it in ways it cannot understand. Small wonder if at times it wishes it had been born half a century later, or earlier, than it was. 'Daddy now, to tell the truth, he was a good man,' a Polish writer of the now central generation recalled in a long article in the main Warsaw cultural weekly in 1966, blaming society's problems with the young on 'feminine liberalism' in upbringing.

He did have a heavy hand, but a just one. And he always explained what it was for. After the punishment, the case was forgotten, crossed off. A good man. He made a man of his son. One should kiss his hand for it – the heavy but wise and friendly hand. And here it is, two o'clock in the morning, and this kid is still not home. . . . Have you heard anything like it, a sixteen-year-old squirt coming home at six in the morning from a drinking party he was not allowed to attend in the first place? Parents might as well not exist for him, he would prefer to exchange them for a steady monthly income, provided the sum were large enough. . . . And one works one's fingers to the bone for this monster, to the detriment of one's health and nerves, condemned to perpetual disappointments: after all, one has placed all one's hopes in one's only son, the precious first-born. My grandfather must be turning in his grave now. He would have settled the matter differently. He would never have permitted the problem to arise in the first place. . . .[8]

Of course today's sixteen-year-olds will themselves become fathers and grandfathers in due course. From having all been 'us' as boys and girls, they will grow into men and women, and then 'them' as at least parents, if not people in posts of some responsibility, and hence authority. This is inherent in their taking over the whole of the world around them, and playing all the roles it provides. And it is at the point where – though versions of order may still be weighing on them from above – versions of spontaneity have begun to heave at them from below, that it will begin to matter how the patterns taught to them since childhood come to the surface. Basically, the whole process of shaping them aims at shaping their standards and behaviour as future owners and rulers of the environment.

In my view, the attitudes of the older and to a lesser extent also the younger of the postwar generations in Eastern Europe can offer their parents and the Party itself a good deal of comfort. Much as the young may at times rebel against authoritarian ways, their own ways very often prove to be versions of the same. The forms of order they have known since birth have imprinted a number of essential patterns on their minds, and often the same young people who actively reject old-style authoritarianism from above are brusque enough in imposing its productionist version on those they themselves have to manage.

A thirty-two-year-old Hungarian agricultural technician, for example, described to me at great length how difficult it was for him and a group of younger people in his collective to get round the ways of the 'elders', led by the chairman himself. But then, as we walked out to the fields and stopped in a vineyard, which he showed me proudly as his own creation on former wheatland, and I asked him how democratic he would be in trying to persuade members of the collective to do what he thought useful, his reply was: 'Democracy, my arse! . . . They're peasants, you can't change them, you have to bully them. You don't know how long it took before they even agreed that what they'd seen as good wheatland for ages could now be put to more profitable use as a vineyard. In the end I had to do most of the work on it myself, and even when we start bringing the money home, I'm sure they'll resent the whole thing. . . . I much prefer working with people I pay in cash, and then they do what I tell them, or get out.'

His rejection of democratic procedures as a waste of time when more important issues are at stake largely reproduced the Party's own argument. It was an expression of what I shall call the attitude of 'purposeful intolerance'. And this central feature of the authoritarian tradition, and of the Party's own dialectical-centralist philosophy and practice, seems also to be central in some cruder or subtler form to the outlook of the majority of today's young East Europeans.

They appear to consider it on the whole justified in public life and, often in still harsher ways, among themselves. As regards politics, for example, a large Polish opinion survey in 1958 found that the majority of its young respondents would have been prepared to see all restrictions short of imprisonment applied to people whose views they 'considered particularly harmful to society'.[9] In interviewing, I myself repeatedly met the belief that the State was entitled to do to the people just about anything, in the interests of what those holding this belief considered progress. A pair of Bulgarian architects, for instance, one in her twenties, the other in his late thirties, explained to me how advantageous it would be to relocate the country's entire population in the mountains, and use the plains for agriculture and industry. They were most surprised when I asked them how they envisaged driving the population up those mountains. The problem seemed not to have figured to any significant extent in their calculations.

Young East Europeans also quite often find it hard to cope with what is less than clear-cut, and thus closer to the spontaneous than they are accustomed to. For example, it can be a dispiriting experience to take otherwise intelligent and erudite members especially of the older of the postwar generations, through an exhibition of new art, and to see them sort every canvas and piece of sculpture aggressively into categories they themselves have had handed out to them by some authority. People offering them the same kind of 'unstructured' challenge are liable to provoke the same kind of aggression. 'You should have seen me in Prague,' a twenty-three-year-old Romanian film director told me in the spring of 1969, having just returned from an international conference of young *cinéastes* held in the then still-free Czech capital. 'I was furious. People were getting up, and putting their views, on and on, without anybody having had a look at what they were going to say. I wanted to shout at them to shut up and sit down and let those who know about things get on with it. I almost did, before I realized that this was democracy, and I just wasn't used to it.'

Of course intolerance is in a way only the expression of a fear to allow phenomena to come forth on their own terms, lest they bring mortal chaos, and of a complementary urge to impose one's inner order on the environment in what seem to be the interests of one's survival. But this fear and this urge, dovetailed in a pattern of defensive-aggressive egotism, are implanted in everyone by his upbringing, and are then either soothed or exacerbated by his life-experiences. Which is why, though young East Europeans differ from country to country, from class to class and from generation to generation, they are all appreciably less tolerant than their coevals and social equals in the West.

Important among the effects of their upbringing is a kind of intolerance towards spontaneity not only around but also within themselves. The more conservative the country, the more they tend to identify during their teens and often even later with discipline, and disciplinarians. 'We've found,' said the young Romanian sociologist whose views on the social pattern of contacts between generations I quoted in Chapter 3, 'that when asked to describe the adults they liked best, the great majority chose parents and teachers who made strict demands on them, whether regarding dress, manners, or results at school.'

They are also likely to form circles of their own which are neither too wide nor too free. On the whole, Jonah will look for a few intimate friends rather than many casual ones. His resulting friendships may be emotionally as taxing as they are rewarding, and they may entail as much interference in each other's lives as they offer support in times of need. Still, these are the friendships he is likely to want, rejecting looser kinds as a bare rubbing of shoulders. His efforts to get to know new people, too, will tend to be aggressive. Often they amount to invasions aiming at conquest, rather than invitations for the other person to come forth on his own terms, and remain sovereign even as a friend. His having fun with friends is likely to be a version of the same bracing thing, whether at parties of drinking and singing, in pranks and explosive laughter, or during intellectual discussions lasting through the night, or combinations of these things.

Jonah's loving – beyond a rather happily frank urge to make love – will also tend to be by tradition a close-knit affair, seeking to recreate two people in terms of one ego, preferably his. The emotions involved are likely to be strong, but possessive rather than freedom-giving and simply tender, and when things go wrong his reactions will be, accordingly, egotistic rather than graceful. In fact a measure of defensive-aggressive egotism in most relationships is what makes his more traditional-type inner structure in particular so 'craggy' and – depending on how self-conscious he has become owing to his social and cultural background and life-experiences – also stiff.

Venturing further from his own centre, he will try in a similarly defensive-aggressive way to impose the categories of his inner order on all he meets. Indeed he will start by imposing strict enough rules on his own appearance and behaviour in public. Walking through provincial cities and even most of the capitals of Eastern Europe it is impossible not to be struck by, for instance, the extent to which even young people seek to dress in a manner that will look respectable, and especially in colours that will not offend by their novelty or variety. While strong traditional contrasts may occur, combinations of many pastel shades or other playful experiments in colour will be rare, creating altogether an impression of dullness cloaking intensity. On seeing western fashions and colours, young East Europeans themselves are often equally struck, and draw very similar conclusions. 'From the very first moment I was aware that they came from another world, almost another planet,' the young hero of the Romanian story I quoted on p. 201 recalled, describing himself as a child in the fifties gazing at westerners in front of their embassies. 'They were always gay and in high spirits, never sullen; one could not see any trace of fanatical concentration on their faces, they were well and tastefully dressed, in light colours, and they behaved openly, harmoniously, freely. . . . As a rule, we used to see couples and we were amazed by the women's grace and elegance, by the sure, balanced but not at all aggressive hands of the men.'

In the circumstances it can hardly be a surprise if such phenomena as hippie life have never caught on among East Europeans. During my first trip through the region, in 1968, I found in fact most reactions to the hippies, then still news, downright philistine. At best they were thought to be 'artists without the talent', as a twenty-six-year-old critic put it, but more in the mainstream was the opinion of the twenty-nine-year-old Hungarian woman I quoted at the beginning of the previous chapter. 'If I got near the hippies,' she said, 'I'd give them a wash and a good hiding, and some work they couldn't get out of.' There was more acceptance of hippie notions in Poland and in Prague, in the first because of ready enough access to western ideas since 1956, and in the second because traditions and sensibilities there have always been closest to those in the West. But despite the formation of small hippie groups, especially in the three northern countries, and even friendly enough appraisals of their ways in the youth press everywhere outside Bulgaria, they remained a foreign curiosity. Nor did I find essential incomprehension of it diminish to any great extent during the three years I spent interviewing young East Europeans.

No doubt modernization will help to ease attitudes in every

East European country, with every passing generation. But for the moment it has chiefly brought new pressures, maintaining the attitudes of purposeful intolerance, and merely changing their manifestations. For example, progress has at best undermined respect for physical aggression, while in some ways it has only increased the value set on certain non-physical forms. The majority of young East Europeans seem in fact to regard personal aggressiveness altogether as a sign not of self-consciousness, but of strength of character, and often to respect it as a promise of success. This is more especially so in the countries most shaken by events and social changes since the start of the Second World War, and among children of families just rising in society. Nor, again, is this surprising. In an environment whose past has been full of dangers and whose present conditions are highly mobile, the stronger a person's aggressiveness, the better he can be expected to prevail over his circumstances.

Similarly, traditions have combined with material conditions turning from harsh to bearable to help young East Europeans to identify almost entirely with the productionist pressures that weigh on them. They see their options as 'do or die' rather than 'do or drop out', and tend to look on others in the same purposefully intolerant way. 'What do you think of Holden Caulfield?' I asked the fifteen- to eighteen-year-old Bulgarians whom I quoted at the start of Chapter 3, apropos of *The Catcher in the Rye*, then playing at the Sofia Youth Theatre. 'I don't really like him, he lives through his feelings,' a girl said. 'But didn't you think he was likeable as a sensitive human being?' I asked. 'Sensitive, perhaps,' an older boy agreed. 'But people who think with their heart can't make good decisions.'

Nor was this just a matter of a group from an élite school, destined to go on to university and emerge into the decision-making strata, articulating its future ethos. Almost every other young Bulgarian I asked about Caulfield gave the same kind of reply. Surveys I shall quote later, carried out among socially representative samples of young people in other East European countries, also showed that respondents overwhelmingly rejected the Caulfield type in favour of the type who will conform and perform.

All this is natural enough. Jonah will have emerged to freedom from his struggle with each form of order largely by adopting the pattern inherent in each. Indeed the more fiercely he has struggled against the pattern, the more he is likely to have been marked by it. And when, having fought and meanwhile absorbed versions of order, he begins to be put on the defensive by versions of spontaneity, he almost inevitably becomes the agent of what he once tried to shake off as an imposition on his own spontaneous being. This is, in fact, what at the end of the whole dialectical process the ordered world recognizes in him as maturity.

There is, however, another dialectical process at work within Jonah's relationship to the world he grows up to own. Everywhere and at all times there are changes in progress affecting the forms of order on which the social environment is structured, and in due course also the people whom these forms shape. But in Eastern Europe, the Party both means to remain for ever central to the order born of the area's traditions, and is proudly engaged in producing changes more rapid than any in the past. It is thus helping to develop a breed of people who, shaped by forms of order the Party's own good work has changed, will fit less and less well into the structure the Party deems existential to itself as Hero in charge.

A more detailed look at the findings of a Hungarian study, to which I referred in passing earlier, will serve to illustrate the point.[10] Based on surveys among children in secondary and technical schools in country towns, provincial cities and the capital, it was an attempt at constructing a mental portrait of the country's adolescents. And it is the very significant differences the survey brought to light between adolescents grown up in less and in more developed areas that I want to discuss here.

Respondents from both country towns and larger cities seemed to attach great importance to social propriety and to productive order. Rural adolescents named 'politeness' as the third and 'cleanliness-orderliness' as the fourth most important quality in a young person, while with urban respondents the same attributes came second and third. But development seemed to have made urban children far more sophisticated about conformism, and the tragicomedy of social life altogether. Whereas a full 50 per cent of country-town adolescents mentioned 'sincerity' as a desirable attribute in themselves, and 21·4 per cent mentioned 'honesty', with children from larger cities the respective percentages fell to 10·7 and 2·3.

Still more interesting was the contrast between their opinions on the need for strictness in parents, and on self-reliance in children. Country-town adolescents, who had clearly had the most traditional type of upbringing, named 'strictness' as the second most important parental quality (while they put 'that he should give me all I need' as only eighth, and 'that he provide an education' only thirteenth). Some even thought that as development brought more affluence and mobility, so parents would have to become still more strict with their children. 'True, sometimes they were too strict with me, but now I'm realizing that they did me good,' wrote an eighteen-year-old from a small-town secondary school. 'There are many examples of parents not having been strict enough with their children, who then took to bad ways and when they left the family and started their own lives, they wouldn't even recognize their parents. . . . In today's world you have to bring up children more strictly because they are much worse, and more prone to bad ways, than they used to be.' But even without going so far, a full 50 per cent of the respondents stated that they wished to bring up their own children as they themselves had been brought up, and only 12·5 per cent that they would not do so (37·5 per cent said 'partly').

The answers of children from larger urban communities proved significantly different. Having had a better life, provincial-city respondents had come to regard the attributes signifying material generosity as altogether most important in parents, while 'strictness' had sunk in their answers to sixth place. They were also more prepared to be critical of their parents. Though among them, too, 48·2 per cent stated that they would be giving their children the kind of upbringing they had had, 27·6 per cent said that they would not, while indicative enough of their ideas seemed to be the following, from an eighteen-year-old girl: 'In many important questions I'd let [my child] decide, after some discussion, of course, and in ways which I too thought were right, for himself. I'd always arrange situations so that he could feel he too had a say, I wouldn't oppress him but treat him as almost my equal. . . . I wouldn't like him to see me as a demi-goddess just because I'm his mother.' As for children from the capital, detailed percentages on their replies were not given, but the drift of their written answers was well enough in keeping with their response to the question of whether or not they would be giving their children the treatment they had received: 50 per cent stated that they would not, and only 15·6 per cent that they would.

However, country-town children, who had named 'strictness' as the second most important parental attribute, also named 'independence' as the second most important quality in them-selves. (As first, they named 'sincerity', in both parents and children.) By contrast, provincial-city children, who did not prize 'strictness' in parents highly, also attached much less importance to 'independence' in themselves. Meanwhile, having seen more affluence and freedom, the quality they considered most important in a young person was 'resistance to vice' (by which they principally meant the vice of drunkenness).

In other words, those more strictly brought up and more likely to impose a strict regime on their own children seemed also to have developed the more self-assertive egos, whereas those who had had a richer and freer time of it, and were likely to impose themselves less oppressively as parents, had also become less closely ordered as individuals. To use a not irrelevant political analogy, those who had grown up under strict rule, and had probably staged full-scale 'revolutions' to assert themselves, could also be expected to try imposing a more authoritarian regime of their own. Meanwhile, those who had been more democratically brought up, and were more likely to have rebelled against authority in less structured ways, were also likely to favour less rigid structures when their time to choose arrived.

Thus there seem to be two dialectical processes at work at an angle, as it were. One interlocks the behaviour patterns of parents and children, while the other is 'softening' the patterns themselves through the effects of development. And though both processes have been going on since time immemorial, the second has been receiving, during the lifetime of today's two youngest active generations in Eastern Europe, a special impetus from the Party. Its work has allowed enormous numbers to move to urban areas and has brought development to the countryside as well, while its deliberate policies have made the social situation more fluid than it has ever been.

It is also in this context that the ways in which young East Europeans differ, as I have mentioned, from country to country, from class to class and from generation to generation assume a special importance, since the differences are related to those prevailing between rural and urban youth.

Of course the differences in the political histories of the countries of Eastern Europe since the Second World War have had their own effect. For example, just as after a period of real liberalization no part of the machinery again behaves with the same tyrannical self-confidence, so no East European age group which has lived through such a period will ever again internalize either dictatorial ways or fears of the machinery to the same extent. At the same time, however, no young generation which has seen its political hopes destroyed will ever again possess the same trust in life, often on a general as well as a political level.

Taking all this into account, once again I would say that those 'in the middle' have been most gravely affected, and single out as such young Poles and to a lesser extent young Hungarians. True, young Bulgarians and Romanians, whose respective countries have seen no real de-Stalinization, show to this day the most profound traces of having been brought up under a one-party system. More important, they are also children of the two most recently (and still least) industrialized countries of Eastern Europe. Altogether, they have grown up surrounded by forms of order closest in style to the traditional ones. But the effect of this seems to me to have been far from negative.

I found young Bulgarians, though the most 'naturally' conservative of all young East Europeans I got to know, also the most open and easily lovable as human beings. And it was actually in young Romanians that I met the most attractive mixture of vital warmth and intellectual brilliance. Nor have I much doubt that the unselfconsciousness about human contacts which distinguishes the young people of these two East European countries has its origins chiefly in the kind of close support they receive as children within their families. And the quite amazing trust in life which young Romanians display amidst quite the worst political conditions in the area is also, I think, due partly to these conditions never having been much better in their lifetimes. True, they have not seen even the controlled de-Stalinization that Bulgarians saw in the early 1960s, but nor have they seen their hopes wholly crushed, as have their coevals in the three northern countries.

Of these latter, young Czechs have emerged as the least harmed and most resilient, even politically. And once again, their having grown up in an environment that had long been the most developed and socially homogeneous in the region and was least shocked by changes in the last twenty-five years, seems to me the most important reason for their having borne the strain so well. Relatively speaking, they knew the fewest traditional and mildest developmental pressures as children; they also lived in a country which between the late fifties and 1968 was an externally conformist but internally ever more tragicomic satellite of Russia. The result is that they have emerged as much the most 'elastically' structured of all young East Europeans,* and hence the most adaptable to new conditions – both at home and in emigration. Except for the fact that the Good Soldier Schweik was, though lovable, a prize idiot, whereas today's young Czechs (if perhaps less lovable in some of their over-civilized ways of conforming and communicating) are subtle and intelligent, they are his true descendants.

Young Poles and young Hungarians, however, have been in the middle, both as regards the shocks of rapid development and as regards political experiences in the last twenty-five years. They also display very similar signs of it. This is in spite of the fact that the history of the two countries in the conscious lifetime of their

* In this connection, I found it interesting to compare the tableaux of school-leavers displayed in shop-windows as I passed through the various countries of the region each year in spring and early summer. Outside Czechoslovakia, all except a few in Budapest and Poland were formal. In Czechoslovakia, however, they usually consisted of snapshots of eighteen-year-olds letting their hair down in all possible ways.

young generations has shown an almost complete contrast: in Poland freedom flourished in 1956, to wither slowly but inexorably until 1970, while in Hungary, savage repression after the 1956 Revolt was followed by a just perceptible liberalization, which began in 1959 and has been progressing ever since. The effect of these contrasting histories on the psychology of the two peoples has, however, only helped to preserve the resemblance between them (previously manifest in their egotistic visions of themselves as the hero-nations of Eastern Europe, and in a number of social and cultural traits they shared). In Poland cruel frustration of all hopes of common progress has been turning each man defensively in on himself and his own, while in Hungary each new measure of freedom and prosperity has proved to be at most enough to satisfy the individual for the day, so keeping him always in fear of tomorrow, and hence on the self-defensive.

All this has, in effect, translated heroic egotism into individual terms. The young people of these two countries now mostly abjure self-sacrifice as 'not modern', but remain strongly self-assertive and avidly self-seeking, while if they are more sophisticated than their brothers in the less-developed south of the region, they are often in the same measure less immediately likeable. Young Poles appeared to me to be altogether the most closely structured of all young East Europeans, in their selves, their ideas and their ways of communicating with each other. They are at the same time much the most achievement-minded and aggressive. 'The only reason one can put up with the aggressiveness and the categoric manners of the girls here is that they're so bloody beautiful,' an English exchange student said to me in Warsaw, rather echoing my own sentiments. Young Hungarians seem more elastic in their social tegument (much nearer, in fact, to the Czechs) but also more enervated in their mental reactions, despite their famous and unquestionable zest for living. In a personally depressing way, it was also among them that I found the largest number of young people without any real 'centres' in any East European country.

The few 'character-studies' that have compared groups of young East Europeans seem to support my admittedly impressionistic conclusions. They show that while certain basic traits distinguish young East Europeans altogether from children of both the much more and the much less developed parts of the world, important differences exist in the degree to which the various groups share these traits. For instance, a detailed survey on the life-outlook of university students, based on an American questionnaire and undertaken in the United States, Japan, India, Norway, Poland and Hungary, found that both young Poles and young Hungarians were significantly more discipline- and less enjoyment-minded, and a good deal less tolerant of pluralism in life-styles, than young Americans. But it also found young Poles much more discipline-minded, as well as more individualistic, than young Hungarians, while in the latter a strong enough attachment to discipline seemed to combine with a crowd-loving bent to produce the highest ratings for intolerance in the whole study.[11]

As regards class, the strongest differentiating signs are visible in those who have come the longest (and hardest) way up from the strata of their parents. Just as it is possible to tell the children of rapidly-developed countries from those brought up in an environment long since industrialized and socially homogenized, so it is possible to tell, especially in the more hierarchy-conscious countries of Eastern Europe, which of two engineers or social scientists comes from a professional intelligentsia family, and which from a family of peasants or miners. The difference in their cultural backgrounds may be apparent enough, but more important is the degree of self-conscious 'orderliness' there is about their clothes, their behaviour and their dealing with others and especially with established members of the same stratum, as well as about their reactions to strange-seeming people and phenomena.

The newcomers will not only tend to have strongly defensive attitudes towards the milieus they have just entered and in which others move with native ease. They will also be more prone to making purposefully intolerant demands on themselves and the world about them, *both* for the worse and for the better. As I shall explain more fully in Chapter 7, having endured the most traditional upbringing and having had to push and discipline themselves hardest to get on, they have less sympathy for the Caulfield type,* and are generally more receptive to arguments imposing order in the interest of the collective's getting on, than children of the established intelligentsia. At the same time, having brought a good many down-to-earth attitudes with them from their background, they are less likely to embrace brands of extremism for the sake of mere theories than children of families in which discussion of ideas and ideals had formed part of daily life.

The generational differences I discussed at some length in a previous chapter, but the reasons for them must be that much clearer by now. As members of the recognized age group themselves often stress, their juniors are more loosely structured, more easily conforming on the outside but more resilient underneath, more absorbed in their sheer existence and drawing more strength from it, in 'much closer contact with life', as the thirty-four-year-old Romanian artist quoted on page 130 put it.

Altogether, the traits characteristic of young East Europeans seem to appear in more 'Platonic' forms in the recognized generation and in more 'Aristotelian' ones in the new generation. Though both are aggressive, for instance, members of the first tend to be more aggressive about imposing order and their own categories, and about wanting security, while their juniors are more aggressive about wanting material things and freedom to enjoy themselves in their own ways. Intolerance, too, is more noticeable and more articulate in the older group, who reject all kinds of cultural and human experiences to which their younger brothers seem prepared to give a chance. Conformity and visible achievements also matter to them in different ways. Those in the recognized generation seem both inwardly more intricate and outwardly more performance-minded, while members of the younger group tend to combine inner elasticity with seeking materially secure but otherwise less structured ways of finding outer fulfilment.

Taking all the differences in attitudes into account, I think it is legitimate to speak of a change occurring in the type of people produced by the East European environment altogether. What

* The Hungarian study I have just quoted had found respondents at provincial universities more discipline-minded than in the capital and, due mainly to their more profound anxiety about results, women in the sample more so than men.

seems to be happening is the decline of a 'Platonic' type and the rise of a more 'Aristotelian' one. The first is more closely ordered and on the whole bad at dealing with spontaneous phenomena on their own terms; the second is more elastic and more adaptable to the unfamiliar in situations and people. The first is more inclined to think in universals, and thus both prone to and responsive to rhetoric and the imposition of comprehensive order; the second is closer to earthy ways both in speech and in attitudes, and offers as well as demands conformity rather than devotion and obedience. The first is more likely to stage revolutions, overturning authoritarian rule to place himself in absolute authority; the second is prone rather to unstructured rebellion, which he can also better tolerate in others. The first is performance-minded and perfectionist in his standards, which for him often have a pure beauty of their own; the second is more private and utilitarian, judging his actual responsibilities to himself and those near him as most important. The first is much happier in shining as a hero, the second in surviving as best he can, in all situations.

It is an aspect of the Party's paradoxical situation that while the Platonic type is clearly closer to its needs as Hero in central charge, as Champion of Progress it is engaged in helping the proliferation of young Aristotelians. In due course, this is likely to prove to be yet another version of the Party's encirclement by the effects of its own good work in Eastern Europe. But even as things now stand, another paradox of the situation is that the Party's call to both types can elicit responses that are only as co-operative as they are treacherous.

There are two main reasons for this. One is that, obliged by its egotistic ideology to pose as the people's warrior command even though times and their tasks are peaceful, the Party sooner or later turns both types of young East Europeans in on themselves. Were there a true war situation, the Platonic type could easily identify himself with the collective as his Universal, whether he became part of the self-assigning soldiery or of the self-imposing command. The Aristotelian type, too, might consider, though less easily, that his life-interests coincided with those of the rest. Peacetime tasks, however, do not lend themselves to heroic simplification. On the contrary, they are bound to become ever more complex and to necessitate involvement as a matter of spontaneity and readiness for intelligent hard work rather than blind enthusiasm. Within this situation, even those Platonists who may at first respond to Party rhetoric soon find themselves entangled in complexities they cannot understand, and so become frustrated, while Aristotelians, better though they may be at managing complex minutiae, are repelled by the Party's centralist rule and rhetoric.

The other reason is that people tend to approach situations not only 'from the self outwards' but also 'from life upwards': under every form of order imposed by 'them' Jonah goes on living his life as one of 'us', and being impelled by this life in directions he himself may barely be able to control. In other words, he will react to both aspects of the predicament that he effectively shares with the Party first in 'animal' ways, and only afterwards in socially useful ones. And while this would be so in any circumstances, his urge to make all the animal use he can of the Party's achievements, concessions and failures alike is made still more avid by the isolation of the Party as Hero in charge of the world which Jonah is said to own.

6 Ways of Life

In 1958 I myself, aged nineteen, had occasion to be interviewed about life as a young animal in Eastern Europe. A recent arrival in England and still stateless, I had applied for a visitor's visa to the United States. I was called in for an interview at the US consulate in London, and there I found myself faced with a long questionnaire, surviving from the McCarthy days and designed to ascertain if I was a Communist or a fellow-traveller of any kind. Among other things, it required me to name all organizations to which I had ever belonged.

One of the organizations I named was a Budapest sports club called *Vörös Lobogó* (Red Flag).

'Red Flag!?' the consul said.

'Red Flag,' I affirmed.

'What kind of a club was that?'

'Sport,' I said, as laconically as only a foreigner can.

'And what did you do there?'

'Swimming. I was in the swimming department.'

'Nothing else? I mean, with a name like Red Flag. . . . '

'No, no, no, we swam. Just swam.'

We spent some time on that question before the consul was prepared to leave it alone. Had he realized that at the time of my joining the club, in 1953, it had been called *Bástya* (Bastion) and had belonged to the AVH, the dreaded State Security Corps, he might have wished to inquire even further. But I did not tell him that. Not because I thought it unwise, but because I myself remembered it only later.

Undoubtedly my club had been part of the political order surrounding young East Europeans like myself. Its prewar name of MTK (Hungarian Physical Exercise Circle) had been abolished when at the beginning of the Stalinist years it was given to the AVH, and its football stars and coaches were made officers in the

Corps. Then in the first bout of de-Stalinization in Hungary, in 1953–4, it was transferred to the textile industry (whence the name Red Flag) and the same football stars and coaches were pulled out of their uniforms and given sinecures in the rag trade instead.* Under either name, the club was part of the vast State establishment promoting 'socialist sport', about whose physical and moral superiority over every other kind of sport no end of speeches were being made. It was a Platonic institution, seeking to generate *mens sana in corpore sano*.

All this, however, had little to do with me. I had joined the club at the age of fourteen quite simply because all schools in my area came under its sponsorship for all sports. Faced with a given form of order, I made use of it to enjoy myself. Irrespective of the club's name, or its Platonic aims, we boys knew it as the thing that paid for our tickets to the pool and our fares to and fro, employed our coaches full time, gave us swimming trunks and bathing wraps and wooden slippers free, entered us for races and took us on a fortnight's holiday each summer. The loyalties that it bred, which we manifested in rooting for our team and shouting abuse at the referee during water-polo matches, had no more to do with State security than with crimson cloth, let alone socialism itself. They were young animal loyalties, pure and simple. In fact it occurred to me to remember my socialist club with gratitude only when I emigrated to the West and found that there one had to pay for tickets to the pool and everything else.

While swimming must have broadened our shoulders and developed our taste for competition, the difference it made to our mental growth was altogether slight. It chiefly enabled us to stand after our training sessions for hours under the hot showers, getting our brains stewed and telling stories that grew progressively more idiotic. To the club's House of Culture we went only on Saturday nights, to hear a jazz trio playing the latest favourites from the West and to dance under soft lights, as slowly as possible, holding the girls whose contours we knew so well from the water, tight in our arms.

* When, after the October 1956 Revolt, every harmless way of soothing the nerves of the population was tried, MTK regained its prewar name, along with a number of other established clubs.

At the same House of Culture we found ourselves in educative contact with a juvenile gang, headed by 'Pinocchio', known as an insanely brilliant high-diver and budding criminal throughout the city. 'I love salami sandwiches', Pinocchio once said to me, taking a comprehensive bite out of the one I had just bought, and staring me in the eye. We had never previously as much as said hello, but the last thing that entered my head was to object. I could recognize might as right when I saw it, and facing the animal form of order manifest in the gang ranged behind him, I made another acquiescent choice.

All this, and a lot else of the same nature, I should have had to explain if my replies to the poor consul's questions were to have any real meaning. Had he asked about any of the other forms of order that had been imposed on us as young animals I should have had to do the same for each. Within the framework each had provided, often simply by herding us together, we had been leading lives which, whether miserable, enjoyable or both, had nevertheless been our own. And though it was after the life we had led that my *émigré* friends and myself later yearned in moments of homesickness, in effect we also wished ourselves back under the grid of the order with which that life had been so closely intertwined.

Part of its fun had in any case derived from the ways that order had forced us to evolve for making it bearable. At school, for instance, though most of us essentially accepted the need for discipline, and respected the hierarchies, the pressures that produced these also forged us into underground groups proud of their tragicomic invention and amoral nerve. Without those heavy pressures we would probably not have begun to cheat so brazenly in our tests and exams, nor have got up to quite the same riotously satisfying pranks. As it was, our brave cadres had our full support in all their diversionist activities, whether these consisted of releasing flocks of sparrows at the height of unpopular lessons, or in disconnecting the central-heating pipes to let the steam billow forth in mid-winter, while we stripped to the waist, presenting Sir with the sight of a Turkish bath.

We behaved in similar ways towards the political forms of order, again irrespective of our levels of involvement and our loyalties. Coming from a family of prewar socialists, I, for example, was an enthusiast of the Left compared to the average pupil, especially in my basic school. Still, what I liked best in the Pioneers was our rare trips to the mountains, and the actual details of what we had to do as members of the organization often bored me stiff. I still remember making feverish efforts as a twelve-year-old to get the boys together for a meeting about the current Five-Year Plan, which in my capacity as speaker I then forgot to attend. And while others spoke at other meetings on similar themes, I very often spent my time daydreaming, like everybody else.

By the time I got to secondary school, at the age of fourteen, the youth organization attracted me even less. But as I was then becoming interested in the theatre and later in writing, and as all activity came under Youth League auspices, it was within the League hierarchy that I rose to the rank of Culture Organizer first of my class and then of the whole school, and that I became Secretary of the Literary Circle. As culture man I got people tickets to theatres at reduced prices, while I took part in and later produced poetry recitals. Though these were propaganda occasions to begin with, their themes changed with the general atmosphere, until the last one we had, in the spring of 1956, could be entirely devoted to the 'Love Poetry of the World' and proved a huge success. I also acted in the school play. Had I applied to enter a university in Hungary, the League would certainly have endorsed me as an 'enthusiastic participant in collective manifestations'.

While school undoubtedly exerted far greater influence over our minds than swimming, it also provided us with underground contacts to shape our behaviour for years if not for life. I myself, in my first year at the secondary school, was best friends with an academically stupid but worldly wise and very lovable character who soon became a semi-professional ping-pong player and under whose influence my involvement with the collective reached its nadir. When he left in my second year, I became friendly with someone very much his opposite. The son of a Zionist imprisoned in 1949, he had worked in a mine and, having missed a year and a half of schooling, was the oldest boy in our class. The girls thought him beautiful and he was nearly always hopelessly in love, and wrote poems, which in imitation of him I began writing too. He and I were together in the drama group, and decided to become poets and/or actors, while our families insisted that we choose 'real' professions like everybody else, or at least read law, as so many Hungarian poets had. As we both left Hungary before finishing school, the crunch never came, but it was the impetus I gained from knowing him that turned me into a writer. He is now an exporter of citrus fruits in Tel Aviv.

School and politics combined, in a way, to acquaint me with love. Having for years been infatuated with a little blonde angel whom I knew only by sight, I met my first more tangible girl friend during a political demonstration which the school attended *en masse*. Dead tired, she and I made our way back in rather a daze, and somewhere along the route we began to hold hands. Later that evening we met again and went to the city park where, under the venerable statue of an eighteenth-century poet, I had my first taste of real kissing. She too then joined the drama group, and later we were seen kissing behind the scenery by our Russian teacher, who next day held a small sermon in class, without naming names, on how much more decent it was to take our girls where nobody would see us, such as home or to the woods.

While thus reminded of moral order from on high, I was brought by my girl face to face with spontaneity in its most elemental form. Though younger, she was years more mature than I was, and as our relationship developed, she offered herself to me again and again. But, much as I wanted her, I would not take her. I was afraid of making her pregnant, but even more important, I held that while one might dream of roaring encounters with one's biology mistress, one should not make love to the girl one loved.

Absurd as this began to seem to me as soon as the pain of our final breaking up had done its work in my mind, at the time I was certainly not alone in believing it – not even among friends of mine who lost their virginities long before I did, and were no more conscious of having been directly affected by either religious or Party teachings on morality than I was. It was just the way in which ideas, received from our romantic culture and from our old-world parents, and also undoubtedly from articulate moral teaching of whatever kind and its reverberations, had coalesced in us, as visions of moral order. The consciously religious among us had still harsher attitudes towards themselves, even while they sinned. As for me, it was when I realized the absurdity of my Platonic pose that I decided to read the Bible, so struck was I by the resemblance between my story and that of Adam's temptation by Eve, offering life and deeper knowledge.

With the outer order we still found it easy enough to deal, partly because so much of it we accepted as just being there. That the world was impenetrably divided into East and West, and that we could not even cross the border into the next socialist country, we took as a given circumstance. Very few of us dreamt about changing it, and even fewer tried to do so by attempting to escape. That the flats we lived in were all about equally crowded seemed to be another given circumstance. If unmarried, and even some married, couples had to try to get round it by borrowing friends' rooms for Sunday afternoons or taking to the hills at night to make love, we thought this in no way peculiar.

That we had to fear the State and all its agents had also become part of our automatic reaction to our given universe. If bureaucrats and policemen tended to behave not as public servants but as a bastard race in power, we might hate them for it at the time but we also accepted their behaviour as on the whole natural. I still remember how angry I became when, stopping to look at the slogans and pictures that bedecked the front wall of a local Party headquarters on the eve of a public holiday, I was moved on by a uniformed AVH guard who carried a rifle and objected to my 'loitering' there. But it was not until the spring of 1956 that I began drawing any general conclusions from this about the Party whose premises had to be so frantically guarded against the people it claimed to represent. And by the time I began properly rejecting not only the political but also the human aspects of that man's behaviour, I was already suffering my own inner death and rebirth as an *émigré*.

Returning to Eastern Europe in 1968 to collect material for the present book, I found that while circumstances had changed considerably, people's patterns of coping with them had remained in many ways the same.

Without question, life had become easier. The forms of order, whether surrounding people or inside them, had softened, while material conditions had improved, and young people's style of living was perceptibly different.

In producing these changes, the results of development and of newer Party policies had inextricably combined. For instance, we used to go hiking in the mountains or on bicycle trips in the surrounding countryside. Teenagers today go hitch-hiking, a thing almost unknown in the fifties, when private cars themselves were as good as unknown. Or they go on their scooters and motorbikes, and not only to the surrounding countryside, but all through the region, and some even to the West.

Their plans, whether for next summer or for this afternoon, simply tend to be different from what ours were. Among other things, they have become less interested in both competitive and mass sports. Pressure on them to participate has declined, while being a sports star has ceased to be the only way of getting a passport. More important, there is a good deal more they can do on their own or in mechanized ways, both at home and out of doors. Combined with higher living standards and the material indulgence of parents, this has in fact created a situation in which papers in several East European countries have begun to complain that urban adolescents are getting too fat, and also retarded for their age in bodily skills.

Perhaps the most important of the combined effects of development and newer Party policies has been to allow the young to retract on front after front into life-styles of their own. The ever more pronounced retraction into pop, from all forms of 'their' order, is very much a case in point. First, as a result of development the spread of transistor radios and then portable tape-recorders began to take western pop music, at a time when it was still banned in several East European countries on radio and TV, literally into the streets, parks and even Youth League camps. Then, in the early to mid-sixties, the changes in style and instrumentation that were making pop music really pop, that is, self-made, had an even more dramatic effect on the situation. They placed the Party in the classically untenable role of a super-organized machine trying to control a thing luxuriant in its disorganization. Whereas professional bands could always be controlled somehow, since they needed a licence, nothing could be done about young animals who just bought guitars and amplifiers, or put together their own, and started to howl. This led to the mushrooming of pop groups, on which final Party benediction merely fell like rain: in Hungary, for instance, where it came in 1963–4, within two years there were over seven hundred pop groups and in another three some four thousand, of which two thousand were known to have started playing in public.

Apart from being non-political and non-adult, pop is also non-class, offering escape from hierarchies at both school and work. 'It's the one thing they can all have in common,' a thirty-one-year-old woman social worker who had formed a free-wheeling 'self-knowledge circle' among fans gathering for weekly pop sessions in the House of Culture of a working-class district of Budapest* told me in 1970. 'Secondary-school kids, and girls working in shops, and kids from the metallurgical plants, and younger students. The way they look there, you can't very easily tell them apart. And once pop has brought them together, they often find they have other things about which they can talk, too. My circle is certainly as mixed as you can get.'

Juvenile delinquency, another 'tribal' manifestation, has been affected in a similar way. Though conservatives still link the two phenomena, rather along the lines of the old maxim according to which '*la musique adoucit les moeurs*', pragmatists have recognized that the real connection between them is the fact that they have been helped in their growth by western-type development, brought to Eastern Europe in a good measure by the Party itself.

---

* The actual method of forming the circle, about whose discussions I shall have more to say, consisted of putting up a picture of the resident pop group, now the most popular in Hungary, with the legend, 'You know us. Come and get to know yourself'. Meetings, which members of the group every so often attend, are devoted to a topic selected by those present. On this an open discussion is held and the questionnaires drafted by the participants are filled up anonymously, for analysis at the next meeting. Topics have included 'Was the personality cult necessary?', 'Social conflicts today', 'Men–women relationships', 'Should one serve power or rebel against it?' and so on. 'When I first told them [the higher-ups] I was having free discussions on all these things, they thought I was mad. They often still act as if they did,' the social worker said.

Whether gangs engage in simple vandalism and bloody fights, or the recruitment of prostitutes for the use of tourists and black-market operations in their currencies, young people's urge to join them derives largely from social and cultural assimilation having been unable to keep pace with sudden progress and rising expectations, as a result of which whole social groups have lost their bearings.

About this the Party is now frank enough. Though speeches and articles may still lay part of the blame for delinquency on 'adventurism encouraged by bad literature and foreign and religious propaganda', or on 'imperialist softening-up tactics aimed at the young', they nearly all admit that the roots of the problem lie in circumstances on the spot, and that these are unlikely to improve for some time. The actual treatment of delinquency depends partly on the outlook of the police force, the more conservative tending to use more conservative methods, and also on exactly what is regarded as delinquent behaviour, which is again decided by the police. But on the whole the approach has become more subtle and more realistic.

Meanwhile, though both the reality surrounding young East Europeans and many of their own expectations have changed, the surviving distance between the two has kept a number of attitudes and conventions of coping very similar to what these were in my young animal time.

For instance, though housing conditions have improved, they remain bad enough to be a factor in making pop music even more of a generational problem than it has been in the West. However irritating it may be to have a teenage son playing records at full volume in his own room, it is a lot more irritating to have him playing them in a room where four other people may be trying to find some peace and quiet. As regards clothes and gadgetry, too, fashions have changed, but many habits of thought and behaviour have survived. Where we might have given anything for a pair of thick crêpe rubber soled shoes, young East Europeans today will give as much for real western jeans, as any visitor will know who has offered to send them what they most wanted from the West. If they carry their transistor sets and portable tape-recorders blaring through the streets more often than western teenagers do, this too is because of the still-surviving novelty of their gear.

They also remain in certain ways genuinely conventional. Though their pastimes have become more mechanized and their sub-culture more self-made and self-centred than ours was, their interest in high culture continues to be more intense and wide-spread than those of their coevals, especially in the Anglo-Saxon West. They read more, and more of such outlandish things as poetry, follow more closely what goes on in the cultural world at home and abroad, and are less shy about being thought serious and intellectual. The programme of the Budapest 'self-knowledge circle' I described earlier gives a fair idea of what a group of pop fans might think worth talking about.

They are also more eager to follow developments in the out-side world, whether these be developments on the pop scene, the political scene or the motoring scene. To some extent this is a matter of letting their minds travel where they themselves cannot, and knowing in intimate detail wonders too distant to touch. The Bulgarian secondary-school children I have quoted several times not only inquired about groups then ascending the BBC pop charts, but also involved me in an argument about an inter-view Stokely Carmichael had recently given a German magazine. The first Hungarians to whom I gave a lift on entering the country were a pair of twelve-year-olds hitch-hiking home from one village to another, and they asked me more about the latest Aston Martin model, of which they had been sent pictures by an uncle, than I had ever even wanted to know.

At the same time, much as their parents and the Party's spokes-men may fear the corruptive effects of the new sub-culture, once left to themselves young East Europeans settle down not just peaceably, but very fast. They are well aware of the dangers of chopping and changing about in the centralist system that will form their working environment. The overwhelming majority often find grooves of their own as soon as they finish their secondary, and especially higher, education. And having done so, they develop ever worse suspicions of the ever-dwindling minority of free-rangers, as being in some way insane. This is in fact a perfect example of how their patterns of coping with given difficulties, for which the reasons may be economic or political, turn into accepted conventions. 'He's wasting his life,' was the judgement I heard more than once applied even to twenty-three-year-olds who were still not in a final groove.

Similarly, their less public and perfectionistic standards of behaviour have made them, if anything, more genuinely responsible for each other. One of the questions in the debate on men–women relationships in the Budapest 'self-knowledge circle' I described earlier had been, 'What would you do if your partner was unfaithful to you a *second* time?' While unhysterical about infidelity, this could hardly be called a promiscuous proposition. Answers varied between, 'I'd clip her one round the ear and never see her again,' and, 'I'd try to find out why, what had I done to her?' but very few people argued that the question was irrelevant.

Also, if they are more matter-of-fact about sex, they are on the whole merely less hypocritical about morality. 'If they have rejected something,' a twenty-seven-year-old educational sociologist said in Poland, 'it is not morals, but the kind of fears, of the Church, of what people will say, on which their parents had based their moral outlook.' The thirty-one-year-old teacher, also from Poland, whom I quoted in Chapter 2, was inclined to take the matter-of-factness about sex with a pinch of salt, too: 'I'm sure a number of our boys have had sex, one or two probably group sex too. But also, a lot of them only try to give that impression. Some time ago we took a bunch camping, and one evening we started a game of confessions, mostly them questioning each other. I was amazed at how many of them turned out to be virgins at seventeen to eighteen.'

And once again, apart from ideas on morality and responsibility, circumstances also help conventions to survive: 'I have the feeling,' an English exchange student who had spent a year in Budapest said to me, 'that unmarried people here lead chaster lives than in England to some extent because of the difference in the flats situation. Very few single people here have places of their own, or even places they share, where they can do what they like. I rent a room which isn't cheap, but you should have seen the fuss the landlady made when a girl as much as came to wait for me there one afternoon. . . . On the other hand, when they get married, that gives them freedom even if they stay living at home, and then I think they make up for lost time.'

Though this is probably true, it once again means only a relativization of standards, which seems to have affected people's sense of responsibility least of all. A large survey on young people's attitudes to marriage, undertaken in the mid-sixties in Czechoslovakia, showed that while they considered absolute fidelity unimportant if not impossible, and had nowhere near the horror of divorce their parents might have had at the same age, their aversion to the latter increased sharply the larger the family broken by divorce.[1] In Poland, a major study on the life-attitudes of sixteen- to twenty-four-year-olds also showed that the moral failing that respondents found least pardonable was 'neglect of family duties'.[2]

Of course changed conditions have affected the views of the young on the family in some very important ways. Higher standards of living, for instance, have made them less immediately conscious of the need for material security to keep a marriage happy than their parents were. This has, among other things, helped to alter the age-structure of families, which in its turn has had further effects. 'In the old days, men more often waited until they had managed to put something aside, or come into property, before they got married,' a distinguished Romanian sociologist explained. 'Especially in the villages, it was almost a custom for rich middle-aged peasants to marry beautiful young girls. Now people not only get married much younger, but there is also very much less difference in age between the partners. And though they have many fewer children, they tend to have them earlier.'

But while as a result of changes young people's view of marriage is now less formal, the partners' contact with each other has become more intense: 'For the under-thirty age group,' a Polish sociologist who had just completed a large survey on marriage told me in 1970, 'marriage is neither the venerable institution it is for the over forty-fives, nor the partnership arrangement the thirty-to-forty-five age group consider it to be, but overwhelmingly a means of self-expression. This is true even in the countryside, where material considerations retain most importance, but where the search for emotional and especially sexual compatibility has been becoming more and more emphatic. You can also see it in the differing attitudes to divorce. The traditionally minded older people see it as a moral catastrophe, while the under-thirties consider it almost as a life-experience like any other, an admission that something they've tried has failed.'

While the thing is going, however, they are also better prepared than their elders were to share the work-load within the house. Recent surveys show the rise of more democratic tendencies even among rural and small-town working youth, reckoned to be the most conservative. This process of change, however, is likely to remain the slowest, not only because a good deal in every family will always depend on the personalities of those involved, but also because not all of the results have proved beneficial. In some surveys girls themselves are found protesting against ideas that would make the husband do the housework 'while the wife sits there reading the paper'. But more important, one of the reasons for the instability of younger families, which has greatly increased divorce rates throughout the region, is thought to be the worsening confusion over roles. In Romania, where draconian anti-divorce laws were put through in 1967, plans were very soon also drawn up for special school curricula in homecraft, child care and family psychology for girls. And whereas I heard a good deal of complaining about the anti-divorce (and anti-abortion) laws during my visits in 1968 and 1969, the idea of reaffirming women's position as central within the home seemed to arouse little hostility.

Altogether, a well-enough developed sense of duty towards themselves and those close to them seems basic to the outlook of today's young East Europeans. This emerges not only in their views concerning morals and the family, but also in their general ideas on the kinds of lives they want to lead. Survey after survey shows them setting the highest value on professional qualifications (or a worthwhile job), prosperity and marital happiness, with the first two aims alternating as the most important. True, social involvement and wider responsibilities tend to be of much greater interest to the highly trained than to those in the manual-working strata. But what respondents in all strata reject most strongly is an unstructured life, whether from the individual, the familial or the social point of view.

Perhaps the clearest expression of this can be found in an analysis by one of Poland's leading sociologists of the success-ideals emerging from the major survey of sixteen- to twenty-four-year-olds to which I referred on page 239.[3] Descriptions of six different types were given to respondents, and they were asked to say which they preferred to which, as well as to give their opinion of these types in relation to themselves. Of the two most-preferred types, the first was a man interested in wealth (though mostly of the 'small-but-mine' sort), a secure job and social position, family happiness and tangible consumption as opposed to spending money on the purer pleasures and ephemeral things of life. The second also valued wealth and consumption, and rejected the pursuit of enjoyment, though less emphatically than the first, while he was more interested in a harmonious family life and in having the respect of his immediate environment. To achieve these goals, he was very much prepared to conform, though he disliked absolutist attempts to impose order on him from above, or to rally him by appealing to his emotions. As a contrast to these two types, the one most emphatically rejected (chosen as an ideal by only 5·6 per cent of respondents and condemned by 62·3 per cent) valued adventure, pleasure in life and freedom of thought and action, and held all duties and restrictive circumstances in contempt. He was also an escapist strongly influenced by films and literature, expected no backing from society and wanted money only to spend it.

Similar results have been obtained elsewhere, too, such as in the Hungarian survey on schoolchildren quoted in the previous chapter, and in the one on working-class youth quoted in Chapter 3. No doubt part of the reason lies in the traditions handed down to the young by their parents. But at least as important is the effect of development having gone far enough in Eastern Europe only to provide outlets for the more immediate drives of the young, but not for any prodigality. In other words, their life-ideals derive from a dovetailing of desires and of possibilities for their fulfilment that are at best no more than sufficient. Instead of wholly destroying former conventions, change and the effects of the Party's social policy have combined to spread formerly middle-class attitudes through almost the whole of what now counts as society.

As regards appearances and visible life-styles, for example, the result is a kind of 'democratic propriety' – democratic in that it makes young bricklayers look indistinguishable from young engineers at a dance; and proper in that both will be wearing suits, shirts and ties of the same 'do-not-stick-out' kind about which I spoke in the previous chapter. Apart from being proper, the same appearances would also be regarded by both young bricklayers and engineers, and their girl friends, as modern[*] – an adjective that is perfectly apt in that the spreading of the style throughout society is very largely due to changes in the last twenty-five years.

A similar democratic propriety is likely to prevail in the way the same couples, on getting married, may furnish their homes. In fact here the stress on modernity may become nothing less than intolerant, mainly as a reaction to the crammed family homes in which the young partners will not only have grown up, but will most often have started their married lives too. Buying their own distinctly 'modern' things amounts for them to an act both of self-assertion and of frenzied escape.

Where the old and the new couples stay living together, one can often walk through ages of interior decorating history merely by stepping from one room into the next. The first may be crowded with heavy chairs and wardrobes and tables covered with lacework and often dominated by a glass cabinet containing family relics and good or bad china, while the second is more likely to contain furniture of smooth lines, usually single beds, steel-wire bookshelves, perhaps some pottery and metal ashtrays, looking altogether carefully unfussy and unobtrusive, if not wholly impersonal. Being democratic, the style varies only so much according to the amount of money spent on it, or to the educational or social levels of the couples concerned, though the

---

[*] The demand that 'he/she should dress in a modern way' is one of the most persistent to crop up in surveys done on partner-ideals.

more self-conscious among the newcomers to the intelligentsia would tend to keep more rigorously to the 'modern' convention in their surroundings.

A meeting of tastes, desires, traditions and circumstances also keeps alive many conventions about the ways in which young East European adults spend their free time. The same people who started out reading a good deal as adolescents go on to fill their bookshelves with much larger and more varied collections than are to be found in the homes of their equals in age and social status in the Anglo-Saxon West, go more to live theatre and even opera, and remain in general more interested in high-cultural events at home and abroad. They are the most important age group of the public that will buy three to five thousand copies of a volume by a young poet, or fifteen to twenty thousand copies of a monthly devoted to foreign literature, in countries of, say, fifteen million people.

The effects of tradition and of their encyclopedic education partly account for this continued interest in high culture. Other reasons include the lack of enough alternative ways in which to use their leisure, while State subsidies make printed matter cheap and maintain stable theatre and sometimes even opera companies in towns of as few as eighty thousand inhabitants. And last but not least, there is the physical and social closeness of East European societies, in which a book, a play or the private life of an opera singer may literally become the talk of a town or even a whole country, from ministers to taxi-drivers and their children. This is also why that old form of self-entertainment, gossip, goes on being practised so vigorously by even the youngest adults, in cafés, at work and just about anywhere large enough to accommodate more than one person.

Their commonest way of banishing the cares of the world remains the oldest, namely the bottle. The use of drugs is very little known. Drinks may be occasionally mixed with chemicals, as happened in Czechoslovakia not long ago when a substance previously used for the relief of asthma became famous as a hallucinogen in combination with beer. A number of young people are also known to have tried hashish and LSD. But that these should become as commonplace as in certain social circles in the West seems unimaginable, and the same applies, only more strongly, to hard narcotics.

Part of the reason lies in the traditional fear of drugs. At the same time, the State machinery's close control over the interior as well as the frontiers of each country makes both the importation and the spreading of drugs far more difficult than in western democracies. As a result, the prices are beyond the reach of all but an insignificant section of societies that are still well below western standards of affluence. Thus once more the strength of traditions and material and social circumstances combine to keep conventional attitudes alive.

Of drinks, however, there is neither the same horror, nor the same scarcity. The result is that not only do a lot of people drink as a natural habit, but alcoholism itself is a major problem throughout the region. It is especially bad in the three northern wine-and-spirit-drinking countries, Hungary, Slovakia and Poland,* of which Poland, importing most of its wine but producing superb vodka, is the worst afflicted. The length and coldness of the winter, age-old habits and certain self-dramatizing tendencies in people's character there have combined with a near-permanent sense of frustration to make drunkenness almost a national disease, to which the young are in no way immune. 'Parties mean drinking and more drinking, just as in the old days,' a student of economics said in Gdansk. 'Students aren't rich, still they'll hardly ever come to a party without a bottle of vodka, and they'll drink it there. And they're not the worst. On pay days, you can't get alcohol in the shops, only in restaurants at double the price, but just as many people buy it.' Nor indeed is drunkenness confined to parties and pay days, as healthy young men staggering through the streets of major Polish cities at midday, or down rural highways at the dead of night in the middle of the working week, sadly attest.

The propaganda line according to which the advent of socialism would put an end to drunkenness now survives only in official

---

* The Czechs are beer-drinkers. When discussing national characters, all kinds of people in Eastern Europe, from wayside philosophers to academicians, are prepared to point to this fact as a major reason for the Czechs being different from everybody else.

references to alcoholism as a 'remnant of the past'. Meanwhile, increased prosperity has tended to make the habit only more widespread. In Hungary, for instance, it has been found that while real incomes rose by 27 per cent between 1965 and 1969, the consumption of alcohol also rose by 26·4 per cent.[4] In Czechoslovakia, according to the surveys on marriage I quoted on page 239, 12 per cent of the divorces at the time were due to alcoholism in one of the partners. Not surprisingly, girls and women questioned named drinking as the least tolerable inclination in their prospective husbands.

The mixtures of time-honoured and 'modern' conventions that shape the lives of young East Europeans will appear as conventions, that is, forms of order, only to an outsider. To people who live by them they represent a continuity of personal choices, that is, their own ways of life. And not only will they enjoy many aspects of their conventional lives, but once the conventions are properly accepted by an outsider, he too will find that many of those living by them emerge as very enjoyable human beings. Several of my own most rewarding encounters in Eastern Europe took place with people who were in every way conventional, and spent their lives in surroundings which at first sight froze my soul. As a matter of fact, some of these encounters never quite abandoned even the conventions of political tragicomedy within which, as a result of official introductions, they had begun.

In Bulgaria, for instance, my interview with the assistant editor of the country's students' paper, whose politic replies to my questions on *protektsio* I quoted on page 156, remained from beginning to end within the tragi-comic convention. As a person too, at twenty-six he seemed stiff and self-conscious. He had received me in an immaculate dark suit in an impersonally neat office, with bottles of brandy and mineral water and an open but untouched packet of cigarettes arranged on a low table, with a few cigarettes even pulled half-way out of the packet for my utmost convenience. To every one of my questions he gave replies couched in the terms of editorials, and often at least as long. Nevertheless, underneath the dark suit and the jargon he struck me as an honest man, whose self-consciousness might have been due as much to his being a newcomer to the intelligentsia as to his being slightly cross-eyed, and I proposed that we meet again.

Two days later I was invited to his home where his wife, fluent in English, was to interpret for us. Arriving after dinner, I was received by the two of them wearing their concert-going best, in a home furnished, rather expensively, very much in the 'modern young couple' style. On the table were once again the bottles of brandy and mineral water and the packet of cigarettes arranged as if for a conference. Our conversation, too, continued more or less where we had left off in his office. Only very slowly did it emerge from the tragicomic convention, despite my efforts to change the tone, and his own knowledge of how comic the convention was. 'Please tell him,' I said to the wife at one point, about an hour and a half after we had started talking and drinking, 'that I find him very likeable as a man, but I wish he'd stop using those bloody long sentences each time he gives me a reply.' 'Tell him,' said he, 'that my replies are so long because I have to explain myself very carefully. And also because at the paper they pay us by length so I'm used to stretching it out as far as I can.'

I stayed until dawn. Talking and arguing, fighting the self-defensive tactics of a non-fanatical but sincere Communist, who would also be left behind to face the consequences of what this foreigner might carelessly print in London, rushing into every breach to find particles of human or political truth, or to retreat where I seemed to have rushed too far, and agreeing to disagree or reaching compromises on points which both of us knew had little relevance outside the tragicomic convention that governed our encounter. Also trying, meanwhile, to get a feel of how he might behave when faced not with my questions and arguments but with live issues, or when discussing them with his perceptibly less self-conscious wife, or when putting uncomfortable questions to someone else who was defending himself or his position. And sipping more and more of the brandy, and taking in the colours and sniffing the atmosphere of the carefully 'modern' scenery of our meeting, and at some level enjoying and honestly loving my conventional hosts all the time.

I may say I also remain grateful to them. Our encounter, early on during my initial trip through Eastern Europe to collect material for the present book, was one of the first to remind me that to understand young East Europeans' behaviour in both the human and the civic order surrounding them, I had primarily to understand the conventions by which they lived.

Most of these, as I have tried to stress, I see now as essentially conventions of coping. People may be trying to cope for themselves and their own families, or for other people, or for parts or the whole of the collective, or combinations of these. But in each case the conventions arise as part of each individual's self-defensive stance in the face of circumstances, be the self private or public. In the case of the young Bulgarian, for example, the formal way he dressed and spoke and had furnished his home were parts of his personal tegument. In the way he answered my questions a defence of his personal position and of the cause in which he seemed to believe was mixed with loyalty to his native country and everyday environment. But beneath all this he was, as became clear when I pressed him, also alive to injustices within the system he was in general defending, and believed in taking up the cause of people slighted by those in power, if he could see himself achieving any results by doing so. This, too, was part of the conventions that governed his daily behaviour, as was no doubt a good deal else that I had no opportunity to discover. And only by taking into account as many as possible of these conventions could he, or any other young East European in whatever position in the civic order, be justly assessed as an individual responding to his given circumstances.

In the majority of cases, the motives for people's coping are, of course, purely or mainly personal. It is human enough for them to feel responsible in so far as they can see the object of their responsibilities as extensions of themselves. And while one of the main purposes of propaganda in the last twenty-five years has been to increase people's sense of being members of a collective, certain more important factors have been at work to produce just the opposite effect.

One of these has been, quite simply, development. It has greatly encouraged people's absorption in their own lives, and though it may have brought marriage partners closer together and made the young more sociable, it has not helped the extension of human sympathies. 'We're warm and hospitable, as everybody tells us,' a thirty-year-old woman said in Budapest in May 1968. 'But we're also becoming more and more callous and unconcerned about each other.' Two days later the papers reported the murder of a gypsy, kicked to death in full view of the morning rush-hour crowd on one of the busiest street corners in the city. No one had lifted a finger in his defence, he was a stranger and people walked on, letting him die.

Development has to a similar extent alienated people from their work and from society at large, by making tasks and relationships more complex and thus the aims less visible. And though such alienation is in no way peculiar to Eastern Europe, it has been aggravated there by two further factors. One is the super-centralism of the economic system. Whether their expectations as heightened by development are private or 'public', in trying to satisfy them people come up not only against stubborn reality but also against a vast Platonic structure, in many ways even more stubborn. And their attempts to cope often drive them into ways which may be either illegal under present conditions, or genuinely against the interests of the community, or altogether counter-productive – but which inevitably become part of the conventions of their lives.

To take an everyday example, the time and energy a working woman has to spend on shopping in Eastern Europe would be liable to undermine the morale of an ox. Shortages of meat and other basic foods, often due as much to bad distribution as to actual scarcity, may already force her to spend hours before or after her work-day on just getting the wherewithal for the family's meals together. This, though bad enough, she would by now regard as simply part of life. But when she finds herself having to spend half a day in a vain search for the right-size shoes for her children, simply because the industry has underplanned, she will not only blame 'them', but also gets her own back by taking off as much time from her job as is necessary to find those shoes.

And this is only the simplest example, involving unselfish motives and a genuine cause for trying to cope by taking out on the system what it does to the individual. Many other ways of coping fostered by circumstances and by the system imposed on them will not be as simple or as unselfishly motivated.

A number of them may still be seen only as perversions of private initiative, stimulated by higher expectations but deprived of proper outlets by centralism. Among these, the most colourful are frauds, impostures and other highly profitable pranks played on the system by people who, on being discovered, immediately enter folklore as tragicomic heroes of the first order. But a good many less heroic ways of privately improving one's lot are also rife in every East European country.

Among the manual-working strata the most popular of these is migration in search of higher wages. Once forbidden, it is now a major headache to managements in every East European country, with one-third to a half of the younger skilled workers leaving some enterprises in a single year. Among the unskilled the figures are usually even higher.

Almost equally popular, both with the manual-working and with the non-manual-working strata, is 'moonlighting' – doing extra work on the side – in which legality and illegality may form a subtle mixture. Manual workers often moonlight as after-work handymen, who are very much in demand owing to the State's inability to provide such services. The tools they use they will as likely as not borrow from work, together with the materials if necessary; or these may be borrowed for them in a similar way by their customers. 'If people can't get spare parts for their cars, which is often a problem,' a twenty-three-year-old Pole told me with some glee in Cracow, 'they'll pinch them off company cars. These get priority on parts available, and if not, that's just too bad, it's the company's problem.' White-collar workers may also moonlight as handymen, but the professionals among them are more likely to take work on private commission from companies other than their own, or to hold several jobs. One can only attempt to speculate, as papers often do, about how much of their time they are bound to spend working for one employer, or resting from overwork, while being paid by another.

There are also side-incomes which people make in occupations quite different from those they declare, so as not to be classed as 'parasites'. The best-paid of these occupations is the oldest – prostitution. In this, all kinds of young women from typists and salesgirls to students find a second source of livelihood, often earning more than ministers. According to an article in a Warsaw daily, in Poland in 1971 there were 'approximately 10,000 prostitutes who have voluntarily registered with the militia ... [plus] innumerable prostitutes controlled by nobody, and [a] still larger number of "freelance broads" soliticing as a supplementary job in addition to their official work'.[5] During my stay in Hungary in May 1970, a radio programme on people's attitudes to money featured a prostitute whose monthly income of about six times the country's average was being discussed as in no way exceptional.

The reason for prostitution being so lucrative is not that East European men will pay anything for a bit of professional skirt. It is rather that the girls lovingly devote themselves to western visitors and especially their currencies, selling the latter on the black market. In Czechoslovakia they are actually called 'Tuzex babies', Tuzex being the firm whose high-quality wares must be paid for in foreign currency. Black-market operations themselves can yield enormous profits. They are rifest in Poland, where the State actually forces its citizens to take part in them: spares for western cars which State agencies sell for Polish money are available only at the Polish equivalent of Tuzex. People not prepared to steal parts off company cars thus have to buy them for western currency, which they can find only on the black market. Not surprisingly, the usual difference between East European official and black-market exchange rates is much the largest in Poland, amounting to between 450 and 550 per cent.

Apart from direct money-making, there are many other purposes for which young East Europeans try to get round the centralist system in various ways. The most important among the latter is *protektsio*, which I have already mentioned. If it is useful for getting into better secondary schools and then universities, its value only increases afterwards, as people begin to make their own way in life, seeking jobs and then promotion. Meanwhile, it also proves to be a supreme aid in all difficulties, whether for getting extra leave from work, jumping the queue for new accommodation or finding, say, brass door-knobs in periods of shortage. Similarly, though counter-selection may be the cancer of the whole system, rather than trying to fight it in vain a good many young East Europeans choose to exploit it. 'I admit it may be a better system than there is, for instance, in West Germany,' the thirty-one-year-old Romanian journalist whose depressed remarks about counter-selection I quoted on page 205 said by way of light relief. 'It's an economic disaster, but it's tolerant. A lot of people would have to starve or work much harder if it were not for counter-selection, and some I think could not stand the change, and would just starve.'

Meanwhile, some of the same conventions for coping may also prove useful to those trying to cope on behalf of more than just themselves. Labour migration, for instance, has been exploited by clever managements to lure together crack work-forces, which are then kept together both by material incentives and by a sense of belonging to crack enterprises. Moonlighting itself may be seen as merely a method whereby the community distributes skills more evenly than the system can and, at a stretch, the same may be said of prostitution. *Protektsio* and even bribes are used to help factories obtain raw materials which, despite plans, they have failed to get, or to enlist support for reform proposals which higher-ups have tried to suppress. Even the tragicomic skills and the habit of intriguing which life in a centralist system strongly fosters in young East Europeans can be of more than personal service. 'What do you do when you can't convince them [older people in power] that they should try your ideas?' I asked a twenty-eight-year-old Bulgarian engineer. 'You either give up after a time,' he said, 'or you try other things. You put your ideas in words they may understand, you look for strings of your own to pull, you make life difficult for them, or in the last resort you start working behind their backs to get them removed or pensioned off.'

The second factor that alienates young East Europeans not only from the system which the collective is said to own and rule but often also from each other is directly political. In essence, one of the conventions by which they live is a need to cope at all times with a fearsome machine, central to that system and tireless in its efforts to recruit new agents, intruding even on people's dreams. This is so almost irrespective of their political convictions. 'Just a minute, if you don't mind,' a twenty-nine-year-old Party member said with a brief smile in the currently most relaxed country, Hungary, as he unplugged the phone while we embarked on discussing some rather involved political matter in his home. He was one of a rare breed of sophisticated but professing Communists, but before going into the ideological aspect of the problem I first wanted to know how we could be overheard through the phone while the receiver was in place. 'You just leave that to our vanguard police force,' he assured me, if this could be called assurance. 'Are you, too, afraid?' I asked. 'We're all afraid,' he said, in smiling earnest. 'Every one of us is afraid at some level, whether they admit it or not. I happen to admit it.'

Fear of the machine is, quite simply, an element of life in Eastern Europe today. 'When they call you in, they start by telling you they know everything,' a thirty-year-old translator said in Poland. 'And you know that it's a trick. I don't mean they might not know everything, but it's still a trick because there's nothing bad to be known about you. All the same, it makes you feel guilty, just the fact that they can harm you in so many ways, and you start defending yourself.' The same kind of thing does not hold true for manual workers, since as soon as they were kicked out of one job they would find another of the same kind. This is one of the reasons why when workers decide to go into the streets, they find themselves faced not just with walls of secret and uniformed police, but with armoured cars and tanks, and more often than not, blood flows. Apart from such occasions, however, there are enough methods of scaring them into not talking politics to anyone but their closest friends. The conviction that there are informers in every working environment is general among young East Europeans regardless of their social circumstances.

As I have mentioned, I myself more than once frightened people by being open with them, and so appearing an *agent provocateur*. This occurred in every East European country during each of my visits to the region. Even in Czechoslovakia in June 1968 I was once suspected of being a Russian agent posing as a

western journalist. In Bucharest in the following year a perfectly
sane writer in his twenties changed, in the middle of our second
conversation, from French into Romanian, and continued in that
language for several minutes, testing me. 'You must understand,'
he said later. 'They try all kinds of things. Kafka's world seems
at times a merry dreamland compared to ours.'

So, living in fear of the machine, East Europeans not only
resort to all possible ways of coping with it, but also extend every
one of these ways to the whole of the world that the machine
seems to own and rule. Having throughout their lives seen their
environment behave in a total manner, they behave in the same
total manner towards it.

It may be said that in so doing they only 'totalize' conventions
many of which are much older than themselves. In fact, it is this
natural extension of these methods to cope with every part of
'their' world, rather than the mere use of these ways, that distinguishes today's young East Europeans from previous generations of copers. On taking power in 1948 the Party had in mind
the abolition of these all-too-human conventions. But through
the imposition of its Platonic-centralist rule on the whole
environment it has further invigorated them, and made them
more general.

For example, to ease one's feeling of impotence in face of the
political machine by devastating it in jokes had been a popular
habit in Eastern Europe long before the Party came to power, and
one the Party duly set out to eradicate. It banned political cabaret
and press caricatures of any but enemy politicians, and made the
telling of political jokes an indictable offence. As a matter of fact,
even in the second half of the sixties jokes about price-rises could
cost people in Bulgaria long-term banishment from all major
cities; and to this day caricatures are not allowed throughout the
region, and cabaret is permitted only in Hungary and to a lesser
extent in Poland.

Meanwhile, however, everything the Party rules, from the
police to foreign trade, has turned into material for political jokes.
The Party's own undeposable leaders serve as more stable comic
figures than any that Eastern Europe has ever seen, while its ever
amended yet always infallible ideology has become rather a joke

in itself. And this was bound to happen, given the Platonic centralism the Party imposed on the whole environment, and is likely to endure for as long as does the Party's centralist rule.

Much the same has happened to a number of other conventions. For instance, to rebel against an aspect of the economic order that one cannot regard as one's own by stealing from it as much as possible had long been a habit of the urban and rural proletariat. The Party's appropriation of the whole of the economy on behalf of the collective only made it more general. The same habit used to be complemented by management overlooking a certain amount of theft as a natural part of employees' pay. And though this is still standard enough, it has meanwhile become compounded by management joining forces on occasions with employees to steal from their common employer, the State. This is, in fact, only the economic version of the irony of Party members often telling jokes of the utmost bitterness about the system and its ideology.

A good many extended conventions of coping, however, hurt only the Party as a Platonic institution, while they benefit the people it claims to represent. *Protektsio*, for instance, can help a man not only in getting on, but also in defending himself against parts or even the whole of the machine. It may provide aid in a fight against the censor as much as in gaining an insight into one's secret police files. At critical times, not only may friends take the risk of giving a dismissed man a good job, but whole organizations may turn into bodies of protective plasma to hide the persecuted from the eyes of those above. 'I don't know how they managed it,' the young wife of a Warsaw academic said to me in May 1970. 'But despite sweeping purges quite a few people we feared for have gone on doing more or less what they had been doing before. They were dismissed as lecturers and then taken on for research posts; or heads of departments would promise the ministry to kick them out and then somehow forget; or the university passed them on to the Academy, or something, until the storm passed. You can only admire the way it works.'

At such times, the sheer inefficiency of the machine, which centralist inertia has done little to diminish, may also be of supreme value. 'It's what saves us from the kind of life the East

Germans are having to live,' said the twenty-three-year-old Hungarian instruments technician I have quoted several times, with a happy sigh. 'You just couldn't keep that kind of thing going here. I'm sure that even in the worst years reports carrying death sentences were made up about people by one section, without the section next door ever getting to hear about them.'

Then, of course, there is humour. Not just the jokes, but 'our' general ability to laugh at, and even humanly to sympathize with, 'them', so making 'them' both less fearful, and less significant in 'our' lives – by, for example, mocking 'their' jargon and slogans in slang, which has contributed a steady stream of sadly untranslatable expressions to each East European language in the last twenty-five years. The secret police themselves have been 'humanized' in almost affectionate slang terms: in Polish they are called *'smutni'* ('the sad ones'), among Transylvanian Hungarians *'szigoru fiuk'* ('the austere lads') and in Hungarian simply *'elvtársak'* ('the comrades'). Nor is this just a matter of names. 'You must understand these people too,' said a thirty-year-old Romanian artist. 'They've been in their jobs for years, it's the only thing they can do, they have to stick to it and produce results, no matter what. So they make inquiries, listen to your phone, have you watched, send you messages through intermediaries that you're not to say such naughty things, and so on. With that they've done their bit, and they make out a report, and can sit back for a while.'

Other ways of coping with 'them' are more structured. Or it may be more accurate to say that, on the one hand, just as all jokes concerned with the civic environment were once taken by 'them' as actionable, so many of 'our' spontaneous attempts at public coping gain a special structure, from seeming to be part of a total challenge to 'their' rule. This is why all strikes are, *ipso facto*, political strikes. It is why when young people speak up for freer discussions at universities or in youth clubs they are seen by all as pressing political demands. It is why when others gather regularly to talk politics in private, or to read out literature the censor has tried to suppress, they are inviting sanctions as 'conspirators'. In 1966 a number of students were said to have been expelled from Sofia University because they had formed a circle in which epigrams and satirical plays with a political edge were being read out. In 1970 in Poland a group of young people who had engaged in bringing *émigré* literary magazines into the country were sentenced in a noisy trial to prison terms ranging up to four and a half years.

On the other hand, 'their' oppressive centralism does often force on 'our' political activities far more of a conspiratorial structure than these would otherwise have. If political trials were freely reported, there would be no need for the speeches of the defendants to circulate in clandestine pamphlets. If the State did not control all printing works and also every duplicating machine in use throughout each East European country, there would be no need for material to be reproduced on typewriters by bands of enthusiasts at considerable risk to themselves. And if people gathering with any regularity to discuss politics were not sure of being closely watched, they would not resort to evasive tactics that are often more complicated than those of Lenin himself in his underground days. In Poland in the late sixties, for instance, it became the habit of leftist groups to get together for 'name-day parties' at which all kinds of inanities were said aloud for the benefit of police microphones, while written messages passed between guests discussing matters of importance.

The question of which of all these ways of coping with 'their' system will be adopted by anyone depends, of course, on a large number of circumstances. Of these I shall mention here only the most important one, namely the personalities of those involved. Some people may be able to absorb fear, and even acts of interference in their lives, and go on living and even fighting back, much better than others. Often husband and wife will describe an interview with the police in very different terms, the one prepared to wait and see if anything worse will follow, the other predicting disaster for both of them, or even a general worsening of the country's political situation. Being forced to act as informers, some people dutifully comply until they grow almost enthusiastic, others become revolted with the system or themselves and commit suicide, and yet others go on turning in banal gossip until they are dropped as idiots. While some people buckle down and others withdraw into isolation in the face of censorship, there is a whole range of individuals in between who will fight for every line of a book and every frame of a film, resorting to all kinds of ruses until the story of their tribulation is common knowledge and so achieves a purpose of its own. When they are kicked out of a job some people collapse, while others lie low for a time, subsisting and reading the books they have long been meaning to read, and others find ways of hanging on, often with signal success.

At the other extreme, the final recipient of all these ways of coping is the Party, as Hero in central charge. The most poignant example of this can be seen, in fact, in the behaviour of its own members towards it. Though far from all of them are careerists, the majority are opportunists, in either the private or the public sense, or both. That is, they continue to see the Party as 'them', with which 'we' have to cope as individuals or as members of the collective, almost independent of ideological considerations, in 'our' best interests and according to conventions 'we' all accept and understand.

Of course, the most important among the interests involved will be, once again, personal – not that people admit this, often even to themselves. On the contrary, it is the young careerists who will be the most eager to hide their aims behind a curtain of phraseology: it is in fact by this curtain that they can be recognized. As a rule, it is made up of the most 'modern' patchwork of Party jargon, slogans and ideas, though less intelligent careerists may not join these up too coherently, and some may even keep putting their feet through the fabric.

But however sound the patchwork, young East Europeans will tend instantly to discern the man behind it. 'Seems a nice person,' I said to my twenty-year-old interpreter, partly by way of soliciting his opinion, after an interview with a member of the Central Committee of the Bulgarian Komsomol, who had in fact struck me as a smooth but humane enough apparatchik. 'Seems,' my interpreter said, in a scathing tone, 'a nice careerist.'

Careerists, however, tend to provoke such contempt only when flaunting their curtain of convictions. Otherwise, the majority of young East Europeans seem to recognize joining the Party for career reasons merely as a human response to a given situation: 'Why would you say your father was a Party member?' I asked a twenty-two-year-old hitch hiker, also in Bulgaria. 'Why? But he's manager of a furniture factory,' was all he answered. It is also a response that many of them expect to have to repeat, according to the tragicomic convention. In fact, a good indication of the extent to which they see entering the central political machine as merely a human response to given circumstances is given in the results of a survey carried out among working-class youth by the Prague City Committee of the Party in the late sixties. Asked why they thought functionaries ever became functionaries, 24·3 per cent thought that they were 'trying to further their careers', while exactly twice that number opined simply that 'somebody had to do the job'.

In addition, personal reasons may themselves be more complex, in which case people will also tend to be more open about them. 'When I applied to joint the Party,' said a young Romanian theatre director, 'nobody could understand, not even the person I asked to second my application. Not that I'm a reactionary, but still, why did I need to be a member? But I know what I'm doing. I'm making sure that when I'm up there directing a play and I tell a stage hand to do this or that, he won't turn round and tell me to go to hell, because he's a Party member and I'm not. I've seen people create chaos that way, and I don't want it.'

'Why are you a Party member?' I asked a twenty-seven-year-old Hungarian social scientist who is a friend of mine. 'If I didn't know you, I'd think you were an *agent provocateur* and give you a speech,' he laughed. 'But I'll tell you. Quite frankly, I *am* a Marxist, and that's one reason. The other is that as a Party member I can have access to all kinds of research material which it would otherwise cost me endless trouble to see. So you may say it's an instance of the unity of theory and practice.'

Equally frank will be many of those who joined to some extent for the purpose of coping on 'our' behalves. 'How can you be politically active in a one-party state?' a twenty-eight-year-old former member of the Czechoslovak Party said in 1970. 'You either go underground or you join the Party and work from within. Even now, though most of the good people have been kicked out of the Party and many are underground, printing leaflets and so on, there are individuals even inside the Central Committee who leak secret reports and speeches and at least keep the rest informed. And before '68, when I joined, the Czechoslovak Party was a huge living organization with all kinds of factions, and though you had to be careful, you could hope to get things done. It was almost like a multi-party system in a one-party state.'

In fact, the successful revolt against the centralist Czechoslovak Youth League between 1965–8 had itself been staged by League functionaries, several of whom were Party members. Many other members and functionaries on many other occasions have also turned out to have genuine purposes in view. In addition, whether the issues involve the activities of a youth club, the distribution of university scholarships or the living conditions of apprentices in a factory, the dynamics of conflict situations themselves may turn some wholly supine careerists into tribunes of the people. And on every occasion those in a position to lead are accepted as leaders when they are seen to be taking 'our' side against 'them'.

Of course, the question that is bound to arise is: if almost everybody even inside the Party is trying for some reason or other to cope with 'them', then who is 'them'? Nothing could better illustrate the validity of the question than the fact that Party members themselves, even while rising in the hierarchy, retain the habit of referring to 'them' doing things. Antonin Novotny, President of Czechoslovakia and First Secretary of the Party, is said to have retained this habit right up to the time he was ousted from his supreme offices in 1968.

The answer to the question is, however, that 'them' is everybody who in any situation is not 'us'. And 'our' alienation from that central version of 'them', the Party, is the sum of our feelings about 'them' in all these situations – regardless of how far we may know any one of 'them' to be as human as 'ourselves'. The perpetuity of the situation between us keeps 'them' for ever alien.

This is the more so as 'we' have seen far too many of them act, in a most human way, less high-mindedly than they preach. 'Very often they tell you they have joined the Party because they want to work at things from the inside,' a twenty-seven-year-old former functionary of the Youth League said in Poland. 'But it's just an excuse. They're careerists, but they talk like that because they don't want to lose their friends.' Equally, they may mean what they say, but not live up to it when the moment of truth arrives. While some careerists may be propelled through their curtains of phraseology to become heroes of the people, many more determined tribunes will be gradually seduced by the advantages of being one of 'them' until they can only rarely take 'our' side in any situation.

And having thus become an alien body, 'they' will make every effort, practical as well as ideological, to defend 'their' position. The fact that 'they' remain human, meanwhile, though it now lessens the dangers of fanatical terror, also gives 'them' a closer grip on 'us'. As humans, they keep in touch with 'our' ways of coping and make use of these in reverse. If 'we' get a good deal of 'our' news through the grapevine, 'they' too will not only sift through gossip for bits of usable information, but also inspire both political and personal gossip to suit 'their' purposes. If 'we' try to get away from 'their' order by burying 'ourselves' in work and making money, 'they' too will know that pressure can be put on 'us' by threatening 'our' careers. If 'we' have people among 'their' agents, 'they' will have agents among 'us'. Any time 'they' want to make inquiries, such as when 'we' apply for a passport to the West, the first person 'they' will come to see will be the caretaker in 'our' block of flats. Nor will 'they' stop there. 'When four really good friends are sitting together, one is sure to be working for "them",' says the East European adage, only slightly exaggerating the situation. In the dark years 'they' went so far as to pressure wives into divorcing their politically disgraced husbands, but nowadays 'they' may still turn girls loose on foreign visitors, and sometimes even locals, whom they want to discredit or blackmail.

'They' also have an effect on 'our' behaviour towards each other. Sometimes directly, as in enabling caretakers to keep whole housefuls of tenants in check. 'Did you see those cherry trees in the courtyard?' a thirty-one-year-old Hungarian acquaintance of mine, living in a four-storey block of flats, asked on one of my visits to his home. 'When I was a child, we could all pick the cherries. Now the caretaker has them for herself, and nobody dares say a thing. Are cherries worth a passport?' But even more important is the effect that 'their' total and unshakeable rule has by adding a special edge to human jealousy and pettiness. 'I live at home, but in a fairly large room which I have to myself now that my husband has gone,' explained a thirty-year-old divorcee whom I got to know during my first trip through the region. 'The other day I had some friends there, and two of them made the most biting remarks about how nice it was to have such a large room all to myself. Good friends of mine, and still they couldn't help remarking. It's the pressure, makes people crazy, makes them want to pry into your life, and gang up against you if you have the least bit more than they have.'

When the pressure changes from claustrophobic to critical, though it brings out the best in some, it brings out the worst in many others. 'That's the saddest thing, perhaps, seeing people turn into cannibals as the situation becomes more hopeless,' a thirty-three-year-old writer said in Slovakia in 1970. 'You see them attack each other for fear they might otherwise be attacked by someone else. Or take revenge for the most ancient sores, even though they know very well they may be doing each other in for years, if not for ever. . . . ' Small wonder if the pressure also crazes some of 'our' jokes to the point of the most bitter masochism. 'A snake was lying by the side of a river, waiting to get across,' ran a story I was told in Romania. 'A horse came by. "Please take me across," the snake asked the horse. "You'll bite me," the horse said. "Of course I won't. If I do, we'll both drown," said the snake. So the horse agreed and took the snake on his back and waded into the water. In midstream the snake bit him. "But why did you do that?" said the horse as they were sinking. "My friend," said the snake, "this is the Balkans." '

There is, of course, a certain amount of perverse comfort in being able to blame all this on 'them'. Whatever 'we' are doing to each other is 'their' fault, 'they' are the ones who are responsible. Nor are 'we' having to invent 'them', or generate theories about some invisible but diabolically clever and powerful 'system'. 'They' oblige by being actually there. Indeed, they advertise 'themselves' as the central rulers of the environment, suppressing all attempts to challenge this position of 'theirs' in the most demonstrative manner. 'We're what has been called a "protectorate generation", and all they did in August '68 was to remind us,' a thirty-two-year-old former Party member said in Prague in 1970. 'And the thing has its advantages. We have no rights, but also we haven't the responsibilities we'd have had if '68 had been allowed to go on. So we live as best we can, and let them worry about things, and take the blame.'

Take the blame, in fact, not only for what 'we' do to each other, but also for most of what life does to 'us'. Again and again I have heard young East Europeans blame everything, from such social ills as endemic theft, alcoholism, and rising divorce and suicide rates to failures in their careers and weaknesses in their friends' and their own characters, on 'them' and 'their' way of running the environment. It may even be said that the Party is to young East Europeans what at the height of the Freudian craze Mother was to many young Americans, the cause of all their problems.

For this, however, the Party has only itself to blame. It takes over in Eastern Europe where 'our' parents left off, never letting 'us' run 'our' affairs as grown-ups, almost regardless of whether 'we' count as its potential enemies or its sworn faithful. 'One of the worst things about being a Party member these days,' said the twenty-nine-year-old Hungarian woman whom I quoted on page 169, in the course of an interview two years after our first, 'is that you can actually criticize more freely than if you were a man in the street. But it doesn't make any more difference to what they do.' However its rule may be moderated, as long as the Party remains Hero in total charge of the environment 'we' are destined to count as its mere children.

The significance of this comes home even more fully to young East Europeans as they grow to adulthood – as indeed does the significance of so much else determining their ways of life. What to the young animal might have been unnoticeable, inconvenient or irritating becomes to the adult, with his needs and standards developed, his energies fully engaged and his nerves strained to their already known limits, important, stifling or deadly. Crowded housing, for instance, which might force a sixteen-year-old to turn down his transistor set, may turn what should be the adult's final refuge into a den of frustrations. 'I have only ever made love in silence,' said the thirty-year-old divorcee I quoted earlier. 'It's a thing you learn and then can't forget it. When for years every time you're with your husband or your lover, you know that in the room on the right are your parents and on the left your younger sister, and everything can be heard through the walls and the doors, you learn to be silent. When you want to shout, you hold yourself back, clenching your fist or scratching in silence.'

Coping itself, in the ways that have become conventional, means something different as people grow older. They realize that the conventions which they got to know as unchangeable during their young animal time, and which some may have criticized idealistically, are in fact both degrading and wasteful. This will not stop them continuing to cope in most of the ways they know. But to do so in ever-growing awareness will embitter and demoralize many of the most responsible and turn an even greater number of others into cynical hedonists. In the three years I spent interviewing young East Europeans I actually saw not a few in the twenty-seven to thirty age group go through this sad process. The twenty-nine-year-old Hungarian woman who I have just quoted again on this subject was herself one of these, becoming disillusioned rather than hedonistic, if that is any consolation.

Homesickness, too, that final form of order most closely inter-twined with one's ways of life, assumes a very different meaning with time. To the young animal, it is a yearning after the life he has led and can see himself leading only under the pressures of his native environment. To the adult, whether or not he feels the same about life under those pressures, being unable to leave is more a matter of entanglements that can no longer be changed. 'Even if I were the sort of person who could leave a wife and child behind me,' said the thirty-year-old Polish translator I quoted on page 252, 'where else could I do what I'm doing here? I'd have to start life all over again, and most likely I'd end up worse off than I am now.'

Altogether, it is on entering the recognized generation and so assuming all responsibility for himself and his own family that Jonah becomes aware of his full predicament as a person alive in Eastern Europe today. While he was a young animal, he saw more or less all authority as 'them', and could make happy use of all the ways of enjoying and coping with the world 'they' owned and ruled. If order or conditions cramped his style, he had known both as restrictive since childhood, and could look forward to the freedom adult years would bring. As a member of the new generation he could still rely on 'them' to some extent, while he learnt the more involved conventions of coping as simply part of life, and continued to blame a number of his problems on the fact that he had only just started to cope for himself. But with his arrival in the recognized generation all that has ever stood between him and the sheer facts of the environment with which he is having to cope falls away. He is left alone in the midst of his circumstances.

Except, of course, for that final version of 'them', the Party, present in every situation, and proposing to remain so for ever. Indeed Jonah's claim to adulthood depends on his admitting that politically he will always remain a child. His full arrival in the recognized generation in Eastern Europe entails his recognition of the Party as the least removable of life's circumstances, completing his predicament on the spot where he was born and is likely to die. 'You see, you little fool,' the Slovak computer analyst of twenty-nine whom I quoted earlier said to his eight-month-old daughter, whom he was nursing while we talked. It was May 1970, two years after our first interview, and not a shred of the hopes of 1968 had been left in Czechoslovakia. 'Couldn't you choose to get born somewhere else? Canada, maybe. And then send a letter of invitation to daddy too, so he can get a passport, going to see a blood-relation who's not an illegal émigré in the West? You're as stupid as your father, getting born here, I tell you.'

Given that they are 'in it together', Jonah's predicament is also, of course, that of the Party. This is so not only because as long as he remains under the Party's tutelage he will always have cause to blame it for all his problems, but even more because, to involve Jonah in its projects, whatever their value, is the gravest problem facing the Party as Hero in charge of Eastern Europe.

In fact, though their common predicament is now harder for Jonah to sustain, it seems bound in the end to ensnare the Party more fatally. Whereas Jonah will go on living for ever, all of the Party's options are suicidal. In so far as it remains the Party it will always alienate Jonah's support, while its tangible successes as ruler of the environment will allow him to escape further from its Platonic order into sheer life, and will feed his spontaneous demands and vigour until they grow beyond the Hero's powers of repression. And as the tasks facing them together become more complex, so the Party's need to involve Jonah will only increase, while to him the simplicity of blaming all failures on the Party will come to seem all the more attractive.

Thus the tragicomic situation between them is likely to grow ever more comic for Jonah and ever more tragic for the Party. As Hero wholly in charge of his world, it will end by taking on itself the whole of his predicament. While his existence under its tutelage will grow ever richer, it will either be suffocated in heroic isolation, or will be overwhelmed by the sheer life that it has helped to grow luxuriant, or both.

Ironical as this may be, to me it seems inevitable, and also just. In proposing itself as the Ultimate Hero of History, Rationality Incarnate and the Sole Champion of Progress, the Party created the situations by which it is now ensnared. These situations will be the subjects of my next three chapters.

7 Heroism, Materialism, Realism

The night after students had set fire to the Paris Stock Exchange, in May 1968, I was sitting with a twenty-three-year-old Maoist poet in a second-rate restaurant in Budapest. We had had something to eat, and were drinking slowly, and arguing furiously.

A group of young Maoists was about to be brought to trial on charges of conspiracy. The conspiracy charge, everyone seemed to agree, had been largely invented, but about their Maoism there was little doubt. What did they want? I asked the poet, who knew most of them. It appeared that they were disgusted with 'frigidaire socialism', with the pursuit of money and lack of higher aims. They were also opposed to policies that promoted social re-stratification, cultural and general westernization, and the growth of the socialist *petite bourgeoisie*. Fair enough, but what would they have instead? They would have a revival of revolutionary purity in spirit and radicalism in practice, such as had been brought about in China, or, as some of those arrested (and a number not arrested) were known to have dreamt aloud, a revival of Stalinism itself.

This then started our argument. Just who did the Maoists claim to represent? Quite apart from a hatred of express Stalinism, people in the country seemed to me to be in no way yearning for revived revolution, but in every way for still more consumer comforts and more westernization. According to my poet, that was because the government, through deliberately promoting consumption, had drugged the masses and destroyed their revolutionary will. This I thought a rehash of the Party's own Platonic rationale from the Stalinist fifties, blaming its failure to rally the masses as their manifest Universal on sadly successful manoeuvres by 'the enemy'. But was consumption not endemic, was the regime not promoting it, and revelling in whatever popularity it gained thereby? the poet demanded to know. Perhaps, I said, but that still did not prove that those who wanted to take consumption from the people and give it heroic slogans, police terror and isolationism instead were its true friends.

Did I think 'they' were, then? A tough question. But I had to admit that if I were the people, between 'them' and the Maoists I would, at least in the current Hungarian situation, still choose 'them'. Because 'they' at least had to a certain extent compromised with 'my' real nature and wishes, while the Maoists had appropriated 'their' formerly Platonic ambitions, on whose behalf I would see mincemeat being made out of me and my brothers once again as enemies of 'ourselves'.

And so on and so forth, with our voices rising. Meanwhile the actual people, at table after table round us, went on with its consumption. In fact, the time being past midnight, certain vanguard elements of the people had begun to show signs of having consumed a bit too much. Others were also catching up with them. Then the small gypsy band on the dais in the centre of the place struck up into a flourish, and fell silent. A man in his forties, beefy, sun-tanned, wearing a light-brown suit and with his hair oiled back from his forehead, stepped up to the microphone. Having tapped it a few times, he let the band lead in, and then began to coo:

> My gracious Madam,
> You look so forlorn. . . .

It was a syrupy dirge, probably older than half the people to whom it was being sung. Yet when he got to the end of the first verse his audience sang the refrain with him. Clearly they were regulars, the clientele as much as the man and his songs, and had been for years.

For my poet, this was too much. 'Look at them, my proletariat, lapping up this hogwash!' he exclaimed, banging his fist on the table. 'Let me get out of here, emigrate! To Paris, there at least you can still light fires! . . .'

An escapist reaction, if ever I saw one, but typical enough – as was my poet's whole line of reasoning – of Platonists of whatever hue in politics. Having tried to impose on reality ideal structures which it is too complex to take, they blame not the structures or themselves, but 'enemy manoeuvres' and reality as such, from which they then try to escape – back into the purer world of theories where their structures belong, or into nature or abroad, or into terror or terrorism or suicide, or whatever else offers a way out of the complexities they heroically wanted to abolish but found too tough to change.

Though an enemy to young radicals now, the Party itself rallied young idealists round such Platonic visions in Eastern Europe in both 1919 and 1945, only to lead them into disasters. From these, due mainly to its romantic contempt for the complex realities of agrarian life, local nationalism and sheer human behaviour, it sought escape initially in terror and then underground and abroad in 1919, and then in more terror and in blaming failures first on 'the enemy' and then on Stalinist 'excesses' in 1945–56. The second time, however, Soviet armed might kept it in power.

This proved both a blessing and a curse. It was a blessing in the obvious sense that the Party wanted to remain in charge, rather than escape underground and abroad; but a curse in that, humbled into varying measures of pragmatism by the complexities with which it thus had to go on coping, it could never again pose as the romantic band of revolutionaries which had so appealed to young idealists in Eastern Europe during the early days. On the contrary, as a body proposing to rule the region for ever, it has had to reject as its own worst enemies those among the young who now embrace its former revolutionary idealism, and look back on its romantic periods with nostalgia.*

It is true, however, that such romantics form a minority among today's young East Europeans. In fact, romanticism is probably less popular in the region now than it has ever been. When asked

* In Hungary itself, the only people who put on a spontaneous demo to mark the fiftieth anniversary of the Commune, in 1969, were young leftists, only to find themselves watched, and sometimes interrogated, by plain-clothes policemen. They also made a film about the Commune, in which one of the two people sentenced in the Maoist trial I mentioned above played his own father, a young Marxist at the time and destined to become Hungary's cultural arbiter under Stalin. The film was never released, and it landed its makers in some very hot water.

what the word 'romantic' means to them, young East Europeans tend to give replies ranging from the barely compassionate to the coldly contemptuous.

My own interviewees thought 'romantic' meant 'starry-eyed', or 'sentimental, sort of gooey', or 'Christian in a hoary way', or 'high-falutin' ', or 'breast-beating' or 'lost to what's going on'. 'Romantics' were 'eager-beaver do-gooders', 'old-type enthusiasts', 'pathetic believers' and even 'idiots'. While some people were ready to grant that 'romantics had their uses in the last century' or 'maybe in the '45–'48 period', nobody seemed to have much use for them today.

The one thing 'romantic' was never thought to mean was 'modern', that synonym for 'supremely good'. In fact people whose egotistic attitudes or assertive eroticism I should have thought most romantic regarded these traits in themselves as 'modern', and held 'romantic sentimentality' in the worst contempt. The few who did think that they were in some sense 'romantics' tended to admit this with a sigh of self-pity. By contrast, a twenty-six-year-old Polish economist I interviewed a few months after his arrival in London said that he was struck by the fact that 'the English are still romantic enough to believe in charity'. A twenty-seven-year-old Romanian woman with obvious Marxist training thought that romantics were altogether 'living with a false-consciousness of the world'. My Maoist poet, who had among other things written a song about the plight of the gypsies as racial outcasts in Hungary, translated and written a bookful of poems about Vietnam, and in 1970 published a sardonic ode to 'Che's Faults', enumerating them as those of a warrior Christ who was much preferable to pragmatic money-changers, was himself described to me by several people during my last visit to Budapest as a 'cheap romantic'.

The 'romantic' attitudes young East Europeans most strongly reject fall into two categories: the 'heroic' and the 'selfless'. Though the idea of self-sacrifice is central to both, they are in fact alternative versions of the same thing. Attitudes of the first kind are often egotistic, those of the second, altruistic; the first are often jealously defensive, the second, by nature indulgent. In political terms, the first often promote a cult of the self, and thus become effectively authoritarian, while the second encourage self-effacement and may help democracy. Altogether, it would be logical for the decline of the first to help the rise of the second. This I think may happen in the future, but for the moment both kinds of romanticism seem to be rejected by young East Europeans as belonging to the past.

Most important among the heroic attitudes rejected is that of battle-enthusiasm, in any officially recognized form. During the debate on the personality cult in the Hungarian 'self-knowledge circle' I described in the previous chapter, while some members argued that certain difficult tasks could be solved by a collective only when it was held together by such unquestioning enthusiasm that it had to find a figurehead in a single hero, most of them maintained that all such enthusiasm was bound to produce blindness to purposes and mistakes that would have to be paid for in blood. In fact, those young East Europeans who are still enthusiastic often arouse suspicions concerning their essential sanity among their friends. 'One of my room-mates thinks he's an idealist,' a twenty-two-year-old Warsaw student said in 1968. 'So we don't talk politics in front of him. He's a nice boy, but you never know what he might do.'

While surviving in battle has come to seem far more estimable than gloriously dying in one, what has come to seem especially mindless is 'dying for a cause' – or killing or hurting others in one. 'Do you believe in necessary cruelty?' I asked the twenty-six-year-old Bulgarian Communist during the all-night conversation which I described on page 246. 'In the heat of a revolution, perhaps,' he said. 'But from that point of view, the revolution has long been over.' In Poland, the survey whose findings on the preparedness of young respondents to apply sanctions against people with views 'considered harmful to society' I quoted on page 213 also found that only an insignificant percentage of the same respondents would have been prepared to spread beliefs by force.

Altogether, for either the collective or individuals to be driven by ideals has come to seem to most young East Europeans a supremely dangerous thing. 'My next short film will be called

"The Hunt",' a Romanian student director of twenty-seven told me in 1968. 'It's a manhunt, really. A man is pursued by beings he's never seen, to his own destruction. He's running through ever worse terrain, losing his youth, the woman he loves, his contact with children, everything human, and all the time you hear the noise of the hunters in the background. . . . When he's all alone, at the end of his strength, he falls down and his pursuers pass him by. He tries running after them, shouting, "It's me, me you've been after!" but they won't turn back or even hear him. He's left behind to die. . . . Who're the hunters? Ideal ambitions. Personal, political, anything the audience wants to make of them.'

Among the second kinds of 'romantic' attitudes, not a few have been denounced by the Party itself, as forms of compromise with the enemy, or as diversions lacking any real purpose. Into this category come charity, tolerance, a belief in *l'art pour l'art*, sheer playfulness, contemplative-religious life-styles, and so on.

The rejection of charitable attitudes is so widespread that though it has been noticed by many other visitors to the region beside myself, young East Europeans tend to become aware of it only when they meet charity in another environment. 'In Oslo, I lived for two months in a commune,' recalled a twenty-year-old student in the Polish seaport of Gdansk. 'They gave me a bed, and food, and everything, and left it up to me whether I wanted to give anything back. I don't think I'd ever find that in Poland. Here, everybody would want their own share first. So if somebody gave you something just like that, you'd think he was an idiot, and give nothing back.' According to all the surveys that I have seen, or that those in charge of them have described to me in detail, 'goodness' is regarded by young East Europeans as one of the least worthwhile of human qualities. Where it is not proposed in a questionnaire, it may not appear in free answers on person-ideals at all. Certainly it is not thought to be a 'modern' attribute, much rather the opposite. The same is true of tolerance, which tends to earn equally low marks when proposed in 'coded' questionnaires. In their personal relationships many young East Europeans, and especially those in the recognized generation, seem to despise it altogether as a quality found in doddering fools.

As regards versions of self-indulgence, not only is '*l'art pour l'art*' rejected by many of those educated enough to understand the notion, but '*l'art-pour-l'art*' has become an epithet of contempt among a number of people who have never thought about what it really means. In general, doing things well for their own sake is looked on as a 'romantic' sort of pastime. In Bulgaria, speakers at the 1962 Teachers' Conference, held in a rare atmosphere of sincerity, complained bitterly about the decline of respect for pure learning among the young and their general unwillingness to indulge in purely artistic or literary experiences. In fact throughout the region teachers now enjoy a lower status than they formerly did, partly because they 'only know things and teach, and don't make money', as a teacher in Bratislava quoted one of his former pupils saying.

Attitudes towards doing things for sheer pleasure are similar, as young East Europeans again tend to notice more clearly when in a foreign environment. 'I find I can't relax, not the way people can here,' a twenty-five-year-old Polish girl said in London, echoing a number of others I interviewed there. 'Even when I'm at home, I must always be doing something, something that has a use. I get nervous when I see the people with whom I'm sharing a flat just lazing about or doing things which to me seem so childish.'

A revulsion from playfulness on the one hand is often combined with rejection of what seems like senile eccentricity on the other. The idea of driving round in the kind of old cars which young westerners may spend countless weekends tinkering with, or wearing the 'granny' styles and second-hand clothing that have become fashionable in the West during the last few years fills most young East Europeans with genuine horror. The only East European capital where young people can be seen driving old cars with relish is Prague, that 'odd city out' of the region. In fact, when I mentioned in an article written for an English weekly about revisiting my Budapest classmates that one of the most likeable of them drove an army surplus jeep, I unwittingly made him the subject of constant ridicule among his friends. His owning such an odd car and spending Sundays under its bonnet had been comic enough, but for this to be known all over England! . . .

Altogether, what governs their attitudes towards both the

heroic and the selfless versions of 'romanticism' is the purposeful intolerance that I discussed in Chapter 5. Basically, this is a version of the Party's own heroic-dialectical rationale, but adopted for material rather than ideological reasons. 'Results are the most important things to them,' a fifty-two-year-old doctor said in Cracow. 'A lot of them, especially if they've had to struggle, hard, are wholly ruthless about this. If you've achieved results, you exist, if you haven't, you don't. And as for living. . . . They have a much better life, but I think they know less about how to live than we did at their age.'

This is how a man comes to be worth not the way he is or lives, but what he does. 'The subject most often raised in the letters we get,' said a twenty-seven-year-old editor of youth programmes on Radio Sofia, 'is education and how to get it. The general feeling is that without proper qualifications you can't enter society.' In surveys on person-ideals, where, as we have seen, 'goodness' emerges as a quality barely worth considering, 'knowledge' and 'professional qualifications' may be marked as twenty or even twenty-five times as valuable. Occupations are also rated by the majority much less according to the satisfaction they offer than according to the money they bring in.

This is, of course, only another version of rating objects according to their novelty and shine, and people according to the amount of new and shiny objects they own and are ready to offer others. Central to this purposefully intolerant vision of the world is a reduction of all its parts to what seems from one's own point of view their most obvious material worths. And used as they are to seeing their own environment in this sadly simplified way, all too many young East Europeans become still more intolerant on their trips to the West. 'I've now got ten pounds and a transistor set out of them,' a very well-brought-up seventeen-year-old Hungarian said to me in London, referring to relatives who had in addition offered to take him to any museums or sights he wanted to see. 'There won't be any more money, so what's the point of going?'

Altogether, the majority of young East Europeans seem to have embraced materialism with a vengeance. Often the more educated are merely more articulate about it. In the Czechoslovak survey on marriage which I quoted on page 239, it was found that when respondents were asked about the relative importance of mutual understanding and material security for a happy marriage, the percentage of those unprepared to trust mutual understanding alone was higher among the better educated.

As regards generations, a similar tendency is apparent. The younger of the two postwar age groups, having grown up in the midst of more affluence, is more demanding of goods and comfort and more concerned with money. Indeed the 'fifth generation' itself seems already to be anxious about affluence. 'Look what my eight-year-old nephew gave us as a wedding present,' said the twenty-two-year-old wife of a Cracow lecturer, showing me a child's painting stuck on the side of the couple's as yet only wardrobe. 'It has on it all the things he wants for us. A little house, a little car, and that train, that means holidays.' In a survey conducted among nursery-school children in Hungary, only 15 per cent of those asked why their daddies went to work could mention any reason other than that 'he brings home cash'.[1]

All this, however, can be of little comfort to the Party. True, its ideology prides itself on being materialistic, and genuinely regards economics as the basis of social, political and cultural developments. But it is also ultra-romantic in its vision of the revolutionary as Prometheus the demigod, bearing fire among men of the earth and so moving them to change the world in one enormous upheaval and for ever. And pragmatic though its purposes may now be, as Hero in central charge and thus obliged to rally the people, the Party must continue to invoke its revolutionary past, use rhetoric about the present and the future and altogether play the warrior prophet.

The kind of response it can expect in this role, especially in the future, may perhaps be seen most clearly in young East Europeans' attitudes towards the figures playing the same role in the region's past. Indeed young poets and writers of today have themselves come largely to reject the prophetic stance. 'Most poets of my generation,' the twenty-seven-year-old poetry editor of the Czech writers' weekly told me in March 1969, 'find the traditional role of the tribune of the people ridiculous. I myself do. Some of us are in politics now, because these are extraordinary times, and it's expected of us, there being nobody else. But I can't tell you how much we're longing to get back to our own proper work.' They were soon forced to do so, under no less extraordinary conditions, when the hard-liners replacing Dubček in power in April 1969 banned all free expression of opinion. In essence, this amounted to the Party asserting itself as Prophet, and suppressing those whom the people had till then trusted in the role.

'Can you see yourself as a revolutionary, another Botev?'* I asked the thirty-three-year-old Bulgarian poet whom I quoted on page 133. 'I know how to handle a gun,' he laughed. 'And I used to see myself as a revolutionary. . . . But nowadays, the kind of poetry I admire is that of T. S. Eliot.' In fact, Eliot came up again and again as an admired example in conversations I had with young poets, while political poetry, often even of the oppositional kind, had lost much of its appeal for them. Yevtushenko, for instance, whom many of them knew personally, had no following at all. He was thought to be serving up oppositional claptrap as poetry, 'making himself a name by protesting about the price of potatoes', as one of the best, if not the kindest, Romanian poets of the recognized generation put it.

'The fact is,' said a twenty-seven-year-old Hungarian poetess, 'we're so fed up with being led by people advertising themselves as the one and only, the Saviour Himself, we don't want to advertise ourselves as such either. When people write that kind of stuff, we find it insufferably romantic.'

The other traditional exponent of the prophetic attitude, the military, seems a good deal less averse to playing the same role again. Not only has it made various bids for power but it also remains the most fervent dispenser of the kind of rhetoric that the majority of young poets have abjured in their style. But whereas poets may still be expected to lead, and speak for, the people at critical times, the military rates nowhere near its former status among those it might want to marshal.

* Hristo Botev (1848–76), one of the greatest Bulgarian lyricists, who not only considered politics the stuff of poetry but was an active revolutionary and died leading a band of guerrillas in a frontier raid against the Turks, then still ruling Bulgaria.

Pacifism has been spreading in every East European country, however heroic its traditions, as articles in the press note with sadness, if not horror. Meanwhile, surveys show the career of an army officer, once among the most highly regarded, to have sunk in esteem to between that of an accountant and that of a railway conductor.[2] It rates very much below other occupations requiring the same amount of education, while at dances girls have long stopped swooning at the sight of a uniform. As for priests, who originally often played both the prophetic roles that poets and the military later secularized and that were again reunited in social revolutionaries, their prestige has also declined. They rate below all other people with a tertiary education, while in Slovakia, where the tradition of priests in political leadership found its ultimate embodiment during the interwar period, a survey on religiosity showed that in a large and representative sample aged eighteen-plus, while 70·7 per cent were believers, only 28·2 per cent thought that priests should 'exercise a politico-public function'.[3]

Perhaps even more important from the point of view of a Party proud of its revolutionary past and retaining its revolutionary ideology even as a body that sees itself for ever in power, the young have become doubtful about the value of revolutions altogether. 'Our history is full of revolutions in which people who just had to be heroes rather than compromisers made a terrible mess of things,' said the twenty-seven-year-old Hungarian social scientist and Party member I quoted on page 258. 'Then they got out and wrote memoirs abroad, blaming treason and everything else except their own stupidity. Meanwhile those they left behind, I mean the people, had to suffer the consequences.' How far such views are a reaction to the actual mistakes of Hungary's past heroes, how far to the Party's own mad heroics in the more recent past, and how far to the Guevaraism of the country's present young Left it is impossible to say.

The important thing is, such views are held. However egotistical many young East Europeans remain in their personal relationships, in public life they largely reject the egotism of leaders and prophets. The same sort of division between their personal and public behaviour towards versions of romanticism promoted by the Party also exists in other forms. For instance, not only is pacifism far more widespread than hatred of the Party's external foes, charity and tolerance too tend to be extended to those the Party has it in mind to persecute. In fact, mercy of a truly revolutionary kind may even be shown to those whom the Party has subdued into acting as its own sly agents. 'I have good friends who only a few years ago worked for the police,' a thirty-one-year-old designer said in Romania. 'We used to shut up in front of them. How can they be still my friends? Because I understand what they've been through, I too have lived here and know what terror can do. Physically or mentally we're all cowards, and some of my friends were just less lucky than others.'

At the same time, the kind of purposeful intolerance which the Party has tried to instil in the young is perhaps practised most strongly with regard to the Party's own efforts to create involvement. 'The question here has long been, what do I get out of it, anything, anybody, what use are they to me?' a twenty-six-year-old Czech journalist said in Prague in 1968. He had just returned from a reporting tour of England, where among other things he had been to see youth clubs and the Boy Scouts. 'One of the things that struck me most was the emphasis on Charity. The Pioneers never taught us that. It was always some great love of the collective, never of the next man. So we've grown up loving neither.'

Of course the reasons for the spread of materialist attitudes have to do with more than propaganda. Some of the main reasons derive, in fact, from the Party's own achievements as Hero in charge of Eastern Europe during the last twenty-five years.

In the first place, people are more materialistic because they have come nearer to having things which they did not previously have. In this situation, a number of old and new attitudes and old and new circumstances combine to produce whole conventions of materialism. For instance, if young people do not want old cars, this is partly because of the surviving anxiety about 'what everybody will say', partly because spares may be difficult or impossible to get, partly because an object which is the first of its kind in the family's history had best be shiny and new, partly because for a lot less money they can buy shiny new motorcycles and scooters, and partly because shiny and new cars are themselves now trickling on to the market.

The same applies, *mutatis mutandis*, to any number of materialistic conventions. If young East Europeans refuse to be charitable, this is due partly to pure selfishness, partly to harsh traditions, partly to recent propaganda and partly to a feeling that they just cannot afford it. If they denounce radicalism as a 'rich kids' pastime', this is partly because so to denounce it saves others (including many rich kids themselves) from having to think about the issues involved, and partly because they do not feel secure enough materially to risk being involved. If on coming abroad they emerge as intolerant and grabbing, this is partly because their expectations have been raised beyond all hope of fulfilment at home, partly because the same expectations are raised still further on seeing the affluence of the West, and partly because no young East European can be sure whether he will see the West, or the people who are being generous with him, again. In fact, the general conventions of intolerance and materialism often spring from the same roots, to produce the same effects. 'It's true I wouldn't want to wear a bright-coloured overcoat because of what people would say,' said a twenty-six-year-old Transylvanian woman. 'But also, if you have a bright-coloured coat, you have to have others to match other dresses you wear with them. And most of us have only one coat for the winter, and another one for the autumn and the spring. So they have to be a colour that'll go with everything, which will be dull.'

For the Hero's children to be governed in their attitudes by such mundane considerations is not just paradoxical. It is also galling for those inside the Party who would genuinely like to see the young behaving or at least posing as the Hero's vanguard. To create such vanguard attitudes has been one of the main aims of each of their renewed ideological campaigns. But not a few older East Europeans themselves look on the mundane concerns of the young as signs of health, on which the Party should congratulate itself. 'People complain that the young are hedonistic and apathetic, and all that sort of thing,' a well-known Polish sociologist, himself in his forties, told me in 1970. 'Because in every survey, and also when you talk to them, they appear to be concerned mainly with their careers and money and having a good time, and then a happy family life. My view is, it's a good thing they are. For the first time in ages, we have a normal generation of young people. Not dreamers and heroes, and people drunk on emergency situations, but people who want to make something out of everyday life.'

At least some of the mundane concerns of young East Europeans also turn out on closer examination to be not so much materialistic as realistic. They reflect not just greed newly aroused but also reason applied to possibilities, and at times even awareness of the possibilities others have to face. I found the best example of such realism in young East Europeans' attitude towards that most romantic of modern adventures, spaceflight. Every time I asked a classful of schoolchildren whether they thought it more important for man to go to the moon or to put the earth in better order, they voted for the earth with a staggering unanimity. Nor was their choice wholly self-centred. 'When we put together a scrapbook on spaceflight,' said the Romanian science master whom I quoted on page 196, 'it was they who insisted that the last page should have nothing on it but the picture of a starving African child, to put things in perspective. They got the picture, and I think the idea too, from *Paris-Match*, but what matters is that the idea appealed to them.'

The second main group of reasons has to do with the Party's work of social transformation since 1945. While the former ruling classes setting the heroic tone by tradition, especially in Poland and Hungary, have been swept away, the children of strata whose outlook had always been more down-to-earth have invaded the intelligentsia and greatly enlarged the middle mass, so rising to form the leadership and bulk of each articulate society.

As a result, the whole outlook of each has become much less Platonic than it used to be. That young East Europeans themselves are at least half-aware of the social factors at work is shown in their rejection of heroism and forms of selflessness not only as 'old-fashioned' but often as 'seignorial affectations'. In fact not only has the intelligentsia been influenced by the earthy newcomers, but the absence of classes that at least affected such seignorial airs has also allowed the new middle mass to grow up less in awe of them.

Social change and the great widening of opportunities for the young are the main factors that have produced, for instance, the decline in the status of that most valorous of careers, the military one. In the old days most officers either came from the gentry or were lower-class boys who had found in the army a rare path upwards. Either way, they were socially respectable – the mere fact of their being in uniform put them a cut above the rest, as indeed it made any doorman a cut above most skilled workers, for example when it came to marriage. Now the gentry has gone, while the roads of upward mobility have opened wide before the young, and the pay and status of skilled workers have themselves risen greatly. In this situation, the career of an army officer offers nowhere near enough advantages to compensate for the rigours of the life and the dangers involved. The same is true, *mutatis mutandis*, of that other old path of upward mobility, the priesthood. It may even be said that workers' and peasants' children who in the old days might have entered the army in order to move up in society now become engineers, while those who might have entered the Church now enter the Party.

The same social situation has also helped to make that ultimate combination of the warrior and the priest, the prophetic revolutionary, much less popular. Only here the effect of changes on the attitudes of the young has been the reverse. Whereas the status of the officer and the clergyman has declined, revolutionary romanticism has become, as I have mentioned, almost exclusively an élitist phenomenon.

This is so irrespective of how democratic the actual programme of any leftist group may be. It has much more to do with the value put on political and generally abstract ideas in the social circles where the young radicals have grown up, and in which they tend to be moving now. Though the young Left in Poland has been more concerned with at the least political democratism than its Hungarian counterpart, it has still consisted mostly of children of the leftist professional intelligentsia, bringing from home (apart from enough security for involvement) a passion for politics. In both countries it has also been overwhelmingly

Jewish* – also true to social traditions going back to the turn of the century. But perhaps the most poignant example of what I am talking about has been the young left in Czechoslovakia. The country's traditions are the most pronouncedly unheroic in Eastern Europe, its society has long been the most homogeneous, and Communism proper looks back to much the strongest proletarian and even peasant traditions. The new-leftist programme, too, has not been merely tilting at the political bureaucratism of the Party, as in Poland, but has always stressed its pro-working-class stand on wages. Still, there, too, leftism has remained very much an elite phenomenon. Though it has included very few 'cadre-kids', virtually all the 'Trotskyites' arrested and tried in 1970–1 were members of the professional intelligentsia. The leftist student group which had spearheaded the pre-1968 revolt against the centralist Youth League had also originated in the Prague faculty of nuclear physics, which concentrated some of the best, and to the regime least dispensable, brains in the whole university.

A further important group of factors 'pulling earthwards' the attitudes of young East Europeans has derived from changes affecting education. While the extension of opportunities has brought lower-class children into the more articulate strata, both the curricula and the professional composition of those emerging from the schools have been transformed.

Science and technology have gained enormously at the expense of the arts. In basic schools, science is taught much earlier and more extensively than it used to be. It has also become much more important in the curricula of the (*lycée*-type) general-secondary schools. Meanwhile, the increase in the number of these has been far outstripped by the increase in technical-secondary

---

* Though viciously exploited by the propaganda machine at the time of the March 1968 student riots this was not a circumstance invented by 'them' for the purpose. 'The fact is,' the twenty-six-year-old Polish economist I quoted on page 269 said in London in 1970, 'no part of the student population was as interested in politics as the Jews. For years before March, whenever politicians came to talk about the country's situation to the students, most of the people who really asked questions and would go on arguing about the answers were Jewish. So when the troubles started, it was easy for the police to pick on them.'

schools, in which scientific subjects predominate as a matter of course. All this has inevitably weighted the minds of young East Europeans towards facts, actuality and utility as against ideas, abstractions and 'ephemera'.

In the case of the manual-working classes, the result has been mostly a confirmation of existing attitudes. In the case of the white-collar and even more the professional intelligentsia, however, it has combined with other factors to produce a qualitative change in outlook.

Among white-collar people, development has made the technician class much larger and more highly esteemed in relation to the clerical staff than it used to be. Meanwhile, the priorities of higher education have changed completely. In Hungary, for instance, whereas in 1937–8 39·8 per cent of students had read law and only 9 per cent engineering, by 1951–2 the percentages had been reversed to 3·8 and 34 respectively,[4] and the trend was to continue during the next two decades. 'The number of those studying in higher technical institutions,' said a Budapest daily in 1971 'has increased fivefold in the last twenty years. . . . While in the arts faculties the number of undergraduates is barely higher than it was in 1949–50, the number of those reading natural sciences has doubled.'[5]

There has thus emerged a young intelligentsia that is different from its prewar counterpart not only in its social origins and the content of its general education, but also in its specific training and its present professional composition and concerns. As a body it is rooted much more firmly in terrestrial facts. Moreover, as children of the manual-working classes have tended overwhelmingly to opt for the sciences rather than the arts, and then to choose careers in industry and the bureaucracy rather than academic and cultural life, they have emerged as dominant in the new intelligentsia not only by their sheer numbers, but also because theirs is the group wielding real power. This has helped them to communicate to their new strata the down-to-earth attitudes which shaped their own educational and career choices in the first place.

The nationalism of the new intelligentsia, for example, is very largely economic. Under pressure, as I shall try to explain in the next chapter, young technocrats may come to embrace heroic nationalism and its variants, but their true concerns lie elsewhere. 'For themselves, they're interested in money and in being able to realize their ambitions,' said in 1970 the thirty-eight-year-old editor of a Warsaw weekly, whose cynical but realistic assessment of the chances of the Party's hard-heroic faction I quoted on page 124. 'And for Poland, not in glory but in modernization. They supported the Partisans because it seemed as if they were going to stand up to the Russians once they came to power and also let the technical intelligentsia have its way. But they're not interested in war films – in fact they're damned annoyed at the money these films cost and are losing. What they want is to pull Poland into the twentieth century before the chance to do so is lost for ever.'

Of course the new intelligentsia's preference for development over heroics is very similar to East European schoolchildren's preference for putting the earth in order over spaceflight. It is realistic rather than purely materialistic. The difference being, in this context, that materialists are interested in coping with circumstances only for themselves, whereas realists also take at least some account of the basic interests of the rest, or even identify the satisfaction of these with their own ambitions. Undeniably the majority of today's young East Europeans emerge as materialists. But a significant minority of them, which grows in size as the level of education and work-involvement of the groups concerned rises, are realists, prepared and often keen to take a hand in coping on behalf of the collective.

Two main factors, however, alienate the realists among young East Europeans from the Party that is in charge of all their lives. One of these is the memory of the Party's abuse of involvement, especially by the young, in the fifties. 'We've seen countless false starts,' wrote the Romanian poet whose play about Jonah I described on page 191:

> Either the pistol failed to fire on time
> or the wind carried off its sound
> and the competitors ordered back to their places
> began fighting in their nervousness

They were rolling in the cinders of the track
broke each others' legs
threw dust in each others' eyes
The racetrack and the stadium
have more than once been flowing with blood
we have seen so many mistaken starts. . . .[6]

The fear that one's gift of oneself to the rest may be abused or wasted has affected both the heroic and the selfless versions of 'romanticism'. 'It seems,' wrote the author of the study on the life-outlook of Hungarian university students I quoted on page 224, 'that a great dread of being exploited and ridiculed exists; in brief that an almost overwhelming lack of self-confidence in three-quarters of those asked lies at the heart of a specifically dual attitude, gregarious but unsympathetic.' Or as the twenty-six-year-old Polish economist who thought that the English were 'still romantic enough' to indulge in charity put it: 'True, I think people in Poland don't give because they're afraid it'll be stolen; so much has been in one way or another. . . . ' This is why those who are still enthusiastic are regarded as not quite sane, and why being sceptical is thought to be perhaps the most important 'modern' quality.

The second political factor 'pushing earthwards' the attitudes of the young is the Party's imposition of Platonic order. In the short term, this may even be of comfort to the Party as a body interested in preserving the *status quo*. If, for example, Left radicalism is far more of an élitist phenomenon in Eastern Europe now than it was in the Party's own heroic days, this is on the one hand because only children of the élite or students indispensable to the regime can politically afford to expose themselves in such a way, and on the other because police control has made the broadening of a non-governmental political organization far more difficult than it was at any time prior to 1945.

But the same Platonic order which isolates the politically most sensitive among the young into minute coteries also isolates the Party from the rest. It forces on people a posture of constant crouching which, though again serving the Party's temporary interests, breeds only resentment and sullen self-seeking, for the inevitable results of which it alone will have to take the blame. 'That was one of the things in '68, you could breathe and walk upright,' a twenty-nine-year-old sociologist recalled in Slovakia two years later. 'It changed people politically as well as in the way they spoke to each other. Now, they've shut up and the country is grinding to a halt. ... ' And even where the Party's centralism is the most relaxed, and progress the most rapid, the pressures that remain often give the young a sense of utter stagnation. 'This is a swamp, you can't rise in it, or even stand up, only crawl around or sink further in,' said a twenty-three-year old Hungarian girl who had just obtained a degree in economics. 'The first chance I get, even on a day-trip to Vienna, I'll get out and stay out.' In essence, she was seeking escape from the same complexities as had depressed my Maoist poet. Only her dream vision was material and his romantic.

Fortunately for the Party, even if her dream appeals to many more young East Europeans than his does, both she and he represent minorities. The majority stop short of the ultimate act of desertion of the Hero which flight to the West or political revolt would signify, and continue to cope with their circumstances on the spot. But among them, while the materialists seek only to cope for themselves, the realists, though ready to cope on a wider plane, also regard the Hero as one of the circumstances with which they have to cope. Thus their staying 'in it together' with the Party barely lessens its heroic loneliness, and only makes the complexities of the situation by which it is ensnared more complex.

Still worse from the Party's point of view, changes now in progress are likely to affect the young in ways which will be to the Party's credit, but often not to its liking. Increased satisfaction of their material desires is likely to make the more sensitive among today's materialists increasingly dissatisfied with sheer materialism. With the concurrent spread of education and social homogeneity, an ever-larger number of them will rise into the ranks of the realists, who are for the moment more significant because of their position in the most articulate strata than because of their numbers in society as a whole. And while seeking to maintain the *status quo* without being able to count on either the romantics or the realists can only force the Party into alliances with the materialist remainder, the effects of its own good work are likely both to swell the realist ranks and to provide the material security and cultural stimulus needed for the emergence of certain neo-romantic currents among them.

Signs of these are already visible among members of the new generation. Having grown up in a more prosperous and peaceful period, they not only have better nerves, are more sociable and have greater wisdom in coping, but they are also less self-conscious about emotions and more socially conscious in their outlook. Their pop songs, for instance, have been becoming frank about feelings and tenderness which their brothers in the older of the two postwar generations would still have been too shy to display in public, and often even in private, without mawkishness. And though greater affluence has made them more demanding about money and possessions in their criticism of the society surrounding them concern with the quality of human relationships has begun to replace mere attacks on shortages, which recede as the shortages themselves slowly recede.

In theory, of course, the realists among the young should be the Party's closest allies. But in practice they are close enough only for discomfort. As Hero in charge of the environment, the Party provokes them as copers into trying to get round its centralism in all possible ways. As the body seeking to maintain the *status quo*, it has to bear the blame for the lack of higher values in society that they criticize. And as an institution bound to employ rhetoric in calling on the young, it alienates what in the realists it could most expect to rally, their romanticism.

The main fact about this is precisely that it is not 'romantic' in the old-fashioned sense. It is much simpler and more direct. It does not seek to strike poses or to employ high-falutin' language. It is a copers' kind of romanticism, altogether Aristotelian rather than Platonic. And as such, instead of responding to the Party's call it combines with the sense of greater security out of which it has grown to give the realists greater courage in trying to cope with the Party.

For the purpose, they may resort to putting on the tragicomic act, or to more direct action, or both. They know how far they can go, and the challenge they present is on the whole oblique, but none the less effective. Some of their songs, for instance, though openly sung, are perilously pertinent. In Romania, I heard a twenty-year-old singer yell at dancing crowds an Italian hit whose local version, just about intelligible, described a world of fear and despair in chilling detail. In Poland, following the March 1968 riots students made up a song retelling almost word for word the Public Prosecutor's version of what had happened, and capped it with abject praise of the Public Prosecutor, the Minister of the Interior and other such dignitaries. This they sang secure in the knowledge that to arrest people who grew hoarse in praise of the Minister of the Interior would be absurd, while the fulsomeness of their hosannas combined with a mere twinkle in their eyes to create a sense of irony as devastating as poison.

In action, while their greater sense of security makes them readier to try, their copers' outlook makes them more resilient. They crouch and retreat, if necessary, with more self-confidence, so minimizing their losses and turning on their attackers more resourcefully as soon as there is a chance to do so. In Czecho-slovakia, as repression began to descend in the autumn of 1968 the students' association kept finding new methods of *legal* resistance, even signing pacts with trade unions which could not be de-nounced without provoking the workers themselves. Elsewhere, too, it is the new generation which is liable to test the nerves of authority in ways that have been out of use for too long. 'The other day the phone rang,' a twenty-two-year-old student of physics recounted in Transylvania, 'and it was a man who said he wanted to have a chat. About what? I said. About things, he said, and it was clear he was from the police. So I asked if the police were interested in me and my friends. No, not really, he said. So what did he want, I said. We argued for a time, then he put the phone down. I thought there would be consequences, but so far nothing. So I've learnt that if you stand up to them, you may win. . . . '

The material security feeding the young's courage has resulted in the main from the Party's own achievements. Equally, when the Party's repression descends on them, the young take refuge in the concerns and pleasures of their lives, which the Party itself has helped to enrich. The dynamics of the whole situation were best described to me by the twenty-one-year-old Cracow student of psychology whose views on the March 1968 events I quoted on page 177. 'Apart from every other reason, students also went out to demonstrate because they needed an experience of that kind,' she said.* 'We're not heroes, but we still want something more than just thinking about our clothes and careers and then babies. . . . There's a song just out here called "The Children of Columbus". It's about Mr and Mrs Columbus who have a great time discovering America, then they buy a house and a wardrobe and have children, and the children have only the house and the wardrobe and no new world to discover. Well, that's us, those children. . . . But then on the same LP there's a song by the same singer about the Wild West, where there's one sheriff to every man. And that's us too, and it's in March that we were reminded. So now we worry only about our clothes and careers and that sort of thing again.'

And so the Party remains alone with its heroic burden, while the process whereby it labours but gains no friends continues. In fact the more successful the Party's labours, the more often and with greater effect the young are likely to unite against it. As affluence increases and education spreads, so the economic, social and cultural gaps which now divide both the romantic minority and the materialist majority from the realists in the middle will diminish. Not only are the realist ranks likely to swell and neo-romantic currents among them likely to develop, but the romantic minority itself, as its isolation decreases, is bound to become more realistic. Thus various tacit or explicit alliances between the three groups for the purpose of coping with the Party's Platonic order will become increasingly possible.

A number of such alliances have already been formed. In Poland in the second half of the sixties the young leftists who

* The idea that 'students in March needed a biography' was put to me again and again in Poland, both by older people and by students themselves. 'We're not afraid of going to prison,' said a student in a Warsaw hostel, talking in his own room beneath a loudspeaker which he himself had just told me he was sure had been installed as a listening device a few weeks after the riots. 'If we can get back to university afterwards, it just makes our biographies richer.'

directly challenged Party speakers during debates held in various university departments attained genuine and widespread popularity among students, and became leading activists in March 1968. And in Czechoslovakia, where the social isolation of the Left has been least acute and its programme therefore most realistic, it managed both to rally the students behind it in the campaign which ended in the destruction of the centralist Youth League and then, as I have mentioned, to conclude actual student–worker pacts in 1968–9.

Of course these alliances, whether tacit or explicit, all had specific purposes round which they had formed. They were practical, not theoretical. I believe that they will also remain so. The reason why Polish students never managed to get the workers on their side in 1968 for instance, was that their demands seemed too 'immaterial'. Though the Czech leftists made more headway, they also gained support only in so far as they could offer visible aims. 'The students who revolted against the Youth League,' one of the leading young radicals told me in Prague in 1969, 'were the same ones who had gone "tramping" and to pop concerts as teenagers in the early sixties. When the police beat them up, they became anti-police. When we started the campaign against the Youth League, and especially after some of us got kicked out of university for it, they accepted us as leaders. But many of our most important ideas, as we found out in '68, were way above their heads. . . . ' 'And would have antagonized a lot of them, if they had understood what these ideas meant to us,' added another Prague radical in another interview. 'Such as our ideas which opposed favouring the managerial élite in the new economic reforms. Many of the students were just about to enter that élite.'

The alienation of the minority of political romantics among the young from the rest clearly helps to maintain the *status quo*. But as it decreases, if the Party is to retain power it will have to rely more and more on combinations of force wielded from above and alliances with sections of the young, based on whatever defensive passions remain alive among the realists and the materialists, and on the sheer materialism of the latter. Meanwhile, as the region becomes better developed and education spreads, so the quality both of these defensive passions and of the materialist remainder can only sink. Thus every alliance that the Party makes with them must further debase it, as was shown by the alliance its hard-heroic faction forged out of anti-intellectualism, anti-liberalism and anti-Semitism in March 1968 in Poland. Having to make further alliances of this kind is a strange prospect for the Ultimate Hero of History. But if the Party is to retain power for ever, as it now intends to in Eastern Europe, it can hardly avoid them. For the same reason, much the same kind of prospect faces the Party as Rationality Incarnate, as I shall now try to show.

8 Passions, Beliefs, Ideas

'I don't like Wajda, he makes films for the Russians,' a twenty-four-year-old prostitute said to me in a Polish seaside resort in June 1968.

'For the Russians?' I said.

'Yes,' she said. 'And for the Jews.'

She had a fresh face, and she was bright, perhaps only a summer prostitute. Still, her passionate dislike of Poland's most famous film-maker for such complex reasons was a surprise to me. Nor did I quite understand the reasons themselves.

'He's making films against Poland,' she said. 'You know what I mean.'

I did not. I had vaguely heard of controversies that had followed some of Wajda's films knocking the Polish heroic tradition. But I had not yet done enough background research for the present book to understand the political significance of these controversies in Poland today. And anyway, did prostitutes normally get so worked up about such things?

Two years later, a historian of the Second World War I met in Warsaw echoed her sentiments.

'We don't like Mr Wajda,' he said. 'He makes films for the West.'

'The West?' I said.

'It's there he wants to be famous,' he said. 'By making Polish heroism look ridiculous. It's good business, they like that in the West.'

By this time, however, I was a little better prepared. To understand both what these charges meant and the dynamics of a situation in which a seaside prostitute and a military historian should echo each other in condemning a Polish Gentile for the pleasure his films might have given to the Russians, the Jews and the West together.

The most important element of this situation, as must be clear by now, is enormous pressure. And the heavier and more complex the pressures weighing on people the more likely they are to seek the causes of all their problems outside themselves and their own group. In other words, to blame 'them' totally, in order to be able to hope for total relief through 'their' downfall. The East European situation thus keeps alive, even in many of those who would now reject active heroism, heroic hatreds of 'enemies', and defensive preoccupations with themselves as a tribe.

Permanent Party rule in the last twenty-five years has not only accentuated the popular tendency to blame everything on 'them', but has also linked 'them' further with alien forces. The Party committed many of its worst blunders, and perpetrated its bloodiest terror, in its period of most complete subservience to the foreign power which has all along been the mainstay of its rule, in some countries under ethnically alien leaders. Thus the hateful visions of 'their' doings and influence may often be distorted only in that East Europeans substitute part of the truth for the whole truth, a classic human reaction under constant pressure. In addition, one of the Party's worst psychological blunders under Stalin was to try spreading 'proletarian internationalism' through propaganda which combined basic insults to each East European nation's spirit with crude attempts to generate loyalty to the alien power maintaining the Party's rule. The reaction to this has been entirely predictable, and is one of the main reasons why such national 'de-heroizers' as Wajda now arouse suspicion and hostility. And lastly, the censorship inherent in one-party rule prevents any real discussion either of the causes of the people's problems, or of its hatreds and defensive preoccupations. Thus instead of issues being clarified and sentiments about 'enemies' being brought to the surface and so perhaps assuaged, blame continues to be laid in total ways on versions of 'them' merging into each other, while 'our' feelings of hatred fester underground.

The most widespread of these is hatred of Russia. Its ferocity has to be seen to be believed, as a number of other visitors from the West besides myself have found to their sad surprise. 'I thought they would dislike the Russians,' a twenty-one-year-old

English girl studying political science told me on her return from a tour of Eastern Europe, 'but what I actually saw was a shock to me. Some of them literally spat on the ground when they spoke of Russia and everything Russian. . . .'

Most young East Europeans do, of course, make the proper distinction between Russians as individuals and Russia as a power. But while feelings about the first nearly always contain at least a measure of sympathy, feelings about the second tend, even among the most educated, to be vicious, and also to reflect on all things Russian.

Hatred of Russia has, of course, been traditional in Poland and Romania, both of which have experienced direct Russian rule followed by major territorial disputes, and to a lesser extent in Hungary. But more important, the fact that Russia is maintaining 'them' in power and forcing certain styles of government on 'them' has also created such hatreds where they used to be largely unknown. 'A lot of people here have always regarded the Russians as liberators,' said a twenty-seven-year-old Prague journalist. 'Partly because of nineteenth-century traditions of looking to Russia as the centre of Slavic culture, and as an aid against Austria, and partly because we were in fact liberated by the Russians in the last war. Feelings of this kind were especially strong in Slovakia. . . . But now, you can imagine. Even children in the street are playing "let's shoot Russians".' In fact, hatred of Russia for maintaining 'their' rule over 'us' is the basic reason why the majority of East Europeans tend to take the side of anyone in the world who is fighting Russian-backed governments. The most poignant illustration of this occurred at the time of the 1967 Arab-Israeli War, when even some of the worst anti-Semites in Eastern Europe became pro-Israelites. Their feelings were best summed up in the Polish saying, 'Our Jews are beating their Arabs', which, referring to the high percentage of Polish-born officers in the Israeli army, in effect appropriated its victories for the Polish heroic tradition.

Sentiments about Russia as an alien oppressor are least pronounced in Bulgaria, where pro-Russian sympathies have always been strongest, and where admiration for Russia's achievement in transforming an agrarian country into an industrial power is most widespread. But even the Bulgarians share the general resentment of Russia as an economic exploiter. Though her brazen tactics in this role are a thing of the past, stories of East European countries having had to sell cheap and buy dear in their dealings with Russia remain vivid. They are told not only by economists, but also by everyone else; in fact the less people know about economics the more vivid their stories tend to become, serving to explain more and more of the distress in which their countries find themselves.

Resistance to Russian exploitation, even under Stalin, cost not a few ranking Communists in Eastern Europe their jobs and some even their lives. But the newer generation of technocrats, for whom, even if they are Party members, modernization of their countries comes first and ideology a long way second, are as a group squarely opposed to any such interpretation of 'proletarian internationalism'. And when this brings them into conflict with Russia's currently integrationist designs within Comecon, which are feared in Eastern Europe as a fresh garb for an old exploitation, they can count on much wider backing than pure ideology ever had. 'It's very dry, here, has been very dry this year,' a Romanian musician of twenty-nine remarked in an ominous tone during a conversation we had in May 1968, clearly referring to more than just his own discomfort. 'We're all worried about the drought,' a friend with him, a poet, explained. 'If it continues, there won't be much of a harvest. We shall be forced to borrow food from our neighbours. And you know who our richest neighbours are. . . . ' I did, and it was all perfectly logical. But I could not help wondering how many musicians and poets might be moved to such thoughts by the weather in, say, Holland.

Finally, reactions against Russia's propaganda about herself as the Vanguard of History, the Bulwark of Culture, the Land of Realized Socialism and so on have been worse than any outsider could imagine. Among the majority of young East Europeans it has virtually undermined belief in Russia's ability to offer the world anything of value at all. 'You mean, you go to see Russian films, in London?' a twenty-three-year-old Polish girl said with amazement when, talking of films I liked, I mentioned Eisenstein's *Alexander Nevsky*. 'I might have said the same,' a twenty-seven-year-old Romanian film-maker commented. 'Of course, Eisenstein was a great director. But I know every one of his films backwards, every frame of every one of his films I have had to study. Wouldn't that make you sick, too?'

Much the same has been true of everything about Russia that the propagandists of crude internationalism have been trying to promote. Sardonic jokes about Russians as inventors of everything under the sun survive from the fifties even in Bulgaria. In fact when the first Sputniks were sent up in the later fifties, large numbers of East Europeans treated the news as yet another of those Russian 'inventions'. And though they nearly all want to see the West, very few young people take the opportunities available to visit Russia, which is next door.

The next most widespread, if milder, hatred is that of neighbouring nations other than Russia. These are largely traditional and temperamental, though some current issues also help to keep them alive. As regards traditions, if pressure within each country often turns neighbours into beasts towards each other, the pressure of imperial powers on the region throughout its known history has had a similar effect on its small nations.

Differences in temperament, often combined with the contempt of the more developed for the less developed nations, and with envy the other way round, cause further friction. The only two nations that seem genuinely to like each other are the Poles and the Hungarians, who are similar in all these respects, while for the same reason nobody likes the Czechs. 'A lot of people here,' a twenty-seven-year-old sociologist told me in Cracow, 'were happy enough in August '68 that the Czechs had got it at last.'

Between neighbouring nations, the least-forgotten issue is that of minorities. In fact, since the catharsis of the Second World War, into which most countries of the area were dragged by Hitler through his exploitation of their minority problems, there has been a recent revival of interest among the young of each mother-nation in their people living beyond the borders. It takes little to provoke young Romanians into passionate talk of their brethren now inside the Soviet Union, and it takes even less to remind young Hungarians of the three and a half million of their kin in the neighbouring countries.

Less general in the area, but sadly more fervent in some of its countries, is hatred of the Jews, which has barely been assuaged by Hitler's appalling success in realizing the wildest dreams of East European anti-Semites. The complaint that 'more Jews came back than were taken away' was common in Poland, Slovakia, Hungary and Transylvania after the war. I myself remember sitting in the summer of 1945 in a playground in Budapest with another middle-class six-year-old, who for no special reason turned to me and said: 'You know, there's nothing worse than the Russians and the Jews.' That the Russians had just occupied the country whereas its Jews had just been massacred had made no difference to the adults who must have handed my playmate this piece of wisdom.

Unfortunately, as he grew up, a number of factors may have reinforced his feelings, always on the pattern of his substituting part of the truth for the whole truth under complex pressures. One of these factors would have been political. Having always constituted a high percentage of Party members, under Stalin Jews rose to leadership in Hungary and Poland, and to a lesser extent in Romania and Czechoslovakia. In addition, though they were usually no more Stalinist than their Gentile colleagues, they tended to belong to the 'Muscovite' rather than the 'national' wing within the leadership, and in Hungary and especially Poland they also became prominent in the political police. And while they thus became associated with the murderous blunders of the Stalinist era, they also distinguished themselves in the cultural campaigns against nationalism in Poland, Hungary and Romania, and in Poland took part in the physical elimination of members of the non-Communist wartime underground.

The memory of all this has remained combustible material ever since. Moreover, though in 1952–6 Jews gradually disappeared from supreme posts throughout the region, in the two most anti-Semitic countries, Poland and Hungary, they retained high enough positions among 'them' to count as 'them' for large numbers of people. And in the same countries some of the genuine reasons that have always separated Jews from the nationalist majority in politics have also survived. 'The truth is, if you look at the young social scientists here,' a thirty-six-year-old Jewish sociologist told me in Budapest, 'you'll find that there's a visible division between the "cosmopolitans" and "de-heroizers" etc. on the one hand, and the nationalists, whether sober or mysticist, on the other. It's the same kind of division that existed in the thirties between the so-called "urbanists" and "populists". Among the first there were, and are now, many more city-born Jews, among the second, many more come from small-town schools and peasant families.' And when quarrels erupt between the two camps, essentially the same insults begin flying about, though in more subtle forms, as were being hurled in the thirties.

Some of the old social reasons for anti-Semitism have also been transformed rather than abolished by the new situation of mobility. In Poland, one of the reasons for the success of the anti-Semitic campaign that began beneath the surface in the early sixties and culminated in the general ousting of Jews in 1968 was that it appealed to parts of the newly risen intelligentsia, who found their upward path blocked by professionally established Jews, or had to compete with their children.

Of course the postwar generations are less anti-Semitic in every East European country than their parents. They are less given to mythical explanations in general, and they have never been subjected to the kind of openly anti-Semitic propaganda their parents knew. The effect is most clearly visible in Romania, where atrocities between the two wars were among the worst but where, due partly to the fact that Jews have not been prominent since the purges of 1952, I found that the topic hardly ever surfaced in conversations. Even in Hungary and Poland, where it came up much more often, it appeared to be inflammable rather than a constantly burning one among the young. But this, in situations of complex pressures, made it dangerous enough. 'My generation,' a twenty-eight-year-old historian said in Warsaw in 1970, 'did not use to watch TV and point at people on the screen saying "Now that's a Jew, you can see it by the look in his eyes, or his nose" or things like that, as many of our parents do. But a lot of young people did get going after the campaign in '68, and now it'll take some years for them to forget it again.' Or as a thirty-year-old Jew, a Party member, said in Hungary – where the absence of a strong anti-Semitic faction in the Party and a much calmer situation altogether have so far prevented any Polish-type campaign – 'If things turned bad, we'd be the first to feel it. Around here, anti-Semitism is like smoking, a constant habit. When people feel nervous, they smoke a lot more.'

As for the West, though it has not come to be regarded as an enemy by any substantial numbers of young people, it has certainly lost much of its former status as a friend. By the time Czechoslovakia was invaded in August 1968, young people in the country had few illusions not only about intervention by the West, but even about the length of time it would take westerners to forget the whole incident. And while this lowering of expectations is in effect healthy, it has been coupled with the growth of a feeling that the nations of Eastern Europe are not only small fry to the West, but inhabit a region whose claustrophobic history, pressures and passions few westerners can be bothered to understand. 'You must be some kind of a specialist in our madnesses', the thirty-three-year-old Bulgarian poet whom I have quoted several times said to me before I had had a chance to tell him that I was Hungarian by birth. 'Mostly, people from the West come here, listen to us, but understand very little and take away the memory of having been with the cast of a sadly comic play.'

It can be no surprise, if, feeling thus threatened, or at the very least friendless, the majority of young East Europeans remain defensively preoccupied with their own tribes. Their preoccupations are much less hysterical than those of their parents, but are still obsessive enough. For instance, their contempt for the nations that surround them is more often than not complemented by exalted visions of their own, usually seen as the one western nation in a sea of semi-orientals. Within this vision, many of the unpleasant features of the national character, if admitted at all, figure as the result of endless foreign rule or its menace – a version of blaming all of one's life-problems and weaknesses on 'them'. The reverse of these attitudes of self-exaltation and excuse is that of seeing the nation as especially worthless and fated never to improve or rise above its troubles. The standard of comparison is, once again, the West.

Because of the pressures and frustrations in the midst of which the postwar generations of East Europeans have grown up, these visions may very often coexist in their minds. They may think of their nation as, on the one hand, uniquely western by culture and given to habits of stealing and corruption only as a result of foreign rule and endless instability, and, on the other, as nomadically unable to manage its affairs and destined to waste itself in political bickering. More than once I found that when I tried to disabuse young East Europeans about such visions, they defended the abject ones even more fiercely than they clung to the brilliant ones.

Of course, one of the most important reasons for this is that both served as a focus for the same defensive passions and preoccupations; and that while even the best-intentioned attempts to disarm these have tended to reach them 'from above', the same passions and preoccupations have been far more generously nourished 'from below'. In other words, they have remained 'ours', as against what 'they' have been trying to promote – with the contrast between the two producing some grotesque effects of its own. 'Until I came to the West,' the twenty-six-year-old Polish economist whom I quoted on page 269 said in London in 1970, 'I'd been a worshipper of Piłsudski. Our history books said only the worst things about him, which even our teachers hardly believed, while to our parents he was the next thing after God. It was only when I got out here and could read books about him by westerners and *émigrés*, which still criticized him, that I began thinking perhaps he hadn't been so marvellous after all.' As I myself found, Piłsudski's shrine in Cracow is flooded with pilgrims young and old to this day.

Faced with such a situation, the Party has gradually changed its approach over the years, until by now little of the militant internationalism of its founders remains. This is a logical enough development in that the Party itself has long ceased to be a band of revolutionaries, and has instead become a body proposing to rule the countries of Eastern Europe for ever. As such it naturally identifies with all sentiments that will help to focus loyalties on it as the tribe's command.

Of course 'socialist patriotism' continues to be identified with 'proletarian internationalism' and friendship towards Russia. But

only the ultras who ascended to cultural power in Czechoslovakia after April 1969 interpret this nowadays in the manner
of the fifties. Meanwhile, anti-Russian sentiments have been used
to create a bond between the leadership and the people in Romania,
and Poland's Partisan faction also gained part of its popular appeal
from the early sixties onwards from posing as a possible spearhead
against Moscow's influence over the country. In fact, the association of Jewish leadership with absolute Russian domination under
Stalin made it possible for the Partisans to use anti-Semitism as a
cover for anti-Russian feelings with great success, and without
provoking Moscow.

Fears and hatreds of neighbour nations and feelings about
minority problems have been used even more extensively. In this
the Romanian leadership proved an absolute pioneer, but in the
course of the sixties the Bulgarians also revived their traditional
dispute with Yugoslavia over Macedonia, assigning an important
role in their campaign to the youth and student press. The
Hungarians, though obliged for historical reasons to tread rather
carefully, have also been showing interest in their brethren outside
their borders in recent years. The official youth monthly features
whole pages of names and addresses of Hungarian-speaking
teenagers in the neighbouring countries looking for penfriends
inside Hungary.

In all this the Party, or factions of it, have been deriving
support from passions to which they should be ideologically
opposed. Meanwhile, however, they have been alienating those
among the young who apply reason to their situation. 'Very well,
we now have many more pages in our history books about our
princes and kings than when I went to school,' a twenty-five-
year-old Romanian writer said. 'But so what? We've already seen
enough idols fall. When I went to kindergarten, we used to
shout "Ana, Teo, Luca, Dej – Battling With The Bourgeois!",
and now they're all gone.* So when I and people like me hear
that now we shall be told more about our princes and kings,
we aren't much impressed. . . . ' Though I heard such arguments

* Ana Pauker, Teohari Georgescu, Luca Vasile and Gheorghiu Gheorghiu-
Dej were Romania's four most prominent Stalinists; Dej purged the first three
in 1952 and was himself posthumously indicted in 1968.

only from a minority in any East European country, for a body posing as Rationality Incarnate to be allied to the half-thinking and the fanatical among the young, and to be alienated from those who think, is no mean paradox.

The struggle for the minds of the young between Party ideology and its other most important enemy, religion, has gone in a similar way. This in spite of the fact that religion retains nothing like the hold over young East Europeans that nationalism has, and that the Party itself has made nothing like the same attempts to identify with it, let alone encourage its rebirth in any form.

Religiosity has certainly declined among the young, and can be expected to decline even further as the countries become more highly developed at least in its hitherto known forms. In all surveys on the subject, children of the intelligentsia and the industrial working class emerge as less religious than children of peasants, and young people of whatever origins now living in towns as less religious than rural youth. Also, the survival of observance about which I spoke in Chapter 1, proves only that many young people continue to take part in rituals. 'The whole family goes to church at Easter,' a thirty-one-year-old engineer said in Sofia, 'but it means different things to each of us. My grandmother believes in the old way, she's praying to God who's an old man with a beard sitting up there. My parents, too, even if they don't believe everything word for word, are moved. I go because I like these old national customs, singing and walking in candle-lit processions and breaking the Easter Egg.'

All this does not, however, constitute the victory over religion of which the Party once dreamt. In the first place, surveys with questionnaires that clearly distinguish between mere practice and genuine belief still show the strong survival of the latter among the young. The major Polish survey on sixteen- to twenty-four-year-olds, to which I have referred several times, found that 78·2 per cent regarded themselves as Catholics, and of the same sample 74·4 per cent wanted to give their children a religious education, and 68·5 per cent believed that God created the world. A survey entirely devoted to religiosity in Slovakia showed that 65·5 per cent of respondents in the twenty-five to thirty-nine age group and 58·7 per cent in the eighteen to twenty-four group were believers, and that in general 'religion proved to be not only a symptom of traditional backwardness, that is, a mere remnant, but also a well-considered attempt to work out a concept of a spiritual-moral model for the life of the people fitting the present time and current problems'.[1]

In the second place, the change of attitudes towards religion has meant for many young people only a change from absolute to relative beliefs. Surveys often show that while, say, only one-fifth of young respondents is prepared to accept religious morality as wholly valid and sufficient, the overwhelming majority regards religious moral principles as basic to life and only an infinitesimal minority would disown them.

But most important, the decline of religiosity has tended to produce not the atheism promoted by the Party, but agnosticism, which the Party itself now deems insufficient. In the Polish surveys I mentioned above, only 4·4 per cent of respondents proved to be atheists, and even more interesting from this point of view were the results of the Slovak surveys. According to these, though the percentage of believers was about one-ninth lower in the younger age group, the percentage of atheists had meanwhile dropped from 19·1 per cent to 15·6 per cent, that is, by more than one-sixth.

At the same time, there remains a certain fresh vigour about religion, such as Party ideology can no longer evince. For one thing, after the absence of religion from compulsory school curricula for a long period, many young people are curious about it, and many fewer are defensive, than in the West. Time and again I came across young East Europeans who first dipped into the Bible at the age of sixteen or even later, to find it a much more profound experience than if they had had passages read aloud to them in childhood. 'When I was at basic school,' a girl doing her second year as a student of biology said in Bucharest, 'there was always something organized for Sunday mornings, so you couldn't go to church. Nor was it advisable. So I knew nothing about religion except what I had heard from my grandfather. But last summer, one day during the holidays I went up to the attic looking for books to read, and there I found an old Bible. I stayed up there reading it all morning. I may be very stupid, but I thought it was beautiful stuff, and it said things to me.'

Further, though religion is no longer the stuff of resistance it was in the fifties, it still remains in countless ways 'ours' as against what 'they' are promoting. To mention only a few examples, not only do large numbers of young people wear the cross as a custom, but several times in the last few years the fad for wearing it as a 'young thing' has been taken up in one East European country after another. Pop stars themselves have appeared on TV with large crosses hanging on their chests. Meanwhile, wearing red stars has neither survived as a custom, nor become a new fashion anywhere.

Similarly, church services with pop music have been held since the mid-sixties in the three northern countries, often drawing capacity crowds. In Budapest in 1968 I was told that the Youth League secretary of the town's famous Secondary School for Music was himself performing in one of the churches. In Bratislava in the same year I attended a 'pop mass' which had filled a large church with people, some of whom had clearly not been to mass for a long time, if ever. By contrast, what there has been of leftist protest singing, mostly in Hungary, has now dried up for lack of popular interest rather than because of official discouragement.

Waves of religiosity proper have swept through the youth sub-culture of various countries, affecting especially students. 'Last year, it was fantastic,' recalled the Bucharest girl. 'Suddenly everybody decided they were going to fast and go to confession at Easter. You came down from the hostel and went to the tram stop, and everybody was there, all at the same time, which meant they could not have had breakfast that morning either. People tried to hide it from each other, but soon you could hear them saying, "You too? . . ." ' Meanwhile, no waves of ideological fervour have developed among the youth of any country in Eastern Europe.

And at the deepest level, whereas those still fanatical about ideology can expect mostly derision, young people who are truly religious tend to arouse respect and even envy among the rest. 'You almost always find,' a thirty-two-year-old former teacher, and Party member, said in Prague, 'that the irreligious are convinced about believers leading much fuller lives than their own.' Nor is this a matter of pure belief. The Polish survey on life-ideals found that the moderately acquisitive type of person whose chief aim lay in harmonious relationships with his family and immediate circle appealed most strongly to believing and practising Catholics.

This, however, can be of comfort to the Party as a body proposing to rule Eastern Europe for ever. Since it is on the stable type that the *status quo* in any society has been chiefly built, the Party can in fact thank God that religion has remained the opium of at least a number of young people in Eastern Europe.

Still from the Party's point of view semi-religious acceptance of its ideology by the young has also been most useful: whenever ideology has been taken seriously, as proposed by the Party, that is, as the sole activist philosophy mankind had ever produced and hence an exclusive guide to action, the results have hurt everyone, including the Party and ideology itself.

By semi-religious acceptance of ideology I mean one involving acts of faith that permit the Party's interpretation to be put on facts that they would not otherwise fit, but make little more difference to people's behaviour than, say, belief in life after death. The best example of this is, in fact, acceptance of the Party's main ideological proposition, namely, that progress is not only a good thing, but is also inexorably leading towards socialism. This is believed by the majority even of those young East Europeans whose natural reaction is to believe nothing the Party says. And the less incredulous tend to take as a basis of any political thinking and discussion that 'capitalism is finished', or at the very least dying.

I myself met this belief both among young people who described themselves as socialists, and among those who might have been described by others as 'reactionaries'. A survey carried out in 1958 among a large number of Warsaw undergraduates whose general views varied a great deal, also found that to the question, 'Do you think the world is moving towards some form of socialism?', 60·2 per cent answered 'definitely yes' or 'probably yes' with the percentage rising to 69·1 in a follow-up study three years later. And an even larger percentage approved of the prospect.[2] In 1958, with the crimes of the Stalinist era still fresh in everyone's mind, to the question, 'Would you like to see the world moving towards some form of socialism?' 21·6 per cent answered 'definitely yes' and 44·7 per cent 'probably yes'. The 1961 percentages were higher still.

In this acceptance of the Party's main ideological proposition, facts and faith have formed a subtle mixture. That young East Europeans should believe in the idea of progress as a good thing can be no surprise. Progress changing the environment has been the main experience of their lives, and for them not to believe in its usefulness would be to deny the facts.

The idea that progress must lead to socialism has never yet been proved. Still, it is easy enough for young East Europeans to believe that too. In the first place, the dialectical model of history taught to them at school, according to which just as feudalism was followed by capitalism so inevitably capitalism will be followed by socialism, is so simple and satisfying that very few people are likely to wonder whether it might not have been purposely thought up by nineteenth-century socialists. And if anyone should so wonder, he would have either to think up something better, or to accept history as meaningless, which is almost as difficult.

Secondly, the progress that young East Europeans have seen changing their environment has been brought about *as* socialism and very few would now declare themselves to be anti-socialists in the sense of wishing back the past. Even in Czechoslovakia, the most developed country and the one that had been socially and politically the most democratic before the advent of Party rule, one of the things I found most persistently emphasized by young people in 1968 was that 'it would be impossible to re-establish capitalism here, nor do we want it'. And finally, the image of the West presented by the media is that of an environment which, despite its now admitted affluence, is plagued by crises, strikes, demonstrations, riots, crime, political scandal, racial strife and general disorientation. Compared to it Eastern Europe is bound to appear a beautifully calm and healthy spot. To reflect that its calm is artificial, and that its health is in about the same measure due to underdevelopment, demands extra mental effort, of which the only reward will be increased anxiety. Thus a combination of genuine facts, pure myth and blurred thinking maintains belief in progress as both a good thing and inexorably leading to socialism.

All this, of course, falls far short of the active allegiance to its ideology that the Party would like to generate. In the Polish survey, for instance, though the majority of respondents thought socialism both inevitable and desirable, to the question, 'Do you regard yourself as a Marxist?' only 0·7 per cent replied 'definitely yes' and 8·2 per cent 'probably yes'. More important, while socialism is thought to be generally a good thing, in practice, few people know just what it is. 'I'm sure if you asked them, they'd all say they're socialists,' a twenty-two-year-old student of economics said in Slovakia in 1968. 'But if you asked them whether the State should own everything or only big enterprises, or if wages should be equalized or de-levelled, everybody would tell you what he thinks best, never mind what the theory is. . . . ' When I did ask them, anywhere in Eastern Europe, I got replies that ranged from the rhetorical through the vague to the slightly embarrassed. Or else people declared themselves to be believers in what a twenty-one-year-old Romanian girl called 'intimate socialism'. By this she meant a system of values and attitudes towards others which elsewhere might simply be called humane.

Still, relativistic as these beliefs in socialism may be, they are much better for the Party than no beliefs at all, or despair on the subject. If a large number of young East Europeans think that the advent of socialism is only a matter of time, this, even if they are doing nothing actively about it, is better for the Party than if they were waiting for its demise. If they associate socialism with worthwhile political changes, this is still better than if they considered it to be only a glorification of the rule of bureaucracy, which it has also been. If it is only their education that makes many young East Europeans call humane values socialistic, then in this respect 'socialist education' has achieved its aims. If others among them think, as a twenty-two-year-old Cracow student put it, that 'Communism is Christianity except for the idea of hating your enemy', at least the same people do not consider the two hated enemies of each other. And, though the East European press has complained on occasions that the young are mixing socialism and religion in their beliefs, little harm can come to the Party from people believing both that the world is inexorably progressing towards socialism, and that this is inherent in the way it was created by God.

More disturbing for the Party is the fact that most young East Europeans who regard themselves as actual Marxists and Communists are also only semi-religious in their devotion. But the reason for this is to be found in, precisely, the damage done by ideology during the 1950s, when it was taken seriously for what it claimed to be, a replacement for religion as well as a total guide to action.

The memory of those years comes to the surface perhaps most clearly when young East Europeans meet people from the West to whom ideology still appeals in its freshness. 'We have an American exchange student here, a leftist,' said a nineteen-year-old Romanian girl. 'He gets into the most ridiculous arguments. He says he wants to teach us what socialism is really about, but to us it sounds much more as if he wanted to teach us concentration camps. . . . ' When Rudi Dutschke, as the most prominent figure of the young Left in West Germany, went to Prague in the spring of 1968, he was given a similar reception. 'At first people only asked ironic questions, to see if he was being serious,' said a twenty-four-year-old student of English, recalling the meeting. 'Then he became more and more categorical in his replies, and angry that we wouldn't agree with him about a bourgeois counter-revolution going on in Czechoslovakia, until somebody said it looked as if Stalin's shadow had begun to rear its ugly head.' Or, as a twenty-seven-year-old Bulgarian Party member summed up the situation: 'It has been said that a young man who is not a Communist can't be honest, but an old man who is still a Communist can't be wise. We've had a lot to age us quickly. . . . '

The same memories are chiefly responsible for keeping the number of pronounced anti-Communists – by whom I mean people actually blaming 'the Communists' instead of 'them' for whatever is wrong with life – far higher even among the newest generation of East Europeans than might be expected. In fact just as individuals retain the habit of blaming 'them' even as they enter the Party and rise in its ranks, so genuine Communists and Marxists can be heard to blame 'the Communists' for such surviving or revived aspects of the dogmatic era as centralism in the economy or blind bureaucratism in dealing with culture. And the generally pro-socialist mass, too, not only balks at embracing Marxist doctrine, but has been actually turned against it by the practice it has inspired. In the Polish survey I quoted earlier, though the majority of respondents clearly supported socialism, to the question, 'Do you regard yourself as a Marxist?' 31·6 per cent replied 'probably not', and 39·8 per cent 'definitely not'. This is especially striking when compared to the very low percentages of avowed atheists emerging from any survey on religiosity in Eastern Europe.

Altogether, while ideology is reckoned to have given young East Europeans little guidance over personal ethics, in the fields where it aims to be paramount, too, its failures have shown it to be at best a dialectical mixture of reason and pure myth. As such, it tends to be either ignored by young practitioners, or accepted as mere 'gravy' – to be poured over decisions made on quite different grounds. 'What really happens, I suppose,' said a thirty-one-year-old Hungarian economist who regarded himself as a Marxist by training, 'is that at university we study Political Economy, and Dialectical Materialism and all that, but then we just do what we think is best, and if necessary call it Marxist. If somebody attacks it in a speech or publication, he will often imply that it's not Marxist, and then we defend it by saying yes, it is Marxist. Or they'll say it's against the interests of socialism, and we will say no, it isn't. And then we carry on with it until somebody stops us.'

In sociology, much the same ground rules prevail. 'We say classes have been abolished,' a twenty-nine-year-old Polish sociologist said, 'but no satisfactory theory exists to fit what we have now. So everybody has to try getting round the problem by using euphemisms, or not talking about it at all, just publishing results and letting readers draw their own conclusions.' In history, its emphasis on infrastructural developments has made Marxism a very useful corrective to previously sacred myths, but it has also introduced not just distortions but whole visions of its own which most young Marxists themselves now regard as purely religious.

The young creative intelligentsia, almost regardless of political attachments, tends to treat Marxism as something which may have been superbly useful in economics, but which has little to teach the arts. This is, in fact, a view of which versions can also be found in other disciplines – among young economists prepared to grant Marx's genius *as a philosopher*, young sociologists who think he was most inspiring *as a revolutionary*, and so on. Meanwhile, in philosophy proper people's views of the only activist system mankind has ever produced seem to have been best summed up in a joke known throughout Eastern Europe. 'Q: What is philosophy? A: Searching in a dark room for a black bed. Q: What is Marxist philosophy? A: Searching in a dark room for a black bed which isn't there. Q: What is Marxist-Leninist philosophy? A: Searching in a dark room for a black bed which isn't there, and shouting, "I've found it!" '

Still worse from the point of view of the only scientific explanation of the world, natural scientists have less use for it even than their colleagues in the social sciences. A certain amount of ideology still survives in the textbooks from the days when Einstein's Theory of Relativity used to be denounced as a hostile manoeuvre, but I did not meet a single young scientist in Eastern Europe who thought that Dialectical Materialism had any bearing on work in hand. In fact, I was given the most comprehensive and personal critique of ideology by a twenty-four-year-old mathematician, following the pop mass in Bratislava which I mentioned earlier. 'You ask me why I go to church,' he said. 'At university I too was put through the usual courses in Marxism, and I thought about them too. And I found Marxism full of holes. Perhaps religion is as well. But religion doesn't claim to be science. It doesn't claim to offer a full explanation of everything which, even if it could be given, would be too difficult for most of us to understand. It just offers peace in God, and that it gives. And guidance on how to live, which Marxism doesn't.'

In these circumstances, the remarkable thing is not that young East Europeans who regard themselves as conscious Marxists and Communists are so few, but that enough such people remain to form a significant minority. Their reasons for their attachments vary. Some still accept the original argument that being a Communist means actively supporting world-wide progress, and in Eastern Europe an industrial and social revolution for which sacrifices have to be made. 'True, it can be hell here,' explained the twenty-nine-year-old Party member whose remarks about fear being an element of life in Eastern Europe I quoted on page 252. 'There are a lot of bastards who have a lot more power than they could have in a democracy. But we can't afford democracy. We've had to industrialize the country, and we still haven't finished. There's much more equality here than there used to be, or than there is in the West now. For all that, and for all that remains to be done, we have to pay a price, and we also have to wait until the Russians can afford democracy for themselves, and will let us have it too. . . . As the saying is, only the first three hundred years will be difficult.'

Others may have more 'intimate' reasons. They may have grown up calling a level-headed approach to phenomena 'Marxist', or have found in Marxism a vision of the world closest to reality, and now put down all counter-evidence to a misapplication of the tools they trust. Or they may equate being a Communist with being compassionate, honest or brave. 'Of course I'm a Communist,' a twenty-four-year-old Romanian artist who had just been describing to me the struggle a friend of his was having to wage against censorship affirmed in reply to my direct question. 'Or at least, I hope I am. And [his friend] certainly is. It's as a Communist he's fighting these people.'

Others may regard their single-minded devotion to their work, or their puritanical approach to morals, as Communistic. If they do, they may very often be accepted by their environment, too, as 'Communists of the best kind'. Or they may believe as a matter of allegiance to their own younger selves. 'When I see ten- or twelve-year-old kids singing and marching in the street,' a thirty-one-year-old woman said in Warsaw, 'I often think to myself I wish I could still believe like that.' She had, however, remained a Party member, and in conversation seemed very much a Marxist.

In most cases, of course, the reasons are mixed, with those most needed coming to the fore in any situation or argument. But whatever the mixture of reasons, the overwhelming majority of young Marxists and Communists are as semi-religious about their beliefs as the mere pro-socialists are about theirs. The number of such fanatics as the Party used to acquire in the fifties is now close to nil. During my 1968 trip through the region I found that of over 260 interviewees only one, a reformed juvenile delinquent in Bulgaria, talked to me about Communism as a utopia to be realized in his own or his children's lifetime. And only among new leftists did I encounter the conviction that, as one of them put it, 'no sane person today can doubt the truth of Marxism'.

The majority of young believers in Eastern Europe are not only more sophisticated than that, but they find behaviour in the fighting manner of the fifties altogether ridiculous. 'Some time ago, we had an English poet here who I think was a Communist,' related the thirty-three-year-old Bulgarian poet whom I have quoted several times. 'Dzhagarov* and I took him out for a drink. I'd just got to know and like Eliot in translation, and as we were drinking, at one point I said, "I want to raise my glass to the memory of the great poet T. S. Eliot." But this Englishman began shouting that he wouldn't drink to that Fascist. . . . Dzhagarov just about fell off his chair. "But this is fantastic!" he said. "Here's a member of the Bulgarian Communist Party proposing a toast to T. S. Eliot, and here's an English poet refusing to drink. . . . " '

This does not mean that they themselves might not behave in the same isolationist manner if they found themselves in the same situation. 'At times when I've been really fed up, I've thought of getting out,' said the twenty-nine-year-old Hungarian Party member. 'But it would be ridiculous. I know that anywhere in the world I'd sooner or later find myself a member of the CP. And to be a Communist in Denmark or England is to be a permanent joke. Even in France and Italy I don't think the Party stands a chance. So. . . . ' But on the spot they tend instead to follow the conventions of coping accepted by their age groups, while their attachment to the Party's ideology becomes ever more a matter of vague yearnings rather than exact conviction. 'If only Marxism

* The head of the Bulgarian Writers' Association.

had remained a philosophy, it could be so beautiful. . . .' a twenty-seven-year-old Party member mused in Prague in 1969. 'But didn't Marx himself say,' I objected, 'something about "philosophers till now have only interpreted the world, our business is to change it"?' 'Well, yes,' my Party member agreed. 'It's what you might call a typical German tragedy.'

That is about the measure of it, especially from the point of view of Marxism itself. Following the blunders due mainly to the monumental conceit it inspired, doubts about all but the vaguest promises of Party ideology have become a distinguishing mark of young East Europeans. 'Not long ago, we had a man from some Party school who came and gave us a talk,' said the forty-eight-year-old Hungarian deputy headmaster whom I have quoted several times in Chapter 5. 'He was speaking mostly about the future, and what Communism would be like, and what the boys asked him immediately was how he could be so certain. They asked politely, but it was clear that they believed almost nothing he said.' And as the Party, though admitting many of its earlier blunders, has continued to rule in the centralist way inherent in its ideology, it has not only forced a number of young socialists in Eastern Europe to denounce what they see around themselves as 'not socialism at all', but has also generated doubts about whether its most essential purposes can ever be realized. 'In 1948 there was socialism,' one of the Prague class of sixteen-year-olds whom I have quoted several times said to me in June 1968. 'Then in 1956, they said that hadn't been real socialism, but now there'd be socialism. In 1963 they said that hadn't been socialism, but now we'd really have socialism. Now they say again we're going to have real socialism. Do you think it's true? I don't think it's possible.'

In fact endless Party rule in the name of an endlessly amended yet always infallible ideology has by now brought about a situation to which another quotation from Marx seems applicable. 'All facts . . . in world history occur, as it were, twice,' he wrote in 1851. 'The first time as tragedy, the second as farce.' After the tragedies that Party ideology brought about in the 1950s, the farce now is that though it still permeates the basic school curricula, begins to be expressly taught in secondary school and remains a major subject throughout everyone's university years, afterwards very few young East Europeans can put it to any use. This makes the majority even of those who might once have found ideology at least interesting tire of it in due course. 'I'm really very pleased you came,' said a thirty-one-year-old Romanian anthropologist with whom, as still rather a recent visitor from the West in 1968, I got into a long ideological discussion. 'It's ages since I've talked about things of that sort to anyone. Brings back memories of my university years. . . . ' As a matter of fact, to most people in the new generation to discuss ideology at all has come to seem not just scholastic, but wholly 'old-fashioned', than which no condemnation could be worse. In this the Party – which once claimed youth as its born vanguard against the old, on behalf of the future that its ideology saw as inevitable – can be said to have fallen victim to its own dialectical rationale.

Faced with such a situation, the Party seems to me to have three main choices. One of these would entail accepting whatever semi-religious beliefs in its purposes it has generated as the best it can hope for, and carrying on with constructing in the most efficient manner possible what the young in turn may accept as socialism. This would begin to weaken the resistance of even the avowed anti-Communists, would gain at least the passive co-operation of the pro-socialist mass and actively involve some parts of it, and would give the genuine pro-Communists a renewed sense of purpose. It is, however, a course the Party cannot envisage taking. Though economically and politically it might be the most rational, ideologically it would amount to suicide.

The two remaining courses open to it are bound to prove suicidal, in ways which are far more important, but which the Party or factions in it cannot rationally admit to themselves. One of these courses entails trying to generate ideological allegiance in the ways that were attempted, to some extent successfully, during the fifties. In today's changed conditions, and with the memory of Stalinist ravages alive in everyone's mind, this can only harden resistance among the anti-Communists, provoke the apathetic into avid selfishness or forms of opposition, alienate the pro-socialist mass from the Party as a madman, and drive the sophisticated Communists to despair.

The Hero's Children

Clear as this may be to any realist, it is 'enemy talk' to the hard-liners now leading the Party along just such a course in three East European countries – Bulgaria, Czechoslovakia and Romania. Indeed, whereas in Bulgaria the spirit of dogmatism is paternal, with Party men mellowed by age haranguing the intellectuals and the young to little effect, in the other two countries it is vigorous. The Czechoslovak ultras, on taking command of culture and education in 1969, went to work in a fighting manner, which has included the purging of education, the reintroduction of oaths of loyalty and the importation of Soviet instructors to teach ideology at the universities. And in Romania the vast ideological campaign which began in July 1971 and has been in progress since has been fully reminiscent of the 1950s, with office workers and professional people forced to attend ideological seminars, librarians having to withdraw even *The Three Musketeers* as a product of 'bourgeois adventurism', and young workers obliged to scrub their lockers clean of nude pictures.

The other course, taken by the Party in Hungary and more recently in Poland, attempts a golden mean. It consists of doing a great deal to put over the Party's ideology, but tries to combine this with a widening of opportunities for political participation by the young. Given the Party's ideological and political situation, this is the soundest policy it can pursue. It will not do much to provoke the anti-Communists; it can establish forms of co-operation with the pro-socialist mass, and it actively enlists the support of at least a number of Communists. Sadly, it is still not sound enough. The Party, being the Party, can go only so far in being either pragmatic about its ideology, or democratic about its practice. And stopping at that 'existential' point, it has to start identifying with the dogmatic Parties in their reliance on attitudes that will help to maintain the *status quo*, and their suppression of reasoned analyses of the situation lest these erode its rule. This position both belies the Party's view of itself as Rationality Incarnate, and is being undermined by its own good work as Champion of Progress.

Most important among attitudes helping the Party to maintain the *status quo* are nationalism and its variants, social alienation and sheer materialism, and apathy in the face of imposed order and of

314

Eastern Europe's 'geographical realities' – in other words, attitudes which allow the Party to pose either as the tribe's true command or as a fatality the tribe must bear.

Concerning nationalism and its variants, I should merely like to add here that, apart from being the Party's strongest rallying agents, they also constitute its most reliable instrument for alienating the rationalists among the young from the rest. Though all too often young East European intellectuals project their own enlightened views on nationalism as those of 'the people', in fact they represent a minority, as at least some of them realize. 'We may be on the best of terms with Hungarian intellectuals here or even in Budapest,' a twenty-nine-year-old Romanian journalist said to me in Transylvania. 'In the villages, too, Romanians and Hungarians may have been living peacefully together for ages. But we mustn't forget that we both have our shoe-maker and bus-conductor nationalism, and that if it came to a choice between that and what we believe in, not even the peasants would side with us. I don't even know how many intellectuals would, really.'

Among socially divisive attitudes, once again the most useful from the point of view of the Party are those which isolate the young professional intelligentsia from the rest, and make such isolation seem a fatality. 'The only reason you're trying so hard to find out what young peasants and workers think is because you don't live here,' a thirty-four-year-old poet said to me in Slovakia in 1970. 'If you did, you'd know that here the people doesn't count, has never counted. I don't mean that workers and peasants are stupid, but without somebody to speak for them they shut off, and they stop thinking anything much about politics.'

Of similar use to the Party is the absorption of people in their own lives and in their pursuit of personal achievements. The result of traditions further activated by development in the last twenty-five years, it is hardly discouraged by the Party. Though its media may denounce money-grubbing or put out romantic calls for enthusiasm, it attacks achievement-mindedness itself only by accident. The result is that, since traditions coincide with the effects of development and the ethos of propaganda, ideas of renouncing achievements in favour of inner values which have long been at least available in the West have very few ways of entering the heads of young East Europeans.

For example, the twenty-seven-year-old Warsaw girl whom I quoted several times in Chapter 5 had never thought of blaming her problems and breakdowns on the pressures she had had to endure since childhood. 'I've always been nervous,' she reflected. 'I don't know why. After all, in my secondary school I'd been the best not only in my form but in the whole school, and still I was always shy.' When I suggested that perhaps she had been pushed too hard and had expected too much inner satisfaction from external achievements, she received the idea with sincere surprise. In fact it was only then that she began to recall how the pressures to perform had been put on her.

Nervousness among many young East Europeans about directly challenging authority or seeing it challenged is another thing that serves to maintain the *status quo*. 'It must be very strange in Prague now,' a twenty-two-year-old Czech girl whom I interviewed half-way through her year's stay in London said in April 1968. 'People writing in the papers and saying openly whatever they like. I can hardly imagine it. I remember when I came to England and saw how people talked about the government on TV, my first reaction was they shouldn't, there's going to be trouble out of that.'

Also, though they may be unruly, and may often pay those in charge no more than tragicomic respect, a feeling that in some sense authority must be right and must represent their true interests, tends to colour their view of it. More than once people, both with and without legal training, put to me the view that the judicial system in Britain and America was 'far too democratic, giving the criminal too many chances to get away when everybody know's he's guilty', as a Romanian lawyer of twenty-nine expressed it. They seemed to find a considerable degree of centralism, too, not just acceptable but essential in life. 'But how can you manage without having identity cards?' asked a twenty-nine-year-old Hungarian friend of mine, when I explained that registering with the police and carrying a personal passport, both compulsory in Hungary, were unknown in Britain. 'And what if the police want to find you, or anything?' Though an intelligent man, he was genuinely shocked by such anarchy in the civilized half of the world.

If the Party does not encourage attacks on achievement-mindedness, at normal times it positively discourages attacks on authority in the media. Certain abuses of power may be singled out, and the subject may be more generally debated at times of sudden liberalization, but on the whole power is treated with awe, even in the most liberal countries. 'It has actually happened,' a twenty-seven-year-old TV director told me in Budapest, 'that in a play set in the 1890s a line about the government being a bunch of idiots had to be cut out. Just in case anybody should think we're being seditious. . . . '

Nervousness about seeing their rulers challenged is combined in many young East Europeans with nervousness about being able to rule themselves. During my 1968 trip through the region I found that young Bulgarians and Romanians were convinced that they did not have it in them to be as politically involved as their coevals further north. Meanwhile, young Hungarians and Poles maintained that they could not be trusted to behave as democratically, or with as much shrewdness and self-restraint, as young Czechs and Slovaks were behaving at the time.

Whatever the temperamental differences, these beliefs are based on young East Europeans' views of their nations' histories, to a great extent as interpreted for them by the Party. Not only does the Party talk, at best, of 'teaching the people democracy'. It also deliberately prevents both the elucidation of the particular difficulties which have on previous occasions doomed democratic experiments to failure, and the recalling of occasions on which an East European nation behaved democratically enough without having ever been instructed in such behaviour by the Party.

A similar mixture of genuine experiences and accidental or deliberate misinformation has been at work to shape young East Europeans' general attitude towards politics. In the first place, they have largely turned their backs on politics since, as a twenty-two-year-old Hungarian film-man put it, 'whatever ideas anybody may have, all means of action here are in the hands of the State.' Such a situation is almost bound to produce in the majority some version of the view expressed by a twenty-nine-year-old sub-manager on an agricultural machine station in southern Poland in these terms. 'I don't care who makes the speeches and what speeches they're making as long as they let me live and get on with my work.'

But even if they do not give up politics altogether, young East Europeans often have only very vague ideas about what they would do in politics if they could. 'We mostly know how to criticize,' a twenty-three-year-old veterinary student close to the Prague radicals said in 1969, 'but we know very much less what we want instead. That was one of the problems last year, not quite knowing what we wanted once we'd got the first things done.' And criticism, too, is usually directed at details, not at central aspects of the system. 'We can't think of anything very different,' one of my interpreters said in Bulgaria. 'We can see that many things are wrong, but we can't envisage an entirely different system.'

Part of the reason is, of course, that to do so would be too much like a revolutionary act, from which most young East Europeans would now shy away. However, the impossibility of public discussion on any such issues is just as important a factor in keeping their views undeveloped – as is the lack of detailed information about democracy in the West. This, in fact, serves the Party as much as does young East Europeans' ignorance of their own countries' democratic past. It is also deliberately fostered by the media for the same purpose – and on the same pattern, which involves always substituting part of the truth for the whole truth.

For instance, young East Europeans very often take it as proven that in the West as in Eastern Europe all the media are controlled by a central machine, so that whatever is written in any western paper is what 'the West' thinks. An equal proportion of the politically interested accepts that western democracy works only for the rich, that the parliamentary process is a puppet show, and so on. They have been carefully prevented from hearing anything about the importance of checks and balances, let alone Churchill's remark about democracy being 'the worst form of government ever invented except for all the others'. If a western paper publishes material embarrassing to a western government, this is reprinted at length, but not a word follows about the salutary effects the paper may have thereby helped to achieve. At best, it is treated as an instance of 'progressive forces' having managed to break through the shield of silence behind which the 'ruling circles' otherwise machinate. Altogether, the body posing as Rationality Incarnate gains part of the assent of the young to its everlasting rule from their ignorance of some of the most instructive details of their own countries' past and of life in the West.

Added to all of this is young people's acceptance of the Party as having been foisted on the region by fate, in the shape of geography. 'In this part of the world,' the twenty-two-year-old Cracow student quoted on page 306 said in 1970, 'we don't dream of "shaking off the yoke". Only of making it more bearable.' Should they forget geography, they will be reminded soon and rudely enough. 'August '68,' a twenty-seven-year-old poet said in Prague in the following year, 'made us think of just where we are in this world, and the patterns of our history on this spot. It didn't make the Russians seem like the Germans in '38 so much as it reminded us of having always been Czechs.' Thus the Party which gains from young people's ignorance of parts of their countries' history gains as much from their consciousness of the chief factor shaping it. Overtly or covertly it then keeps emphasizing this, in the countries to which the shock has been administered as well as in the rest of the region, until nothing less than a geo-political fatalism becomes basic to people's outlook.

In fact, all the attitudes and feelings helping the Party to maintain the *status quo* are in a sense fatalistic. They amount to either a passionate response to the tribe's fate as hero besieged, or a semi-religious assent to socialism as historically inevitable if not pre-ordained by God; or they may accept the *status quo* in society, in individuals' relationships to authority and in politics as unalterable, leaving each person only the choice of working away at his own material aims.

As against the fatalism prevalent in one form or another among the majority, and helping the Party to maintain the *status quo*, there is the rationalism of a minority, which it has to ignore or actively suppress in order to stay in power. For a body posing as Rationality Incarnate this is paradoxical enough. What makes the paradox even more poignant is that most of the rationalists are, at least palpably and often radically, of the persuasion which should be dearest to the Party. 'You'll find,' I was told by a twenty-four-year-old Hungarian sociologist engaged on a study of political and ideological involvements among the young, 'that the ones who are really interested are almost all on the Left. By this I don't just mean the radical leftists, but people who think in essentially Marxist terms, and would want change only on a socialist basis. Very simply, Marxism is the only ideology there is, so anybody interested in thinking systematically about politics, or about change on any scale, is almost bound to be a leftist. Whether he'll ever end up as a Party supporter is another matter. Most likely not – the radical leftists are in fact young Communists rejected by a bureaucratic-Communist regime.'

Along with them are rejected a good many others whose differences with the Party are much less radical. As regards nationalism, a good enough illustration is the fact that the young Polish historian whose reasoned approach to the problem I quoted earlier in this chapter carefully made me promise that I would not quote his name. As regards religion and ideology, while the religious can simply accept that the two have a good deal in common and are free enough to express this, Marxists, to whom the realization that their ideology mixes reason with myth comes as more of a shock, cannot elaborate on this in public. 'And yet it's quite clear,' a thirty-one-year-old Bulgarian Communist said to me, 'that if there's a decline of belief in God and an after-life, this is only a matter of people living in a less religious age, which has equally affected belief in Marx and a Communist future.'

Though most rationalists are of the Left, far from all are in any way conscious Marxists. As regards society, for instance, they may simply realize that alienation between the strata is not as hopeless as the fatalists believe it to be. 'If you talk to workers here,' said the twenty-three-year-old Cracow student of English quoted in Chapters 3 and 4, 'you'll find that if they think of politics, they're often more progressive than the established intelligentsia. Especially here in Cracow, where the social structure has survived intact since before the war, the intelligentsia are far more conservative than the workers.' But this hardly leads them to Marx's Messianic visions of the working class. 'That was one of the basic mistakes he made, to pronounce the proletariat as the revolutionary class of society,' said the twenty-four-year-old Hungarian sociologist I have just quoted. 'They aren't – there's no such thing as a revolutionary class. There are revolutionary situations, in which a lot of people get together under the leadership of a conscious élite and overturn the social structure. But a revolutionary class. . . . You have to be a romantic to believe in any such thing.'

Naturally enough, it is in politics that the rationalists find themselves most strongly opposed to the Party. In the most general sense, this results from the dynamics of a one-party system. 'I'm a socialist and I don't want the old days back,' a twenty-one-year-old student of physics said in Poland in 1968. 'But I'm also convinced that the people who run this country suffer from sclerosis in their brains, and will ruin us. So what can I do? I must be against them.' Or as the twenty-three-year-old veterinary student said in Prague in the following year: 'When leftists from the West come here they talk as if the choice lay between technocracy and democracy. We say, both are better than bureaucracy, which is what we have here.'

More explicitly, the rationalists criticize what they see around themselves in terms which may often be the Party's own, but which it would dearly wish not to be used to describe the situation it rules. 'It's true, we can't expect to have democracy until international alignments change,' a twenty-two-year-old Hungarian writer said in May 1970. 'But meanwhile, how about changing what we have inside the country, and in people's minds? So we can have democracy when the chance arises. What we have at the moment is more or less a socialist reproduction of what there was before the war. Instead of feudal capitalism, we have feudal socialism. And inside people's heads too, a feudal mentality, of either ordering others about or waiting to be ordered about. If there's going to be change, that's where it'll have to start as far as I'm concerned.'

And where it comes to actual programmes, the Party finds itself facing the actual new Left. In Hungary, these programmes have been on the whole self-defeatingly élitist in their conception and romantic in their aims. But in Poland, and in Czechoslovakia, they have included both realistic critiques of conditions and some very appealing proposals for change. In Poland, a basic leftist idea has been the creation of a workers' party to balance the power of the Party, which is now dominated by management and often represents its interests. In Czechoslovakia, in addition to taking definitely trade-unionist stands on economic reforms and wages, the new leftists also envisaged the formation of 'self-awareness circles' in all occupational groups in society, enabling each group to articulate its views first within small circles and then in ever-widening circles, and to put forth ideas rather than have these simply handed down by the Party.

As both proposals have struck at the roots of the Party's centralist rule, they have been rebuffed even more forcefully than the less well-thought-out ideas of the Hungarian New Left. Or to be more exact, in Poland the Party demonstrated in March 1968 that it had no intention of giving up its heroic role in charge of the country, and as part of this demonstration it used the trial and imprisonment of some leading new leftists. In Czecho-slovakia, where at the same time it looked as if the Party might allow the development of genuine democracy, the Russians demonstrated the same centralist lesson on its behalf, dismissing the democratizing leadership as revisionists.

I had a chance to observe the contrasting reactions of fatalists and rationalists among young East Europeans to these events which had reimposed the Party's order. The fatalists saw them as essentially examples of what was bound to happen to the small countries of Eastern Europe if they allowed themselves too many internal or external liberties. Nationalism and its variants also influenced their thinking. In Poland, even students who smarted under repression often responded to the anti-Semitic propaganda put out by the same repressive machinery with a view to exploit-ing the Jewishness of most student radicals, while following the invasion of Czechoslovakia dislike of the Czechs in Poland and of both Czechs and Slovaks in Hungary strongly mitigated sympathies for the occupied population.

The reactions of the rationalist minority were very different. 'The invasion actually created an understanding between the Slovaks and us, which we had never known before,' a thirty-one-year-old Hungarian poet said in Bratislava. 'Partly because they've seen us offering no welcome to the Hungarian troops, and partly because they were reminded of being a small nation, just like us.' The feeling that the small nations of Eastern Europe, instead of letting their enmities be exploited or simply giving in to imperial pressure, should unite in their adverse situation was in fact the rationalist response in several countries to this latest reminder of the area's 'geographical realities'. Federalism became the topic of many late-night conversations, especially in Prague and Budapest.

Many other attitudes helping the Party to maintain the *status quo* were similarly affected. In Poland the majority of students concluded after March 1968 that the workers were simply too stupid to join them in any political move. But at least a few drew the conclusion, which by 1970 I found had permeated the whole student body, that they themselves had been too stupid in 1968, putting forward programmes which could be of no real interest to the working classes.

The shock of repression had much the same sort of effect on people's concerns, and on their attitudes to order imposed from above. 'Czechoslovakia confirmed the materialists in their materialism,' the twenty-two-year-old writer quoted on page 321 said in Hungary. 'It made us realize that you either have to go underground, or have to think of much more careful tactics. Not even anti-heroes like Dubček will do. Even he was too romantic. You have to have somebody at the top with a spine like rubber to take the strain of Russian pressure, and with hands hard enough to keep the people and especially us writers and journalists from going wild, and yet with some quality people can trust.'

The effect of the shock was, of course, most acute in politics. It turned not a few even of the people whom I got to know as rationalists and realists during my first trip through the region in 1968 into fatalists who were often hardly above sheer materialism. 'All you can do is not think about it,' a thirty-one-year-old social scientist said in Romania in 1969. 'I have friends who remember August last year only as a time when they were down by the sea and got a good suntan. And I don't blame them. The only way to keep sane here is to stop thinking about politics.' By May 1970, when it was clear that not even the superb self-discipline and realism of the people of Czechoslovakia following the invasion had saved them any of the achievements of 1968, an engineer of the same age in Poland summed up his feelings in these terms: 'Realism is no better than anything else. . . . All you can do is breed bees and grow cabbages in your spare time, and forget about everything else.'

Yet at least some rationalists managed to react in a more constructive way. 'You ask me what I'd like to see done,' said the twenty-three-year-old Hungarian instruments technician whom I have quoted several times in this book, also in 1970. 'It's very difficult, as Czechoslovakia has shown. You have to analyse to yourself everything that's involved, geography, history, the external situation, the internal situation, interest groups, personal motives, personalities, everything. Then when you have got some idea of what you want to do, you have to talk it over with people whose opinion you can trust, and also who won't give you away, and then find other people who have some power and still understand what you're talking about. Then you have to let them find others who're on their level, so a group forms round your ideas, and then carry them out so the people at the top, or the Russians, won't object, but still you've done some good. This is the only way, every other way is irresponsible, and we've seen enough of irresponsibility.' All of this may seem finicky to the point of paralysis. But I consider it to be the most genuinely heroic course in the circumstances.

And though it is close enough to the Party's own course at least in Hungary today, it is also likely to prove more dangerous to the Party than any other, because it is the most realistic and the most rational. In fact, while the various groups among the young may intermingle, mostly due to the realists becoming more rational in more peaceful times and more fatalistic under pressure or in response to shock, what is chiefly characteristic of the situation is, again, the paradox of the Party's stance. It poses as the Ultimate Hero of History and Rationality Incarnate. Yet it must find comfort in the sheer materialism and fatalism of the young, against those whom their realism and rationalism turn into heroes ready to cope with its Platonic rule.

Besides being paradoxical, this is also a position which can only undo the Party. True, each time it applies pressure or force the divisions between the materialists and the fatalists on the one hand and the realists and rationalists on the other re-form, and the size of the first group gains at the expense of the second. But each time, also, lessons are learnt by the young as copers in general. And on each successive occasion the gains in the size of the second group, on which the Party seeks to rely, are reduced. Also, though geographical realities now place at the Party's disposal all the force it could ever need, in the shape of Soviet armed power, should the international situation really change, not only could that force be withdrawn, but the geo-political fatalism of the young would go with it. In addition, the materialist and fatalist attitudes that may cement the *status quo* are useful to the Party only because they do not interfere with its rule. They do not provide it with any positive help in sharing its burden as Hero in central charge. On the contrary, they turn each man and each group further in on themselves and their own material lives and aims, so increasing the Party's heroic loneliness.

But worst of all, even if no upheavals or violent changes intervene, the Party's own work must undermine fatalistic attitudes among the young as much as the attitudes of sheer materialism. In the simplest terms, peace provides a better atmosphere for thinking, and affluence provides more time. Both decrease the pressures which at the moment help so powerfully to maintain versions of fatalism (and of sheer materialism) in many young East Europeans. Meanwhile the spread of education, which has already made the young far more knowledgeable and enlightened than the majority of the Party's stalwarts, is bound to make the difference between the two groups ever more acute. And as development makes complexities more complex, the young can only grow ever less tolerant about simplist heroics and useless ideology, while they become ever better equipped to cope with their circumstances, and with the Party itself. In other words, its position both as Hero seeking to remain in charge of Eastern Europe for ever and as Rationality Incarnate is likely in the end to fall victim to the Party's own achievements as Champion of Progress.

9 Past, Present, Future

Anybody visiting Eastern Europe is likely to find that one of the things people there dislike most is the idea of their living in the East. I found so during my first trip through the region, in 1968. To Bulgarians, their country had been a bridge between East and West for over a thousand years. Romanians talked of themselves as a people at – but only at – the Gates of the Orient and looked down on the Bulgarians as Balkan peasants; they saw the Russians as awesome barbarians, and generally pronounced their nation a Latin island above a sea of Slavs. Hungarians, having barely forgotten their traditional view of the country as a Bastion of the Christian West against hordes from the East, continued to look with a mixture of fear and contempt at the nations living to the east and south of them. Poles, having only just abandoned their vision of Poland as Christ Crusading, considered themselves, as a doctor in his thirties put it to me, 'westerners placed by geographical accident in the East'. And in Prague, the western-most capital, I found that when I asked a twenty-eight-year-old journalist what the local version of the same idea was, he said, 'But these are only expressions of an East European mania about belonging to the West. We Czechs have no such manias. We're a Central European nation!' And then he laughed, but only just.

It has long been part of the same 'mania to wester' for East Europeans to see not just themselves but their environment, too, in western terms. Bucharest, for instance, is proud of being the 'Paris of the East', the City Park in Budapest has been called the 'Hungarian Bois de Boulogne', and the great textile town of Poland, Lodz, the 'Polish Manchester'.

The last epithet may seem to all except Mancunians to confer a dubious distinction. But it does provide the main clue to the origins of the mania I am describing. They lie in the – by now obsessive – urge of East Europeans to escape from the conditions of underdevelopment.

The mania to wester is in fact a wish-equivalent of emigration, which itself has accounted for over nine million East Europeans in this century. It is, of course, mixed with a certain horror of the East, whence the nomad invasions, fearful in themselves and also to some extent responsible for the area's backwardness, all came. But as the same backwardness which has been putting East Europeans to flight also formed part of the reason for their countries' inability to withstand pressure and conquest from both East and West, it is really the basic factor generating the escapist urge. 'We're much too near to the West not to know what it's like, and want the same thing for ourselves,' the twenty-three-year-old instruments technician in Budapest said. 'But we've never been quite near enough to have it.'

Naturally, the urge to escape from the mire has manifested itself in many other ways apart from emigration and its wish-equivalents. In fact emigration itself has usually been the extreme course, taken before the war mainly by the landless peasantry, who had least hope of escaping from its conditions at home. And even among the peasantry, before emigration came dreams, looking not westward but to heaven – dreams of some version of the Messiah descending to turn the wretched into the rulers of the earth, in waiting for whom tens of thousands crazed with hunger and dying of cold and sickness huddled together in millennial movements. In fact, it was as the most realistic of these millennial movements that the Communist Party itself appealed, not to the peasantry but to the intelligentsia and sections of the working class on behalf of the whole of the people in Eastern Europe.

And before emigration and millennial visions, each almost as dreamlike as the other, came thoughts of rising from the mire in ways more immediate and realistic, and thus much more difficult. Among them were thoughts of escaping from the countryside to the towns, where employment, however degrading, seemed plentiful and was in normal times certainly more steady; thoughts of escape from the ranks of the landless, and often even the landed, peasantry into the unskilled employee strata and the industrial working class, and, exceptionally, into the ranks of the white-collar and professional intelligentsia. One could escape by just taking one's life in one's hands and moving to town; or, better, by learning a trade; or, best of all, by getting an education. It was only those who found all these routes blocked (and a number of people from the higher social strata who did not find enough scope for themselves) within the conditions of underdevelopment who took the route West.*

The Party's main achievement in charge of Eastern Europe in the last twenty-five years has been the opening up of realistic routes of escape from the mire. It had always been the most realistic of the area's millennial movements in that it proposed economic and social revolution as part of the advent of paradise. In power, for all its murderous mistakes, blatant oppression and mad rhetoric, it has proved a Messiah on the ground. Its policies of rapid industrialization and its extension of unprecedented educational and social opportunities to children of the manual-working classes have made it possible for people to rise from conditions that had long oppressed them, not in their dreams and through emigration, but in reality and within their own countries.

In Bulgaria, at the end of the sixties the industrial labour force was about four and a half times its size in 1948.[1] In Poland, between 1946 and 1970 the urban population had grown from 31·4 per cent to 52·4 per cent of the total.[2] In Hungary, a statistical survey in the late sixties found that in a large and representative sample of householders, while 63·6 per cent of the unskilled and semi-skilled industrial workers came from the peasantry, 72·6 per cent of those belonging to the white-collar or professional intelligentsia were of worker-peasant origins.[3]

The most immediate result of the Party's opening up of escape routes has been an increase in the urge to escape. Distant places and dreams may be attractive but their attraction is nowhere near as powerful as that of immediately achievable reality. The

* To all of these must, of course, be added the Jews, who were fleeing persecution. But this too was largely a matter of their trying to escape from the conditions of underdevelopment, and the urge which the same conditions had generated in the local populations to find scapegoats in aliens.

Party's propaganda, extolling industrialization and constantly reminding the young of their educational opportunities, has naturally helped. But propaganda would have generated only resentment had the Party not at the same time gone to work developing the region and transforming its social structure in earnest, so opening wide the roads of migration, and providing room in its long-cherished 'target areas'.

Of the many more complex results, two seem to me important here. One is that while the urge to escape has greatly increased, the quality of migrants in the two main directions has changed. Essentially, the people who used to make up the bulk of westward migration now head for industry and the towns, whereas the people who once thought it enough to arrive or remain in the ranks of the professional intelligentsia have become dominant among those seeking to escape westwards. Of course the ban on passports to the West, still unrelaxed in three of the five East European countries, has put a major obstacle in the path of westward migration, and this obstacle is somewhat easier for professional people – with better access to *protektsio* – to overcome. But far more important have been the effects of development and of deliberate social engineering, not only in offering new occupational and social scope to children of the peasantry and the industrial working class, but also in raising the expectations of members of the professional strata, and in increasing the competition they have to face in every field. Even if the frontiers were wholly open, what we would see would be not a repetition of the largely peasant exodus of former years, but a brain-drain.

The other change that seems to me relevant here is also demographic. It consists in the drastic reduction of the size of East European families. Countries of Eastern Europe which in the 1920s registered birth-rates of between 30·2 and 39·9 per thousand had rates ranging between 13·6 and 16·7 by 1966.[4] This has worried both conservative moralists and nationalists, still in thrall to the idea of fertility or in awe of the death of the nation, or both, and also Party leaders, for basically the same reasons. In my view, however, the phenomenon is not just inevitable but actually a measure of how far the Party's policies of development and social engineering have succeeded. In fact the changes affecting migration and the birth-rates seem to me to be connected, and in a genuinely encouraging way.

Large-scale emigration was a result of people's inability to satisfy their ambitions, or more often sheer hunger, in the conditions of underdevelopment. But virtually the same conditions were also responsible for the very high birth-rates. In fact Czechoslovakia, the country with much the lowest birth-rates before the war (26·7 per thousand in the peak years of 1920–4) was also much the most highly developed; the rates of the other countries, too, almost directly reflected their degree of backwardness, with Hungary's the lowest, and Bulgaria's the highest.

Nor are the reasons difficult to guess. Apart from the fact that in the less developed countries child mortality was expected to take a hideous toll of the numbers born, the children who survived most often represented their parents' sole investments. After all, the reason the proletariat has ever been called the proletariat is that it owned and could offer for sale nothing but its children. In the mainly agrarian countries of Eastern Europe before the war this held true for as much as one-third to half the population.

Since the war, much the same changes as have helped to abate the urge to emigrate have also decreased the urge to proliferate. With the improvement in economic conditions, fewer and fewer parents regard their children as their investments. At the same time, rising expectations and widening consumer choices have brought ever larger numbers of people face to face with the kind of alternative summed up in the Hungarian pun *kicsi vagy kocsi* ('baby or car'). The number of things they can do in their spare time – as opposed to what used to be the poor man's only pleasure – has also increased, while with the decline of absolutist religious beliefs contraception has become far more common, and development has helped to spread modern methods of it. Abortion itself has lost nearly all its former moral stigma, and even in the countries where it is not available on the health service, people can much better afford it on the black market than they once could.

But most important of all, intentions concerning children have changed. With education wide open before the young and with their parents' expectations for them commensurately heightened, instead of regarding their offspring as investments, people now want to invest the maximum in each child's future. And as urban housing conditions are still execrable due to sudden industrialization and bad planning, and an average couple's earnings are still enough to feed and clothe only three people, whose other expectations will take years of fulfilment before satiety may be reached, birth-rates were bound to plummet. But this should be no cause for alarm such as East Europeans and some of their Party leaderships have shown. In fact several of their countries are losing no more and some a good deal less of their populations due to the lowering of birth-rates than they once lost through emigration, never mind infant mortality.

Meanwhile, inside each country migration to industry and the towns has been heavy indeed. Of the three countries where rural over-population had been worst before the war, Poland had by 1970 reduced the percentage of its people dependent on agriculture to about half of what it had been at the time of the Depression.[5] In Hungary, too, where in 1949 55 per cent of the population lived by agriculture, by 1970 the percentage had been halved.[6] And in Romania, where the Party's industrialization policies took effect somewhat later, the share of the agricultural population in the total was reduced by one-third in the twenty years preceding 1969.[7]

The effects of industrialization and movement to the towns have been momentous. It is no exaggeration to say that they have formed the major experience of the East European peasantry during the Party's twenty-five-year rule. And as the peasantry has provided all the new recruits to the urban working strata, making a very serious impact on them, and has still remained the major class in four of the five countries of Eastern Europe, its experience has in fact been the crucial experience of the region as a whole in the same twenty-five years. Not just economically and socially, but also in human terms, and regardless of how they related to it in politics, the nations of Eastern Europe have experienced the Party in the main as the Champion of Progress.

And none more so than their young. To take movement to

industry and to the towns, it has been natural for those who were as yet least settled to be the fastest on their feet. And they have been, too, almost with a vengeance. In Poland, where private farming has largely survived, the flight of the young from the countryside has resulted in many older peasants now working their lands only as a pathetic rearguard action, until they die. 'The father wished so much to educate both his children,' wrote a fifty-year-old farmer, describing the life of his village family by family, in a long entry for a contest in a Polish weekly in 1970, 'that when he could no longer walk behind his plough, he fixed a stool to it and forced himself to go on ploughing the field in a sitting position. To be able to harrow, he again devised something to stand on, fixed to the harrow, such was his determination. He struggled mightily and so did his wife . . . to secure a better life for their children, to give them an education, and to enable them to earn their living outside farming. . . . The old farmer was so spent, his heart so weak, that a bee's sting killed him while he was feeding his horses. He fell down, the old tired heart refused to rally the worn-out body. . . . In similar manner died his neighbour, a woman with an overworked, damaged heart.'[8] In Hungary, where most of the land has been collectivized, in the late sixties the average age of collective farmers was 54·2 years, while only 7·6 per cent of them were under 26.[9] And in Romania, of those who had left for the towns between 1956 and 1966, including some of the heaviest years of migration, 81·7 per cent had been between 14 and 29 years of age.

Not that the newcomers find it easy to adapt to the towns. In fact their problems are very similar to those of masses of newcomers to higher social strata in today's Eastern Europe, which I discussed earlier and which the problems of being a newcomer in a town may often aggravate. The result is a feeling of isolation and loss of bearings within their new environment, a collapse of identity and the adoption of defensive manners and postures, which may stay with them for life. The greater the distance between them and their native environment, geographically and socially, the worse the effect. 'You'd think students are good mixers, but there are in fact two separate societies among them,' said a twenty-seven-year-old lecturer, born and now teaching in

Cracow. 'To one belong people who live here or whose parents have been able to afford to rent private rooms for them. To the other, students living in the hostel, who are all from out of town and of course from poorer families. During my university years I belonged to the first lot, and I don't remember a single party where we might have invited people from the hostel. We met them at lectures, but otherwise it was as if they lived in a ghetto. Even though a lot of them try to break out of it – now that I'm teaching I sometimes get them coming to me to ask what I think they should wear to go to the theatre, and that sort of thing. But still, it'll show a mile off that they're newcomers.'

Perhaps even worse is the loss of bearings. In Budapest, for instance, the overwhelming majority of juvenile delinquency cases are brought against newcomers: in the late sixties, they accounted for 80–85 per cent.[10] 'It is they who make up our "socialist mob",' said the twenty-eight-year-old woman Party member I quoted on page 131. 'It's not their fault, they're rootless in large cities, they can't understand what's happening round them or to them. They can't put it into village terms, it wouldn't fit, and also they've kicked the village. But the way they are, they could be used for anything that might give shape to their lives, as Fascism did in the thirties. It's a terrifying thought.'

Part of the reason is, of course, that though town life attracted them from a distance, on reaching it they find that they can enjoy or participate in it only at basic levels. 'Most of them never go to the theatre or even to the cinema,' said a twenty-nine-year-old lawyer in a provincial town in Romania. 'If they go out in the evening at all, rather than watch TV, which they could also do in the village by now, they go out to drink, not to sit in cafés and talk. They simply haven't yet got what it takes to live in a city.' In fact surveys show not only that peasants' children constitute much the smallest percentage of applicants to university and prefer learning trades, but also that within present city populations the children of newcomers have the least interest in opportunities for further education. They are still too busy securing what has long been their families' major goal of geographical and social migration, and enjoying the first fruits of achievement, to be able to set their sights any higher.

A version of this is also one of the reasons why students from the countryside are known to be by far the hardest workers at university, and the least relaxed. 'I may go to a concert,' said the twenty-two-year-old Cracow student whose views on religious belief I quoted in the last chapter, and who was from a small town further east, 'and perhaps to the theatre. But for student clubs and dances, I just haven't the time. I've got too much to catch up with.' This, however, is still the more creditable, and more difficult, of the defensive attitudes taken. The majority of newcomers have only enough resources to denounce what they themselves cannot enjoy in city life as pointless, and to make whatever material use they can of the rest.

They also partially communicate this attitude to their host environment. In fact, just as newcomers to higher social strata have in various ways informed the attitudes of these, so large new masses in town have had more than just a numerical impact on urban life. If, for instance, many East European cities and even some capitals have a distinctly country air about them, this is where the main reason lies. 'Almost every one of us here,' said the thirty-three-year-old Bulgarian poet I have quoted several times, in Sofia in 1968, 'comes from a village, or if he doesn't his parents or at most grandparents did.' In most cities of Eastern Europe not only are there crowds wearing clothes which, whether dirty and torn or Sunday-clean and well looked after, are obviously from the countryside, but an even larger number of people is wearing what is just as obviously their first set of city clothes. This is yet another reason for the general dullness of colours that I mentioned earlier, and the visible anxiety not to stick out, complemented with intolerant staring at those who do.

The influence of newcomers on urban atmosphere and appearances, however, only reflects the deeper effect they have had on average behaviour and attitudes. For example, if interest in material possessions rather than ideas has greatly increased among all strata, partly as a result of new down-to-earth masses invading them, another part of the reason has been the rural invasion of the cities. The proverbial peasant who on getting money went to town to buy whatever he could show off at home has now moved to town, taking his attitudes with him. And being able to afford

things his ancestors only dreamt about, he has also become far
more avid in his materialism, which he naturally enough helps
to confirm among the people he has just joined in town. His
rejection as pointless of the non-material things he cannot yet
enjoy similarly strengthens the attitudes of purposeful intolerance
that are anyhow well enough rooted in his new environment.

The one thing newcomers to town have not communicated
to their hosts has been a love of peasant life. The most important
reason for this is that the overwhelming majority of them had
never felt any such love. The idea of the peasant as the Noble
Savage, and of the agrarian way of life as inherently healthy,
invigorating and altogether a form of mystical communion with
God, has always been an upper- and middle-class urban fancy.
In Eastern Europe, even a good many intellectuals born of peasant
stock have long rejected it as something that only people who had
never been starving in the middle of parched plains, nor had had
to clean out the pigsties – more especially someone else's – could
entertain. Most peasants, too, even if they owned some land, had
always preferred their sons to learn a trade or if possible to get an
education, and their daughters to marry men who had.

Of course the ideology behind the Party's industrialization
programme has not been free of its own middle-class fancies.
On the contrary, its championship of industrial progress and its
mystique of the proletariat as the Heroic Class were twin versions
of conservatives' attachment to agriculture and their mystique of
the peasantry. Both had their origins in the Rousseau-esque
vision that posited 'the people' as the source of all good, and its
'enemies' as the cause of all corruption. Only, while the conservatives looked on industrial development itself as an enemy
of the people, Marxists exalted it, and in this they were much
closer to the way the peasantry – especially its landless majority –
itself viewed things in Eastern Europe. Thus even though the
Party never really understood the peasants, as was shown by the
folly of its proposing in 1919 in Hungary and Poland to nation-
alize rather than distribute estates, when it returned for the second
time, on the firm shoulders of the Soviet Army in 1945–8, and set
about industrializing the region, it did what 'the people' wanted.

And needed too, as the thirties had meanwhile shown. The

Depression, with agricultural prices sinking much further and taking longer to recover than industrial ones, had caught the four eastern countries of the region, in which the peasantry then constituted half to four-fifths of the population, in the deadly 'price scissors'. Driving millions of peasants mad with hunger, this had been the main factor in making even populists in these countries reflect on the myths some of them had till then cherished, and cast around for more practical ideas. In other words, the Party's industrialization programmes after the war only combined the conclusions many East Europeans had already drawn from the horrific lesson of the thirties, with the Marxist mystique of progress and the proletariat. And whatever violence to people and their feelings the execution of these policies has involved, it has at the same time helped to realize the dreams and abate the hunger of just that major segment of the area's population, the peasantry, that the Party has least understood.

It has been part of essentially the same paradox that while the Party has failed to change that mentality from above, the changes it has brought about in the life of the people have irresistibly transformed a number of the latter's attitudes from below. But if these changes have been beyond the control of the people, they have proved even less controllable by the Party. Results have followed which by now the Party would often wish away, even though they are fully in the spirit of its own progressivist mystique and, indeed, of its original promise of mankind's rebirth to a higher state of consciousness.

There can be little doubt about the Party's success in giving the major push necessary to the industrialization of the area. To give only a few examples, according to Polish statistics in 1970 the volume of the country's industrial production was 7·5 times what it had been in 1950, and accounted for 20 per cent more of the national income.[11] In Romania, during the years of rapid industrialization since 1958 output rose by a yearly average of 13 per cent, and wholly new industries – from steel manufacturing to synthetics – were being introduced.[12] In Bulgaria, whereas industrial machinery and equipment had formed no part of the country's exports in 1939, by 1968 it accounted for 24·5 per cent, and the share of unprocessed agricultural materials had dropped from 63·8 per cent to 13·0 per cent.[13] And throughout the region the production of electricity and of heavy industrial and (more recently) consumer goods has soared.

Apart from what all this has done to people's lives, one of its main effects has been to turn them into fanatical progressivists. I have more than once quoted their use of the word 'modern' to mean 'supremely good'. Let me now quote from a poll carried out among sixteen- to eighteen-year-olds in Romania in 1964.[14] To the question, 'What do you mean by "being modern"?', the enthusiastic answers ranged from, 'having automatic equipment at your disposal', to 'adjusting yourself to modern fashion, which changes from year to year'. In between, people thought to be modern meant 'to have at your disposal all the things you need', or 'to be well-dressed but not make a display of yourself in the street', or 'to know the latest conventions of society and adapt to them', or 'to adjust oneself quickly and thoroughly to new conditions'. In other words, modernity meant a sense of affluence as well as the traditional anxiety about 'what people will say', and a knowledge of what was fashionable as well as a readiness to conform in the most elastic manner. Only one respondent thought that 'to be modern is a thing to be condemned'.

The love of modernity affects their choice of occupations as much as their taste in people. Newer industries not only have little trouble in finding manpower, but they can usually pick and choose the best among school-leavers, though the wages they pay are not disproportionately higher than elsewhere. In Hungary, for instance, in the late sixties in the telecommunications and precision industries the percentage of under twenty-fives was 48·9, much higher than the average, and 20 per cent of the young skilled workers had been through the *Maturita*.[15] 'What emerges from the questionnaires on person-ideals,' a Polish sociologist in charge of a large survey on the young told me in Warsaw in 1970, 'is that young people want to be, above all "modern". By this they mean a person who "knows how to manage", who is properly educated and qualified, who is straightforward and unfussy, and who gets on well with the rest. They both use the word "modern" to describe this person and explain him as such.'

All of which could be perfectly acceptable to the Party, were it not for the fact that by 'modern' young East Europeans also tend to mean 'western', whether they are conscious of it or not. Even though the music or ties or washing machines they call modern may by now be home-produced, they remain part of a way of life that has come to the region from the West, where higher levels of affluence, sophistication and homogeneity have already been attained.

How seriously the Party takes this phenomenon could be seen from the fact that President Ceausescu himself stressed, at the start of the vast new ideological campaign in Romania in July 1971, the need to teach the young that if a piece of imported machinery was well produced, this did not mean that 'capitalism' was good. And it was as part of this didactic effort that western and western-type pop music on TV and radio were replaced with home-produced jingles and folk-tunes, the latter beautiful in themselves but of little interest to the young.

However, the effort is likely to prove as vain as it is misguided. It is, in fact, an example of the Party trying to counter from above effects which the results of its own work in transforming the environment have produced from below. Whether or not young people equate good machinery and the western way of life with 'capitalism', they no longer live in the conditions amidst which the folk-songs were born. Instead, and thanks mainly to the Party, they live among conditions that are similar to those generating today's pop sub-culture in the western world. If, as Marxists believe, existence determines consciousness, young people working in factories, living in towns and thinking in terms of an industrialized future cannot be expected to dance to the tunes of an agrarian past.

On the contrary, it is inevitable that they should be looking westwards even more eagerly than their fathers and grandfathers ever did. To the older generations, the West was either a distant land of civilization and opportunities, or a potential Saviour from foreign oppression. Among today's East Europeans the idea of the West as Saviour is almost extinct, but instead they see it as the example of what their countries are about to become, and as the source of the necessary knowledge and technology. Its attractions are all the more powerful in that rather than being distant and half-mythical, they are immediate and almost tangible.

On this the Party should congratulate itself. If the outlook and expectations of the young have become strongly westernized, this is because the Party has succeeded in westernizing their lives to the same extent. Its policies of rapid industrialization and deliberate social engineering have also created the kind of economic and social opportunities in search of which previous generations used to migrate westwards. The majority of young people now seek the same opportunities within their own countries because the Party has in effect brought the West to them. Large-scale emigration has been replaced by internal movement to industry and the towns, at the same time as young East Europeans are becoming even more eager than previous generations to see themselves and their countries as genuinely part of the developed West.

But, useful as this may be to the Party's own modernizing purposes, in other respects it is entitled to regard the results of its own good work as threatening its position in charge of Eastern Europe. By this I do not mean that the measures it may take to defend itself must succeed, but that its sense of being in mortal danger is justified.

In the first place, the Party as the Champion of Westernizing Progress was put in charge of the region in 1945–8, and has been directly or indirectly maintained there ever since, by a superpower further to the East – namely Russia, a country which the majority of East Europeans, with or without reason, have always seen as behind their own in level of development. Nor have they abandoned this vision, regardless of political allegiances. 'Do you know what the Russians call a man who can either read or write?' the twenty-nine-year-old Party member whom I quoted among the genuinely convinced in the previous chapter, had asked me in Budapest. I did not. 'They call him a specialist. . . . And a man who can both read and write? A preposterous know-all.'

Even where the expression of their view of Russia and Russians is not vicious, central to it is a sense of their own superiority. 'The Russians are good people,' a twenty-one-year-old hitchhiker said in Poland. 'But they're so very naive. If their government told them the midday sky was black, they'd at least believe it wasn't blue.' Many young East Europeans have good friends in Russia, but this only colours their condescension with more sympathy. 'They've been so backward, and isolated, they can't help being naive,' a thirty-year-old Party member, who had studied in Moscow, said in Romania in 1968. 'I knew people doing aesthetics who really thought Impressionist painting was already incomprehensible, never mind anything more up to date. There's, of course, a tiny minority who're Europeans, apart from being wonderful people, which a lot of the rest are as well. But even these "Europeans" are affected by their isolation. So imagine what it does to the rest.'

Very often, in fact, young East Europeans talk of their visits to Russia as western travellers in the last century talked of their journeys to the mysterious East. 'If you want to go somewhere, Russia is the place,' a twenty-five-year-old Czech sculptor enthused. 'I've been to Vienna and Italy and England, it's all nothing compared to what you see there. The faces, the expressions, the fantastic patience people have, the drinking, the squalor, and more than anything, the religiosity. I don't think anybody can really understand what's been going on in Russia in the last fifty years without seeing how the pilgrims flock to holy places, how they feed the beggars sitting at the church doors, fat and unmoving and just munching all day long the food old women keep pushing into their mouths as a sacrificial offering. And then the crowds, really queueing all night in the dead of winter to get in to see Lenin's body at the Mausoleum. It's the same Russia, Holy Mother Russia, and that's where anybody should start trying to understand them. . . . '

And if the Party's successes in modernizing the region have turned its young only further westwards, it has to the same extent confirmed their view of Russia as being behind them in development. Polish marine engineers, for example, designing ships for export to Russia, go to pick up new ideas at boat shows in Copenhagen and further west. 'And when I'm there, I'm ashamed of our backwardness,' one of them told me in Gdansk in 1968. 'We must catch up with them, or we're lost.' No one talked, in Gdansk or anywhere else, about catching up with Russia. On the contrary: 'To the Russians we're the West,' said a Hungarian journalist who had travelled widely. 'When they're posted here, they get themselves spruced up, they make all kinds of preparations, and once they're here, they revel in it and do everything not to be recalled. It's the same as when our people are posted to a commercial outfit in Italy or America. Everybody has the West God gave them. . . .'

Much as the Party may rail against 'unprincipled admiration of the West', the truth is that it too has come to equate 'modern' with western. Instead of propaganda extolling 'vanguard Soviet methods' in everything from agriculture to sport, it is far more common for both specialists and publicists, discussing progress achieved in any field, to take as their standards of comparison statistics and phenomena from 'the advanced capitalist countries of the West'. It makes as little difference to them as it does to the young whether the comparisons made refer to the production of welding machines or plastic toys. The standard is the same. In fact, even official pop festivals invite western celebrities as guest jurors, whose opinions are then quoted as authoritative by the youth press, and who often decide who gets the prizes. The guests no doubt add glamour to the festivals and so may do the Youth Leagues organizing them some good. But nothing could better illustrate how well the Party knows which way the young are looking, and how best they can be pleased.

Still more important from the point of view of the Party's intention to remain in charge of Eastern Europe for ever is a second paradox. The Party has been put in charge of the region and set about westernizing it not only as the protégé of an eastern power but also as an essentially 'eastern' type of institution. A centralism unknown in the West has been characteristic of its rule in every sphere: indeed its claim to power over every sphere from agriculture to sport is the essence of its existential philosophy. And though centralism, whether in politics and the economy or in control over education and the media, is germane to the East European tradition itself, the heroic form in which the Party has been maintaining it now seems to many young East Europeans to be an 'eastern' accretion to Communist ideology and practice – that is, developmentally beneath them. This is especially so in the three more highly developed northern countries (of which the northern two never saw Ottoman rule, and the southernmost, Hungary, only for a period brief in comparison to the four or five centuries that it survived in Romania and Bulgaria). For example, almost every time Marxists in Poland, Hungary and above all Czechoslovakia make an attempt to defend their faith by separating it from the gigantic mistakes and awesome terror perpetrated in its name, they do so in part by putting down the latter to what they call 'Asian-type Communism', a type Marx never envisaged, and would not have approved.

Nor is this purely an illusion on the part of East European Marxists to excuse their views. True, centralism of a type is what makes Marx's vision of the world systematic at all. But beyond the fact that Party centralism took its ultimate form under Stalin, who was a Georgian, Lenin's own centralist methods, definitive of the Party since 1903, had also been developed to fight an orientally despotic form of government and its secret police, many of whose traditions Soviet Russia inherited as a matter of course, and handed on to its East European protégés. In addition, the Marxist passion for central planning was almost bound to inspire absolute centralism in the Russian, and later the East European, context. As seen by many Party people at the time and on the spot, only through centralist methods could such a vast, backward country as Russia in the 1920s, and also the smaller and less backward countries of Eastern Europe in the 1950s, be developed with the speed they have in fact registered since. And, finally, the centralism inherent in the idea of the élite as Hero in command of a besieged collective was historically rooted in the circumstances which in both Russia and Eastern Europe had been left behind by the invasions from further East since the ninth century.

Every one of these reasons justifying the Party's heroic centralism, however, point further east, and into the past, whereas the Party's main achievement as Champion of Progress in Eastern Europe has been, precisely, to give the area the major push it needed towards the West and a different future. In other words, the Party's most tangible successes in the last twenty-five years are enabling the region 'to escape' in both space and time from under its centralist rule.

Nor is the Party unaware of this. Every one of its attempts to decentralize has been described by its own spokesmen and ideologues as an effort 'to adapt to today's conditions of development'. In the terminology I have been using in this chapter this means to westernize its hitherto eastern methods of rule as much as it has westernized the region. The accuracy of these geographical terms in the context has also been shown by the reaction of the super-power further East to any East European Party's actually proceeding with decentralization. Each time the process has looked like going beyond the point where the Party might still contain it, and so stop the country at least half-way between East and West, the Russians have intervened – directly, as in Hungary in 1956 and Czechoslovakia in 1968, and as bogeymen in Poland from early 1957 onwards. Should Bulgaria and Romania, where the Party has never really attempted to westernize its rule, do so and go too far, they would be taught the same geographical lesson.

Thus the Party whose main achievement in power has been to westernize the region can never expect to westernize itself. It must remain a Platonic institution, irremovable and taking decisions whose sheer size must simplify them into universals, even while it forges ahead with the basically Aristotelian work of development, inducing motion and the proliferation of complexities. This position is as paradoxical as it is bound to prove untenable.

Put at its simplest, each of the Party's own successes can only diminish what need there has ever been for it as central Hero, and what appeal it has ever possessed as a Messiah. In fact, having given the area the major push it needed, the Party has set in motion changes which will not only continue by themselves, but will also bring the Party ever closer to facing two main options, both of them suicidal. One consists of trying to clamp down on processes its own good work as Champion of Progress in Eastern Europe has begun, until these prove too powerful for it to control. The other consists, however, of gradually giving up its position as Hero in charge of the environment, and so ceasing to be the Party as founded by Lenin.

As regards economic development, for example, though there remains a good deal to be done, the ground-work has on the whole been completed, and even a number of benefits have begun to roll in. One of the things that distinguish today's teenagers in Eastern Europe from the three older active generations is precisely that they have grown up enjoying the first fruits of development, instead of fearing it as a new monstrosity in the manner of the generation that is now senior, or suffering its worst deprivations and problems, as the two age groups now in the middle have. Meanwhile, the complexity of the tasks ahead will render the Party's centralist methods inadequate, and it will itself at the centre become an obstacle to further progress.

As regards the more general transformation of the environment and of society, the situation is similar, if more involved. A number of processes that the Party set in motion are now either coming to an end, or slowing down, or taking directions it never anticipated, or going into reverse of their own accord. The effect is to make the Party's original propaganda less and less appealing, its presence as the motor of change less and less necessary, and its political 'function' more and more that of a scapegoat for whatever evil side-effects develop.

Migration to industry and the towns, for instance, is no longer the stampede it once was. It is continuing, but at a considerably slower rate, and certain countries have in fact begun to witness a return to the countryside. At the moment, those re-migrating belong mainly to the professional intelligentsia, but in the two most developed countries, Czechoslovakia and Hungary, some manual workers have also begun to trickle back. A village-bound exodus is unlikely, but the relatively stable situation now prevailing in such semi-agricultural countries as Denmark may be coming into view.

Both of the main reasons for the slowing down of movement to the towns, and the measured re-migration and stabilization that are likely to follow, result essentially from the Party's success in realizing the people's dreams. One of these reasons is that the target areas of migration from the countryside, geographical as well as occupational and social, are becoming overcrowded or have begun to disintegrate. The other, that living and working in the countryside has come to seem much less repulsive than it was when the dream of escaping became maniacal.

Geographically, there is not enough room in the towns. Housing construction has lagged far behind the demand for it and many towns have also deliberately refused to grow, guarding themselves against newcomers through administrative measures. If Budapest, the largest city of the region, today contains two million people, this is only because it had acquired almost half that number of inhabitants by 1914, as the second capital of the Austro-Hungarian Empire. And most of its newer citizens live in suburbs which, as villages become urbanized, are becoming less and less distinguishable from small country towns. Nor can there be much question that policies of urban dispersal will remain dominant throughout Eastern Europe, especially as they have been becoming more and more pronounced in the West itself.

Occupationally, even where no decrees for directing manpower to the countryside exist, the law of supply and demand has begun to force people out of industry and the towns. In a number of professions, from engineering to medicine, graduates are finding it increasingly difficult, if not almost impossible, to land their first jobs in cities. As regards manual workers, too, even though East European countries pride themselves on the absence of unemployment, in several this has long been a matter of 'unemployment within the gates' – that is, employment of far larger labour forces than are, according to East European economists themselves, necessary for efficient production. As it is, Poland – until recently much the most fertile country of the region – has long been on the verge of an unemployment crisis, and it is expected that once economic rationalization is implemented, a measure of industrial unemployment will become as constant in the more developed East European countries as it has been in the West.

Meanwhile, living and working in the countryside has become a good deal less repellent. Of course to a westerner used to paved streets and at least basic amenities even in small villages, much of rural Eastern Europe may still look like the back of beyond. But to a native East European on a return visit, as I was, the improvement in people's houses, clothes and even faces, in the supply of water, electricity and services, in the availability of such aspects of civilization as cafés and libraries, in the road and communication systems, is striking. (Such a 'mirror-effect' would in fact be likely to prevail in almost everything I have said in this chapter, and indeed the whole of this book: what to those from the West may seem poor, backward and hidebound, may represent by local standards the result of basic changes for the better in conditions, and in formerly traditional attitudes.)

And though many East Europeans themselves consider the countryside to be the back of beyond, once they have had a closer look at it, or especially settled there, they too begin to notice and then take pride in the changes. 'When we got here, two years ago,' said the thirty-one-year-old Budapest-born lawyer of a collective farm in western Hungary, 'the street in which we live had no water and no pavement. Six months of the year you had to wade through mud, or skate along, before you got to the main road. Now there is water, and at the top of the street, as you must have seen, they've started paving at least with stones. Give it another few years, and there'll be asphalt.'

In other words, the slowing down of townward migration, and the beginnings of its reversal, are due to much the same kind of changes as had 'internalized' rural migration in the first place. If the peasantry's urge to escape westwards has abated because the West is in effect being brought to Eastern Europe, the urge to flee to the towns is now beginning to abate because the towns (and thereby the West) have begun coming to the village.

The process is, of course, still in its initial stages. In fact, within each East European country it has affected western districts first, and has left many areas in the east almost untouched. Also, it has affected life in the countryside more than the actual working conditions from which the peasantry has been trying to flee. This is why the professional intelligentsia has been in the forefront of the return – attracted by jobs and deliberately supplemented wages, easier housing conditions and the chance of being part of a local élite rather than remaining small fish in large ponds, and also best able to afford cars and so make use of developing road systems. 'I may well go and work on a collective farm,' said an engineering student in his final year in Bratislava in 1968. 'But I'll be received with open arms, and stay "Mr Engineer". I wouldn't go if I had to mind the cattle.'

However, if agricultural work itself has remained hard, dirty, irregular and altogether unattractive, the peasantry's life has changed as much as the villages themselves. This is particularly the case in the two most developed countries, Czechoslovakia and Hungary – in the latter special efforts have also been made by the Party during the last decade to raise the peasantry's living standards faster than those of the industrial working class – but there can be little doubt that it will spread eastwards as much as it is spreading in eastern parts of the region from the top down. 'Of course the superficial things come first,' a Romanian sociologist said. 'Urban dances, western dances, urban clothes and so on, which people see on TV and adopt. But also, where they used to build with adobe they have begun to build with bricks; instead of soup and bread and cucumbers they eat at least some meat; and ideas as well as dances come through the TV or are brought back by commuters from town.'

All this is partly a matter of spreading urbanization and rising prosperity. But another crucial factor lies in the peasantry's changed attitudes towards life and, in particular, money. Whereas previously those who had some money, rather than just children, used to invest it in land or hoard it in mattresses for their old age, with collectivization land has lost its value while pension schemes have become the rule. As a result most of the money peasants earn, which, in the countries where they can sell the produce of household plots freely on the market, may mean considerable sums, they spend on themselves. They buy town clothes and rebuild their houses, and then get such town goods as refrigerators and washing machines and finally even cars. 'I wouldn't want the land back if they threw it at me,' a fifty-seven-year-old former kulak said in Slovakia. We were sitting inside his large, newly built house, furnished as any suburban home in Eastern Europe might be. 'You couldn't get the men to work it, and anyway, it would just be all the bother again, and getting up at all hours, and saving for more land. Now, I'm living – I've just been on a [package] tour to Hungary and next year I'll go somewhere else – and I don't blame my children for wanting to work regular hours and to get regular wages.'

Altogether, if a certain re-migration has begun and at least a stable situation can be expected to arise, the reasons lie in facts, not in the myths that were once so dear to all shades of romantics. 'For five years I was a company solicitor, lived in a single room with my wife and two children; I earned just enough to keep us going, and abhorred the idea of living anywhere outside the capital,' said the thirty-one-year-old Budapest-born lawyer quoted earlier. 'Here, I have a five-room house, the children can play as much as they like, I earn more, and get produce I can sell or we can eat. I've started growing grapes, and I'm still only an hour by car, which I coudn't have otherwise afforded so soon, from the great life.' In the less developed countries, and among manual workers, the same sort of attitude is only just beginning to emerge. But whatever changes have occurred in outlook, these too, are due to factual rather than ideological reasons. 'The pride in being a peasant, which used to be part of the ethos of the pre-war peasant youth movement, is gone,' said a thirty-three-year-old sociologist in Poland. 'But instead, we're beginning to have our first generation of young peasants aggressively interested in new crops and methods, and that's far more important.'

Changes that are perhaps less radical but are of the same kind have begun to affect occupational and social migration. Originally, the Party's vision of itself as Social Messiah was justified by the fact that it had made it possible for people to escape from the manual-working strata, first through direct promotion and then through education. Nor, of course, has movement into the white-collar and professional intelligentsia stopped. But it has begun to slow down, and there are signs that here, too, something of a reverse migration has begun and a situation of dynamic balance is within sight. Not only have the percentages of children of the manual-working classes among university applicants been falling for years, but some people with higher qualifications have also begun, casting aside almost maniacal prejudices, to take to manual work.

Initially, this was a matter of moonlighting, rather like a version of what commuting is to the area's many worker-peasants. That is, engineers supplementing their incomes as taxi-drivers in the evening, geologists sinking wells over the weekend, and so on. But more recently there have been instances of professionally educated people taking manual jobs as their main source of income, and in considerable numbers.

> A worker in a textile factory in Skocz [the main Warsaw weekly reported in 1971] was given a rise, and told to sign up for an evening class to obtain an engineering degree, necessary for the post to which he had been promoted. He then took a diploma out of his pocket. He explained that he had concealed the fact that he was an engineer because he had a wife and two children, and as a skilled worker he made twice what he would have obtained as a novice engineer. In Lodz, 2,060 persons have been found to be concealing their intermediate and higher technical education. Really, the things people conceal in Poland![16]

Considering that the report was talking about a single town, namely the Polish Manchester, in whose textile mills workers' wages were at much the same time being attacked as lower than the country's average, the number of people concealing their qualifications in order to do manual work in the whole of Poland must be impressive.

Nor are these numbers likely to decrease. The reasons for the slowing down of movement towards the intelligentsia and the beginnings of what promises to develop into another ever more homogeneous situation are versions of those that have affected migration to industry and the towns – the overcrowding of target areas, and the simultaneous improvement in the conditions of the strata from which people began by trying to escape.

As regards overcrowding, when it first became apparent it was blamed, popularly and to some extent officially too, on sheer bad planning. But then it was realized that several East European countries had simply acquired more secondary and higher school graduates than they could employ in the jobs hitherto reserved for them. For example, Hungary today has about as many engineers per head of the population as France, though it is much less industrialized.[17] In Poland, as early as the end of the fifties trained people began attending western language courses in large numbers, with a view to emigration. In general, the expansion of education without a proportionate increase in the need for white-collar and professional people has created, in Eastern

Europe as much as in the West, a brain-pool ready to be drained.

The difficulties of emigrating have been partially responsible for trained people beginning to remigrate towards the manual-working classes. But far more important has been the upgrading of manual occupations, and social strata, as a result both of development and of Party policies. In fact, beyond the actual improvements it has brought about in their lives, the Party has also helped to decrease in children of the manual-working classes the urge to enter the roads of upward mobility, precisely by opening wide these roads before them. Being a worker is now much less a fate to which they find themselves condemned, and much more the result of a choice they have freely made, and can leave their children to reverse at will.

Meanwhile, development has seriously changed the nature and status of manual work, making much of it more hygienic and less tiring, and some of it a lot more complex. It has also brought a number of wholly new industries, offering the young far more sophisticated kinds of work than their parents could have found, and with little of the social stigma that may still be attached to older manual occupations. In fact, jobs in such 'modern' industries as electronics are now as respectable as a good many white-collar occupations, while they offer much more money, both in official wages and in what moonlighters can make as – licensed or unlicensed – private handymen.

And here again, what are beginnings now are likely to grow into dominant phenomena, due mostly to further development. Automation, for instance, is almost bound to speed both the reduction in the size of the bureaucracy, and the elevation of a good deal of manual work towards the level of present white-collar occupations. It will certainly make further areas of skilled manual work more hygienic and less physically exacting, as well as reducing the length of the working day or week – as it has already begun to do in several East European countries.

But, once more, the reasons for whatever remigration towards the manual-working class has started, and whatever dynamic balance and degree of homogeneity will result, are factual, not mythical. Young people do not choose to remain part of, or to enter, the manual-working class because of any passion for the proletariat as the revolutionary element in society. They do so because there is room for them there, and the jobs are more satisfying in every way than they used to be, and mean less of a separation from 'proper' society than they once did. In fact, the country in which development has long ago created the most homogeneous society of the region, Czechoslovakia, is also the one where upward migration is now the slowest, and the difference between the strata is least noticed. 'I'm surprised by what you tell me about the social divisions among students in Poland,' a twenty-four-year-old student of English said in Prague in 1970. 'Here, we're just not very much used to wondering about who comes from what sort of family.' *Mésalliance*, Czech sociologists told me, was among the least important of the causes of divorce.

And while the Party becomes less and less necessary as the motor of social change, it will also become more and more clearly unnecessary as an élite in charge of the environment. Not that the élite itself will become redundant. If anything, development is likely further to increase the need for it, for practical as well as psychological reasons. 'We simply must allow the growth of an élite,' a well-known Polish sociologist said in May 1970. 'At the moment, there's almost nothing people with above-average abilities can do. Why else do you think they're taking all these second and third degrees, when we already have countless PhDs doing the same jobs as before they took their doctorates? They're all looking for something to do with the extra they have in their heads, but all they can do is put letters after their names, which is no use to them or to society. We must allow them to rise above the rest, so they can give us what they have.'

Rising through ability and rising through Party membership, however, are two different things. And, increasingly, the élite needed will be a professional rather than a semi-theological élite. That is, a genuine meritocracy, making only the Party redundant. 'Already the situation is almost laughable,' said a twenty-eight-year-old engineer, himself a Party member, in Hungary. 'Everybody knows that we have what's called "double management" – management by management plus management by the Party. It's expensive, unnecessary, and only leads to the left hand interfering with what the right hand tries to do.'

Nor is there much doubt about which the left hand is. In Hungary itself, where expertise has long been preferred over political criteria in management selection, young graduates often do not say in their applications for jobs that they are Party members, so as not to arouse doubts about their professional qualifications. This only highlights the fact that in East European countries where no rational policies of management selection have been introduced, a very high percentage of the managerial personnel are Party members and even more of them lack the qualifications for their jobs. In Romania, for example, even prior to the re-emphasizing of political criteria as part of the ideological campaign begun in July 1971, whereas only about a quarter of skilled workers were Party members, 46 per cent of engineers were.[18] In Czechoslovakia in the mid-sixties (that is, again before political allegiances assumed paramount importance in the post-invasion purges of both Party and management) less than a quarter of the deputy directors of all enterprises were qualified, while of those 'with higher education between the ages of 25 and 59, only 11 per cent [held] leading positions in industry at the director or deputy director level'.[19] Small wonder if, just as the 1969–70 purges got under way, a lecturer in ideology should have found his seminar students voice the subversive view that 'if the situation is to improve, the leadership of the nation must be taken over by the intellectual élite.'[20]

As development proceeds, this can only become more the case, not less. In fact, as the value of the trained élite increases, so in country after country the Party will be forced either simply to confer membership on experts, or to let them have managerial jobs without holding Party cards. While the first course would mean sheer tragicomedy, the second must lead to a situation where the old and once unfair popular adage that 'only the good-for-nothings turn Communist' will hold sadly true.

Some centralists within the Party appear to see the advent of the computer as their salvation. But this is a very short-sighted view. Central planning will, of course, become easier and probably more efficient when large amounts of information can be collected and processed rapidly, and corrective measures can be instituted at equal speed. But even if the use of computers should lead to recentralization in Eastern Europe, it would do little to bolster the Party's rule. On the contrary, it would further increase the value of the trained élite in comparison with Party hacks. The only material worth feeding into the computer will be factual, and only experts will be able to formulate the alternatives for it to work on and draw the relevant conclusions from the patterns it may project. And above all, the computer will be impervious to rhetoric and retain no use for ideology.

This will also be ever more characteristic of the élite itself. That is, just as the masses will cease to need the Party to keep open the roads of geographical and social migration, along which they can now walk forwards and backwards well enough by themselves, so the élite will cease to use the rhetoric and the myths of ideology which the Party has employed for trying to communicate with the masses. This will be partly because as the region becomes more highly developed, so aims will become more man-size, and rewards more visible, making the heroic appeals of the past first ludicrous and then unnecessary. But even more because as tasks become increasingly complex, and as educational and social homogeneity spread, so changes in the style of managing people are almost bound to superannuate the Party's inherently centralist methods.

Signs of this are already visible, in the economy as much as in other spheres. From having been largely authoritarian, employing combinations of force and rhetoric, the style of management has been gradually becoming productionistic, relying on pressure and material incentives, and is heading in the direction of becoming manipulative, based on forms of what is best called 'triangular participation', involving the managers, the managed and the purposes of their work together.

In several countries of Eastern Europe management trainee institutes are now making conscious efforts to further this process of change, for economic reasons. Still more important from the point of view of people's behaviour and outlook, an analogous process has meanwhile been affecting the East European family, not so much as a result of conscious efforts from above, as of development changing people's lives from below. In the treatment of children, paternal authoritarianism and its forceful and haranguing approach have been giving way to 'maternal-productionist' methods working mostly through pressure, which themselves are likely to be replaced by a 'fraternal-manipulative' style, based on a greater community of interests, and a widening pattern of participatory 'games' between parents and children.

The reasons for these analogous changes are not merely analogous, but basically the same. In fact, they are part of one major phenomenon: homogenization in all spheres. As regards management in general, the factors involved are the spreading of affluence and the widening of consumer choices, lessening the economic distance between managers and managed and making the tasks they face together more manageable; combined with a decrease in the social and educational distance between them, providing greater scope for a growth of trust and possibilities for intelligent compromise.

The same factors have been at work in changing the atmosphere and structure of families in Eastern Europe, and in the same direction. Greater affluence has brought a lessening of the age difference between marriage partners, once made necessary by the man's need to put something aside before he took on the responsibilities of a paterfamilias. Meanwhile, the spread of educational and social homogeneity has helped to produce closer integration between the partners and more equality in the distribution of roles. Factors I mentioned earlier have reduced the number of children, but because of the same factors these children are now born to younger parents. Less difference between the generations means, in turn, more shared interests and activities, more of the patience and sheer playfulness on the part of parents needed for participatory games, and generally more egalitarianism in family management.

Sadly enough for the Party, the analogy also works in the reverse. Indeed it is only too exact. The authoritarianism inherent in the Party's vision of itself as Hero in central charge of the environment is becoming superannuated in phase with its membership, consisting ever more of paterfamilias, if not grandfathers. And just as the Party is becoming increasingly conscious of being left behind as an eastern-type institution by western-type development, so it is increasingly aware of the choice developing between itself and the new élite. Not only have its hard-liners more than once engaged in whipping up ideological fervour so as to defend themselves as politically sound hacks in positions where they might be replaced by proper experts; party ideology has itself developed a distinct fear of the élite. This is why the Prague lecturer I quoted on page 352 had adduced his students' views as not just 'guided by prejudice' but as 'threatening the justifiability of the Party's leading role', and altogether 'anti-socialistic'.

As each time liberalization has swept through an East European country to the point of endangering the Party's heroic position intellectuals have been in the forefront of the struggle, the Party's fear of them is understandable enough. Nevertheless, it shows yet another aspect of the Party's paradoxical situation. Not only have the Party's own founders and ideologically most brilliant cadres come from the professional intelligentsia, but whole sections of the newly trained élite owe their educational chances to the Party, and were given their training by the Party specifically so that they could carry on the good work it began. In rejecting them, the Party is doing nothing less than offering the classic challenge to the children to kill the father so that they themselves may rule the house.

Meanwhile, the decline in the Party's functions as Champion of Economic and Social Progress in Eastern Europe is to be compounded by the decline in whatever general appeal it has possessed. In fact, a further aspect of its paradoxical tragedy is that the realization of the material part of the Hero's original promise may enable the Hero's children to realize a spiritual part of that promise for themselves, but without the Hero's guidance, if not in direct opposition to it.

Essentially, the enthusiasm the Party has all along sought to command, and as Hero cannot do without, is pre-materialistic. Millennial to begin with, it has been bound, within sight of its actual targets, to result in the purposeful intolerance on which the Party's centralist rule is still based. But the attitudes likely to grow after the realization of the Party's main economic and social purposes in Eastern Europe belong to the post-materialist family. Their chief characteristic will be to let growing numbers of people try to do their own thing, which society will be better able to afford, and will tolerate more easily. Another way of putting the same thing would be to say that the first kind of spirituality, to which the Party once genuinely appealed and in some hearts still does, has been Platonic, while the second will be Aristotelian. And as the Party is ideologically and politically bound to the first, it can expect at best only mercy from the second.

For the moment, the majority of East Europeans are still 'in the middle' of the continuum. This is shown in their avid materialism as much as in every other result of the developmental process the Party has championed, beginning with migration to industry and the towns and the non-manual-working strata, and ranging through changes in management methods that they have experienced in the family, at school and in the economy and society at large, to educational and cultural homogenization. From all these points of view, they are in the middle, and showing every sign of it too, not only to me, but also to other visitors. It may be to the purpose to quote here the reactions of two of these, from countries between which young East Europeans know themselves to be in the middle only too well.

'We had a Russian girl here not long ago, an actress, she wasn't poor,' a thirty-year-old Hungarian film-director related. 'A friend and I, both of us Russian speakers, took her out for an evening. It was terrible. She heard us talk about things that interested us. I was wondering about when I could change my car, the other man whether he could get a tourist passport to Italy and whether his uncle would then transfer some money from Sweden, and suddenly she broke down. She was crying, and screaming that we must stop the car, she wants to get out, she can't bear the way only things and money interest us. And she did get out, too, and we had to run after her, and console her that, all right, we know they're more idealistic in Russia, but we aren't so bad either, after all.'

'I get very depressed here sometimes,' a twenty-five-year-old American exchange student said to me in Warsaw. 'They're so incredibly materialistic. When people ask me about the West, it's almost always about how much you can make there and what

sort of car you have, and that kind of thing. It's all that interests
them, here too. The kind of post-materialistic generation which
has grown up in the last few years in America is missing here.'

As yet. It is understandable if as yet, when they are just beginning to realize dreams historic in their families, and are mostly
new in the cities and the social strata to which they had long
aspired, the majority of young East Europeans are materialistic
and often intolerantly so. In a similar way, it is in phase for the
newcomers to town and to the higher strata to be especially
careful about decorum in their clothes, and the colours they wear,
to be rather stiff in their manners and conventional in their life-
styles, and altogether to observe the propriety whose democratic
extension has just reached them, and often to be intolerant in
expecting others to do likewise.

In fact the purposeful intolerance of the newcomers is in phase
not only with that of an age group, but also with that of whole
populations in the countries of Eastern Europe. All three are,
from the point of view of their particular histories, 'in the middle'.
Having worked hard to rise to their present state, they still lack
the material security and general ease which to ever larger
numbers in their children's generation will be almost natural.

The first of these children are already there, having grown up
in circumstances which have been becoming increasingly homogenized in all respects, and showing the effects too in their attitudes.
Of course as yet only initial changes are apparent. But just as
remigration towards the countryside and towards the manual-
working strata has only just begun but can be expected to grow,
so if (as Marx held) there is any correlation between changes in
the environment and in the attitudes it nurses, then from these
beginnings too more widespread effects must develop.

In fact young East Europeans themselves have begun to note
these changes in just the terms that belong to our continuum.
'When you ask them, say sixteen-year-olds, why they think they
don't get on with their parents,' a thirty-seven-year-old sociologist interested in youth problems told me in Budapest, 'one of
the things they'll tell you is, "My parents are too materialistic."
Then you say, "Well, don't you think they're grubbing the
money up so you can have a better life too?" and they say, "Per-

haps. But I won't be like that with my children, I'll talk to them more than give them things." '

The same initial signs are also noticeable as regards other attitudes. For example, as we have seen, the majority of young East Europeans still despise charity as 'romantic'. But in Prague, the most westernized capital, I found them spontaneously collecting in 1968 for Biafra; it was also the picture of a starving Biafran child that the Romanian schoolchildren I mentioned in Chapter 7, insisted on placing at the end of their scrapbook on spaceflight, to put the costly pyrotechnics in perspective in 1969. And how far this was a matter of generational differences became especially clear to me during an interview I had, also in Romania and in the same year, with a group of sociologists engaged on a major survey concerning the outlook of the young. The head of the group was in his early forties, his assistants in their mid- and later twenties, and their response to a query of mine highlighted the contrast in their attitudes.

In a coded part of their questionnaire they had asked people to choose from a set of alternative human qualities. One of the alternatives had been 'honesty or tolerance'. I thought this apposition recalled the slogan, 'You can love only if you know how to hate', and I asked the leader of the group why the two qualities had been offered as alternatives. At first he did not understand the question at all. I explained that, as given, the two seemed to exclude each other. 'But they do,' he said. 'You're either honest or you're tolerant. . . . If, for example, you're a factory manager and some man makes a mistake, are you going to cover it up or make him pay for it? Perhaps it's different in England, it's a richer country, but here we have to struggle hard, and we can't just let people get away with things.'

In brief, he was giving me the Party's own purposefully intolerant argument, which for him still had its full meaning. But it had much less meaning for his assistants. 'It's true,' one of them said. 'Might have been better to give them some other choice of qualities. Like beauty or tolerance, for instance.' I seconded him. 'Perhaps,' said the leader of the group. 'But that's not where the real choice lies, is it. . . . '

He was, however, right in pointing out that much of this

had to do with circumstances. More affluent societies can afford more charity and tolerance. And more educated societies can rely rather less on bullying, and more on understanding between the rulers and the ruled. The thirty-two-year-old agriculturist whom I quoted in Chapter 5, had come to wish he had only paid labourers to order around because his collective farmers would not be persuaded to change from traditional wheat to more profitable grapes, and had left him to do most of the work involved by himself. But he might not have come to the same desperate conclusions if he had been faced with the more enterprising and better schooled peasants described by the young Polish sociologist in this chapter as the new rural generation. And the future throughout Eastern Europe clearly lies with attitudes and modes of behaviour and management born of greater general affluence, and of more social and educational homogeneity, not with those born of the privations and caste systems of the past.

This will amount to development from below, succeeding essentially where the Party failed in its efforts from above. It will be true to the Party's own thesis that existence determines consciousness. In fact the realm of consciousness is itself likely to offer further proof of it. The Party's cultural revolution, which in the fifties and to a large extent since has amounted to trying to spread culture from above, has on the whole failed because the people below had neither the time nor the energy after a full day's work to take it. But when development changes their lives, the thing may have a second chance: if not as a revolution, then as an evolutionary process, in which people with more money, more leisure and more life left in them after work to enjoy both begin to make more of their own culture and also to assimilate more of the high culture of the present and the past.

Such a process of fusion can already be seen to have taken place in the culture most important to the young, namely, pop music. Not only has it proved, as I mentioned in Chapter 6, a mixer among strata that are otherwise still fairly alien, but among those making the music too it is much less of an upper- and middle-class phenomenon than classical music used to be and mostly still is. True, in Eastern Europe many more pop musicians still come from middle- and higher-income families than in the

West, largely because good equipment is imported and so expensive that only better-off children can buy it. Also, a striking percentage of them are musicians trained in academies, again mainly because occupational and social strata are still too firmly separate. But all this does not prevent myriads of pop groups producing good or bad music on good or bad instruments up and down each country.

Beyond being democratic, pop is also the kind of music that is most naturally sensitive to the moods of the young. What it expresses is definitely 'ours', not 'theirs'. This makes it all the more significant that, in addition to becoming frank about emotions and tenderness in ways that teenagers even a decade ago in Eastern Europe would have found unbearably 'romantic', pop should now be turning to themes that are all too close to what the young have consistently rejected when it comes to them from above:

'Tomorrow, somebody will have to conquer the darkness,' runs a song released by the most popular Hungarian pop group in 1971:

> Tell me, who would you choose?
> Tomorrow, somebody will have to rewrite the old myths,
> tell me, who would you choose?
> Tomorrow, somebody will have to redeem the world,
> tell me, who would you choose?
> Tomorrow, somebody will have to tear off his chains,
> tell me, who would you choose?

You could not get more romantic, indeed millennial. But there is between the spirit of this song and the enthusiasm the Party has been trying to engender a crucial difference. The song has charity. Called 'Oratorio for Human Rights', it is full of that 'generalized love of mankind' which the heroic-dialectical ideology of the Party has all along rejected as a version of compromise with 'the enemy'. It has done so for reasons which, in a revolutionary élite, are understandable enough, but which to the young, growing up in times of peace and rising prosperity, have less and less meaning. And as the Party can give up its hatred of the enemy only along with the rest of the heroic ideology which defines it as the Party, though the spirit now growing from below may be close to what it once promised as the essence of human rebirth it can never hope to pose as its focal church.

And once again, it will be to a considerable extent, as a result of the Party's own good work in Eastern Europe, and of the affluence and homogenization it has brought, if the young now go their own ways: in their humanism as much as in their choice of where to live, in their occupations as much as in their choice of social strata, in their behaviour towards each other as much as in their choice of how to cope with their circumstances. More and more, and materially as much as mentally, they will be wanting and able to do their own thing.

All this, denuding the Party of one guiding role after another, will make it increasingly absurd as a purely political erection above the landscape, until in the end yet another of its original promises will become due for fulfilment – namely, its promise about the withering away of the State. It will be fulfilled not in absolute terms, which, like all of the Party's original promises, belong in the realm of Platonic utopia, but in earthy, Aristotelian ones, as has happened with every other promise, presenting the Party with more of an elemental threat. As specialists take over one specialized function after another, and as each new generation becomes better at managing for itself, so the State, while remaining a live body, will cease to have any room for the Party at its centre.

I am not indulging here in fancies about the future. On the contrary, the thing I am describing is already visible in the East European economy. Throughout the region the Party is faced even now with the choice of letting the experts take charge, co-opting them as its nominal members, or reasserting its own dilettante rule, with effects that will grow predictably worse as the situation becomes more complex. In other words, it has the choice of three courses: one pragmatic, one tragicomic and one neo-centralistic, liable to end in tragedy. A number of such choices have come up in social management, too, each Party reacting to them according to its general outlook.

For example, the fall in the birth-rates that I mentioned earlier has alarmed each leadership. But reactions to the phenomenon have varied from country to country. In fact the Polish leadership, already faced with an unemployment crisis, has done very little to increase birth-rates. In the later sixties, in Czechoslovakia and even more pronouncedly in Hungary, the Party took the pragmatic course of giving new mothers partially paid leave for up to three years, and offering other family benefits. At the same time in Romania and Bulgaria, it forbade abortions, reduced the supply of contraceptives and banned their import, and in Romania as good as put a stop to divorce: following legislation, the number of divorces fell from 25,804 in 1966 to 48 in 1967.[21]

The pragmatic course led to a slow but appreciable rise in the birth-rates. The neo-centralist course, which in effect reproduced Stalin's own policies in the mid-thirties in Russia, which were copied throughout Eastern Europe in the early fifties, brought a jump in the birth-rate, but it also increased the number of female suicides, sent the price of back-street abortions soaring, and in Romania seriously reduced the number of new marriages too. And then to this spectacle of counter-productivity, the Bulgarian Party reacted in the tragicomic manner, leaving laws in force but effectively allowing them to lapse, whereas the Romanians stuck to centralism. The result was that whereas the Bulgarian birth-rates continued to rise slightly, in Romania, within three years following their jump to 27·4 per thousand, they declined by about a quarter.[22]

To almost every other choice presented by the effects of development, the reactions of the various East Europeans Parties have similarly depended on their individual outlook. The need for specialists in the countryside, for example, is solved by increasing the attraction of advertised posts in the three northern countries, and by the obligatory placing of graduates in the southern two. The first often leads to competition for jobs, and certainly makes those who can get nothing better than far-flung appointments try to present these to themselves and others in a more favourable light, by way of justifying their existence there. The second breeds resentment, and a mad scramble involving every kind of corrupt practice to get back to the towns, leaving, as the Party press itself complains, sections of the countryside wholly without trained people and only swelling the ranks of bureaucracies at the centre, which are already too large. And though the effects are clear, once again the conclusions drawn by the Bulgarian Party are closer to the tragicomic, and those by the Romanian Party to the centralistic. As the Party is, so the Party does.

And so it will be called on to do increasingly often. If its work as Champion of Progress in Eastern Europe has been worth its heroic effort, as clearly I think it has been, then the Party can expect to face the same set of choices in sphere after sphere that its work has affected. And since its being Hero in central charge of the environment has meant its having gone to work on all spheres, and seeking still to rule them all, the growth in the number of times it will be forced to choose must prove exponential. Until the paradox of its situation as a Platonic body irremovable from central power, and yet championing a process whose central feature is the increase of mobility, reaches its final stage.

It will be final, however, only for the Party – not for the generations it once claimed as its natural vanguard, who will survive its demise very successfully. Already its age structure is the reverse of the region it rules: at the end of the sixties, whereas about 48 per cent of the population of the five East European countries was under thirty, only one-fifth to one-quarter of its Party members were. The average age of Party members was between the middle and late forties, with people over fifty greatly outnumbering those under twenty-five. All this in spite of deliberate efforts in several countries to rejuvenate the Party. In fact, the Hungarian and Czechoslovak Parties, which have lowered the age of eligibility to eighteen, have found that they still cannot keep up with the natural ageing of their memberships.

Very simply, the Party is powerless against the causes of its own superannuation. And just as it has developed an ideological fear of the intellectual élite from which it derives, so it has come round to denying, at least by implication, the Leninist thesis that, as vanguards of the future, the Party and youth are one. The reason is that in reality the two have diverged, and of the alternatives born the Party, excusably enough, prefers itself in power. 'Both sectarian dogmatism and revisionism met their ends in

1956,' the First Secretary of the Hungarian Communist Youth League stressed in an otherwise wholly pragmatic interview in 1969,[23] with the purpose of adding. 'Similarly, fashionable notions current elsewhere which deny the leading role of the proletariat [i.e. the Party], and regard the intellectuals and the students as the vanguard of progress, have had their day with us.'

This also works in reverse. If the Party has come to see itself competing for leadership with the professional intelligentsia and the young, once its chosen allies, then for them it is the Party that has had its day. And while the progress it has championed can only go on increasing the value of the professional élite, biology is bound to bring the young to triumph over all those who opt to be their rivals.

Denying the conflict, however, would be of no more help to the Party. All it can do is choose the manner in which the conflict should be resolved. This might be pragmatic, with the Party giving way in due course, tragicomic, with the élite and the young remaining obsequious to those they continue to ease out from below, or tragic, with centralism reimposed and lasting until force brings it down.

The Party's choices are thus clear. Losing its former heroic functions and appeal, it either follows every one of its roles in being absorbed by the people, or becomes a hollow structure, such as the winds of history have always blown down with ease.

I sincerely hope it takes the first course. True, this will mean that instead of the Revolution trying heroically to devour its children, this time the children will slowly incorporate the Revolution, and its Hero. But in my view, no death could be more fitting for a Messiah.

Notes

Abbreviations

EE *East Europe* (formerly *News From Behind the Iron Curtain*) (New York 1952–70)

Radio Free Europe Research Reports are indicated by the letters BR (Background Report) or PS (Press Survey), both abbreviations preceded by that of the country to which the report refers (B = Bulgaria; CS = Czechoslovakia; H = Hungary; P = Poland; R = Romania)

I The Hero

1 *Constitution of the Polish People's Republic* (Warsaw 1964), p. 44

II The Hero's Call

1 Lenin: *On Youth* (Moscow 1967), p. 145
2 M. Rákosi, *Válogatott beszédek és cikkek* (Budapest 1955), p. 413–14
3 E.E. Vol. II, No. 3 (March 1953), p. 44
4 *Magyar Nemzet* (Budapest), 16 May 1952
5 Zhdanov, *On Literature, Music and Philosophy* (Moscow 1950), p. 15
6 M. A. Zinoviev, *Soviet Methods of Teaching History* (Moscow 1948); English translation (Ann Arbor 1952), pp. 3–4
7 *Szabad Ifjúság* (Budapest), 14 December 1952
8 K. Csala (ed.), *Érettségizők, felvételizők zsebkönyve* (Budapest 1969), pp. 62–3

III The Hero's Children

Chapter 1

1 *The Times* (London), 11 March 1968
2 *Valóság* (Budapest), XIII, 2 (February 1970), pp. 10–22
3 *Vecerni Praha* (Prague), 29 May 1965; in CSPS, 1656

Notes

4 G. Gheorghiu-Dej, *Discours Prononcée au Congrès des Instituteurs de la R.P.R.* (French translation) (Bucharest 1952), p. 6
5 *Przegląd Kulturalny* (Warsaw), 8 September 1960, in EE, ix, 11 (November 1960), p. 43
6 G. Gheorghiu-Dej, *op. cit.*, p. 31
7 B. Zadura, in *Życie Warszawy* (Warsaw), 25–6 June 1967; in PPS, 2086

Chapter 2

1 Czeszław Miłosz (ed. and trans.), *Post-War Polish Poetry* (London 1970), p. 78
2 Text in *Valóság* (Budapest), xiii, 4 (April 1969), pp. 56–69
3 *Literarni Noviny* (Prague), 23 May 1964; in CSPS, 1494
4 *Narodna Mladezh*, 19 June 1967; in EE, xvii, 1 (January 1968)
5 *Život Strany* (Prague), 22 March 1971
6 *Sociologia* (Bratislava), 1 (1970); in CSPS, 2308
7 Antonin Brousek, 'The Monument', in G. Theiner (ed. and trans.), *New Writing in Czechoslovakia* (London 1969), p. 202
8 *Po Prostu* (Warsaw), 25 March 1956; in EE, v, 6 (June 1956), p. 39

Chapter 3

1 *Lidove Noviny* (Prague), 17 March 1950; in V. Busek (ed.), *Czechoslovakia* (London 1957), p. 162
2 R. Nyers, 'Problems of Profitability and Income Distribution', *New Hungarian Quarterly*, 40 (Winter 1970) and 41 (Spring 1971)
3 *Życie Warszawy* (Warsaw), 17–18 January 1965; in EE, xiv, 3 (March 1965), pp. 42–3
4 M. Petrusek, 'Sociálni kontakty a sociopreferenčni orientace', in F. Machonin (ed.), *Československa Společnost* (Prague 1969)
5 A. Cazacu, 'Structuri integrative in relaţiile dintre generaţii', in M. Constantinescu (ed.), *Integrarea Socială a Tineretului* (Bucharest 1969)
6 *Ifjusági Magazin* (Budapest) (May 1970)
7 Z. Bauman, interview in *Sztandar Młodych* (Warsaw) 9 June 1964; in PPS, 1728
8 *Ifjusági Magazin* (Budapest), May 1970
9 *Trybuna Ludu* (Warsaw), 18 March 1970
10 This, and all other figures relating to 1947–8, are taken from

R. V. Burks, *The Dynamics of Communism in Eastern Europe* (Princeton, NJ 1961), p. 52

11 A MSZMP X. Kongresszusa (Budapest 1970), p. 21
12 *Rudé Právo* (Prague), 27 February 1970

Chapter 4

1 B. Weber, 'Youth and Modern Times', paper presented at Seventh World Congress of Sociology (Varna 1970)
2 K. Csala (ed.), *Érettségizők, felvételizők zsebkönyve* (Budapest 1969), blurb
3 *Kulturny Život* (Bratislava), 13 May 1966; in CSPS, 1798

Chapter 5

1 Result quoted in J. Materényi, *Parbeszed* (Budapest 1967)
2 All figures are taken from *U.N. Demographic Yearbook* (New York 1970)
3 P. Popescu, 'Recollections with Twins', *Luceafarul* (Bucharest), 20 March 1971; in RPS, 882
4 *Ifjúsági Magazin* (Budapest), May 1970
5 K. Katona, *Ifjúságunk problémái* (Budapest 1967), pp. 63–4
6 *Mladezh* (Sofia), May 1969; in BBR, 21/1969
7 *Kortárs* (Budapest), November 1969
8 Jerzy Lovell, in *Kultura* (Warsaw), 20 March 1966; in PPS 1986
9 *Nowa Kultura* (Warsaw), 9/1958
10 K. Katona, *op. cit.*, pp. 63–4, 78, 92
11 K. Varga, 'The View of Life of Hungarian Students', *New Hungarian Quarterly*, 35 (Autumn 1969)

Chapter 6

1 *Smena* (Bratislava), 30 June 1965; in CSPS, 1674
2 *Polityka*, 25 April 1960; in *Poland's New Generation* (mimeographed) (Munich 1963), p. 162
3 Z. Bauman, 'Wzory sukcesu życiowego młodziezy warszawskiej', in R. Dyoniziak (ed.), *Młodziez epoki przemian* (Warsaw 1965); further details in *Poland's New Generation, op. cit.*, pp. 180–7
4 *Valóság* (Budapest), XIV, 6 (June 1971), p. 12
5 *Życie Warszawy* (Warsaw), 25–6 April 1971; in PPS, 2306

Notes

Chapter 7

1 A. Hermann, 'A gyermek ismerkedése a világgal', in *A 3–6 éves gyermek átalakuló társadalmunkban* (Budapest 1966)
2 For instance, *Polityka* (Warsaw) 21, 23, 24 (1959); in *Poland's New Generation, op. cit.*, p. 156
3 *Sociologia*, 1 (1970); CSPS, 2308
4 *Magyar Statisztikai Szemle* (Budapest), February 1953; in EE, II, 10 (October 1953)
5 *Magyar Nemzet* (Budapest), 12 May 1971
6 M. Sorescu, 'Start', in *Tineretea Lui Don Quixote* (Bucharest 1968), p. 128

Chapter 8

1 *Sociologia*, 1 (1970); in CSPS, 2308
2 Quoted in *Poland's New Generation, op. cit.*, p. 188 ff.

Chapter 9

1 *Statistical Pocket Book of Bulgaria* (Sofia 1970)
2 U.N. *Demographic Yearbook* (New York 1955); and *Concise Statistical Yearbook of Poland* (Warsaw 1971)
3 Zs. Ferge, *Társadalmunk rétegződése* (Budapest 1969), pp. 291–2
4 U.N. *Demographic Yearbook* (New York 1966 and 1970)
5 *Concise Statistical Yearbook of Poland* (Warsaw 1971)
6 *Közgazdasági Szemle* (Budapest), February 1968; and *Magyar Mezőgazdaság* (Budapest), 13 January 1971
7 *Lupta de Clasa* (Bucharest), June 1970; in RPS, 849
8 *Tygodnik Powszechny*, 20 September 1970; in PPS, 2257
9 *Magyar Mezőgazdaság* (Budapest), 13 January 1971
10 I. Balogh, *Munkásifjúságunk helyzetéről etc.* (Budapest 1968), p. 49
11 *Concise Statistical Yearbook of Poland* (Warsaw 1971)
12 EE, XVIII, 4 (April 1969), p. 23, quoting *Scinteia* (Bucharest), 27 February 1969
13 *Statistical Yearbook of Bulgaria* (Sofia 1969), 1970
14 *Luceafarul* (Bucharest), 19 December 1964; in RPS, 545
15 Balogh, *op. cit.*, p. 43
16 *Polityka* (Warsaw), 11 June 1971; in PPS, 2312
17 *Elet es Irodalom* (Budapest), 18 September 1971
18 *Scinteia* (Bucharest), 20 March 1970

368

Notes

19 *Rudé Právo* (Prague), 13 May 1965; quoted in M. Gamarnikow, *Economic Reforms in Eastern Europe* (Detroit 1968), p. 115
20 *Vysoka Skola* (Prague), October 1970; in CSPS, 2350
21 *U.N. Demographic Yearbook* (New York 1970)
22 *U.N. Demographic Yearbook* (New York 1971)
23 *Magyar Ifjuság*, 25 July 1969

Bibliography

T. Aczél (ed.), *Ten Years After*, London, 1966
N. Apanasewicz and S. M. Rosen, *Education in Czechoslovakia*, Washington, 1963
N. Apanasewicz and S. M. Rosen, *Education in Bulgaria*, Washington, 1965
N. M. Apeland, *World Youth and the Communists*, London, 1958

I. Balogh, *Munkásifjuságunk helyzetéről, etc.*, Budapest, 1968
N. Bellu (ed.), *Tineretul şi idealul moral*, Bucharest, 1969
Y. Blumenfeld, *Seesaw, Cultural Life in Eastern Europe*, New York, 1968
R. Braham, *Education in Romania*, Washington, 1963
A. Bromke, *Poland's Politics, Idealism v. Realism*, Cambridge, Mass., 1967
J. F. Brown, *The New Eastern Europe*, London, 1966
J. F. Brown, *Bulgaria under Communist rule*, London, 1970
Z. K. Brzezinski, *The Soviet Bloc, Unity and Conflict*, Cambridge, Mass., 1967
N. Buhler and A. Zhukovski, *Discrimination in Education in the People's Democracies*, New York, 1955
R. V. Burks, *The Dynamics of Communism in Eastern Europe*, Princeton, N.J., 1961
V. Bušek and N. Spulber (eds.), *Czechoslovakia*, London, 1957

M. Constantinescu (ed.), *Integrarea socială a tineretului*, Bucharest, 1969

L. A. D. Dellin (ed.), *Bulgaria*, London, 1957
I. Deutscher, *Trotsky*, 3 vols, London, 1959
I. Deutscher, *Stalin* (Revised Edition), London, 1966
R. Dyoniziak, *Młodzieżova 'podkultura'*, Warsaw, 1965
R. Dyoniziak (ed.), *Młodzież epoki przemian*, Warsaw, 1965
M. K. Dzyewanowski, *The Communist Party of Poland*, Cambridge, Mass., 1959

Bibliography

L'Evolution de l'Enseignment dans les Démocraties Populaires, Paris, 1956 (mimeographed)

J. Faragó, *Fiatalok vallomásai világnézetről, erkölcsről*, Budapest, 1968
Zs. Ferge, *Társadalmunk rétegződése*, Budapest, 1969
S. Fischer-Galati (ed.), *Rumania*, London, 1957
S. Fischer-Galati, *Twentieth Century Romania*, New York, 1970
C. J. Friedrich and Z. K. Brzezinski, *Totalitarian Dictatorship and Autocracy*, Cambridge, Mass., 1956
P. Fryer, *The Hungarian Tragedy*, London, 1956

I. Gáll (ed.), *Naponta Más*, Budapest, 1969
M. Gamarnikow, *Economic Reforms in Eastern Europe*, Detroit, 1968
K. Grzybowski, *The Socialist Commonwealth of Nations*, London, 1964

E. Helmreich (ed.), *Hungary*, London, 1957
A. Hermann and others, *A 3–6 éves gyermek átalakuló társadalmunkban*, Budapest, 1966
O. Halecki (ed.), *Poland*, London, 1957

Gh. Ionescu, *Communism in Rumania, 1944–62*, London, 1964
Gh. Ionescu, *The Politics of the European Communist States*, London, 1967

G. D. Jackson, *Comintern and Peasant in Eastern Europe*, London, 1966
M. J. Jászai, *Kinek higyjen?*, Budapest, 1966
Z. A. Jordan, *Philosphy and Ideology*, Dordrecht, 1963

L. Kardos, *Egyház és vallásos élet egy mai faluban*, Budapest, 1969
A. Kassoff, *The Soviet Youth Programme*, Cambridge, Mass., 1965
K. Katona, *Ifjúságunk problémái*, Budapest, 1967
L. Kolakowski, *Toward a Marxist Humanism*, New York, 1968
P. Korbel, *The Sovietization of the Czechoslovak School System*, New York, 1954

V. I. Lenin, *Selected Works*, 2 vols., Moscow, 1950
V. I. Lenin, *On Literature and Art*, Moscow, 1967
V. I. Lenin, *On Youth*, Moscow, 1967
R. Littell (ed.), *The Czech Black Book*, New York, 1969
E. Loebl, *Sentenced and Tried*, London, 1969
K. London (ed.), *Eastern Europe in Transition*, Baltimore, 1966

Bibliography

C. A. M. Macartney, *October Fifteenth, A History of Modern Hungary*, Edinburgh, 1961

C. A. M. Macartney, *Hungary*, Edinburgh, 1962

C. A. M. Macartney and S. Palmer, *Independent Eastern Europe*, London, 1962

P. Machonin (ed.), *Československá Společnost*, Bratislava, 1969

J. Materényi, *Párbeszéd*, Budapest, 1967

P. Mayewski (ed.), *The Broken Mirror*, New York, 1958

K. Mehnert, *Stalin versus Marx*, London, 1952

P. Meyer, *Jews in the Soviet Satellites*, Syracuse, 1953

Cz. Milosz, *The Captive Mind*, London, 1953

Cz. Milosz (ed.), *Post-War Polish Poetry*, London, 1970

D. Mitrany, *Marx Against the Peasant*, New York, 1961

Poland's New Generation, Munich, 1963 (mimeographed)

D. Pryce-Jones, *The Hungarian Revolution*, London, 1969

H. Ripka, *Eastern Europe in the Post-War World*, London, 1961

H. Rogger and E. Weber (eds.), *The European Right*, Los Angeles, 1965

H. Roos, *A History of Modern Poland*, London, 1966

M. Rura, *Reinterpretation of History, as a method of furthering Communism in Romania*, Washington, 1961

T. Schreiber, *Christianisme en Europe Orientale*, Paris, 1961

B. Simon, *Education in the New Poland*, London, 1954

Gy. Simon and J. Szarka, *A magyar népi demokrácia nevelésügyének története*, Budapest, 1965

G. H. Skilling, *Communism, National and International*, Toronto, 1964

R. F. Staar, *Poland 1944-62, The Sovietization of a Captive People*, New Orleans, 1962

J. V. Stalin, *Our Tasks*, Moscow, 1931

J. V. Stalin (and Lenin), *On Youth*, London, 1940

J. V. Stalin, *Concerning Marxism in Linguistics*, London, 1950

J. V. Stalin, *Problems of Socialism in the U.S.S.R.*, Moscow, 1952

E. Taborsky, *Communism in Czechoslovakia*, Princeton, N.J., 1961

G. Theiner (ed.), *New Writing in Czechoslovakia*, London, 1969

I. Vitányi (ed.), *Beat*, Budapest, 1969

Bibliography

H. Seton-Watson, *Eastern Europe Between the Wars, 1918–1941*, Cambridge, 1945

H. Seton-Watson, *The East European Revolution*, London, 1956

H. Seton-Watson, *The Pattern of Communist Revolution*, London, 1967

R. W. B. Seton-Watson, *A History of the Roumanians*, Cambridge, 1934

R. W. B. Seton-Watson, *A History of the Czechs and Slovaks*, London, 1943

C. Wieniewska (ed.), *Polish Writing Today*, London, 1967

E. Wiskemann, *Czechs and Germans*, Oxford, 1938

J. Woolfe (ed.), *European Fascism*, London, 1968

A. A. Zhdanov, *On Literature, Music and Philosophy*, London, 1950

P. Zinner, *Revolution in Hungary*, New York, 1962

M. A. Zinoviev, *Soviet Methods of Teaching History*, Ann Arbor, Mich., 1952

Index

abortion, 240, 330, 362
achievement-mindedness, 200, 206, 220,
273, 315–17, 333–4
age-structure of Party, 128, 354, 363–4
aggressiveness of youth, 124–5, 223, 225,
214–27
agrarian way of life, 330, 335;
improvements in 345–8; *and see*
collectivization, peasants
agriculture, 331, 332, 346–7; in
Depression, 335–6; improvements,
post-Stalin, 80; nationalization of, 335;
and see collectivization, peasants
Albania, 12
alcoholism, 243, 244–5, 262
alienation: caused by development,
247–51; caused by Stalinism, 40, 41;
and fear, 251–7; and the political
machine, 248, 254–65
anti-Bolshevism, 27, 28, 29
anti-Communism, 307, 313, 314
anti-Semitism, 27, 28, 30, 296; and
Arab-Israeli War, 293; in Poland, 26,
50, 112, 166, 281 n, 290, 291, 296, 322;
and youth, 297–8
Antonescu, General, 20–1, 147 n
Arab-Israeli War, 1967, attitudes to, 293
Aristotelianism: and élite, 13; growth of,
198 n–199 n, 225–7, 356, 361; of
Party aims, 33, 56, 68, 343; and
romanticism, 286
army: attitudes to, 276, 280; bids for
power, 275; centralists in, 50; and
sports clubs, 64
arts: decline in study of, 281–2; post-
Stalin liberalization of, 92–3, 116–18;
and see censorship, culture, films,
literature, poetry, theatre
Austria, 16, 24, 44
Austro-Hungarian Empire, 23 n, 345
authoritarian régimes, pre-war, 26–30,
31, 33, 50
authoritarianism: effects of, social,
191–227; effects of on youth, 213–15,
219–27, 232–3, 237–8, 270, 316–17; and
élite, 354
automation, 50, 350
AVH (Hungarian State Security Corps),
64, 228–9, 233

Balkan wars (1912–13), 17, 25
Bessarabia, 17
Biafra, collections for, 358
birth-rate, fall in, 329–30, 354; Party
reactions to, 361–2
black market, 250
Bohemia, 16, 24
Bolshevism, 27, 31 n, 37 *and see*
anti-Bolshevism
Botev, Hristo, 275 n
bourgeoisie, growth of, 161–2, 266 *and see*
middle-mass
Bratislava, 109, 178, 185, 303, 309, 323,
346
Bucharest, 113–14, 116, 117, 147, 177,
191, 302, 326
Budapest, 59, 100–1, 105, 109 n, 119, 128,
131, 136, 147, 151, 155, 163, 176,
185–6, 193, 197 n, 228, 235, 237, 238,
248, 266, 269, 282, 296, 297, 303, 317,
326, 327, 333, 339, 346, 348, 357;
population of, 345
Bulgaria: abortion laws, 362; attitudes
to East, 326; to Soviet Union, 293–4;
to West, 116, 298; authoritarianism
in, 213–14; backwardness of, 23, 26,
330; birth-rate in, 362; censorship in,
253, 255; centralism in, 23, 43, 48, 51,
84; Communism in, 33, 246, 307, 311,
314, 320; de-Stalinization in, 44, 47;
education in, 108, 140, 198–9, 209,
272; family life in, 103, 104, 222;
historical background of, 18–31;
industrialization in, 210, 293, 328,
336–7; and Nazi Germany, 30;
nationalism in, pre-war, 15 n, 18, 22,
24, 27–8; Party membership in 257–8;
Party rule in, 44, 47, 48, 51, 84, 128,
343, 362–3; peasantry in, 26, 153, 210;
peasant migration in, 334; police in,
fear of, 253; poetry in, 275;
pragmatism in, 83; private enterprise
in, 251; propaganda in, 116; religion
in, 110, 301; social changes in 210;
Stalinism in, 75, 133–4; tourism in,
116; travel restrictions in, 89, 116;
Turks in, 18, 24, 28, 275 n; and
Yugoslavia, 300; Zhivkov régime,
90 n

375

Index

Index

films—*cont.*
68–9, 70, 116–17; Russian, 294–5
First World War, 12, 14, 18, 24, 25, 28, 61
Five-Year Plans, 18, 69, 231
food-shortages, 248
France: Communism in, 311; illiteracy in, 62 n
freemasons, 177
Frejka, Ludvik, 67, 102
French Revolution, 13
Freud, Sigmund, 105

gangs, juvenile, 230, 236
Gdansk, 175, 244, 271, 340
generation gap, 124, 125–32, 137–8, 225
Georgescu, Teohari, 300 n
German-Soviet Treaty (1939), 30
Germany, East, 254–5
Germany, Nazi, 26, 30, 33, 34 n *and see* Hitler
Germany, West: and Czechoslovakia, 89; illiteracy rate in, 62 n; New Left in, 307; propaganda against, 66, 137
Gheorghiu-Dej, Gheorghiu, 90 n, 106, 108, 300 n
Gierek, Edward, 43, 89
Gomulka, Wladyslaw, 44, 46 n, 83–4, 89, 90 n, 187–8
Greece, 12
Guevara, Che, 269, 279
gypsies, 248, 269

Habsburg dynasty, 16
Hacerstwo, 61, 63
Hegel, Georg Wilhelm Friedrich, 37
Heisenberg, Werner Carl, 71 n–72 n
hippies, attitudes to, 216
history; Communist view of, 37–8; and de-Stalinization, 81, 90; dialectical teaching of, 70–1, 73, 305, 308–9, 317
Hitler, Adolf, 26, 30, 124, 295, 296
House of Culture, 229–30, 235
housing conditions, 236, 238, 242, 262–3, 331, 345, 348
humour, 253–4, 255, 261, 209
Hungary: agriculture in, 80, 331, 332, 335, 346; alcoholism in, 244–5; anti-Russianism in, 28, 30, 293, 296, 339, 340–1; anti-Semitism in, 28, 296–8; and Czechoslovakia, 322–3; attitudes to East, 326; attitudes to West, 89; birth-rate, fall in, 362; censorship in, 317; Commune (1919), 28, 269 n; Communism in, 31 n, 33–4, 136, 308, 312, 314 *and see* Party; de-centralization in, 51; demonstrations (1966), 46 n; economic reforms in, 80, 84, 164–5; education in, 62 n, 88, 109, 151, 197–8 n, 199–200, 207, 209, 282; elections in, 44; family life in, 100–1,

104, 193, 195, 219–20, 357; Fascism in, 29, 107; floods in (1956), 185–6; historical background of, 16, 18–31; industrialization in, 210, 328, 337, 349; incomes in, 144; Jews in, 112–13, 231, 296; Kádár régime in, 43, 90 n; liberalization in, 84, 223, 233–7, 253; management in, 122, 351–2; Maoism in, 266–7, 269; mass culture in, 151; materialism in, 356; nationalism in, 18, 22, 27–8, 296–7, 335; and Nazi Germany, 30; New Left in, 118, 165, 166, 276, 280, 321, 322; peasants in, 26, 154, 213, 347; Party membership in, 115, 258, 262, 351–2, 363–4; Party rule in, 43, 44, 45, 83, 276, 341–2 *and see* repression; People's Front in, 65–6; personality cult in, 45; police in (AVH), 49, 64, 228–9, 233, 252, 255; pop-music in, 118–19, 124, 235, 360; prostitution in, 250; repression in 83, 187, 223, 260–1, 285: relations with other countries, 300, 315; relations with Poland, 295; religion in, 109, 110, 304; Revolt, October 1956, 43, 44, 47, 83, 84, 85, 223, 229 n, 322–3, 363–4; Russian invasion of 1956, 111, 114, 186, 187, 343; social attitudes in, 153, 154, 155, 212–13, 216, 218–20, 248; social changes in, 143, 154, 209; social divisions in, 24, 147–8, 151, 161; sociology in, 93; Stalinism in, 47, 266; suicide rate in, 209; surveys in, 100, 218–19, 241, 274, 320, 328; trade unions in, 47; travel from, 89, 116; university entrance in, 158, 159, 180; urban population of, 345; workers in, 159, 164, 176–7, 344
Hungary, youth in: and culture, 173, 231–2; and discipline, 224; and delinquency, 333; political apathy of, 173, 174, 270, 317; political attitudes of, 115, 124, 130, 221, 222–3, 230–1, 285, 308, 320, 321, 324; social attitudes of, 154, 155, 185–6, 218–20, 224, 229–38, 272, 284; social life of, 131, 228–32, 235 & n; student trials (1968), 163, 266–7, 268 n; and Youth League, 59–60, 85, 174, 203, 228–31, 364; and youth organizations, 61, 235 & n, 237, 270; *and see* Hungary, education in, Maoism in, New Left in, pop-music in, Revolt, 1956

ideological revival campaign, Romania (1971), 48, 84, 86, 314, 338, 352
ideology *see* Communist ideology, Dialectical Materialism, Marxism, Socialism
illiteracy rates, 62 n
incentives: need for, 176–8; schemes, 166–7

378

Index

incomes: de-levelling of, 162, 166–7, 177;
of intelligentsia, 348–9; levelling of,
143–4; *and see* wages
industrialization; effects of, social, 121,
127–8, 142–3, 210, 328–38, 344–51;
effects of, on youth, 331–2, 338–41;
Party programme for, 35
industry; employment of youth in, 337;
and sports clubs, 64
integration, 27–8, 30
intelligentsia: and communication, 156,
162; division of from workers, 148–53,
156, 158–9, 164–6, 315, 320; education
of, 207, 211; and emigration, 329;
low pay of, 348–9; and Marxism,
31–2, 309, 320; nationalism of, 282–3;
and New Left, 280–1; and Party
membership, 164, 355; in Polish
riots, 152, 163, 165–6; pragmatists in,
50; realism of, 282, 283; and religion,
282, 283; return to countryside,
344–8; return to manual work,
348–51; revolt of post-Stalin, 78–81,
81; support of Communism, 31, 35,
40, 60, 327; workers' movement into,
141, 142–3, 151, 156–7, 207, 279, 282,
328, 348
internationalism, proletarian, 294, 299–300
intolerance of youth, 213–17, 224, 225,
273, 277, 278, 357
irredentism, 18, 27–8, 30
isolationism, Party propagation of, 66,
68, 81, 92
Italy, 12; and Czechoslovakia, 89;
Communism in, 311

Jews: emigration of, 328 n; in Hungary,
112–13, 231, 296; and jokes, 194; and
New Left, 280–1 & n; and Marxism,
32; in Poland, 26; rise of under Stalin,
296–7; *and see* anti-Semitism, Zionism
juvenile delinquency, 90–1, 235–6, 333

Kádár, János, 43, 90 n
Khruschev, Nikita, 42, 84
Komsomol (Hungary), 59, 85, 174, 257

labour camps, 86, 87
Legion of Archangel Michael, 147 & n
Lenin, Vladimir Ilyich, 31 n, 36–7, 39,
40, 51, 59, 73, 137, 340, 342, 343
Leninism, 163 *and see* Komsomol,
Marxism-Leninism
Levente, 61
liberalization, post-Stalin movements
towards, 83, 84, 85, 89–94, 107–12,
221, 233–40, 355 *and see* Dubček
libraries, Party control of, 66, 117, 314
literature: attitude of youth to, 129–30,
180, 217, 243; control of, 66–7, 68–9,
117, 118; and de-Stalinization, 81
Lodz, 326, 349

Lysenko, Trofim, 76

Macbeth, 117
McCarthyism, 288
management: changes in, 353–4, 355,
361; growth of, 143; and labour
migration, 249, 251; Party control
over, 48, 121, 182, 203–4; and Party
membership, 48, 122, 123–4, 351–2;
and theft, 254
manual work, attitudes to, 149, 151–2
Maoism, 163, 266–7, 268 n, 269
marriage, attitudes to, 239–40, 242,
247–8, 274, 354
Marx, Karl, 36, 37, 73, 309, 312, 320–1,
342, 357 *and see* Marxism
Marxism, appeal of, 31–3, 36–7, 269;
centralism of, 36, 342 *and see*
centralism; and industrialization,
335–6, 338; and New Left, 163, 311;
and youth, 306–12, 320
Marxism-Leninism, 92, 108, 309
Masaryk, Jan, rehabilitation of, 99
Masaryk, T. G., 19, 24, 25, 27, 61, 70,
99, 100, 108
materialism: increase of, 334–7; of,
Marxism, 32–3; of youth, 273, 277–9,
283, 285–91, 323, 324, 355–6 *and see*
prosperity, effects of
Maturita, the, 200–1, 337
middle classes: denunciation of, 141–2,
143; discrimination against, 160;
education of, 160; reintegration of
146–7, 154–5; *and see* middle mass
middle mass: growth of, 144, 161–2;
social attitudes of, 161–2, 207
migration of workers, 249, 251, 328,
329, 331–6, 344; and return to countryside, 344–8, 357
modernity, admiration of youth for, 223,
242–3, 271, 337–8
moonlighting, 249, 251, 348
morality, attitudes to, 238–9, 302 *and see*
sex
Moscow government, 41, 42–56 *and see*
Soviet Union
Munich conference (1938), 26, 30

nationalism: pre-war, 14–15, 18, 22–4,
27–8, 61, 50; post-Stalin, 79, 90, 121,
128, 175–6, 282–3, 291–6, 314–15, 320,
322; and youth, 62
nationalization, 31 n, 35, 141, 335 *and see*
collectivization
neurosis and social pressures, 106,
209–10, 225 n, 262, 316
New Course, the, 42
New Left: failure of, 174–5; in Germany,
307; ideology of, 163–7, 276; and
Marxism, 163, 311; opposes Party,
321; repression of, 166; social origins
of, 163, 165–6, 280–1

379

Index

Poland, revolt, October 1956, student riots March 1968; political apathy of 318, 319, 324; political attitudes of, 270, 280–1 & n, 306, 308, 317, 321; and protest songs, 119; social attitudes of, 149, 152, 153, 155, 222–3, 271, 272, 278–9, 284, 337; social life of, 101; students' circles, 177, 256, 288–9; student riots (March 1968), 93 111, 112, 124, 132, 134, 148, 281 n, 287, 288 n, effects of, 177–8, 181, 183, 288, intelligentsia in, 152, 163, 165–6, 180, 280–1, 289, 290, reasons for, 288, repression following, 166, 181, 322; students and workers' riots, 182; and youth movements, 61, 62, 63, 85, 86, 152; *and see* Poland, education in, university entrance in

police: centralists in, 50; fear of, 134, 182, 252, 256, 277; humour and, 182, 255; Jews in, 296; Party control of, 182, 284; powers of, 47, 49, 132, 182, 233, 255, 284; and sports clubs, 64, 228–9; Stalinist, 40; and youth, 132, 134, 287, 289

political attitudes of youth: 124, 128, 156, 171–90, 213, 221–3, 230–1, 237, 251, 270, 274–5, 276, 280–1, 285–91, 305–25; activities of, 152, 255–6, 266–7, 284, 287–9, 317; apathy of, 113, 169–77, 180–6, 188, 231, 233, 270, 278–9, 285, 317–19, 323–4; desire for involvement, 115, 132, 171, 177–8, 184–7, 266–7, 281, 288, 323, 324; *and see* Maoism, New Left, Party, the, attitudes of youth to, propaganda, students, Youth League

politics: and age-groups, 125; and education, 107, 232; fear of discussing, 134, 179–80, 182, 235 n, 246, 252–3, 255–6, 270, 285, 316, 318; and family influence, 101–3, 104; jokes on, 253–4, 309; Party control over, 48–9; pragmatism in *see* pragmatism

pop music: and class, 359–60; denounced, 118, 388; and emotions, 286, 360; festivals of, 340; and politics, 287, 360; popularity of, 115, 118–19, 124, 234–5, 286–7; as propaganda, 69; and religion, 303, 309

population: rural, 331; urban, 194, 345

pragmatism, post-Stalin spread of, 42–52 *passim*, 78–87 *passim*, 158, 178, 187, 268

Prague, 99, 100, 108, 110, 111, 129, 135, 150, 166, 176, 185, 188, 198, 214, 216, 258, 262, 272, 289, 293, 304, 307, 318, 319, 321, 326

Pravda, 40

priests, decline in prestige of, 276, 280

private enterprise, 146–7, 178–9, 249–51 *and see* moonlighting, *Protektsio*

Pro Prostu, 135

proletariat *see* peasants, workers

propaganda: and alcoholism, 244–5; and anti-Semitism, 281 n, 297, 322; and the Church, 67, 72–3, 75; and culture, 39–40, 71, 231; and delinquency, 236; and de-Stalinization, 45, 47, 91–2; and education, 91–2, 101, 106–7 *and see* history, dialectical teaching of; and industrialization, 329; Party control over, 39, 48; reactions against, 121, 292–3, 294–5, 300–1; Stalinist, 39–40, 77, 92, 114, 133; and the West, 66, 69, 70, 71, 72, 73, 88–9, 116, 137, 305, 318–19, 341; and women, 91; and workers, 121, 149; and youth, 61–77 *passim*, 100–1, 110–13, 116, 126, 128, 136–9, 170–2, 179–80, 202, 278, 329 *and see* Pioneers, Youth League; and Soviet Union, 74–5, 81, 294–5

prosperity, effects of, 128, 136, 205–8, 219, 234–7, 239, 241, 273–4, 277–8, 286, 288–91, 330–1, 325, 354, 359, 360 *and see* materialism

prostitution, 250, 291

protektsio, 155 & n–156, 250–1, 254, 329

protest songs, 119

purges, 84, 107, 108; Stalinist, 40, 296, 300 n

radio: control of, 68; increased freedom of, 111; jamming of, 66, 81, 88–9

Radio Free Europe, 114–15

Radio Sofia, 273

Rákosi, Mátyás, 59 60, 63

rationalism: and de-Stalinization, 42–3, 45–6, 78; and opposition to Party, 319–25

realism: in culture, 92–4, 117; of Marxism, 32; and nationalism, 15–16; of New Left, 163–4; of Party, 22, 23, 48; necessity for, 188–90; of youth, 279, 281–91, 323–4; *and see* pragmatism

Realist Party (Czechoslovak), 18, 22, 25

Red Army, 30, 33, 34, 38

religion: and de-Stalinization, 81; and family influence, 101, 104; teaching of, 108, 109; and youth, 109–10, 131, 232–3, 276, 301–4, 307, 309, 320; *and see* Catholicism, Church

Romania: abortion laws in, 326; agriculture in, 331; anti-Russianism in, 43, 293, 294, 300, 340; anti-Semitism in, 28, 297; backwardness of, 23, 26, 145; birth-rates in, 362; censorship in, 150, 191, 310; centralism in, 23, 51, 326–3; Communism in, 33, 310 *and see* ideological revival campaign; counter-selection in, 205, 251; divorce laws in, 240, 362; education in, 62 n, 158, 196–7, 199, 201–2, 208; élite in, 148; family life in, 104, 222,

381

Index

Index